Special Economic Zones

Special Economic Zones

*Progress, Emerging Challenges, and
Future Directions*

Edited by

Thomas Farole
International Trade Department
World Bank

Gokhan Akinci
Investment Climate Department
World Bank

 THE WORLD BANK

 BANK-NETHERLANDS
BNPP
PARTNERSHIP PROGRAM

 International
Trade
Department
PREM The World Bank

 IFC | International
Finance Corporation
World Bank Group

 World Bank Group
Multilateral Investment
Guarantee Agency

© 2011 The International Bank for Reconstruction and Development/The World Bank
1818 H Street NW
Washington DC 20433
Telephone: 202-473-1000
Internet: www.worldbank.org

This volume is a product of the staff of the International Bank for Reconstruction and Development / The World Bank. The findings, interpretations, and conclusions expressed in this volume do not necessarily reflect the views of the Executive Directors of The World Bank or the governments they represent.

The World Bank does not guarantee the accuracy of the data included in this work. The boundaries, colors, denominations, and other information shown on any map in this work do not imply any judgement on the part of The World Bank concerning the legal status of any territory or the endorsement or acceptance of such boundaries.

ISBN: 978-0-8213-8763-4
eISBN: 978-0-8213-8764-1
DOI: 10.1596/978-0-8213-8763-4

Cover design: Naylor Design, Inc.

Library of Congress Cataloging-in-Publication Data has been requested.

Contents

Acknowledgments   *xv*
Contributors   *xvii*
Abbreviations   *xix*

Chapter 1   **Introduction**   1
             Thomas Farole and Gokhan Akinci

             Attracting Investment and Creating
                Jobs: Old Models and New
                Challenges   8
             Moving from Static to Dynamic Gains:
                Can SEZs Deliver Structural Change?   13
             Social and Environmental Sustainability:
                Emerging Issues For SEZs   17
             Conclusion   19
             Notes   19
             References   20

PART I   **Attracting Investment and Creating
                Jobs: Old Models and New Challenges**   **23**

Chapter 2   The Thin End of the Wedge: Unlocking
                Comparative Advantage through EPZs
                in Bangladesh   25
                Mustafizul Hye Shakir and Thomas Farole

                Introduction   25
                Historical Development of EPZs in Bangladesh   27
                Performance   29
                Key Success Factors   33
                Challenges for the Future   38
                Conclusion   43
                Notes   44
                References   45

Chapter 3   Success and Stasis in Honduras' Free Zones   47
                Michael Engman

                Introduction   47
                Historical Development of Free Zones in
                    Honduras   48
                Performance   49
                Key Success Factors   54
                Challenges for the Future   61
                Conclusion   65
                Notes   67
                References   68

Chapter 4   China's Investment in Special Economic
                Zones in Africa   69
                Deborah Brautigam and Tang Xiaoyang

                China's Overseas Special Economic Zones:
                    Aims and Objectives   69
                China's Overseas Zones in Africa:
                    Current Situation   72
                China's Overseas Zones: Mechanisms   80
                Progress, Challenges, and Potential   91
                Appendix 4.A. China's Official Overseas
                    Economic and Trade Cooperation Zones   96

Notes   97
References   98
Interviews   100

Chapter 5   Partnership Arrangements in the China-Singapore
             (Suzhou) Industrial Park: Lessons for
             Joint Economic Zone Development   101
             Min Zhao and Thomas Farole

             Background   101
             Introduction to Suzhou Industrial Park   102
             The Strategy of the Chinese and Singaporean
                 Governments   104
             Partnership Structure   105
             The Knowledge-Sharing Process   107
             Challenges to the Partnership   110
             Overcoming Partnership Challenges and
                 Implementing Innovations   113
             Conclusion   115
             Appendix 5.A. Selected Indicators:
                 Developments at SIP, 1994–2008   121
             Appendix 5.B. SIP Timeline and Major Milestones   122
             Notes   124
             References   125

Chapter 6   SEZs in the Context of Regional Integration:
             Creating Synergies for Trade and Investment   127
             Naoko Koyama

             Introduction   127
             Regional Trade Agreements   129
             Implication of RTAS for SEZs   134
             Harmonization of SEZs: Beyond Tariff Issues   143
             Conclusion   149
             Appendix 6.A Regulations and Handbooks of
                 Regional Trade Agreements   150
             Appendix 6.B Summary of Tariff-Related
                 Measures Taken by Regional Trade Agreements
                 for Special Economic Zone–Processed Goods   151
             Notes   154
             References   155

PART II   **Moving from Static to Dynamic Gains:**
           Can SEZs Deliver Structural Change?   **157**

Chapter 7   When Trade Preferences and Tax Breaks Are No
           Longer Enough: The Challenge of Adjustment in
           the Dominican Republic's Free Zones   159
           Jean-Marie Burgaud and Thomas Farole

           Introduction   159
           Free Zones in the Dominican Republic   162
           Performance and the Challenge of Adjustment   166
           The Policy Response   172
           Current Situation and Conclusions   175
           Notes   180
           References   181

Chapter 8   Fostering Innovation in Developing Economies
           through SEZs   183
           Justine White

           Introduction   183
           SEZs as an Instrument for Innovation   184
           The Need for Absorptive Capacity and
              Local Linkages   189
           A Staged Approach to Building an
              Innovative SEZ   197
           Conclusion   200
           Notes   202
           References   202

Chapter 9   Early Reform Zones: Catalysts for Dynamic
           Market Economies in Africa   207
           Richard Auty

           Context   207
           The Confused Definitions and Aims of
              Special Economic Zones   210
           Examples of Successful SEZs   214
           The Potential Role of ERZs in Sub-Saharan Africa   220
           Conclusions: ERZs and Economic Reform in
              Sub-Saharan Africa   223

| | | Note | 224 |
| | | References | 224 |

| Chapter 10 | Planned Obsolescence? Export Processing Zones and Structural Reform in Mauritius | | 227 |
| | Claude Baissac | | |

	Introduction	227
	The Policy Environment	227
	Overview of MEPZ Performance	230
	Today's Challenges	235
	The MEPZ and Economic Reform	237
	Conclusion	240
	Notes	243
	References	244

| **PART III** | **Social and Environmental Sustainability: Emerging Issues for SEZs** | | **245** |

| Chapter 11 | The Gender Dimension of Special Economic Zones | | 247 |
| | Sheba Tejani | | |

	Introduction	247
	Background on Trade and Gender	248
	The Economics of Female-Intensive Production in SEZs	253
	Evidence on Gender in SEZs	255
	Quality of Female Employment in SEZs	262
	Defeminization of Employment	266
	Conclusion and Policy Implications	269
	Notes	272
	References	274

| Chapter 12 | Low-Carbon, Green Special Economic Zones | | 283 |
| | Han-Koo Yeo and Gokhan Akinci | | |

	Introduction	283
	Low-Carbon, Green SEZs: Overview	284
	Low-Carbon (Green) SEZ Framework	287

Low-Carbon, Green SEZs around the World:
Current Status and Future Trends   304
References   306

Index   309

Boxes

2.1   Incentives Offered in Bangladesh EPZs   37
2.2   The Labor Counselor Program   40
2.3   The Korean EPZ: The First Private EPZ in Bangladesh   42
2.4   The Economic Zones Act   43
3.1   Incentives in the Honduras Free Zones   50
3.2   San Pedro Sula: Key Agglomeration for the
       Export Sector   58
3.3   The Critical Role of Domestic Investors in
       Attracting FDI   60
3.4   Instituto Politécnico Centroamericano   65
4.1   Timeline: Tianjin TEDA in Egypt   75
4.2   Challenges in the Lekki Free Zone in Nigeria   93
5.1   SIP Free Trade Zone Development   116
7.1   The Apparel Sector in the Dominican Republic   160
7.2   Gulf and Western Establishes the Dominican Republic's
       First FZ in 1969   162
7.3   Profile of the Dominican Republic's Free Zones in 2010   164
7.4   Grupo M Pioneered the Strategy of Production Sharing
       between FZs in the Dominican Republic and Haiti   174
8.1   The First Modern SEZ, Shannon, Ireland   186
8.2   The Development of Backward Linkages:
       A Successful and Less Successful Example   194
8.3   SEZs and Labor Circulation: A "Domestic Diaspora"?   195
8.4   A Tale of Two Countries: Investment Climate Reform   196
8.5   SEZs in Cambodia   199
10.1   Targeting Productivity Improvements in the EPZs   234

Figures

2.1   Exports (US$ millions) and Contribution to
       National Exports (percent) of EPZ Enterprises   30
2.2   Employment Generation in EPZs
       (Year-Wise and Cumulative)   32

2.3	Comparison of Average Wages and Benefits of Unskilled Workers in SEZs	34
3.1	Employment in Free Zones	53
3.2	Gross Value of Production in *Maquilas*	63
5.1	Governance Structure of SIP	106
5.2	Current Ownership Structure of CSSD	108
6.1	Total Notifications Received by Year, 1948–2009	131
6.2	Network of Plurilateral Groupings in Africa and Middle East	132
6.3	Evolution of the Share of Intra-PTA Imports in Total Imports, 1970–2008	135
6.4	Classification of Various Tariff-Related Measures by RTA	140
7.1	Index of Growth (1995 = 100) in the Free Zone Program	165
7.2	Free Zone Value Added (US$m) and Contribution to GDP, 1995–2008	167
7.3	Free Zone Exports (US$ million) and Share of National Exports	168
7.4	Index of Free Zone Exports: Textile versus Nontextile (1995 = 100)	169
7.5	Comparative Growth in U.S. Imports of Knitwear by Key Countries, 2004–08, and U.S. Imports of Apparel and Textiles by Key Country, 2009 and 2010	170
7.6	Evolution of FZ Employment, 1969–2008	171
8.1	The Republic of Korea's Gradual Buildup of R&D Capacity	192
8.2	Island to Catalyst SEZs	200
8.3	SEZs from Linkages and Technological Capabilities to Upgrading	201
10.1	Employment Data	230
10.2	Investment Data	231
10.3	Exports	232
10.4	Sectoral Share of Exports	233
10.5	Exports per Employment	233
10.6	Measures of Export Productivity	234
11.1	Female Share of SEZ Employment and Nonagricultural Employment, 2005–06	258
11.2	Female Share of SEZ Employment and Nonagricultural Employment in African Countries, 2009	259

11.3   Female Share of Employment in SEZs by Sector,
        Select Countries, 2009   260
11.4   Female Share of Employers and Managers,
        Select Countries, 2009   261
11.5   Female Intensity of Manufacturing Employment and
        Manufacturing Value Added per Worker, Average
        Annual Growth, Southeast Asia and Latin America,
        1985–2006   268
12.1   Spectrum of Environmentally Sustainable Zones   285
12.2   Main Components of a Low-Carbon, Green SEZ
        Framework   287
12.3   Trajectory of GHG Emission and Mitigation Target   289
12.4   Example: Some SEZ GHG Emission Structures by Sector   290
12.5   Example of Industrial Symbiosis Networking Map,
        Republic of Korea   293
12.6   Global Greenhouse Gas Mitigation Marginal Cost
        Curve Beyond 2030 Business-as-Usual   295
12.7   Low-Carbon, Green SEZ Policy Framework   298

Tables

1.1   Summary of Types of Zones   2
2.1   Summary of EPZs, 2009   28
2.2   Operating Enterprises in the EPZs by Sector, 2009   30
3.1   FDI in Manufacturing Activities   51
3.2   FDI in Manufacturing by Country of Origin   51
3.3   Value-Added Contribution by Manufacturing in
        "Industry" and "*Maquila* Industry"   52
4.1   Structure of Investment in China-Africa SEZs   84
5.1   SIP Key Statistics   103
5.2   FDI Utilized, US$ Billion   112
8.1   Direct and Indirect Benefits of SEZs   185
8.2   Training for Workers in SEZs   191
8.3   Staged Approach to the Development of an SEZ:
        The Shenzhen Case   201
8.4   Some Policies Aimed at Stimulating Innovation
        through SEZs   202
9.1   Export Processing Zone Performance, Six Asian
        Economies   212
9.2   Ratio of Firms, Workers and Profits to Urban Population
        Share, Chinese Regions, 1996   219

11.1	Female Wages as a Percentage of Male Wages in Manufacturing	250
11.2	SEZ Exports as a Percentage of Total Exports	256
11.3	Total Employment and Female Share of Employment in SEZs	257
12.1	Some Examples of CDM Projects of IDA Countries	302
12.2	Interlinkage between CDM and FDI	304

Acknowledgments

The editors extend their sincere gratitude to all the authors who took the time to contribute to this volume. In addition, they thank the peer reviewers whose comments and feedback provided invaluable guidance to the authors and editors: Magdi Amin, Kishore Rao, Marilou Uy, and Michael Wong. Thanks also are extended to others who provided comments on the book or individual chapters, including Sumit Manchanda, Martin Norman, Harun Onder, and José Guilherme Reis.

Thanks also to Cynthia Abidin-Saurman, Igor Kecman, Charumathi Rao, Marinella Yadao, and Aimee Yuson for support on administrative and financial matters, and to Stephanie Chen and Stacey Chow for support on publishing and marketing matters.

Finally, thanks to the Bank-Netherlands Partnership Program, which provided the generous financial support under which this project was conducted.

The book was produced under the overall supervision of Mona Haddad (sector manager) and Bernard Hoekman (sector director) in the International Trade Department of the World Bank.

Contributors

Editors

Thomas Farole — Senior Economist, International Trade Department, World Bank, Washington, D.C.

Gokhan Akinci — Lead Investment Policy Officer, Investment Climate Department, International Finance Corporation and World Bank, Washington, D.C.

Other Contributing Authors

Richard Auty — Senior Lecturer, Geography, University of Lancaster, UK

Claude Baissac — Secretary General, World Economic Processing Zones Association and Executive Director, Eunomix Consulting, Johannesburg, South Africa

Deborah Brautigam — Professor, International Development Program, School of International Service, American University, Washington, D.C.

Jean-Marie Burgaud	Independent Consultant, trade and economic development, Santo Domingo, Dominican Republic
Michael Engman	Economist, Finance and Private Sector Development, Africa Region, World Bank, Washington, D.C.
Naoko Koyama	Project Leader, Dalberg Global Development Advisors, Nairobi, Kenya
Mustafizul Hye Shakir	Consultant, Finance and Private Sector Development, South Asia Region, World Bank, Washington, D.C.
Sheba Tejani	PhD Candidate, Economics, New School for Social Research, New York, NY
Justine White	Operations Officer, World Bank Institute, Washington, D.C.
Tang Xiaoyang	Ph.D. Researcher, Philosophy Department, New School for Social Research, New York, NY
Han-Koo Yeo	Senior Investment Officer, Investment Climate Department, IFC and World Bank, Washington, D.C.
Min Zhao	Senior Economist, World Bank, Beijing, China

Abbreviations

ADOZONA	Dominican Association of Free Zones
AFTA	ASEAN Free Trade Area
ASEAN	Association of Southeast Asian Nations
BAU	business as usual
BEPZA	Bangladesh Export Processing Zones Authority
BICF	Bangladesh Investment Climate Fund
BPO	business process outsourcing
BSCIC	Bangladesh Small and Cottage Industries Corporation
CACM	Central American Common Market
CADF	China-Africa Development Fund
CBD	Central Business District
CBI	Caribbean Basin Initiative
CBTPA	Caribbean Basin Trade Partnership Act
CCECC	China Civil Engineering Construction Corporation
CCX	Chicago Climate Exchange
CDM	Clean Development Mechanism
CEMAC	Economic and Monetary Community of Central Africa
CER	Certified Emission Reduction
CNMC	China Nonferrous Mining Company

CNZFE	*Consejo Nacional de Zonas Francas de Exportación* (National Free Zones Council of the Dominican Republic)
COMESA	Common Market for Eastern and Southern Africa
CSSD	China-Singapore Suzhou Industrial Park Development Company, Ltd.
DEDO	Duty Exemptions and Drawback Office
DR-CAFTA	Dominican Republic–Central American Free Trade Agreement
EAC	East African Community
ECCI	Egypt-Chinese Corporation for Investment
ECOWAS	Economic Community of West African States
EDB	Singapore Economic Development Board
EFTA	European Free Trade Association
EIA	environmental impact assessment
EPA	Economic Partnership Agreement
EPZ	export processing zone
EPZDA	Export Processing Zones Development Authority
ERZ	early reform zone
ESCO	energy service company
FDI	foreign direct investment
FIDE	Foundation for Investment and Development of Exports
FOCAC	Forum on China-Africa Cooperation
FTA	free trade agreement
FZ	free zone
GAFI	General Authority for Free Zones and Investment
GATT	General Agreement on Tariffs and Trade
GCC	Gulf Cooperation Council
GDP	gross domestic product
GHG	greenhouse gas
GVC	global value chain
ICT	information and communication technology
IFC	International Finance Corporation
IFEZ	Incheon Free Economic Zone
IFTZ	Integrated Free Trade Zone
ILO	International Labour Organization
INFOTEP	*Instituto Nacional de Formación Técnici Profesional*
IPC	*Instituto Politécnico Centroamericano*
IPR	intellectual property rights
JICA	Japan International Cooperation Agency

JSC	China-Singapore Joint Steering Council
JTC	Jurong Town Corporation
KCER	Korea Certified Emission Reduction
LDC	least-developed country
LED	light-emitting diode
LFTZ	Lekki Free Trade Zone
M&E	monitoring and evaluation
MDC	Main Development Company
MEDIA	Mauritius Export Development and Investment Authority
MEPZ	Mauritius Export Processing Zone
Mercosur	Southern Cone Common Market (*Mercado Commún del Sur*)
MFA	Multi-Fiber Arrangement
MFEZs	Multi-Facility Economic Zones
MFN	most-favored nation
MMM	*Mouvement Militant Mauricien*
MNC	multinational corporation
MOFCOM	Ministry of Commerce
NAFTA	North American Free Trade Agreement
NIC	newly industrializing country
NPCC	National Productivity and Competitiveness Council
PKCC	Pingxiang Coal Group
PMSD	*Parti Mauricien Social Democrate*
PPP	public-private partnership
PTA	preferential trade agreement
R&D	research and development
RMB	Renminbi
RPS	renewable portfolio standards
RTA	regional trade agreement
SACU	South African Customs Union
SADC	Southern African Development Community
SAFTA	South Asian Free Trade Agreement
SCM	(Agreement on) Subsidies and Countervailing Measures
SEZ	special economic zone
SFADCo	Shannon Free Airport Development Company
SIP	China-Singapore Suzhou Industrial Park
SIPAC	Suzhou Industrial Park Administrative Committee
SME	small and medium enterprise
SOE	state-owned enterprise

SPF	SIP Provident Fund System
SPO	Software Project Office
t CO_2e	tons of carbon dioxide emissions
TEDA	Tianjin Economic-Technological Development Area
TFP	total factor productivity
TVE	township and village enterprise
UNFCCC	United Nations Framework Convention for Climate Change
VAT	value added tax
WAEMU / UEMOA	West African Economic and Monetary Union (*Union Économique et Monétaire Ouest-Africaine*)
WTO	World Trade Organization
ZIP	*Zonas Industriales de Procesamiento*
ZOLI	*Zona Libre*

CHAPTER 1

Introduction

Thomas Farole and Gokhan Akinci

Ask three people to describe a special economic zone (SEZ) and three very different images may emerge. The first person may describe a fenced-in industrial estate in a developing country, populated by footloose multinational corporations (MNCs) enjoying tax breaks, with laborers in garment factories working in substandard conditions. In contrast, the second person may recount the "miracle of Shenzhen," a fishing village transformed into a cosmopolitan city of 14 million, with per capita gross domestic product (GDP) growing 100-fold, in the 30 years since it was designated as an SEZ. A third person may think about places like Dubai or Singapore, whose ports serve as the basis for wide range of trade- and logistics-oriented activities.

In fact, all three of these are correct descriptions of this diverse instrument: Table 1.1 provides a brief summary of the different types of zones in existence. This table highlights the many ways in which the concept of "special" economic zones has been operationalized and underscores the challenge of attempting to say anything specific about such a heterogeneous policy tool. But despite the many variations in name and form, all SEZs can be broadly defined as— .

Table 1.1 Summary of Types of Zones

Type of zone	Development objective	Typical size	Typical location	Activities	Markets	Examples
Free trade zone (commercial-free zone)	Support trade	<50 hectares	Port of entry	Entrepôt and trade-related activity	Domestic, re-export	Colon Free Zone (Panama)
Traditional EPZ	Export manufacturing	<100 hectares	None	Manufacturing or other processing	Mostly export	Bangladesh, Vietnam[1]
Free enterprises (single unit EPZ)[2]	Export manufacturing	No minimum	countrywide	Manufacturing or other processing	Mostly export	Mauritius, Mexico
Hybrid EPZ	Export manufacturing	<100 hectares; only part of area is EPZ	None	Manufacturing or other processing	Export and domestic	La Krabang, Thailand
Freeport/SEZ	Integrated development	>1,000 hectares[3]	None	Multiuse	Internal, domestic, and export	Aqaba, Shenzhen

Sources: Derived from FIAS (2008) and Farole (2011).

Note: EPZ = export-processing zone; SEZ = special economic zone.

1. Bangladesh passed a new Economic Zones Act in 2010 that will open up the potential of zone activities beyond the traditional EPZs; Vietnam has various forms of economic zones, among which are EPZs.

2. Many EPZ programs offer licenses for both EPZ industrial parks and "single unit" EPZs. Examples include Dominican Republic, Honduras, and Kenya.

3. Some multiuse SEZs, particularly those that do not include a resident population, may be smaller in scale.

demarcated geographic areas contained within a country's national boundaries where the rules of business are different from those that prevail in the national territory. These differential rules principally deal with investment conditions, international trade and customs, taxation, and the regulatory environment; whereby the zone is given a business environment that is intended to be more liberal from a policy perspective and more effective from an administrative perspective than that of the national territory. (Farole 2011, p.23)

In this book, we use SEZ as a generic expression (as per FIAS, 2008) to describe the broad range of modern economic zones discussed in this book (see table 1.1). But we are most concerned with two specific forms of those zones: (1) the export processing zones (EPZs) or free zones (*zona francha* in our case studies on Honduras and the Dominican Republic), which focus on manufacturing for export; and (2) the large-scale SEZs, which usually combine residential and multiuse commercial and industrial activity. The former represents a traditional model used widely throughout the developing world for almost four decades. The latter represents a more recent form of economic zone, originating in the 1980s in China and gaining in popularity in recent years. Although these models need not be mutually exclusive (many SEZs include EPZ industrial parks within them), they are sufficiently different in their objectives, investment requirements, and approach to require a distinction in this book.

SEZs have a long-established role in international trade. *Entrepôts* and citywide free zones that guaranteed free storage and exchange along secure trade routes—such as Gibraltar, Hamburg, and Singapore—have been operating for centuries. The first modern industrial free zone was established in Shannon, Ireland, in 1959.[1] Before the 1970s, most zones were clustered in industrial countries. But since the 1970s, starting with East Asia and Latin America, zones have been designed to attract investment in labor-intensive manufacturing from MNCs. These zones became a cornerstone of trade and investment policy in countries shifting away from import-substitution policies and aiming to integrate into global markets through export-led growth policies.

SEZs normally are established with the aim of achieving one or more of the following four policy objectives (FIAS 2008):

1. *To attract foreign direct investment (FDI)*: Virtually all zones programs, from traditional EPZ to China's large-scale SEZs aim, at least in part, to attract FDI.

2. *To serve as "pressure valves" to alleviate large-scale unemployment*: The SEZ programs of Tunisia and the Dominican Republic are frequently cited as examples of programs that have remained enclaves and have not catalyzed dramatic structural economic change, but that nevertheless have remained robust, job-creating programs.
3. *In support of a wider economic reform strategy*: In this view, SEZs are a simple tool permitting a country to develop and diversify exports. Zones reduce anti-export bias while keeping protective barriers intact. The SEZs of China; the Republic of Korea; Mauritius; and Taiwan, China, follow this pattern.
4. *As experimental laboratories for the application of new policies and approaches*: China's large-scale SEZs are classic examples. FDI, legal, land, labor, and even pricing policies were introduced and tested first within the SEZs before being extended to the rest of the economy.

In achieving these objectives, SEZs have had a mixed record of success. Anecdotal evidence turns up many examples of investments in zone infrastructure resulting in "white elephants," or zones that largely have resulted in an industry taking advantage of tax breaks without producing substantial employment or export earnings. Moreover, many of the traditional EPZ programs have been successful in attracting investment and creating employment in the short term, but have failed to remain sustainable when labor costs have risen or when preferential trade access no longer offers a sufficient advantage. Empirical research shows that many SEZs have been successful in generating exports and employment, and come out marginally positive in cost-benefit assessments (cf. Chen 1993; Jayanthakumaran 2003; Mongé-Gonzalez, Rosales-Tijerino, and Arce-Alpizar 2005; Warr 1989). Many economists, however, still view zones as a second- or even third-best solution to competitiveness, whose success is restricted to specific conditions over a limited time frame (Hamada 1974; Madani 1999; World Bank 1992). Concerns also have been raised that zones, by and large, have failed to extend benefits outside their enclaves or to contribute to upgrading of skills and the production base (cf. Kaplinsky 1993).

A number of examples, however, also illustrate the catalytic role zones play in processes of economic growth and adjustment processes (cf. Johansson and Nilsson 1997; Willmore 1995). For example, many of the zones established in the 1970s and 1980s in East Asia's "tiger economies" were critical in facilitating their industrial development and upgrading processes. Similarly, the later adoption of the model by China, which launched SEZs on a scale not seen previously, provided a platform for attracting FDI and not only supported the development of China's export-oriented manufacturing sector, but also served as a catalyst for sweeping economic reforms that later were extended throughout the country. In Latin America, countries like the Dominican Republic, El Salvador, and Honduras used free zones to take advantage of preferential access to U.S. markets and have generated large-scale manufacturing sectors in economies that previously were reliant on agricultural commodities. In the Middle East and North Africa, SEZs have played an important role in catalyzing export-oriented diversification in countries like the Arab Republic of Egypt, Morocco, and the United Arab Emirates. And in Sub-Saharan Africa, Mauritius is an example of zones operating as a central policy tool supporting a highly successful process of economic diversification and industrialization.

Although the nature, scale, and scope of their success or limitations will no doubt continue to be debated for decades to come, what is clear is that the attraction to policy makers of SEZs as an instrument of trade, investment, industrial, and spatial policy is undiminished. In fact, since the mid-1980s, the number of newly established zones has grown rapidly in almost all regions, with dramatic growth in developing countries. For example, in 1986, the International Labour Organization's (ILO's) database of SEZs reported 176 zones in 47 countries; by 2006, this number rose to 3,500 zones in 130 countries (Boyenge 2007), although many of these zones are single companies licensed indiviudally as free zones. SEZs now are estimated to account for more than US$200 billion in global exports and employ directly at least 40 million workers (FIAS 2008).

This rapid expansion in SEZs is happening in the midst of substantial changes in the macro context in which they are situated. Most important, the global trade and investment environment is changing in a way that may no longer support the traditional EPZ model. The rapid growth of EPZ programs around the world over the last two decades, and their success in contributing to export-led growth in regions like East Asia, is due in part to an unprecedented globalization of trade and investment that took place since the 1970s and accelerated during the 1990s and 2000s, which saw trade grow 85 percent faster than GDP between 1983 and 2008. This growth was enabled by the vertical and spatial fragmentation of manufacturing into highly integrated "global production networks," particularly in light manufacturing sectors like electronics, automotive components, and especially apparel, which have accounted for the large majority of investment in traditional EPZs. Especially for countries with low labor costs, scale economies, and preferential access to major consumer markets like the Europe, Japan, and the United States, economic zones—with their access to duty-free inputs, quality, flexible infrastructure, and often generous fiscal incentives—proved to be a powerful instrument through which to capture increasingly mobile foreign investment.

This era may well have come to an end, however, for several reasons. Although trade has recovered significantly from the depths of the 2008 and 2009 economic crisis, it is clear that the United States and European economies can no longer be the ony engines of global demand. Responding in part to the crisis as well as longer-term strategic trends, lead firms in global production networks are increasingly consolidating their supply chains, both in terms of suppliers and production locations. Much of this consolidation increasingly is being entrenched in "factory Asia." Linked closely to the issues discussed thus far, the expiration of the Multi-Fiber Arrangement (MFA)[2] at the end of 2004 has had a huge impact on the cost competitiveness of textile and apparel manufacturing in EPZs in Latin America, Africa, and Eastern Europe in relation to low-cost Asian producers.

Thus, for countries that have not yet established economic zones programs, the traditional variety targeting multinational assembly activities within global production networks is far from the sure thing that it used to be. In the absence of massive labor cost advantages (e.g., Bangladesh and Vietnam) or scale (e.g., China), most countries will need to design more sophisticated strategies—beyond the basic EPZ—to attract MNCs. For countries that already have established EPZ programs, the challenge is perhaps more acute. It is about remaining competitive, which in the absence of aggressive, long-term dampening of real wages, means upgrading production capabilities and attracting investment in higher value-added activities. But, as we will see from the examples in Parts I and II of this book, this is precisely where the EPZ models have often let down countries by creating an incentive environment that restricted adjustment processes.

Indeed, recent years have seen a shift away from the traditional EPZ model. In its place, zone development is moving toward the SEZ model, with emphasis on physical, strategic, and financial links between the zones and local economies, and a shift away from fiscal incentives to value added services and a greater focus on differentiation through the investment climate in the zone. Although many of these zones eschew the narrow focus of traditional EPZs in favor of multiuse developments encompassing industrial, commercial, residential, and even tourism activities, others are moving to highly specialized developments focused on specific high-end services like information and communication technology (ICT) and biotech. Another notable trend has been the growing importance of zones that are privately owned, developed, or operated (FIAS 2008).

In the postcrisis environment, in which competition for FDI likely will remain much more intense than it has been in the past, SEZs likely will continue to grow in importance. But it is not the existence of an SEZ regime, of a master plan, or even of a fully built-out infrastructure that will make the difference in attracting investment, creating jobs, and generating spillovers to the local economy. Rather, it is the relevance of the SEZ programs in the specific context in which they are introduced, and the effectiveness with which they are designed, implemented, and managed on an ongoing basis, that will determine success or failure.

But recognizing the importance of context should not mean approaching each situation anew, ignoring the substantial body of knowledge that has been built up over the past three decades on what determines success in implementing SEZs. While this book cannot hope (and does not attempt) to provide any such thorough review of the state of the art in SEZ knowledge, it is designed to offer policy makers, practitioners, and researchers with an interest in SEZs (and trade and investment policy more widely) a chance to take stock of the past and current role of SEZs, and their potential for the future. Combining theoretical discussions with practical examples from the field, through the use of case studies from (mainly developing) countries around the world, the book will discuss some of the well-known challenges facing both traditional EPZs and newer SEZs around the world and also will look forward to some of the emerging issues in the field, which will not only present further challenges to many SEZ programs, but will also open up new opportunities.

Specifically, the book is structured around exploring three main issues of critical interest to policy makers:

1. *How to make economic zones successful in attracting firms that create jobs:* This could be called a first-order or static measure of success.
2. *How to ensure that zones are economically sustainable and deliver positive externalities, including facilitating upgrading and structural transformation and catalyzing economic reforms:* This could be called a dynamic measure of success.
3. *How to ensure that economic zones are sustainable from an institutional, social, and environmental perspective:* This means not only minimizing negative externalities but, if possible, delivering noneconomic benefits to the society.

Using this framework, the book is organized in three parts. Part I: *Attracting Investment and Creating Jobs: Old Models and New Challenges* includes case examples from South Asia, Latin America, and Africa combined with a technical discussion of new issues in the trade environment that will offer both opportunities and challenges for first-order success. Part II: *Moving from Static to Dynamic Gains: Can SEZs Deliver Structural Change?* follows a similar approach, combining case examples highlighting the challenges with discussions of models for delivering dynamic benefits from SEZs. Part III: *Social and Environmental Sustainability: Emerging Issues for SEZs* discusses the issues related to gender and labor, as well as environmental sustainability.

The remainder of this chapter discusses the themes of these sections in more detail and summarizes some of the main findings and policy conclusions based on the contributions in this book.

Attracting Investment and Creating Jobs: Old Models and New Challenges

The fundamental benefits of SEZs derive from their role as instruments of trade and investment policy. These static benefits result from capturing the gains from specialization and exchange. They include employment creation, the attraction of FDI, the generation of foreign exchange through exports, and the creation of economic value added. Traditional EPZs were designed to capture these benefits by enabling countries to better exploit a key source of comparative advantage (low-cost labor) that otherwise was underutilized because of low levels of domestic investment and barriers (regulatory, infrastructure, etc.) preventing FDI. These EPZs have operated under simple principles: allowing investors to import and export free of duties and exchange controls, facilitating licensing and other regulatory processes, and usually freeing these firms from obligations to pay corporate taxes, value added taxes (VAT), or other local taxes. To maintain control, EPZs normally have been fenced-in estates with strict customs controls at entry, and sales are typically restricted mainly to export markets.

The model has been extremely successful in many countries. For example, it allowed the Dominican Republic to create more than 100,000 manufacturing jobs and shift dramatically away from reliance on agriculture. Similar stories of industrialization and job creation can be seen in Mauritius, the Republic of Korea, and Taiwan, China; in Honduras, El Salvador, and Madagascar; and more recently in Bangladesh and Vietnam.

It is clear, however, that the model is now increasingly reaching its limits. Indeed, it is perhaps no longer fit-for-purpose, given the changing macroeconomic and regulatory environment in the global economy. This creates significant challenges for developing countries that are in the early stages of developing their zone programs. As we will see from the case studies in Part I, some of the basic principles at the heart of traditional EPZs are no longer (or perhaps never were) sustainable sources of competitiveness.

But regardless of the model, it is also apparent that some countries have been more successful than others in using zones to attract FDI, to encourage export-oriented production, and to create jobs. Indeed, reviewing the experience of economic zones across many countries over the past three decades, some clear principles emerge regarding the policies and practices that are associated with static success. The case studies in part I—of Bangladesh and Honduras, and of the experience of the recent Chinese investments in SEZs in Africa—highlight many of these principles.

In chapter 2, we examine Bangladesh, a country that perhaps highlights the contrasting recent fortunes between zones programs in low-cost Asian countries and those that have been established in Latin America and Africa. Mustafizul Hye Shakir and Thomas Farole describe how Bangladesh's EPZ program has become part of the latest wave of beneficiaries from multinational outsourcing in the classic low-wage-based garment sector. While the expiration of the MFA (for the garment sector) and the continuing trend of tariff liberalization has eroded the benefits of trade preferences for most zone programs, wage-based competitiveness can still be critical in many sectors. The case of Bangladesh emphasizes the importance of positioning the zone program to leverage the country's comparative advantage. Indeed, while the program in Bangladesh initially aimed to attract high-technology investment, it took off only when it made a concerted effort to focus on the garments sector, in which it had a clear comparative advantage. The case of Bangladesh also highlights another observation about SEZs—that is, their incubation period. Even the biggest SEZ success stories like China and Malaysia started slowly and took at least 5 to 10 years before they began to build momentum. In Bangladesh, the program started in the early 1980s, but it only began to attract investment on a large scale in the early 1990s (a similar evolution is seen the Honduras case study). From a policy perspective, this means that governments need to be patient and to provide consistent support to zone programs over long time periods, a particular challenge in countries whose political cycles are rather shorter.

Beyond the wage-based advantages of Bangladesh, the critical contribution of the zones program was not, in fact, incentives (which exist but
are relatively modest in global terms), but rather the provision of serviced
industrial land infrastructure and relatively reliable supply of power.
Indeed, recent research (Farole 2011) shows that on a global basis
infrastructure reliability has a significant impact on SEZ success, while
incentives have no measurable effect.

The test of success for Bangladesh will be whether it can continue to
attract investment in the program in the face of rising wages.[3] The recent
adoption of a modern Economic Zones Act in 2010, which opens up
greater potential for private sector participation and for zones of various
forms, and the adoption of programs to address labor and environmental
issues, suggests that efforts are being made to modernize and diversify the
program to ensure that it avoids stagnation.

In chapter 3, Michael Engman relates the case of Honduras, which has
also been highly successful in attracting investment in the garment sector,
but has faced challenges in maintaining competitiveness. Although the
Honduran free zone program was built on the back of trade preferences,
labor cost arbitrage, and a certain amount of good timing, this was just a
starting point. The case study shows the critical importance of dynamic
local entrepreneurs in catalyzing foreign investment (indeed, the success
in Bangladesh also may be partly attributed to local investors, avoiding a
reliance simply on footloose FDI).

Beyond this, the case study highlights three additional critical factors
for successful zone programs. First is the role of the private sector.
Although it is too simplistic to say that private sector development of
zones is better than public sector development (bearing in mind the success of many East Asian countries and of Mauritius with public sector–led
models), the private sector can be much more dynamic in implementing
zones in many countries and, regardless, is an important source of expertise and risk management. In the case of Honduras, a stagnant government-
run zones program was transformed when the law was changed to allow
for private developments of zones. Second, the government focused on
providing not only the regulatory framework in which the private sector
thrived, but also critical infrastructure and services, most notably a high-
quality port and road connections to the zones. Finally, it provided effective on-site customs services that allow investors efficient import and
export procedures.

Ironically, as Engman points out in chapter 3, some of these sources of
competitiveness may also prevent the zones program from diversifying

outside the garment sector. Specifically, it relies on investors that are entrenched in the garment sector (most zone developers are not real estate developers but rather garment manufacturers). Moreover, the privileges long enjoyed by the sector have become a powerful disincentive for reform, which has acted as a brake on innovation and competitiveness.

Surely China is at the top of any list of success stories in attracting investment and promoting exports through SEZs. At the bottom of the list probably sits Africa, where, outside of Mauritius (and partial success in Kenya, Lesotho,[4] and Madagascar), most zones initiatives have been failures. In chapter 4, Deborah Brautigam and Xiaoyang Tang explore a recent development that seeks to leverage the Chinese model to create successful zone development in Africa. Specifically, they look at the recent Economic and Trade Cooperation Zones, an initiative which the Chinese government is supporting in six African countries. These initiatives have high-level government support and are implementing proven successful models (ironically, with one major difference—that is, they are being led by private developers[5] rather than by provincial and local governments). Although most of these zones remain in the early stages of development, troubling signs have emerged that highlight some important lessons in zone development.

First, it is important to separate political support from political objectives in zone projects. Although strong commitment from the government is needed, projects must be designed carefully on the basis of clear strategic plans. The commercial case must be present. Moreover, that commercial case must be based on sustainable sources of competitiveness, not on fiscal incentives. Second, despite the concept of zones as enclaves, in practice, their success is almost fully entwined with the competitiveness of the national economy and the national investment environment. Most of the Chinese zone projects in Africa are operating in an environment of poor national competitiveness (weak local and national value chains). Regardless of what is done inside the walls of the zones, these projects face challenges in linking the zones and global markets, including critical infrastructure like ports, roads, and electricity.

Third, the policy and legal framework in which they operate, and their *de jure* implementation, are critical. An effective legal and regulatory framework is a necessary first step to zone program development. Putting in place a clear and transparent legal and regulatory framework codifies the program strategy and establishes the rules of the game for all stakeholders involved in the process. This framework plays a fundamental role in addressing often-difficult land issues, facilitating the provision of the required infrastructure, and ensuring compliance with labor and environmental standards. But *de facto* implementation is of equal importance. In many of the African SEZs involved in the Chinese developments discussed in chapter 4, the authority responsible for developing, promoting, and regulating the program lacks resources and capacity to carry out its mandate. Of equal importance, it often lacks the institutional authority to do so. The lack of a clear and transparent legal and regulatory framework and an authority with the capacity to enforce it has led to disputes and delays in several of the projects.

One critical aspect of the Chinese Trade and Economic Cooperation Zones is their potential to transfer knowledge to developing-country governments on how to effectively plan and manage the implementation of SEZ programs. In fact, one the principal determinants of success or failure of SEZ initiatives has little to do with EPZ or SEZ models and much to do with the strategic planning, project implementation, and management capabilities of governments and their zone regulatory authorities specifically. With this in mind, chapter 5 looks back at China's own experience in establishing SEZs, during which it took advantage of similar turnkey partnerships to learn from the expertise of other countries. Min Zhao and Thomas Farole present the case of the partnership between China and Singapore in development the Suzhou Industrial Park (SIP), which is a telling example of how host governments in Africa and elsewhere should approach zone partnerships to take advantage of the learning opportunities and set the stage for the sustainable development and management of zones programs. The case study highlights a number of key principles for success of partnership initiatives and zone program institutional development more widely, including (1) the importance of high-level political commitment; (2) the need to align fiscal incentives among all partners (including local government); (3) the need to balance investments in infrastructure with a strong focus on "software"; and (4) the critical importance of putting in place an *institutionalized* process for learning and knowledge transfer between partners. Although the SIP partnership was not without its problems, the proactive, institutionalized approach to learning in the partnership played a critical role in ensuring that the host government took maximum advantage of the SEZ opportunity.

In addition to the competitive challenges emanating from the changing macroeconomic environment, economic zones (particularly, again, the traditional EPZ model) also are facing threats from changing regulatory environments. In chapter 6, Naoko Koyama highlights how one particular regulatory issue—the growing importance of regional preferential trade agreements—presents both challenges and opportunities for zones programs. Although the multilateral trade agenda has failed in recent years, bilateral and regional trade agreements are growing rapidly around the world. Many regional blocs are making substantial progress in integration efforts. A consequence of this progress is that the rules around which many traditional EPZ regimes were based suddenly may change. If an EPZ is prohibited from selling to the domestic market, but suddenly the regional trade agreement makes its neighboring countries "domestic" from a customs perspective, this change will have an enormous impact on the business model of investors and on the attractiveness of zones. From an institutional perspective, it will be increasingly critical for zone programs to look beyond their borders and develop integrated or at least harmonized approaches to SEZ legal and regulatory frameworks, most notably on the treatment of exports, rules of origin, and fiscal incentives.

But beyond the regulatory issues, Koyama's chapter also highlights another critical factor to the success of zones programs—that is, market access. One of the clear findings from research on SEZs (and on FDI in general) is that market access is often the number one investment location determinant. Koyama points out that regional agreements for smaller countries, particularly in Africa, offer the potential advantage of scale that these countries otherwise would not have. This is clear for export markets; but perhaps more important, Koyama discusses the potential for using zones to link up regional suppliers and leverage economies of scale in production. Indeed, linking regional SEZs to infrastructure investments to create growth corridors may be a powerful new route to competitiveness.

Moving from Static to Dynamic Gains: Can SEZs Deliver Structural Change?

Economic zone programs that are successful in contributing to long-term development go beyond the static benefits of attracting investment and generating employment. They leverage these static benefits for the creation of *dynamic economic benefits*. Ultimately, this means contributing to structural transformation of the economy, including diversification, upgrades, and increased openness. Critical to this process is the degree of integration of zones in the domestic economy. Countries that have been successful in deriving long-term economic benefits from their SEZ programs have established the conditions for ongoing exchange, and the accompanying hard and soft technology transfer, between the domestic economy and investors based on the zones. This includes investment by domestic firms into the zones, forward and backward linkages, business support, and the seamless movement of skilled labor and entrepreneurs between the zones and the domestic economy.

From a policy perspective, this suggests shifting from a traditional fenced-in EPZ model to an SEZ model that eliminates legal restrictions on forward and backward links and domestic participation. But it also will require implementation of much broader policies beyond the scope of any SEZ program, including the following: promoting skills development, training, and knowledge sharing; promoting industry clusters and targeting links with zone-based firms at the cluster level; supporting the integration of regional value chains; supporting public-private institutions, both industry specific and transversal; and ensuring labor markets are free to facilitate skilled labor moving across firms.

Chapter 7 presents the example of the Dominican Republic, one of the pioneers in establishing economic zones programs in the Western Hemisphere. Jean-Marie Burgaud and Thomas Farole illustrate how the traditional EPZ model initially had a transformative impact on the Dominican Republic, not just in terms of investment, exports, and jobs but also in shifting the economy radically away from a reliance on agricultural commodities. At its peak, the zones program contributed 7.5 percent of total GDP and was responsible for 90 percent of the country's exports.

However, the nature of the zone regime, including its reliance on fiscal incentives and wage restraint, and its enclave nature, which contributed to its prolonged failure in establishing significant forward and backward links with the Dominican economy, ultimately condemned it to an inevitable deterioration of competitiveness. Indeed, the recent macroeconomic trends discussed earlier in this chapter have accelerated these processes so that the competitiveness gap is now too large to be closed by the "artificial sources" of the EPZ regime, exposing the adjustment challenge for the zones program.

The case of the Dominican Republic highlights that while low labor costs, trade preferences, and fiscal incentives each can play a role in catalyzing a zone program, they are almost never sustainable. Indeed, they create pressure for further distortions and race-to-the-bottom policies, including extending and increasing incentives (rather than addressing more difficult factors of the investment environment) and granting exemptions on minimum wage and labor rights (rather than addressing productivity or labor market rigidities).

For the Dominican Republic, and many other lower middle-income countries whose zones programs have focused on basic assembly manufacturing and trade, the main growth opportunities are now in services sectors, especially ICT, business services, and in more knowledge and research and development (R&D)–intensive sectors. As Justine White illustrates in chapter 8, this means fostering innovation. And this highlights the need for zones to avoid becoming enclaves and instead facilitate an ongoing exchange with the local economy. Chapter 8 reinforces the importance of skills development and training, bringing in examples not only of the Shenzhen case, but also of the Republic of Korea, Malaysia, and others. Finally, it establishes a clear set of guidelines for how to ensure that an SEZ plays an ongoing role in fostering innovation, and brings in rich examples of countries whose SEZ programs not only catalyzed a process but also provided the necessary spark to fuel continuous innovation and upgrading.

But facilitating structural transformation through SEZs is not a mechanical process that simply requires the right policies. In fact, the principal factors explaining why many countries have distorted economic structures and lack sufficient dynamism are political in nature. In many cases, political and economic elites benefit from the status quo and thus have little interest in structural change. It is in this context that SEZs can perhaps be most effective, in catalyzing processes of economic reform. Indeed, this is the classic case of China's SEZs, which were used to test liberal economic reforms and to introduce them to the wider economy in a gradual way. Thus, although the idea of integration between SEZs and the domestic economy is ultimately the key to structural transformation, where economic reforms are politically sensitive to implement, it is *precisely* the enclave nature of zones that can be their key to success.

In chapter 9, Richard Auty explores this issue from a theoretical perspective, looking at the political economy of SEZs and their potential to play a catalytic role in facilitating economic reform in environments in which the barriers to such reform within the domestic economy are substantial. Auty introduces the concept of early reform zones (ERZs) as a dual-track strategy to overcome barriers to economic reform in rent-distorted economies. Although his model is relevant in many situations, perhaps most notably in natural resources driven economies, in chapter 9, he discusses specifically the context of Sub-Saharan Africa, where many economies have entrenched patronage systems that undermine reform, resulting in stagnating competitiveness. Drawing lessons from the experiences of China and Mauritius, as well as from Malaysia and others, Auty points out that the ERZ approach turns the often-criticized enclave nature of zones into "a virtue." By using the enclave approach to address reform, necessarily in isolation from the rent-distorted economy, it later can allow for spillover and integration.

In chapter 10, Claude Baissac describes the case of Mauritius. He argues that although the country is often cited as an example of EPZ success, the true success story of the Mauritius EPZ program was not job creation, investments, or exports per se, but rather the reform process, both economic and (critically) political, that it catalyzed. It is this reform that facilitated the structural transformation in the economy. Several important lessons can be drawn from the Mauritius case. First, it highlights the importance of the political process and the importance of having a specific political champion behind the zones program, a lesson that we also see from cases such as China and Malaysia (especially Penang). Second, not only does the Mauritius case emphasize the importance of domestic investment in the zones program, it shows that integration of the zone program must go beyond the physical and financial—it must also be integrated strategically. Indeed, one of the main differences between zone programs that have been successful and sustainable and those that have either failed to take off or have become stagnant enclaves is the degree to which they have been integrated in the broader economic policy framework of the country. In Mauritius, the EPZ program featured as a pillar of the country's development strategic. Zones generally have failed to have a catalytic impact in most countries in part because they have been disconnected from wider economic strategies. Zone programs often are put in place and then left to operate on their own, with little effort to support domestic investment into the zones, to promote links, training, and upgrading. Unlocking the potential of zones requires strategic integration of the program along with the government playing a leading, active role in potentiating the impact of the zones.

Finally, Baissac observes that in the process of achieving adjustment, the zones program effectively made itself obsolete. Although this is true, it is important to note also that Mauritius continues to use instruments of SEZs to promote emerging industries, such as ICT and financial services, and indeed many argue that its duty-free island initiative effectively turns the whole country into an SEZ. And so, although the Mauritius case suggests some life cycle of traditional EPZs, the instruments on which they are based may remain relevant in facilitating the ongoing transformation process.

Social and Environmental Sustainability: Emerging Issues For SEZs

Both measures of success discussed in part III—static and dynamic—are concerned with economic efficiency alone. But SEZ impacts on host societies go well beyond this. There has been much (mainly critical) documentation of the social and environmental impacts of zones over the years. It is important to recognize that these issues should not, in fact, be viewed as completely segregated from the economic ones discussed earlier. Indeed, over time social, environmental, and economic outcomes are closely entwined. Zone programs that fail to offer opportunities for quality employment and upward mobility of trained staff, which derive their competitive advantage from exploiting low-wage workers, and which neglect to provide an environment that addresses the particular concerns of female workers are unlikely to be successful in achieving the dynamic benefits possible from zones programs and likely will be forced into a race to the bottom. By contrast, zone programs that recognize the value of skilled workers and seek to provide the social infrastructure and working environment in which such workers thrive will be in a position to facilitate upgrading.

In chapter 11, Sheba Tejani addresses an issue that has important social as well as economic implications for zones programs and the people who work within them. Several studies of employment in SEZs have found that firms located inside zones have a much higher share of women in their work force relative to the overall economy. (Kusago and Tzannatos 1998; Milberg and Amengual 2008; United Nations Centre on Transnational Corporations-International Labour Organisation 1988). In this regard, zones have created an important avenue for young women to enter the formal economy. On the other hand, zones have long been criticized for poor labor standards and, more generally, for failing to provide quality employment for female workers. But, it also is critical to understand the structural nature of the link between female workers and SEZs. Indeed, it is not a direct one. SEZs do not attract female workers per se. But they do attract the firms in sectors whose basis of competition is highly dependent on the available supply of low-wage, flexible, and unskilled or semiskilled workers, a set of requirements that often results in a concentration of female workers due to prevailing social and cultural conditions. These firms have been attracted to traditional zones in part because they (1) minimize costs (through fiscal incentives and administrative efficiencies); (2) provide access to serviced land and more reliable infrastructure; and (3) reduce the investment requirement, lowering risk and providing operational and strategic flexibility.

So it is probably more appropriate to refer to sectors and tasks that are gender concentrated rather than zones per se. This is important for more than theoretical reasons. The evidence shows that as firms and zones upgrade—both into higher value added sectors and to higher value added activities within existing sectors—the share of females in the labor force tends to decline. Thus, countries that remain reliant on traditional labor-intensive, low-skilled activities will be forced in time to adjust, and it will be critical to consider some of the economic and social implications these adjustments may have.

Ensuring that the rights of workers are upheld and, beyond this, that efforts are made to provide the training and social infrastructure needed to enable individual workers to thrive, ultimately will be critical to ensuring the sustainability of zones programs, and their potential to deliver the dynamic economic benefits discussed previously. Thus, zone programs will need to strengthen their approach to social and environmental compliance issues, establishing clear standards and putting in place effective monitoring and evaluation (M&E) programs. At a national policy level, economic zones should be seen as opportunities to experiment with policy innovations.

These same principles—of policy experimentation, clear standards, and robust M&E—also are applicable in the environmental field. In chapter 12, Han-Koo Yeo and Gokhan Akinci explore a seldom-discussed issue in the zones literature, but one that will become increasingly critical in all economic policy discussions: climate change and the role of SEZs in supporting environmentally friendly development and production. Some zones have been criticized as promoting "dirty" industries and failing to meet environmental standards. SEZs, however, offer an ideal environment for environmental policy experimentation, not only because of their enclave nature but also because they have built-in compliance mechanisms that normally do not exist outside the zones, such as the ability to issue licenses, to monitor firms in a short time frame, and ultimately to revoke a license, terminate a lease, or impound containers. This context could offer interesting opportunities particular to innovations in both social and environmental policy. As Yeo and Akinci discuss in chapter 12, the concept of developing low-carbon "green" zones is in its infancy, but already is being adopted in many SEZs around the world.

Conclusion

With more than 100 countries worldwide operating SEZ programs and several thousand individual zones, it is perhaps not surprising that huge diversity exists in terms of their objectives, design, and implementation. As a result, policy makers, donors, and private sector investors have a vast range of challenges and opportunities to consider. This book addresses only a small set of them, but in doing so, it sets out a substantial policy and operational agenda.

As SEZ programs continue to proliferate around the world, particularly in developing countries, it will be critical for policy makers to learn from past experiences and to anticipate the implications of the emerging and future issues discussed in this book. Under the framework of attracting investment and creating jobs, facilitating dynamic benefits, and ensuring sustainability, this section set out a number of key principles for policy makers to consider. There is no need to enumerate these principles here. However, it is worth repeating that achieving success with SEZ programs in the future will require adopting a more flexible approach to using the instruments of economic zones in the most effective way to leverage a country's sources of comparative advantage, and to ensure flexibility to allow for evolution of the zone program over time. Most fundamentally, this will require a change in mind-set away from the traditional reliance on fiscal incentives and wage restraint, and instead focusing on facilitating a more effective business environment to foster firm-level competitiveness, local economic integration, innovation, and social and environmental sustainability. It also will require proactive, flexible, and innovative policy approaches to address today's significant macroeconomic constraints and the many unanticipated challenges that no doubt will shape the environment in the years to come.

Notes

1. However, a form of industrial free zone was established in Puerto Rico as early as 1948 (Farole 2011).
2. The MFA, which originated in 1974, was a system of quotas and voluntary export restrictions that resulted in quantitative restrictions on the textile and

garment exports used to protect the markets of the main importing countries of Europe and North America.

3. The recent doubling of the minimum wage in the garment sector shows that wage restraint is not likely to be a policy of the government.

4. Lesotho does not, in fact, operate any formal zones program.

5. Most of the developers are state-owned enterprises.

References

Boyenge, J. P. S. 2007. *ILO Database on Export Processing Zones, Revised.* Geneva: International Labour Organization.

Chen, J. 1993. "Social Cost-Benefit Analysis of China's Shenzhen Special Economic Zone." *Development Policy Review* 11 (3): 261–71.

Farole, T. 2011. *Special Economic Zones in Africa: Comparing Performance and Learning from Global Experiences.* Washington, DC: World Bank.

FIAS (Foreign Investment Advisory Service). 2008. *Special Economic Zones. Performance, Lessons Learned, and Implications for Zone Development.* Washington, DC: World Bank.

Hamada, K. 1974. "An Economic Analysis of the Duty Free Zone." *Journal of International Economics* 4: 225–41.

Jayanthakumaran, K. 2003. "Benefit-Cost Appraisals of Export Processing Zones: A Survey of the Literature." *Development Policy Review* 21 (1): 51–65.

Johansson, H., and L. Nilsson. 1997. "Export Processing Zones as Catalysts." *World Development* 25 (12): 2115–28.

Kaplinsky, R. 1993. "Export Processing Zones in the Dominican Republic: Transforming Manufactures into Commodities." *World Development* 21 (11): 1851–65.

Kusago, T., and Z. Tzannatos. 1998. "Export Processing Zones: A Review in Need of Update." SP Discussion Paper 9802. Washington, DC: World Bank.

Madani, D. 1999. "A Review of the Role and Impact of Export Processing Zones." World Bank Policy Research Working Paper No. 2238. Washington, DC: World Bank.

Milberg, W., & M. Amengual. 2008. *Economic Development and Working Conditions in Export Processing Zones: A Survey of Trends.* Geneva: International Labour Organization.

Mongé-Gonzalez, R., J. Rosales-Tijerino, and G. Arce-Alpizar. 2005. "Cost-Benefit Analysis of the Free Trade Zone System: The Impact of Foreign Direct Investment in Costa Rica." *OAS Trade, Growth and Competitiveness Studies,* Organization of American States, January.

United Nations Centre on Transnational Corporations-International Labour Organization. 1988. *Economic and Social Effects of Multinational Enterprises in Export Processing Zones.* Geneva: International Labour Organization.

Warr, P. 1989. "Export Processing Zones: The Economics of Enclave Manufacturing." *The World Bank Research Observer* 9 (1): 65–88.

Willmore, L. 1995. "Export Processing Zones in the Dominican Republic: A Comment on Kaplinsky." *World Development* 23 (3): 529–35.

World Bank. 1992. "Export Processing Zones." Policy and Research Series No. 20. Washington, DC: World Bank.

PART I

Attracting Investment and Creating Jobs: Old Models and New Challenges

The Thin End of the Wedge: Unlocking Comparative Advantage through EPZs in Bangladesh

Mustafizul Hye Shakir and Thomas Farole

Introduction

Bangladesh is an extremely densely populated country (150 million people living on less than 150,000 square kilometers). Despite this density, the country relies mainly on agriculture to support the majority of its population. Although Bangladesh has a historical reputation for producing the finest quality textiles and jute products, and long has been a hub for trade, the country has a low industrial and manufacturing base. Jute was the main export of Bangladesh for decades: during the 1950s to the 1960s, almost 80 percent of the world's jute was produced in Bangladesh. However, from the 1970s onward, the global jute industry faced a long period of decline as a result of the development of synthetic substitutes.[1] The gap in exports was filled by the textile and garment sectors, which gained a quick foothold in international markets, taking advantage of Bangladesh's low labor costs to attract investors from other Asian economies (particularly the Republic of Korea;

Taiwan, China; and Hong Kong SAR, China) that faced quotas resulting from the MFA.

But the country's phenomenal growth in garments was experienced only in the last decade. Indeed, in the early 1980s, Bangladesh had only 50 garment factories, employing only a few thousand people. It was during this time that the EPZ program was established—a move that would prove to have a substantial impact in catalyzing the development of the garment sector in the coming decades.

Bangladesh now has nearly 4,500 garment manufacturing units, employing almost 2 million workers (50 percent of the industrial workforce in the country), and contributing 75 percent of the country's total export earnings (Bangladesh Bank 2009). Garment exports in Bangladesh have continued to grow strongly despite the recent global economic crisis. Although accounting for a minority of employment and exports, the EPZs are at the heart of Bangladesh's dynamic garment sector. By providing serviced land, a supporting infrastructure, a transparent and relatively efficient regulatory environment, and a regime of incentives, the EPZs have played a critical role in attracting large-scale FDI. This environment has had a knock-on effect, catalyzing additional investment by domestic entrepreneurs in recent years.

As of 2009, the EPZs in Bangladesh employ more than 200,000 and account for a substantial share of national exports and investment. However, the program faces a number of challenges going forward. Chief among these challenges are how to maintain competitiveness while also upgrading wages and working conditions for EPZ workers, and how to achieve diversification outside of the garment sector. This diversification will require changes in the zones program itself. Indeed, the traditional EPZ model on which the program is based has become increasingly archaic, and a number of reforms are necessary to ensure that it remains an engine of economic growth into the future—in particular, private sector development and management of zones, implementation of World Trade Organization (WTO)–consistent policy and incentive frameworks, and more innovative regulatory frameworks. A new Economic Zones Act, which was passed in July 2010, represents an important step in addressing these challenges.

This chapter provides a brief history of the development of EPZs in Bangladesh and discusses its successes and the factors that have contributed to it. It then assesses the key challenges facing the Bangladesh's export sector going forward and the role of the EPZs in addressing these challenges.

Historical Development of EPZs in Bangladesh

Bangladesh's EPZs were conceived of at a time when the trend among many developing countries was to shift toward import substitution. The industrial structure in Bangladesh was built around nationalized mills and factories. With the loss of many jobs in the jute sector, however, the government was anxious to create jobs and was open to establishing a more liberalized environment for trade and investment. The garment sector appeared to offer the main source of hope for large-scale job creation. Initially, this came through domestic entrepreneurs who invested in the industry with a small-scale production base. In addition, a cadre of about 130 Bangladeshis, who were trained by the Daewoo Company in the Republic of Korea, returned home and started brokering deals to accommodate foreign investment in the sector (e.g., buying houses and factories). These ex-Daewoo trainees, in conjunction with a few Sri Lankan garment companies relocating during their country's civil war, catalyzed the growth of the sector.

The government was quick to recognize these signals from the private sector. It acted decisively to take advantage of this opportunity by creating a secure environment for exporters to realize the industry's potential. With the initiation of the Foreign Investment (Promotion and Protection) Act (1980), the foundations were set to attract foreign investment on a large scale. Nevertheless, the issues with land accessibility and administrative and logistical obstacles were a major hindrance to attracting investment. The establishment of EPZs was coined as an innovative and quick way to deal with the issues while nationwide reforms were slowly unfolding. The Bangladesh Export Processing Zone Authority (BEPZA) was established in 1980 and the first EPZ was built in Chittagong in 1983.

The establishment of EPZs is quite remarkable for several reasons. The concept of industrial serviced land was not new in the country, but never before was any piece of land declared as "extraterritorial" and dedicated to manufacturing of products for export. Significant changes were brought into the fiscal incentives scheme and administrative procedures for the import and export of goods. The range and quality of services provided were superior to what was ever offered by any government agency. The Bangladesh Small and Cottage Industries Corporation (BSCIC) already operated a number of estates around the country,[2] which catered to the small and midsize local entrepreneurs. However, the BSCIC estates typically are small (less than 40 hectares), land is leased for long periods (99 years), and the maintenance of the estates is minimal.

EPZs, on the other hand, typically are larger (the smallest ones are in excess of 40 hectares), walled, secured, and considerably well maintained and managed. Moreover, the package of incentives available in the new EPZs for export-oriented activity was not available in any other industrial estate in the country (see Section 3, Performance, for a detailed discussion on the incentives regime).

Despite this progress, the EPZs caught on only gradually. It took almost 10 years for the zone to host a meaningful number of companies. But with the growth in global production networks in the garment sector during the 1990s, Bangladesh's EPZs took off. A second EPZ was started outside Dhaka in 1993 (and later expanded) and an additional six have been opened since then, with several more in the pipeline.

Today, eight EPZs are operating under BEPZA, with two new zones in the planning stages. In addition, a privately developed zone, operated by the Youngone Corporation of the Republic of Korea, is under construction near Chittagong. Although the zones are spread throughout the country, in reality, economic activity in the EPZs is highly concentrated: of the eight operating zones, just two of them—Chittagong EPZ and Dhaka EPZ—account for more than 80 percent of the companies operating in the EPZs (see table 2.1).

Other than Chittagong and Dhaka, all the EPZs have been launched since 2000. The Adamjee and Karnaphuli EPZs were established on the grounds of suspended state-owned enterprises (SOEs, the former an old jute milling complex and the latter a steel mill), which the government had handed over to BEPZA. The Adamjee EPZ is fully operational and has been attracting investment at a fairly rapid rate. Karnaphuli is partly in the project stage, but it too already has attracted some investment.

Table 2.1   Summary of EPZs, 2009

Location	Year Established	Size (Hectares)	No. of active enterprises
Chittagong	1983	183	140
Dhaka	1993	140	96
Mongla	2000	186	12
Ishwardi	2000	125	3
Uttara	2000	93	5
Comilla	2001	108	18
Adamjee	2005	119	12
Karnaphuli	2006	109	4

Source: BEPZA.
Note: Data represent the 2008/09 fiscal year.

Similarly, the Comilla Zone—located on the Dhaka-Chittagong corridor—has grown steadily, if gradually. The Uttara, Ishwardi, and Mongla EPZs have performed poorly, however. These zones, located at great distance from the port and Dhaka, have combined to generate less than 3,000 jobs.

Performance

After a modest start, the EPZ program made substantial advancements within a short period of time. The EPZs employ a large number of workers and account for a substantial share of exports and FDI in Bangladesh. Given the size of the Bangladesh economy, however, the contribution of the zones to GDP and employment is modest. Moreover, the program remains highly concentrated in labor intensive, low skill manufacturing.

The remainder of this section reviews the results of the EPZ program in terms of (1) firms and investment, (2) exports, (3) employment, and (4) domestic market linkages.

Firms and Investment

The EPZ program has been quite successful in attracting investment, particularly taking into account that Bangladesh has historically one of the lowest levels of FDI in the region. Between 1994 and 1999, average annual investment flows into the EPZs were US$52 million; this grew to US$88 million in the subsequent five years (2000–04) and has since nearly doubled to US$172 million in the period since (2005–08). As of 2009, accumulated investment in the EPZs was nearly US$1,500 million. This is equivalent to about 15 percent of the total FDI flows into the country since 1995.[3] In 2008 and 2009, the EPZs accounted for 18 percent and 22 percent (respectively) of FDI in-flows. Approximately 290 active companies are operating in the EPZs.

The majority (61 percent) of companies in the EPZs are fully foreign owned. Of these, by far the biggest group of investors comes from the Republic of Korea, followed by Japan; Hong Kong SAR, China; and Taiwan, China. In addition, a number of investors from across the European Union and the United States are prevalent across the zones. Second most prevalent are 100 percent locally owned enterprises, which account for 25 percent of all EPZ enterprises. Indeed, the number of Bangladeshi-owned enterprises is about on par with Korean-owned enterprises across the EPZs. Joint ventures account for the remaining 41 enterprises in the EPZs.

Of the active companies operating in the EPZs, nearly two-thirds are in the garment sector (see table 2.2), with a number of other labor intensive manufacturing sector making up the rest.

Exports

Promotion and development of exports is a key objective of BEPZA. In this regard, it has been quite successful since the early 1990s (see figure 2.1). Exports have grown rapidly, at an average annual rate of 23 percent since 1993, to reach nearly US$2.5 billion by 2008. EPZ

Table 2.2   Operating Enterprises in the EPZs by Sector, 2009

Sector	No. enterprises	Percent
Textile and apparel (garment)	189	65%
Electrical and electronics	15	5%
Footwear and leather	13	4%
Metal products	12	4%
Plastic products	12	4%
Food and beverages	8	3%
Other manufacturing	31	13%
Services	3	1%

Source: BEPZA.

Figure 2.1   Exports (US$ millions) and Contribution to National Exports (percent) of EPZ Enterprises

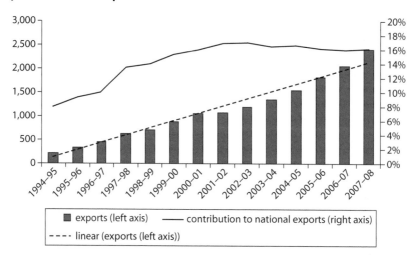

Source: BEPZA.

contribution to national exports peaked at more than 18 percent in 2003 and stood still above 17 percent in 2009. It is worth noting, however, that the EPZs still represent only 20 percent of total garment exports from Bangladesh.

Employment

In a country with millions entering the workforce annually, the contribution of the EPZs to employment generation is crucial. In terms of this objective, the EPZ program has been modestly successful. As of 2009, about 220,000 jobs had been created in the EPZs. Although this represents fairly substantial job creation over a short period of time (most of it has taken place only since the early 1990s), it is important to put this number into perspective. With a workforce of 70 million in Bangladesh, EPZ jobs are virtually a drop in the ocean. Even relative to the industrial workforce, the EPZ jobs contribute only about 3 percent of total employment. In fact, even in the garment sector up to 90% of jobs exist *outside* the EPZs, although evidence suggests that at least some of these jobs exist because of the competitive export sector inside the EPZs.

Nevertheless, EPZ jobs have had an important, positive impact on the economy, particularly because the majority of jobs created within them are held by women (data from BEPZA indicate that women account for 64 percent of employees in the EPZs). Nearly 60 percent of all jobs in the EPZs are in Chittagong, which accounts for nearly 136,000 jobs; another 72,000 jobs are in Dhaka EPZ. Unlike many other EPZ programs globally, the Bangladesh EPZs do not rely extensively on foreign labor. In fact, 99.5 percent of all employees in the EPZs are Bangladeshi—foreign workers account for less than 1,200 jobs in the EPZs.

Figure 2.2 outlines the annual and cumulative rates of employment in the EPZs. Over the past 10 years, nearly 15,000 new jobs have been created annually in the EPZs. Over this time, evidence indicates that labor productivity has been increasing steadily, if not spectacularly. Exports per worker in the EPZs rose by an average of 2 percent annually between 1998 and 2008, reaching a level of more than US$11,000.

Domestic Market Linkages

Linkages with the domestic market are relatively limited as a result not only of business strategies of FDI, but also of the policies and practices of the EPZ program. Evidence, however, demonstrates that increasing supply links have been developed in recent years.

Figure 2.2   Employment Generation in EPZs (Year-Wise and Cumulative)

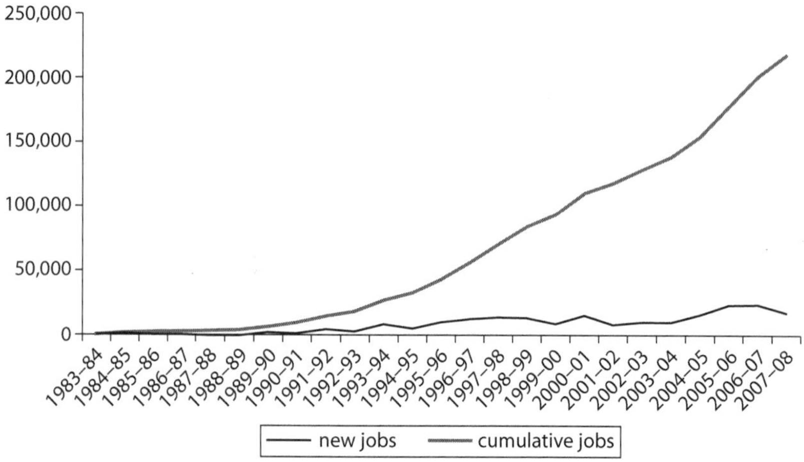

Source: BEPZA.

In terms of forward linkages, the EPZ program has restrictive policies in place, limiting local market sales to only 10 percent of production. Most important, for textiles and garment companies, who make up the bulk of EPZ enterprises, no local sales are allowed. The local market restriction attempts to protect against unfair competition, which is understandable given the size of the local industry and the substantial incentives available to EPZ-based companies. Given the large domestic market, however, FDI increasingly is looking at Bangladesh not only as a location for an export platform, but also as an opportunity to tap into the local market. This is particularly relevant in industries like metal products and processed food. In general, FDI is looking to have flexibility to tap into both local and international market demand; the domestic market restrictions place significant limits on this. For example, a company that wanted to set up a US$500 million steel mill recently approached the Korean EPZ. The company, however, wanted access to the domestic market for this investment and decided against investing because of the local market sales restrictions. For those sectors that are allowed to sell 10 percent into the local market, administrative procedures act as an additional barrier. Firms are first required to obtain authorization from BEPZA; they then must pay customs duties, the procedures for which are said to be particularly burdensome.

Backward linkages, however, are not actively prohibited and, in theory, are encouraged. However, a number of regulatory, administrative, and general market factors place significant barriers in the way of backward linkages. In theory, local producers selling into the EPZs can obtain duty drawback on imported inputs (as an indirect exporter), putting them on a level playing field with foreign suppliers to the EPZs. But for a small producer of garments accessories or a dying and washing unit servicing larger units inside EPZs, this turns out to be extremely difficult in practice. The Duty Exemptions and Drawback Office (DEDO) is severely understaffed, the system of drawbacks is heavily bureaucratic, and the process suffers from total lack of trust between the service receiver and provider.[4] Small, indirect exporters often complain that they cannot claim drawback because they cannot attach the original bill of export with their claims with the DEDO. As a result, small suppliers rarely claim duty drawback.[5] Second, because of security concerns and EPZ products leaking into the local market, BEPZA has restricted the movement of trucks from the domestic territory into the EPZs. This has made the process of getting supplies from local companies more difficult—for example, trucks are prohibited from coming in and out of the zone outside specifically designated hours.

Despite these problems, the large local supply base is making some inroads into the EPZ exporters. BEPZA points to the case of a Swedish contractor to H&M, which sources inputs from 27 different local suppliers. This certainly may be the exception to the rule, but it does underscore the size of the local supply base and the diversity available, something that is not the case in many EPZ programs in Africa, for example.

Key Success Factors

A number of exogenous factors explain the rise of Bangladesh as an export location for the garment sector, but several aspects of the EPZ regime have played an important role—in particular, the availability of serviced land and supporting infrastructure, the transparent and relatively efficient administrative regime in the zones, and the incentives regime that is available to zone-based firms. This section discusses each of these factors after an initial introduction to two critical exogenous factors that also are affected by the EPZ program: wages and market access.

Exogenous Factors: Wages and Market Size

Whatever role the EPZs have played in supporting the rapid growth of garment sector exports in Bangladesh, the most critical factor behind

Figure 2.3   Comparison of Average Wages and Benefits of Unskilled Workers in SEZs

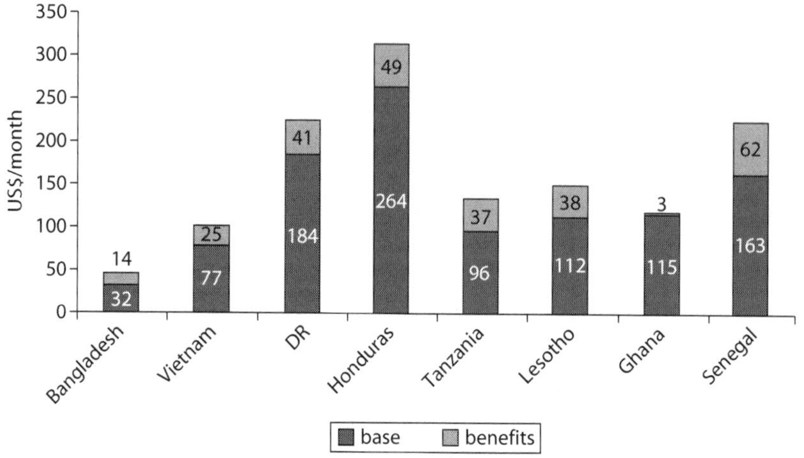

Source: Farole (2011).

Note: The data presented in this figure on wages in Bangladesh were obtained before the July 2010 decision to raise the national minimum wage substantially.

growth of the sector in Bangladesh is the country's labor cost advantage. Low-skill garment workers in Bangladesh receive among the lowest wages paid in formal employment anywhere in the world, with starting wages only around US$30 per month.[6] Figure 2.3 shows a comparison of average wages in free zones around the world, based on a recent World Bank survey (Farole 2011). The labor cost advantage for Bangladesh is striking—wages are 2.5 times lower than the next cheapest country (Vietnam), and more than three times lower than in most African SEZs. Even accounting for relatively low productivity, for labor-intensive activities like garment processing (where wages often account for 50 percent or more of total production costs) the case for locating in Bangladesh is compelling.

In addition to the significant labor cost advantage, Bangladesh also benefits from its huge market size. Despite limited purchasing power, producers in Bangladesh are interested in accessing the 150 million people living in the country. In addition, the scale of the market—particularly around Dhaka and Chittagong—ensures access to critical material and service inputs to producers, which may be unavailable in smaller markets.

Offsetting these advantages, however, Bangladesh, like most low-income countries, struggles with a poor investment climate. The private sector remains weak, and regulations and weak institutions make setting up a business extremely difficult, for both foreign and domestic investors. Bangladesh ranks 119 of 183 countries in the World Bank's *Doing Business* index for 2010 (World Bank 2009). In some key components of the index, in which Bangladesh has fared worst, it is clear that the EPZ environment helps investors to overcome significant constraints. In particular, these constraints relate to accessing and developing serviced land (Bangladesh ranked 176 of 183 countries on the measure "registering a property"), obtaining licenses, and other regulatory constraints. Other important investment climate constraints identified—for example, in the World Bank's Enterprise Surveys (World Bank 2008)—include corruption and unreliable power. The environment for both of these constraints is at least partly improved inside the EPZs. Finally, companies operating inside the EPZs report that internal security protects them from such issues as labor unrest, vandalism, and petty extortion, which are problematic outside the zones.

Provision of Serviced Land and Supporting Infrastructure

Because Bangladeshi land titling issues present a major constraint to investment and the country's industrial land market is severely constrained, BEPZA's provision of land and factory shells plays a critical role in attracting investment. BEPZA offers land on 30-year leases, which may be renewed, and enterprises construct their facilities in designated plots of typically 2,000 square meters. BEPZA also rents prebuilt factory units on shorter lease periods, which attracts investors that are not in a position to invest substantially upfront and are looking to set up operations quickly and with little risk. Given the high costs of land access and development in Bangladesh, it is widely believed that the rates charged are highly subsidized.

As of end 2009, no space is left in the two main zones of Dhaka and Chittagong. Although company turnover allows some new investors to move in every year, most investors are now limited in their options—they must either move to another EPZ in a less desirable location or set up outside the EPZs. BEPZA has been looking to expand in Dhaka for several years, but the high cost of land acquisition is making this problematic.

Another key area of infrastructure provision by BEPZA is electricity and gas. Outside of the zones, power is a major problem in Bangladesh, and most companies must rely on their own generators. Inside the zones, BEPZA purchases power from the national grid and sells it to enterprises in the zones, adding a 10 percent surcharge (this is an important revenue source for BEPZA). Although the country faces an acute power shortage, BEPZA's power supply takes priority over other national usage. BEPZA also has allowed companies to produce power within the zone for the zone's use only, and several of these power plants (some under public-private partnerships (PPPs)) are expected to be in operation soon.

In addition to this core infrastructure, BEPZA also develops and maintains a wide range of key supporting infrastructure in the zone, including business and commercial infrastructure, administrative infrastructure, and infrastructure to support leisure, family, and quality-of-life issues. These include the following:

- *Business*: Bank, business center, courier, post office, clearing, forwarding, and shipping agents
- *Administrative*: Customs office, police station, in-house security, fire station, public transport, medical clinic
- *Support and quality of life*: Restaurant and canteen, health club, investors club, recreation center, school, sport complex

Efficiency of the Administrative Regime

In the bureaucratic environment of Bangladesh, BEPZA offers the best service in terms of ease of obtaining licenses and approvals. BEPZA's recommendation to other agencies is taken seriously and BEPZA's officials make an effort to guide the processes through the various channels. The administrative functions within BEPZA's own domain work quite well, and investors seem to be quite satisfied with the speed and efficiency of the system within BEPZA. The BEPZA executive board has the capacity to make its own decisions and execute them. Moreover, certain activities have authority delegated to BEPZA, including registering a business, foreign investments and loans approval, and outsourcing services such as power generation. The fact that BEPZA reports directly to the prime minister's office is seen as a critical factor that supports its efficient delivery of services to investors.

Incentives Regime

The core fiscal incentive offered in the zones is a 10-year tax holiday, followed by an additional five years with a 50 percent reduction (the normal corporate tax rate for industrial companies ranges from 27.5 percent for publicly traded companies to 37.5 percent for nonpublicly traded companies[7]). This incentive is broadly in line with international norms; however, it actually is less generous than in many EPZs, which either offer unlimited tax holidays or allow the tax holiday to begin only after a ramp-up period or when the company first reaches profitability (in Bangladesh, the tax holiday begins the first year of operation). In addition to corporate tax, expatriate workers receive a three-year exemption from paying income tax. Other fiscal and nonfiscal incentives, offered in most EPZs around the world, are available in Bangladesh (see box 2.1).

Another important part of the package to attract foreign investors is a regulatory framework that provides confidence of across-the-board investor protection. This includes the Foreign Investor Protection Act of 1980,

---

Box 2.1

Incentives Offered in Bangladesh EPZs

Fiscal incentives

- 10-year tax holiday; additional 5 years at 50 percent
- Duty-free import and export of raw materials and finished goods
- Duty-free import of construction materials, equipment, office machinery, spare parts
- Relief from double taxation
- Exemption from dividend tax
- Duty-free import of two to three vehicles for use in EPZ
- Expatriates exempted from income tax for three years
- Accelerated depreciation allowance on machinery or plant
- Remittance of royalty, technical, and consultancy fees allowed

Nonfiscal incentives

- 100% foreign ownership permissible
- No ceiling on foreign or local investment
- Full repatriation of capital and dividend
- Foreign currency loans available directly from abroad
- Permission to hold nonresident foreign currency deposit account
- EPZs enjoy most-favored nation (MFN) status
- Operation of foreign currency account allowed for all companies not 100% locally owned

Source: BEPZA.

the availability of insurance through the Overseas Private Investment Corporation (OPIC, a U.S. government agency) and the Multilateral Investment Guarantee Agency (MIGA, part of the World Bank Group), access to arbitration through the International Settlement of Investment Disputes, and safeguarding of copyrights through the World Intellectual Property Organization.

Challenges for the Future

Despite the rapid growth of exports in recent years, Bangladesh's manufacturing export sector will face a number of significant challenges in the years to come. The EPZ program has the potential to play an important role in confronting these challenges; but to do so, the program will need to undertake some significant reforms of its own. This section discusses some of these key challenges and the implications for Bangladesh's zones program.

Balancing Competitiveness with Sustainable Wages and Working Conditions

Bangladesh's competitive positioning in the global garment sector is built around its significant labor cost advantage relative to alternative production locations. But even with millions of new workers entering the labor force each year, the huge wage differential is unlikely to remain sustainable. Indeed, the recent decision to nearly double the minimum wage (to 3,000 *taka* per month, up approximately US$43 from 1,662.50 *taka*) in the garment sector is evidence of the upward pressure on wages. In addition, although the EPZs have created substantial employment opportunities for low-skilled workers and have had a particularly important impact on poor families through the creation of wage-earning opportunities for females, they also have been criticized for quality of work, working conditions, and worker rights. Maintaining a competitive labor cost (or productivity) position while also delivering quality, sustainable employment opportunities will be a significant challenge for the zones program.

Most evidence indicates that wages and working conditions inside the zones are better than outside the zones. For example, wages in the zones are on average 20–30 percent higher than what is offered for the same job outside the EPZs, and factories outside the EPZs are infamous for delaying wage payments. Moreover, benefits (transport, meals, access to health clinics, holidays) and mandatory annual wage increases make employment inside the zones superior to what is available outside.

Despite these benefits, worker rights in the zones were poorly protected for a long time. EPZs have been exempted from national labor regulations. The EPZ Act, in an apparent effort to provide a more favorable investment environment, suspended the application of the 1969 Industrial Relations Ordinance and subsequent amendments, which provide for the right to organize labor unions and enter into collective bargaining agreements, as well as other labor-related legislation. Consequently, labor unions have been prohibited in the zones.

In 2004, against international pressure, Parliament passed the EPZ Workers Association and Industrial Relations Act 2004 (amended October 2010). This granted the workers some leeway to establish a franchise of workers. Although limited to only certain types of collective activity, the act allows the workers to organize elections to represent their demands and participate in collective actions in harmony with BEPZA's other regulations. This is a step toward rights to free collective union. Under this legislation, however, a ban on strikes and lockouts remained. The legislation was originally set to expire at the end of 2008, but BEPZA was able to extend it through October 2010.

In the absence of national regulations, BEPZA follows a suggested set of instructions regarding labor relations, which are referred to as "Instruction 1" and "Instruction 2." These instructions have been the rules and regulations bible in terms of the worker-owner-BEPZA relationship and compliance, and therefore they provide an established reference point. The problem is that, although the de facto situation in most firms in the EPZs is relatively good, the de jure situation as per Instructions 1 and 2 not only offers weak protection of workers' rights but also specifies lower benefits to what is available under the national labor regulations. In addition, capacity to monitor and enforce regulations is limited.

As a result of this inconsistency, and in light of the recent labor unrest and the massive protests against some of the factory owners, BEPZA has made efforts to improve worker-owner relations in the zones. One component of this effort was the establishment of a Labor Counselor Program (see box 2.2). After an initial pilot, 67 counselors were recruited to act as go-betweens and resolve problems between workers and managers. These counselors worked closely with the workers and the management and reported progress to BEPZA. They were extension workers of BEPZA and became solid advocates for the workers' concerns and rights. This project, originally funded by the World Bank, has been slightly modified and sustained through funding by the Bangladesh Investment Climate Fund (BICF).

Box 2.2

The Labor Counselor Program

The Bangladesh Export Processing Zones Authority (BEPZA) is endowed with the responsibility of ensuring compliance on social and labor issues within its zones. Acknowledging that BEPZA's resources, especially in the areas of social and labor aspects, are thinly stretched, BEPZA initiated an innovative program in 2005. The program, funded by the World Bank, recruited approximately 67 counselors to work closely with the workers and their respective management with the intention of proactively addressing issues related to wages, working conditions, food, childcare, benefits, and security. These counselors worked on behalf of BEPZA but were perceived more like facilitators than regulators and enforcers. These young recruits paid almost daily visits to their designated factories to work with management on the correct application of labor issues and compensation practices. They also acted as informal arbitrators between management and workers to resolve grievances. They also reported to BEPZA any existing or potential issues. The International Finance Corporation (IFC) estimated that the better implementation of existing rules thanks to the role of these counselors resulted in an increase of 32 percent in wages for the workers in the EPZs.

The program was valued both by BEPZA's management and the workers. The initial funding for the program expired in 2009. At BEPZA's request, the IFC BICF put in additional funding to continue the counselor program. Realizing the benefit of the program, BEPZA is committed to integrating the program into its mainstream operational budget. Following allegations of unpaid wages, the country experienced massive demonstrations and unrest. In 2006, two factories were set fire in the Dhaka EPZ. This case of unrest was one of the worst in recent times. The role of the counselors in avoiding such situations in the future has been established and acknowledged by all stakeholders.

Despite significant unrest that shook Bangladesh's garment sector in 2010, no incidents were reported in any of the EPZs in the country. The work of the labor counselors since the BICF started employing them in 2007 has been instrumental in the stark contrast in unrest inside and outside the zones. The counselors have acted as an effective and informal arbitration mechanism and have built a relationship of trust between worker and employer in all the EPZs. As evidence of this, in the Dhaka EPZ, grievances have declined from 2,000 in 2007 to 400 in 2009.

Source: Authors.

Diversification

When the Board of Investment established the first EPZ in Chittagong, the mandate was to accept only high-technology companies and not to attract labor-intensive garment companies. This, in part, explains the long delay in filling up the EPZ. Apparently, it was only after one garment company called itself "Hi Tech Knitwear" that they were allowed into the zone. This paved the way for other garment companies and the EPZs subsequently took off.

Since that time, there has been much talk about diversifying the industrial base of the EPZs, but little to no concerted action has been taken to effect such change. Across all the EPZs in Bangladesh, garment production accounts for two-thirds of companies and close to 90 percent of jobs. Despite the BEPZA's repeated statements of intent to deny any more garment investments into the EPZs to promote diversification, as late as December 2009, new garment projects had been accepted. In recent years, the EPZs have shown little to no diversification and no apparent targeted investment promotion strategy that will effect such a change.

Within the garment sector as well, upgrading over the years has been limited. Although the EPZs have suppliers across the range of inputs, assembly, and finishing, few companies have become full-package suppliers, with the vast majority carrying out simple cut, make, and trim activities.

Reform of Existing EPZ Regime

To address these and other challenges facing the export sector, in the coming years, reforms to the existing EPZ regime are needed in several areas.

First, BEPZA needs to realign its program of fiscal incentives. Like most traditional EPZ programs, BEPZA's incentive scheme is tied to exports, which makes it incompatible with the WTO Agreement on Subsidies and Countervailing Measures. As a least-developed country (LDC), Bangladesh remains exempt from these prohibitions for the time being. However, as the leases in the EPZs are set for 30 years, it may be difficult to phase out the incentive schemes in the future (when Bangladesh does graduate from the low-income country exemption) if the adjustments are not made ahead of time. This adjustment likely will involve a phasing out of the core fiscal benefits over time.

Second, there is a need to promote much greater private sector development and management in the zones program. BEPZA's role as regulator and operator has been identified as a major obstacle to the continued success of the zones, both in terms of regulatory compliance and private sector–led growth. Until very recently, BEPZA has had an implicit monopoly on developing and managing EPZs. Although the Private EPZ Act of 1996 makes a provision for private entities to develop and run EPZs, it lacks any clear criteria for approving such zones and the nominal regulator of private zones (an Executive Cell, which is essentially a parallel regulator to BEPZA) has no capacity or resources to perform its responsibilities. Thus, 13 years after the passage of the legislation, only one private sector–led EPZ has been initiated, and it has not yet managed to become operational (see box 2.3).

The Economic Zones Act, which was passed in July 2010, will result in substantial changes to the existing zones regime in Bangladesh and

---

Box 2.3

The Korean EPZ: The First Private EPZ in Bangladesh

The Youngone Corporation was the first company to obtain a license from the Government of Bangladesh to build and operate an EPZ. Youngone is a Republic of Korea conglomerate that has been operating in the Bangladesh EPZs since the early 1980s. It is one of the largest and most reputable companies in BEPZA's zones, with at least eight companies operating in textiles, garments, footwear, sportswear, and plastics. The "Korean EPZ" will, when it becomes operational, be the largest EPZ in Bangladesh.

Youngone purchased 2,500 acres of land in Chittagong to build an EPZ in the mid-1990s. The land has since been prepared and the site has been zoned. Equipped with housing, hospitality, independent jetty, and an 18-hole golf course, the Korean EPZ is designed to host an array of activities and service within its boundaries, including both light and heavy industry. The master plan for the project estimates that it will attract US$1 billion in investment, resulting in at least 100,000 jobs and US$1.25 billion worth of exports.

However, the process of establishing the EPZ has proceeded far from smoothly. Licensing of the EPZ took almost eight years and an operational license was only obtained in May 2007. This delay is attributed to problems in gaining environmental clearance, bureaucratic procedures in setting up the zone, and the lack of institutional capacity to support private sector zone development. In addition, the project suffered long delays because of the inability to access electricity and gas supplies. Indeed, access to gas still was not resolved as of late 2009 and continues to delay development.

Source: Authors.

Box 2.4

The Economic Zones Act

The Economic Zones Act, which was passed by Parliament in July 2010, has the following strategic provisions:

- Establish one law to govern all economic zone programs in the country
- Create a broader and more flexible model for zones allowing exports as well as local sales
- Bring larger areas under special regimes, which may include existing EPZs and industrial estates
- Set clear and objective criteria for site selection and mandatory feasibility studies to eliminate discretionary powers and erratic decision making
- Facilitate an increased role of the private sector in ownership, management, and operation of zones
- Allow a light-handed approach to the regulation of zones
- Ensure that all zones are operated on commercial principles and the market to drive the price of services
- Allow the conversion of any zone into an SEZ with parameters fulfilled
- Make a provision for declaring large geographic areas to be brought under special administrative and incentive regimes to allow "brownfield" approach

Source: Authors.

will address many of the reforms (see box 2.4). The act moves Bangladesh beyond the traditional EPZ regime to embrace a broader SEZ or "economic zone" model. Specifically, it allows for much larger scale zones and takes a more flexible approach to the types of activities that can be undertaken within the zones. In addition, not only does the new act put greater emphasis on private sector participation in zone development, but it also substantially alters the role of BEPZA by splitting its regulator function from its development and management role. Finally, it ensures more private provision of public goods in the zones as well as PPPs.

Conclusion

In 2008, BEPZA celebrated its 25th anniversary. What started as a pilot program has now become a large and substantial element of the government's investment attraction and industrialization efforts. Bangladesh's EPZs have been highly successful in attracting investment and creating jobs, particularly for low-skilled female workers. It also has played a part in creating a more efficient investment environment in the country and, indeed, in putting Bangladesh on the map as a low-cost location for FDI in the garment sector. Given the size of the national economy, the overall impact of the EPZs on employment and exports has been relatively modest; however, they are likely to have played at least some catalytic role in supporting the growth of the garment sector outside the walls of the EPZs.

On the other hand, the EPZs have been less successful in facilitating upgrades and diversification in the economy. Indeed, they arguably have further entrenched the reliance on garment assembly. In addition, the EPZs have been widely criticized for their treatment of workers and for environmental failings. Although, in fact, the situation in both these respects is generally much better inside than outside the EPZs, it is true that the EPZs have not yet met their potential as modernizing influences in the industrial system in Bangladesh. That said, several recent initiatives discussed in this paper—most critically the adoption of a modern Economic Zones Act—suggest that the EPZs still have a potential to play a role in facilitating a transition toward a higher quality, more sustainable manufacturing sector for Bangladesh.

Notes

1. Although in recent years, demand for natural fibers has grown, leading to a substantial rise on the global market and prices for raw jute (de Vries 2007).

2. As of March 2009, BSCIC operated 74 industrial estates.

3. Assumes that approximately 80 percent of EPZ investments accrue from FDI.

4. In a survey conducted in 2006, DEDO had more than 2,000 pending applications, 30 percent of which were from 2004; in most cases, drawback takes 3–18 months and significant amounts of paperwork to be processed.

5. An estimated less than 10 percent of eligible duty drawback is claimed through the system.

6. The data presented here on wages in Bangladesh were obtained before the July 2010 decision to raise the national minimum wage substantially.

7. The vast majority of EPZ companies are not publicly traded.

References

Bangladesh Bank. 2009. Available at http://www.bangladesh-bank.org (accessed December 14, 2009).

BEPZA (Bangladesh Export Processing Zones Authority). 2009a. Available at http://www.epzbangladesh.org.bd/.BEPZA 2009b. "Investment Opportunities in the EPZs of Bangladesh." Presentation to the World Bank Group, Dhaka, March 2009.

BEPZA (2010) Available at http://www.epzbangladesh.org.bd/bepza.php?id=YREMPL.

de Vries, Johan. 2007. "Export of Jute Products from Bangladesh to Europe: Analysis of Market Potential and Development of Interventions for GTZ-PROGRESS." Available http://essay.utwente.nl/639/ (accessed December 16, 2009).

Farole, T. 2011. *Special Economic Zones in Africa: Comparing Performance and Learning from Global Experiences.* Washington, DC: World Bank.

World Bank. 2008. *Harnessing Competitiveness for Stronger Inclusive Growth: Bangladesh Second Investment Climate Assessment.* Washington, DC: World Bank.

World Bank. 2009. *Doing Business 2010: Country Profile for Bangladesh, Comparing Regulation in 183 Economies.* Washington, DC: World Bank.

CHAPTER 3

Success and Stasis in Honduras' Free Zones

Michael Engman

Introduction

How did a small, unremarkable Central American country with a turbulent political past (and, indeed, present) manage to become a leading exporter of clothing and apparel to the United States and, in doing so, create in excess of 100,000 new jobs? Although not without peers in the region, Honduras has achieved notable success with its free zones. The Honduran free zone/*maquila* program was established as early as 1976; however, it was not until the 1990s that it reaped dividends for the economy, as a confluence of factors, including external political events and economic trends, government policies, and a dynamic private sector, enabled the country to attract large-scale FDI and become a location of choice for offshoring in the U.S. apparel sector.

Over the last two decades, the free zone industry has expanded rapidly in terms of investment, exports, and employment. However, the global economic downturn began to affect the sector in the second half of 2008. By mid-2009, the poor economy resulted in sizeable layoffs and some companies closing down their operations in Honduras. The global economic crisis has exposed possible weaknesses in the competitive position of the traditional labor-intensive processing activities on which Honduras' free zones have relied and highlighted the urgency of diversification.

In facing this challenge, Honduras can draw on many of the strengths that allowed it to build a successful free zone export sector. Some of these same factors also may be a source of "lock-in" that prevents the government and the free zone sector from making the decisions necessary to achieve diversification and upgrading in the sector.

This chapter analyzes Honduras' experience with free zones over the past three decades. It discusses the factors that contributed to its success and the key challenges the industry faces today.

Historical Development of Free Zones in Honduras

The *maquila*[1] (or *maquiladora*), which in Latin America and the Caribbean refers to factories that use duty-free imports of materials and equipment to assemble products that are exported predominantly to the U.S. market, was introduced in Honduras in the mid-1960s. The interest in this factory concept stemmed from a wave of initiatives in Central America, the Caribbean, and East Asia to integrate industrial parks into national development plans. By establishing geographically limited enclaves with dedicated infrastructure, streamlined public administration, and various fiscal incentives, the underlying idea was that developing countries would be able to attract foreign capital and technology used for labor-intensive, export-oriented production activity. This capital would generate employment and foreign exchange that by extension would stimulate economic growth and facilitate the payment of imports.

Political disturbances including the 1969 war with El Salvador, which destroyed infrastructure, alarmed investors, and shifted policy attention, were partly responsible for Honduras failing to follow Mexico and the Dominican Republic as early adopters of the *maquila* policy. In 1976, however, the country enacted its first free zone law,[2] which allowed export-oriented companies established in Puerto Cortés to enjoy a number of mostly fiscal incentives.

The early years following the passing of the Free Zone Law saw limited investment and business activity—eight companies chose to invest in the Puerto Cortés free zone in its initial years of operations. To broaden the choice of location for investors, the Free Zone Law was in 1979 extended to another five counties: Amapala, Choloma, La Ceiba, Omoa, and Tela. In 1984, the Temporary Importation Regulations Law extended many of the fiscal incentives to export-oriented companies based outside the free zones to create a domestic supply base and soften the economic distortions that the zones gave rise to. The Export Processing Zone (EPZ) Law of 1987 later provided similar fiscal incentives to both export-oriented companies and real estate owners who invested in the physical infrastructure of industrial parks anywhere in the country. Finally, on May 20, 1998, after 22 years of selective enlargements, this process was complete as the National Congress declared the entire national territory a Free Zone Area (Decree No. 131-98), allowing privately owned and managed EPZs (or "ZIPs," *Zonas Industriales de Procesamiento*) to be established anywhere in the country.

Honduras offers several advantages as a base for manufacturing of light goods, including (1) the proximity to the U.S. South and East Coast markets; (2) the efficient deepwater port of Puerto Cortés; (3) the sizeable cluster of textiles and clothing companies in the San Pedro Sula region; (4) preferential market access through the Caribbean Basin Trade Partnership Act (CBTPA) and the Dominican Republic-Central American Free Trade Agreement (DR-CAFTA); and (5) a comprehensive free zone regime with favorable fiscal incentives (see box 3.1). In addition, although higher than in neighboring Nicaragua and in some other large exporting countries like Bangladesh, China, and Vietnam, labor costs are relatively low in Honduras compared with other countries in its region.

Performance

Honduras has experienced rapid growth in the free zone program, particularly in the period from the early 1990s through 2007. This section provides a brief summary of progress of the zones program across the main components of performance: firms and investment, exports, employment, and local market linkages.

Firms and Investment
The free zone sector in Honduras consists of a fairly large cluster of light goods manufacturers concentrated around the city of San Pedro Sula near Puerto Cortés. As of the end of 2008, 342 free zone companies, predominantly in the textiles and clothing sector, were based either in one of two dozen privately operated zones or operating as "single zone enterprises." Most of the companies operating in the zones are foreign owned, while the owners and operators of the free zone industrial parks are predominantly Honduran investors. The dominant position of the textiles and clothing sector is confirmed by the data available on FDI (see tables 3.1 and 3.2). The sector received on average 64 percent of total FDI in the manufacturing sector in 2004–2007. "Electronic components,"

Box 3.1

Incentives in the Honduras Free Zones

The fiscal incentive structure that the Government of Honduras offers companies with free zone status is generous from an international perspective. Free zone–based companies are exempt from all federal and municipal taxes as well as duties and charges associated with trade. What makes the fiscal incentive structure in Honduras rather unique is the fact that there is no time limit attached to the fiscal incentives. The boxed table summarizes the incentive structure offered in the various laws that cover companies in Honduran free zones.[3] The legal framework that currently governs the free zones is tailor-made for the manufacturing industry and does not cover the provision of services. However, in practice, the government does not enforce this rule and it is said to allow those zones that move into the business of call center services.

Incentives	Free Trade Zone (ZOLI)	Export Processing Zone (ZIP)	Temporary Import Law
Imported duties on raw materials, components	100% exemption	100% exemption	100% exemption
Export taxes	100% exemption	100% exemption	100% exemption
Local sales and excise taxes	100% exemption	100% exemption	100% exemption if imported
Taxes on net assets	100% exemption	100% exemption	Subject to payment
Taxes on profits	100% exemption	100% exemption	Subject to payment
Municipal taxes and obligations/ duties	100% exemption	100% exemption	Subject to payment
Taxes on profits repatriation	100% exemption	100% exemption	Subject to Central Bank
Capital repatriation	100% exemption	100% exemption	Subject to Central Bank
Currency conversion	Unrestricted	Unrestricted	Subject to Central Bank
Customs	Cleared on site	Cleared on site	Through a customs agent
Sales to local market	5% of total production paying customs duties	Only paying customs duties authorized by the Secretariat of Industry and Trade	Only paying customs duties authorized by the Secretariat of Industry and Trade

(continued next page)

Box 3.1 (*continued*)

Incentives	Free Trade Zone (ZOLI)	Export Processing Zone (ZIP)	Temporary Import Law
Eligibility requirements	Industrial and commercial companies can be established	Industrial and supporting companies can be established	Industrial and commercial companies can be established

Source: Asociación Hondureña de Maquiladores (2009).

Table 3.1   FDI in Manufacturing Activities
(US$, million)

	2004	2005	2006	2007	Average 2004–2007
Textiles	92.2	76.3	127.3	197.6	63.7%
Input services	20.7	22.9	32.0	20.0	12.3%
Commerce	−3.3	8.0	16.3	5.8	3.5%
Agriculture and fishery	7.7	7.8	8.2	4.3	3.6%
Cardboard products	3.8	3.3	−9.1	1.9	0.0%
Plastic products	0.0	0.6	0.4	0.1	0.1%
Chemical products	0.0	2.7	0.0	0.0	0.3%
Furniture & wood products	0.5	−0.4	0.5	−1.5	−0.1%
Tobacco	22.4	5.3	−0.1	−3.6	3.1%
Electronic components	28.7	65.3	2.3	−5.3	11.7%
Other industry	2.2	3.9	6.9	0.2	1.7%
Total	174.9	195.8	184.7	219.6	

Source: Central Bank of Honduras (2008).

Table 3.2   FDI in Manufacturing by Country of Origin
(US$, million)

	2004	2005	2006	2007	Average 2004–2007
Canada	37.9	4.5	65.6	112.6	28.5%
El Salvador	1.4	0.9	0.2	1.0	0.5%
Germany	2.2	0.8	0.4	−2.8	0.1%
Korea	16.8	17.5	10.9	10.9	7.2%
Mexico	0.2	0.6	7.0	−3.4	0.6%
Spain	4.3	1.3	3.9	0.1	1.2%
Switzerland	0.0	7.0	6.6	7.2	2.7%
Taiwan	4.2	6.4	10.6	5.7	3.5%
UK	−0.1	1.0	4.1	5.0	1.3%
United States	75.8	140.0	75.9	81.7	48.2%
Other countries	32.2	15.8	−0.5	1.6	6.3%
Total	174.9	195.8	184.7	219.6	

Source: Central Bank of Honduras (2008).

which includes wire harnesses, generated significant amounts of FDI in 2004–05, but this sector has been largely defensive in the 2006–2009 period, and some companies have closed down their operations in Honduras. Canada and the United States were by far the largest sources of FDI inflows in 2004–2007. Overall, the free zone industry captured 34.4 percent of total FDI in 2007 (EIU 2008).

Production and Exports

Table 3.3 shows that in 2007, the value added contribution of the free zone/*maquila* industry to the overall economy (GDP) and to the country's overall industry production was 7.7 percent and 42.7 percent, respectively. The share of the *maquila* industry to GDP has been stable in the years following the expiration of the MFA (at least until the beginning of the global economic crisis starting in 2008), which suggests that one or more of the following is happening: the industry is maintaining competitiveness in its traditional apparel-processing activities despite the growing competition from Asian producers; it is shifting to higher value added segments of the sector; or it is diversifying away from clothing.

Free zone exports have grown rapidly since the early 1990s. Value added export earnings reached US$3.3 billion in 2007 (EIU 2008), a level 10 times higher than in 1993 (equivalent to 20 percent average growth each year over that period). Recent data by the Central Bank of Honduras also indicate that this expansion continued in 2007 but that the global economic downturn, which started in Honduras' main export market, the United States, had a negative impact toward the end of 2008 and a strong negative impact in 2009. According to the *Maquila* Association of Honduras, the country is now the fourth-largest supplier of clothing (garment) products (5.9 percent market share) and the second-largest supplier of electric harnesses to the United States. It is also

Table 3.3   Value-Added Contribution by Manufacturing in "Industry" and "*Maquila* Industry"

Year	GDP (Lempira mn)	Gross value added industry (Lempira mn)	Gross value added Maquila (Lempira mn)	Maquila industry (percent)	Maquila/GDP (percent)
2005	183,749	35,066	13,898	39.6	7.6
2006*	204,685	38,129	15,558	40.8	7.6
2007*	232,817	42,209	18,029	42.7	7.7

Source: Central Bank of Honduras (2008).
* = preliminary.

the world's largest importer of U.S. yarn (US$799 million in 2008). Honduras' producers excel in particular at producing small orders for expedient delivery to the U.S. market. This is a key comparative advantage given rapid shifts in fashion and taste as well as retailers' effort to reduce the costs of inventory. U.S. orders of textiles and clothing in the mass market are increasingly being sourced from more cost-effective locations like Bangladesh, China, and Vietnam.

Employment

The main objective of the government's free zone policy is employment creation—in this regard, the program has been quite successful. In 2007, employment in the free zone industry reached 134,000 workers; up by 3 percent year on year in 2005 and 2006. Seventy-seven percent of the workers were employed in the textiles and clothing sector. The only other product category with more than 3,500 employees was "car parts and wire harnesses" for vehicles, which accounted for about 10 percent of free zone employment (13,600).

Figure 3.1 illustrates the development of employment in the free zones since 1995. The figure indicates that rapid growth of employment took place mainly in the 1990s. Following recent declines, however, the estimated employment in 2008 was only 15 percent higher (114,000) than employment 10 years earlier (99,000). This is partly a result of capital deepening and increases in productivity—important factors to stay competitive and to move up the value chain—since exports have increased more rapidly over the same period (see WTO 2003). But it also reflects declining competitiveness in the labor-intensive assembly activities

Figure 3.1   Employment in Free Zones

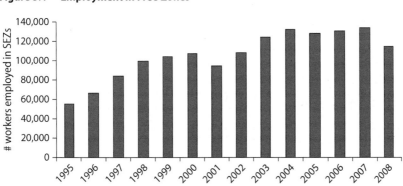

Sources: WTO (2003) for 1995–2001; Asociación Hondureña de Maquiladores (2009) for 2002–08.

that traditionally have been at the heart of the *maquila* program. Thus, although the free zone policy generally has been a success, free zones may have limited scope to absorb more than a small share of the growing labor market in the future.

In 2007, 169 textiles and clothing companies were based in the free zones, but a small handful of MNCs accounted for the majority of the 103,377 workers in the sector. Canadian company Gildan, which assembles a wide range of products, including socks, fleece products, and knit products such as T-shirts and underwear across several factories, is the largest employer in the Honduran free zones. Gildan, along with U.S. multinationals, such as Fruit of the Loom and Hanes, each employs more than 10,000 workers.

Local Market Linkages

Forward linkages are limited, in part, because the dominant apparel production sector is geared almost exclusively for the U.S. market. But policy barriers also restrict forward linkages by free zone companies. To protect local producers based outside the free zones (those that do not enjoy tax free status or other incentives available to free zone firms), Honduras restricts free zone firms to selling a maximum of 5 percent of their output into the local market.

Honduras has been fairly successful at developing backward linkages (i.e., establishing a domestic support industry that provides locally produced goods and services for the free zone–based manufacturers). The original *maquila* concept was essentially a "job shop" in which imported inputs were assembled and stitched together by local labor and then exported to foreign markets. This situation held for Honduras during the early years; however, local suppliers based in Honduras now are providing a number of locally produced intermediary goods in the production chain, in particular, textiles used in the apparel sector. As of 2011, Honduras had 10 to 12 mills producing textiles for the clothing and apparel sectors.

Key Success Factors

As noted, although the free zone program in Honduras began in the mid-1970s, it was by no means an immediate success. In fact, it took at least 15 years before the investment in the sector really began to take off. A number of factors contributed to this eventual success, including a willingness to evolve the legal framework for the program; effective use of preferential trade agreements; government support to develop the necessary infrastructure and support services for the zones; support for agglomeration; effective institutional support, particularly in marketing and promotion; and, most important, a dynamic, entrepreneurial domestic private sector. But what appears most critical to this success is that all of these factors came together at the same time. Moreover, they did so at a fortunate time when external political and economic factors also favored investment in Honduras—specifically, the U.S. recession of the early 1990s, which helped to trigger offshoring of labor-intensive production in the apparel sector, and Honduras' position as a relatively stable environment in the midst of civil strife throughout the region. This section reviews each of the main components that contributed to the success of the free zone program.

Experimentation and Evolution to Reach a Sound Legal Framework that Facilitated Private Investment

It took Honduran legislators almost a quarter of a century to find a legal framework for free zones that conformed to the demand of all stakeholders. The enactment of the first piece of legislation in 1976 created a small publicly run enclave near Puerto Cortés, which targeted export-oriented foreign investment. Over time, the government enacted several pieces of new legislation that broadened the geographic reach of the free zone policy. Most critical in this regard was the 1987 Export Processing Law, which (1) abandoned the previous policy discriminating against domestic private investors, and (2) opened up the fiscal incentives of the free zone program to export-oriented companies and real estate developers who invested in the physical infrastructure of industrial parks anywhere in the country. As discussed in the following section, this law helped to unlock investment from local entrepreneurs in developing the industrial parks, which in turn catalyzed investment from U.S. multinationals.

Further development of the legal framework sought to create more backward linkages by extending many of the tax-free and duty-free incentives to local producers outside the free zones. The evolution culminated in 1998, with the declaration of the entire national territory as a Free Zone Area (Decree No. 131-98).

Effective use of Preferential Trade Agreements

The United States traditionally has been Honduras' largest trading partner, and U.S. policies providing preferential treatment to Honduran products have had a significant impact on Honduran exports. The Caribbean

Basin Initiative (CBI) was initiated by U.S. President Ronald Reagan and came into effect on January 1, 1984, as a unilateral and temporary program. It offered preferential market access to several countries in Central America and the Caribbean for exports of clothing and apparel to the United States. It was part of U.S. policy to combat political movements through aid and trade. With CBI in place, Honduran producers did not have to pay duties on reexported inputs, such as textiles and fabrics, of U.S. origin, but only on local value added. In 1990, the U.S. passed the Caribbean Basin Economic Recovery Expansion Act (CBI II), which made the incentives in the CBI permanent. Thus, in the period from the late 1980s into the early 1990s, when the legal framework was fine-tuned to facilitate investment in industrial parks and to attract FDI, the development of preferential trade agreements was also working strongly in Honduras' favor.

The impact of CBI-induced trade preferences was reduced significantly following the passing of the North American Free Trade Agreement (NAFTA) in 1994. Mexico was a major competitor in the clothing and apparel sector, and the implementation of NAFTA offered Mexican producers new preferences to the U.S. market in relation to Honduran producers. However, in 2000, the U.S. passed the CBTPA, which provided renewed trade preferences for Honduras' producers. In particular, the CBTPA extended preferential tariff treatment to textile products assembled from U.S. fabric that previously had been excluded from the CBI. This boosted the use of local content in the production value chain and resulted in significant investment in textile mills in Honduras. According to the *Maquila* Association of Honduras, CBTPA shifted the incentive structure from the previously preferred solution of importing all input material from the United States to using locally produced input material. Today, roughly 60 percent of inputs are produced in Honduras, although most of the intermediary goods used in the production process are produced in the domestic free zone environment. This production used to be less than 10 percent in the 1980s and parts of the 1990s.

On April 1, 2006, Honduras ratified and implemented DR-CAFTA, which covers the Dominican Republic, Costa Rica, El Salvador, Guatemala, Honduras, Nicaragua, and the United States.[4] DR-CAFTA provides additional trade preferences to Honduran producers, although in this case the rules of origin clause in the agreement led to mixed results for Honduran producers of clothing and apparel. Rules of origin are applied to discriminate between suppliers, and DR-CAFTA favors U.S. producers of fabrics to suppliers from cost-effective producers in Asia. These rules of origin have weakened the supply chain of Honduran clothing manufacturers since uncompetitive U.S. mills already were starting to close down during the DR-CAFTA negotiation.

Government Support for Key Infrastructure and Services

In the initial years of the free zone program, key infrastructure, including factories, roads, and port facilities, was not yet in place to support the large-scale investment. The government played a critical role in facilitating targeted investment for the free zone program, again beginning the late 1980s and early 1990s. One key program derived from the private sector debt crisis that affected the country in the late 1980s, forcing several important domestic companies to default on their loans. As a part of a deal to address this crisis, the government agreed to buy corporate bonds that were then valued at only $0.08–0.12 each for US$1; in return, the private sector agreed to invest the proceeds in free zones and other infrastructure. Thus, several free zone industrial parks and the surrounding infrastructure were financed by this debt-swap deal, in particular, in the San Pedro Sula and Puerto Cortés regions.

The government also has played an important role in providing adjacent infrastructure. For example, the Honduran government invested in a number of roads, including between San Pedro Sula and Puerto Cortés, which attracted investment. Some of these roads are publicly operated roads with toll systems that recoup public investments. Significant investments also were made in the port itself, including (most recently) the designation of Puerto Cortes as a SAFE (Security and Accountability for Every Port) port under the U.S. Secure Freight Initiative, one of the few such ports in the hemisphere. Finally, the government also ensured the implementation of an expedient and effective customs regime for the free zones. This customs regime has allowed free zone operators to enjoy rapid and simplified customs procedures, with on-site customs officials inside each free zone.

Support for Agglomeration

Many countries have sought to use free zones as regional development tools, and plenty of political leaders have targeted remote or poor areas where they perceive jobs to be particularly needed. The government of Honduras initially sought to promote geographic diversification by selectively expanding the zone policy to targeted regions, including the capital Tegucigalpa, but this approach had little success. As discussed, the government slowly abandoned this regional development approach and, in parallel with opening up the sector to domestic investors in the late 1980s, it permitted investors to choose to locate where it best suited them. The market response was to agglomerate around San Pedro Sula (see box 3.2). Almost 80 percent of all employment in Honduras' free zones is concentrated in the Cortés region.

Institutional Support in Marketing and Promotion

FIDE (Foundation for Investment and Development of Exports), the national export and investment promotion agency, was established in 1984. From its inception, FIDE's objectives have been to promote investment, develop export markets, and work closely with the government and other private organizations to create new legislation aimed at improving the business climate in Honduras. A key initiative of FIDE was to

---

Box 3.2

San Pedro Sula: Key Agglomeration for the Export Sector

Although the government had an objective to develop an export sector around the capital Tegucigalpa (as well as in peripheral regions of the country) and initially aimed to use the free zone program as an instrument to attract investment toward Tegucigalpa, it failed to shift capital from the Cortés region, particularly San Pedro Sula, for several reasons. First, the cost of living is higher in Tegucigalpa. There is also a scarcity of suitable land. Transporting containers overland is always a challenge in Honduras given the country's hilly landscape and security problems. Manufacturers based in San Pedro Sula benefited greatly from its proximity to Puerto Cortés, which is the country's entry and exit point of seaborne goods.

The San Pedro Sula region also had a first mover advantage. It hosts a number of influential industrial families, including the Rozenthal, Canahuati, and Facousse, who had established small clothing and apparel businesses even before the enactment of the free zone Law. The availability of local suppliers was attractive to investors who sought proximity to the value chain. In addition, the San Pedro Sula cluster offers economies of scale in the supply of input services for the kind of service support sectors required by local entrepreneurs and foreign investors, like international schools, health services, financial institutions, supermarkets, and recreational activities like golf courses. Access to international transport services, logistics, land, human capital, local entrepreneurs, and so on has been crucial in San Pedro Sula's rise as a hub of the free zone manufacturing sector.

Source: Author.

establish export promotion offices in Florida, Atlanta, and New York to nurture networks and connect Honduran exporters and zone operators with companies in leading U.S. centers of textiles and clothing production. This policy was successful and much valued by Honduran-based companies that benefited from the contacts established by FIDE and the investment that was generated through its work. FIDE also worked closely with key leaders in the domestic sector, for example, organizing visits in the middle of the 1980s, during which a number of local leaders of industrial families visited free zones in other countries, including in Asia and the Dominican Republic, to learn from their experiences.

Dynamic and Entrepreneurial Domestic Private Sector

The Honduran government realized early the need for private sector participation in the establishment of free zones. It was not until the enactment of the EPZ law in 1987 and the associated end in government discrimination between domestic and foreign manufacturers that investment in free zones gathered momentum. The domestic industry's investment in zone infrastructure and the establishment of manufacturing companies catalyzed FDI. The free zone industry now is almost entirely made up of private zone operators and private companies. The ZOLI (*zona libre*) Puerto Cortés is the only publicly operated zone—this zone never expanded much beyond its initial development phase and now hosts only 11 total companies.

Although domestic entrepreneurs have played an increasingly important role as investors in free zone companies—for example, between 2000 and 2007, Honduran companies in the free zones grew by almost 700 percent, or from 13 to 103 companies—it was the role of local industrialists in establishing the free zone industrial parks in the later 1980s and early 1990s that was critical to catalyzing FDI into the sector, which in turn spurred rapid growth in exports and employment (see box 3.3).

The poorer the business environment in a country, the more important is the role of the zone operator and the quality of the services it provides. The zone operator offers a security buffer to a sometimes-turbulent external business environment as well as a range of support and facilitating services that are tailored to the client's specific needs. This has very much been the case in Honduras, which ranks 141 out of 183 countries in the World Bank's *Doing Business* Index (World Bank 2009), behind all the countries in Latin America and the Caribbean except Bolivia, Haiti, Surinam, and Republica Bolivariana de Venezuela. In this context, Honduran zone operators also have played an important role in providing

Box 3.3

The Critical Role of Domestic Investors in Attracting FDI

Investment in the establishment of an industrial park takes several years to provide a return on the investment: in good conditions, around 7–12 years. It is a chicken and egg problem in which companies want to locate to free zones where everything is in place. Thus, there are large upfront investments that take time to recoup. This is arguably the main reason why the free zones in Honduras are owned and operated by domestic companies.

In a historically volatile region like Central America, foreign investors also want to see that domestic companies are taking on the risk and commitment by investing in bricks and mortar. Investment by domestic entrepreneurs signals to foreign investors that returns are possible. For Honduras, attracting an anchor investment— a leading MNC like Arrow, Gildan, Hanes, or Sara Lee—sent an important signal to prospective investors. It created interest among competitors who routinely benchmark their operation to those of their competitors and thus positioned Honduras on the map for production centers of textiles and clothing. In addition, it was equally important for the first greenfield investors to get a good start in Honduras because they soon became "salespeople" for the country.

Source: Author.

an environment that allows manufacturers to focus on their operations without major distractions from the challenges that affect entrepreneurs outside the zones. As one zone operator expressed it, "a customer [foreign investor] who gets exposed to government-related corruption and other problems gets scared and wants to leave. The *maquila* operator functions as the interface that sorts out all the issues behind the scene, leaving the companies to do what they do best, which is manufacturing."

The increasing sophistication of the services offered by zone operators is striking. For example, some parks offer "shelter plans" for particularly footloose companies. These plans include everything from servicing the real estate to the provision of administration services, such as payroll and human resource services. The zone operator provides the labor for lease to manufacturers. Free zones like ZIP Buena Vista and ZIP Choloma provide engineers and builders that can be hired for short-term jobs. Some zone operators thus are becoming manpower agencies as well as real estate agents. And manufacturers increasingly are willing to pay for these value-added services.

Challenges for the Future

More than three decades following the enactment of the Free Zone Law, Honduras can boast a fairly sizeable export industry. However, it faces a significant challenge to diversify, both in terms of product categories that are being exported and the geographic coverage of the zones. Diversification will require a significant shift in the approach by both government and the private sector. Most important, the government must be willing to forego protecting existing interests and thus avoid the risk of stasis in the free zone sector, which ultimately will result in the continuing stagnation and decline of investment, exports, and, perhaps most important, employment.

After several years of sustained investment and increased exports, the *maquila* industry was hit by the global economic downturn that struck in 2008. The downturn affected U.S. sales of both automobiles and clothes, which make up the great majority of exports from Honduran free zones. The former sector was severely hit as sales by the three U.S. automobile manufacturers dropped and General Motors and Chrysler went into Chapter 11 administration. Honduran textiles and clothing producers already were affected by Asian competition in the post-MFA environment, and the global economic downturn may well have accelerated the shift of U.S. clothing assembly to Asia. From a peak of 134,000 workers in 2007, employment in Honduras' free zones had, according to estimates provided by industry experts, dropped to approximately 100,000 workers in May 2009. The *Maquila* Association of Honduras argues that many zone operators are in debt and 50 percent of their plots of land are empty. Workers who lose their jobs often move to the informal sector or seek employment opportunities in the United States. However, migration to the United States has become increasingly risky as many migrants are losing their jobs there. Workers who have been employed in the free zones for many years are not necessarily attractive candidates on the job market, and many workers struggle to find new jobs.

Next to the global economic downturn, the free zone industry has faced several external shocks in the last few years. First, the domestic currency, the lempira, which is pegged to the dollar, has appreciated in relation to other currencies of leading exporters of wire harnesses and textiles and clothing products. For example, the Mexican peso depreciated by 28 percent in relation to the U.S. dollar (and hence the lempira) on the year to June 30 2008 to 2009. The macroeconomic climate is not favorable and the risks associated with inflation keep interest rates high and, as a result, for those who can (many cannot) borrowing from abroad is the favored option. Second, on January 1, 2009, the national minimum wage was raised by 60 percent to 5,500 lempira (US$297). Although the free zone industry managed to negotiate an exemption from this raise, it still increased the cost of many of the goods and services in the production supply chain.

Third, Honduras' growing crime—fueled in part by a squeeze on organized crime in Colombia and Mexico and the subsequent migration of criminal elements to the region—is scaring off some investors and adding security costs to company operations. For example, security personnel need to protect the factories and the zones, all workers are screened to ensure that criminal gangs do not infiltrate businesses, and containers need to be protected during transportation.

Finally, international competition, especially from China, is increasing the pressure on free zone companies to make more use of technology and raise labor productivity. The big dislocation of textiles and clothing production from the United States to Latin America and the Caribbean that took place in the 1990s is to a large extent complete. North American clients are now benchmarking their production matrixes in Latin America with those in Asia. Consequently, Honduras is facing competition from China and Bangladesh rather than Atlanta, North Carolina, or Mexico. And the requests by foreign investors are increasing. Twenty years ago, they would be pleased with the cost of labor, the proximity to the U.S. market, and the services offered in the port. Today, as one zone operator put it, "they ask if the country has global ambition; if we have FTAs with other countries; about the sources, cost and reliability of electricity; how many training centers we have; the level of expertise, etc., because Honduras is not so inexpensive anymore."

Employers in the free zones have responded by attempting to address productivity through increased training and incentives like production-linked bonus schemes, free breakfast and dinner for workers who arrive early to the factory or leave late, childcare provided on weekends, and so on. But while improving productivity with the help of capital, technology, and incentives is reducing the demand for labor, this improvement may be somewhat at odds with the government's main objective of employment creation through the free zone program.

Although productivity increases certainly are required, in light of the challenges the free zone sector is facing, it is clear that a competitive position based on low-cost production of garments (and wire harnesses) for sale to the U.S. market, is unlikely to be sustainable. Therefore, the strategic focus of the free zones must be on diversification outside the traditional garment sector and upgrades (moving into higher value added activities inside or outside the garment sector).

The relatively recent establishment of the wire harness industry was a significant step in terms of product diversification. UTI, later Lear Corporation, located in Nacu, outside San Pedro Sula, and suppliers like Alcoa (metallic wires) and a number of French companies (producing tubes) followed in its steps. Honduras lacks the establishment of the entire value chain, which makes them sensitive to competition. One of the key strengths of the country's free zone sector is the comprehensive and efficient services package offered by the zone operators, but these operators often are garment manufacturers. These operators have found it difficult to diversify into new sectors and largely have failed to attract a more diverse set of investors. Despite an industry-neutral incentive structure, only textiles, clothing, and wire harnesses have gathered significant investment (see figure 3.2).

The textiles, clothing, and apparel sectors still have scope for diversification. For example, Honduras does not produce synthetics and this is a multibillion dollar market. Honduras may be the leading producer

Figure 3.2   Gross Value of Production in *Maquilas*
(lempira, millions)

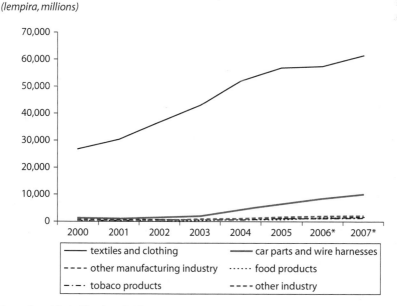

Source: Central Bank of Honduras (2008).

of underwear and T-shirts for the U.S. market, but it is not one of the 10 leading producers of nylon production. Tariffs are lower for the former two products, but they have not taken advantage of the tariff preferences they enjoy in the U.S. market. Additionally, agriculture, fishery, and tobacco processing activities exist in some free zones, but these are relatively small businesses. The Atlantic Coast is processing fruits and the Pacific Coast hosts shrimp and melon farms. Currently, interest seems to be high in the export potential of call center services. Some zone operators are assessing the requirements to attract foreign call center companies. As of May 2009, however, no call center company had yet located to Honduras.

One critical factor in the challenge of diversification is the need to upgrade the skills of the free zone workforce. The traditional garment assembly operations, however, historically have provided only minimum training and skills development. The *maquilas* have worked in PPPs to develop vocational training for *maquila* workers. But, in general, *maquila* workers are relatively low skilled and possess limited formal education (see box 3.4 for an initiative to address vocational training).

Despite the significant success of domestic investors in the free zone sector, and the critical role played by the effective interaction between the government and the private sector, they may also be a source of lock-in, limiting the scale and speed by which the necessary processes of adjustment take place. One reason for this limitation is that the majority of free zone developers and operators in Honduras are not real estate developers, but rather they have direct interests in the textiles and garment manufacturing sector. As such, their primary interest tends to be on salvaging competitiveness in their traditional activities, rather than perhaps focusing on attracting more diversified tenants into their zones.

More broadly, the privileges enjoyed by the free zone sector can be a powerful disincentive to reform. For example, in the 1980s and early 1990, the Honduran government offered exchange rate convertibility in the free zones. This policy is likely to have accelerated the devaluation of the Honduran lempira. The government faced increased pressure from the free zone industry to provide greater exchange rate incentives. This led to a macroeconomic distortion, which is likely to have undermined the currency. Indeed, while the government of Honduras at times has been open to reforming the legal framework to better suit local and foreign market conditions, it has not strategically leveraged the free zone policy for more comprehensive policy reform that could benefit all investors and entrepreneurs.

Box 3.4

Instituto Politécnico Centroamericano

Instituto Politécnico Centroamericano (IPC) is a nongovernmental, nonprofit, vocational training institute that was founded in 2005. An assessment of Honduras vocational training system had concluded that the system was broken: instructors were incapable of teaching and 95 percent of equipment was stolen, broken, or irrelevant. Based on these findings, IPC was established to design courses for current and future workers in all sectors of the economy, including in manufacturing and textiles and clothing. The institute's objective is to provide workers with relevant skills demanded by industry. Its curricula hence are influenced strongly by input from employers. IPC strives to offer the best technical equipment, curricula, and test instructors in the region. For example, a majority of the 12 instructors are brought from North America, Europe, and Latin America. In the spring of 2009, IPC had 270 full-time students and some 1,400 workers that were upgrading their skills in courses lasting between 2 and 18 weeks. A majority of the graduates join the free zone companies: for example, Gildan, the Canadian company that sponsored the above-mentioned study, hires 60 students from IPC every year.

Nine students out of 10 come from large families earning less than US$300 per month and the fee for a year of full-time training is US$1,500. The expenses are partly covered by companies, charitable organization, and governments—for example, a U.S. nongovernmental organization (NGO) covers transportation and a daily meal; a Swiss company that supplies chemicals to the textiles industry donated a chemistry lab; a French company provided design equipment; and an Italian company donated sewing equipment. Roughly 95 percent of the students receive a corporate scholarship that covers 75 percent of the fee. In return, they commit to work for the sponsor for two to four years. Foreign MNCs are carrying most of the expenses, whereas Honduran companies are less willing to invest in training and retraining—a pattern that is common throughout the developing world.

Source: Author, based on information supplied by IPC.

Conclusion

Honduras has more than three decades of experience of hosting free zones. It took approximately a decade and a half following the enactment of the Free Zone Law in 1976 before the policy had a significant economic impact. In addition to U.S. demand, the key to takeoff in the early

1990s was the fact that all the crucial conditions with regard to infrastructure, free zone policy, trade policy, and committed domestic investors were in place. When foreign MNCs started to shift their assembly lines to Honduras, the small Central American republic with its turbulent political past (and present) quickly developed into a leading exporter of textiles and clothing products to the United States.

Over the course of 22 years, the Honduran government enacted several pieces of new legislation that broadened the geographic reach of the free zone policy to finally cover the entire country. The government learned from its early mistakes: for example, the implicit discrimination against domestic manufacturers up until the enactment of the EPZ Law reduced domestic investors' interest in developing the local free zone environment and consequently had a discouraging effect on foreign investors. In more recent years, manufacturers have suffered from the unfavorable macroeconomic climate and the difficult security situation, which raise the cost of capital and risk of doing business.

The country has gotten many things right. The in-house customs solution is a widely lauded PPP that is expedient and efficient. The professionally managed Puerto Cortés has been crucial to the competitiveness of the free zone industry. The zone operators' decision to differentiate their free zones from other free zones in the region by investing in quality infrastructure and focus on providing high-quality services appears to have been the right strategy. Foreign anchor investments helped signal to foreign investors that Honduras was a potentially attractive supply base of clothing for the U.S. market. A professional trade and investment promotion agency also plays a seemingly important role.

Honduras has been fairly successful at developing backward linkages. The lesson for small economies is that the design of the rules of origin in trade agreements may have a huge impact on the country's ability to sustainably integrate new industries into the domestic economy. Honduras benefited greatly from preferential market access to the United States extended first in the CBI and later in DR-CAFTA. The rules of origin incorporated in these agreements, however, had a huge impact on the types of textiles and clothing product categories the country exports: at times, the rules have had a negative effect, and at other times, they have had a positive effect.

Despite the success of the free zones program, it remains highly concentrated in terms of exported product categories and geographic coverage of the zones. The government's selective geographic expansion of free zone policy did not have any significant effect, and the zone operators have not been particularly effective at broadening the scope of investors. This situation indicates the bluntness of the free zone policy tool and the difficulty of using it for industrialization purposes. Increasing international competition, especially from China, has taught the free zone industry that it constantly needs to adapt, make use of technology, and raise labor productivity if it wants to remain in business. Addressing the latter will require a greater attention to skills development at all levels.

Finally, the fiscal incentive structure that the government of Honduras offers companies with free zone status, including time unlimited exemption from taxation and duties, is generous from an international perspective. This incentive regime undoubtedly has played a role in attracting investment into the free zones program both from FDI and local investors. But it also has created a dual economy that is sustained by the government's disinclination or inability to address issues that impede the private sector. The application of the Free Zone Law discriminates against small and midsize manufacturers, and prospective exporters thus may be left out of the business. The private sector would benefit in the long term if the government provided a more equal incentive structure for small and large companies, producers of services and goods, and exporters and companies producing for the domestic market alike.

Exclusivity has proven to be a powerful force against comprehensive reform and has contributed to stasis in the free zone sector. Although the government of Honduras at times has been open to reform the legal framework to better suit local and foreign market conditions, it has not strategically leveraged the free zone policy for more comprehensive policy reform that could benefit all investors and entrepreneurs.

Notes

1. The term *maquiladora* derives from the practice of millers charging a *maquila* ("miller's portion") to process other people's grain. This chapter uses the terms *maquila* and free zone interchangeably.

2. Law Establishing the Free Zone of Puerto Cortés (*Ley Constitutiva de la Zona Libre de Puerto Cortés*, Decree No. 356).

3. On some rare occasions, the government has provided fiscal incentives linked to training to specific companies. For example, Lear Corporation received some fiscal incentives to train 100 employees.

4. In addition, Honduras has signed trade treaties with Mexico and currently is in the process of negotiating preferential tariff arrangements (PTAs) with Chile, Colombia, the European Union, Panama, Taiwan, China, and Canada.

References

Asociación Hondureña de Maquiladores. 2009. "Honduras: Analisis del Comportamiento de la Industria Maquiladora Periodo 2000–2009." Power Point presentation, San Pedro Sula, May 2009.

Central Bank of Honduras. 2007. "Actividad Maquiladora en Honduras Año 2006 y Expectativas Para el Año 2007." Subgerencia de Estudios Económicos, August.

Central Bank of Honduras. 2008. "Actividad Económica de la Industria de Bienes Para Transformación (*Maquila*) y Actividades Conexas en Honduras, 2000–2007 y Expectativas 2008." Subgerencia de Estudios Economicos, September.

EIU (Economist Intelligence Unit). 2008. "Country Commerce: El Salvador, Guatemala, Honduras," June. London: Economist Intelligence Unit.

MSN (*Maquila* Solidarity Network). 2005. "Honduras: The Gildan Story." Toronto: *Maquila* Solidarity Network.

World Bank. 2009. *Doing Business 2010: Country Profile for Honduras, Comparing Regulation in 183 Economies.* Washington, DC: World Bank. www.doingbusiness.org/ExploreEconomies/?economyid=86

WTO (World Trade Organization). 2003. "Trade Policy Review Honduras." Report by the Secretariat, WT/TPR/S/120, August 29. Geneva: World Trade Organization.

CHAPTER 4

China's Investment in Special Economic Zones in Africa

Deborah Brautigam and Tang Xiaoyang

China's Overseas Special Economic Zones: Aims and Objectives

In 2006, as part of the implementation of its 11th five-year plan, the Chinese government announced that it would establish up to 50 overseas economic and trade cooperation zones. In the experimental manner that characterizes many Chinese policy innovations, the rollout of these zones has been gradual. In Africa, two competitive tenders (discussed in section 2) have led to the selection of seven proposals for overseas zones, all of which became eligible for incentives from the Ministry of Commerce and other Chinese government agencies. This chapter outlines the background of this policy innovation, describes the current status of the seven African zones, sheds light on the variety of mechanisms by which these zones have been established and operated, provides a preliminary assessment of the benefits and drawbacks of the zones, and provides recommendations that might be helpful in allowing African economies to fully maximize potential benefits from these investments. The chapter draws on the authors' field research,[1] as well as on a literature review and telephone interviews.

Background

China's efforts to attract foreign investment relied at first on SEZs. In 1979, four SEZs were established in the southeastern coastal region of the country (a fifth zone was later added on Hainan Island). These were patterned after similar zones established in Taiwan, China; the Republic of Korea; Singapore; and Hong Kong, China. In 1984, 14 Chinese coastal cities set up industrial and technological development zones, many of which nurtured clusters targeting a particular industry. More than a hundred zones of various kinds now have been established around the country, offering low taxes[2] and infrastructure at international standards. These zones have become one of the principle means by which the Chinese government, at the local, provincial, and national levels, provides preferential policies to foster the development of technology and industry.

China has some experience with international partnerships in the development of these zones. In 1983, the Japanese government helped develop a master plan for the port of Qingdao, and in the early 1990s, Japan's International Cooperation Agency (JICA) provided foreign aid for the Jiaozhou Bay Highway, a railway, and a sewage treatment plant, all connected to the Qingdao Economic Development Zone. In 1993 and 1994, the Jiangsu province cities of Wuxi and Suzhou developed industrial parks with Singaporean partners to learn from Singapore's model. These zones were run on a commercial basis, as joint ventures. The Singaporean interests held majority shares, and took the lead in developing and marketing the zones until around 2001–02 when the capital and management were restructured and Chinese interests became the major shareholders and decision makers in both zones. The Chinese government closely followed this process: the Suzhou zone even had a vice premier as chairman of its board. In recent years, several Chinese development zones have invited institutes from the U.S., Japan, Australia and U.K. to participate in planning.

In the mid-1990s, after nearly 20 years of "bringing in" (*yin jinlai*) foreign investment, technology, and skills, the Chinese government began to emphasize "going out" (*zou chuqu*) or "going global." Going global involved finding new markets for Chinese goods and services, building up Chinese brand names, and ratcheting up China's own foreign investment. In an experimental fashion, the Chinese government and Chinese companies began to establish overseas industrial and trade zones, as early as 1998. In 2006, a policy decision was made to establish up to 50 special economic cooperation zones in other countries as a central vehicle for this aim.

The China-Africa Development Fund (CADF), a venture capital instrument set up by one of Beijing's policy banks, China Development Bank, is one of the key tools for the going global strategy. First announced at the November 2006 Summit of the Forum on China-Africa Cooperation (FOCAC), CADF was established with US$1 billion in assets and is expected to rise to US$5 billion over time. CADF's role is to invest in Chinese companies, Sino-Africa joint ventures, or African companies, with the commercial objective of at least breaking even. CADF has taken equity shares in some of the overseas zones projects.

Objectives

Overseas economic zones were believed to meet several strategic objectives. First, they would increase demand for Chinese-made machinery and equipment, while making it easier to provide postsales product support. Second, by producing overseas and exporting to Europe or North America, Chinese companies would be able to avoid trade frictions and barriers imposed on exports from China. Third, the zones would assist China's efforts to boost its own domestic restructuring and move up the value chain at home.[3] Fourth, they were intended to create economies of scale for overseas investment, and in particular, to assist less experienced small and midsize enterprises to venture overseas "in groups." Finally, fifth, they were viewed as a way to transfer one element of China's own success to other developing countries, a strategy that the government believed would be helpful for recipient countries, while also benefiting China. These multiple objectives mean that Chinese companies also have a variety of objectives in constructing and investing in these zones. Indeed, evidence from the zone in Egypt, which is the most advanced of the projects, supports the perspective that companies investing in the Chinese zones are not following one model. Some Chinese manufacturers in the zone are producing for the European market (garments), others are serving the Egyptian market (oil rig assembly, women's sanitary products), and yet others are exporting back to China (marble).

Brief History of China's Overseas Economic Zones

The policy established in 2006 built on earlier overseas experiments. For more than a decade, Chinese companies already had ventured into establishing a variety of overseas industrial and trade zones. For example, in 1999, the Chinese government signed an agreement with Egypt to assist in the establishment of an industrial zone in the Suez economic area. Also in 1999, the giant Chinese appliance firm Haier built its first industrial complex outside of China: a 46-hectare industrial park in South Carolina, United States. Fujian Huaqiao Company built an industrial and trade zone in Cuba in 2000. In 2001, Haier and a Pakistani company, Panapak Electronics, constructed a joint industrial park near the Pakistani city of Lahore. A Chinese company began to implement an industrial zone in the Chambishi area of Zambia in 2003. In 2004, China Middle East Investment and Trade Promotion Center and Jebel Ali Free Trade Zone constructed a US$300 million trade center, designed to host 4,000 Chinese companies in Dubai. Similarly, also in 2004, Tianjin Port Free Trade Zone Investment Company and the United States Pacific Development Company set up a Chinese trade and industrial park in the South Carolina city of Greenville.

Thus, the decision to establish overseas zones as a part of the going global policies was made after Chinese companies already had set up industrial and trade zones overseas. China's Ministry of Commerce and the National Development and Reform Commission studied the experience of these companies in formulating the policies of support.

China's Overseas Zones in Africa: Current Situation

Chinese support for the development of "economic and trade cooperation zones" is not limited to Africa. To date, the Chinese government has selected 19 overseas zone proposals (see appendix 4.A) across 15 countries for official support under the going global policies. Seven of these projects, across six countries, are in Africa (five projects in four countries are located in Sub-Saharan Africa with two in North Africa), with the goal of developing at least 10 overseas Chinese economic and trade cooperation zones during the 11th five-year plan (2006–10), and stimulating overseas investment of US$2 billion from some 500 Chinese companies.[4] These zones are not expected to conform to a single model. They can be science and technology parks, manufacturing and processing bases, or multiuse facilities. They can emphasize domestic markets (import substitution) or export processing. In addition, some mainland Chinese and Hong Kong, China, companies have established industrial estates and other spatially delimited areas for trade, logistics, or manufacturing in Africa and elsewhere, outside of the scope of official government support.

This section outlines the overall plans for the zones. Their results to date are discussed in Part IV, "Progress, Challenges, and Potential."

China's Seven Approved Zones in Africa

China's Ministry of Commerce has approved seven African zones for special funding under the going global initiatives; six had commenced construction as of November 2009. These zones are located in Zambia, Mauritius, Egypt, Ethiopia, Nigeria (two), and Algeria. This section provides an overview of the seven zones, including their location, participants, investment, industry focus, and current status. It discusses the future of the Chinese initiative and briefly looks at Chinese investments in industrial parks and other SEZs in Africa, but outside of the special initiative. In addition to these seven zones, other Chinese companies and provincial governments have experimented with the establishment of industrial parks and free trade zones in Africa. Some of them sent proposals to the Ministry of Commerce (MOFCOM) tenders, but did not win. Most are quite recent, and their experiences vary widely: some failed at an early stage, but others have survived and grown. In comparison with the seven official zones, their sizes vary, forms are more diversified, and strategies are more flexible. Among these are the Guoji Industry and Trade Zone in Sierra Leone, the Nigeria Lishi-CSI Industrial Park, Linyi (Guinea) Industrial Park, China Daheng Textile Industrial Park in Botswana, and the Shandong Xinguang Textile Industrial Park in South Africa. Several other proposals for industrial parks or zones have been mentioned in various media, but they either are at an early stage, remain under discussion, or failed to begin.

Zambia-China economic and trade cooperation zone/Chambishi multi-facility economic zone. China Nonferrous Mining Co. (CNMC Group) began planning the Zambia-China Economic and Trade Cooperation Zone in 2003 in Chambishi, about 420 kilometers north of the capital of Lusaka. CNMC's decision to open a zone for mineral processing and related industries allowed the company to make full use of the 41-square-kilometer surface area of its Chambishi copper mine. In 2006, CNMC won official support from MOFCOM for the Chambishi zone. In a sign of the political importance of this initiative, in February 2007, China's president Hu Jintao presided at the opening ceremony of the zone.

The Chambishi Zone focuses on the value chain of copper and cobalt: mining, processing, recycling, machinery, and service. It aims to attract 50 to 60 enterprises, create some 6,000 jobs for Zambians, and reach an annual output of more than US$1,500 million by 2011. By July 2009, 11 enterprises had been established in the zone, including the Chambishi copper mine, copper smelters, a sulfuric acid plant, and a foundry, for a total investment of US$760 million.

CNMC's Lusaka subzone project, adjacent to the Lusaka airport, was launched, at least symbolically, in January 2009. The zone is planned to have an area of 5 square kilometers. A master plan for the zone is expected to be completed by the end of 2009, with construction slated to begin in 2010. Although the focus of the zone remains to be determined, CNMC has indicated a wish to focus on services (hotels, a conference center), light industries such as food and tobacco processing, and assembly of home appliances and electronics. The strategic purpose of the Lusaka subzone may be to diversify out of resource-intensive investment as well as to accommodate the Zambian government's desire for urban employment opportunities. China Development Bank has set up a Zambia team to provide funding support for the zones and CNMC activities in Zambia. The Chambishi and Lusaka zones were the first of five Multi-Facility Economic Zones (MFEZs) planned by Zambia. Malaysian interests are also constructing an MFEZ near Lusaka, with technical assistance from JICA.

Egypt Suez Economic and Trade Cooperation Zone. Egypt Suez Economic and Trade Cooperation Zone is located in Sector 3 of the North-West Suez Canal Economic Area just outside Egypt's new deep-water Sokhna Port, just below the southern entrance of the Suez Canal, 120 kilometers from Cairo. It is being developed by Egypt TEDA Investment Co., a joint venture between Tianjin Economic-Technological Development Area (TEDA) Investment Holdings, Egyptian interests, and the China-Africa Development Fund. The Suez project has a long and complicated history (see box 4.1). Discussions on a transfer of China's experience were initiated by Egypt in 1994. TEDA Investment Holdings was tasked by Beijing to set up a zone project in the Suez area in 1998. A joint consortium, Egypt-Chinese Corporation for Investment (ECCI), was set up to implement this initial project. TEDA relied on the experience of their Egyptian partners to learn how to operate in Egypt. The venture began long before the area infrastructure was complete and the initial years were not very successful, but with time a number of companies have set up operations in Sector 3 of the zone.

In November 2007, TEDA participated in the second tender of MOFCOM for overseas zones. After winning the bid, they bought additional land in Sector 3 of the zone and formed a new joint venture with Egyptian interests. The zone builds on the earlier investment and will be

Box 4.1

Timeline: Tianjin TEDA in Egypt

1994   Egypt and China begin discussion of cooperation in economic zone development.

1998   Chinese and Egyptian governments sign a memorandum of understanding to construct a free trade zone in North-West Suez. TEDA assigned the task. Sets up Suez International Cooperation Co.

1999   ECCI was formed by TEDA, Arab Contractors Co., National Bank of Egypt, National Investment Bank, and the Suez Canal Authority. TEDA had 10 percent of the shares. ECCI acquires rights to 21.95 square kilometers of land in NWSEZ (all of Sector 3).

2000   TEDA sets up Suez International Cooperation Co., which is 100 percent TEDA because they believed the joint venture business plan was not viable. They plan to develop 1 square kilometer for small and medium enterprises (SMEs) on their own. They started construction.

2003   After slow start, ECCI releases most of its land rights in Sector 3, retaining 6 square kilometers. The infrastructure is established. Some companies are established (a marble company).

2004   January. Egypt-China Joint Working Group established to boost cooperation at zone. TEDA concentrates on Sector 3 of North-West Suez, 1 square kilometer. White Rose (a Chinese textile machine company), drilling equipment joint venture, and companies in steel tableware, luggage, and women's sanitary products.

2004   October. International Development Ireland wins contract to design overall plan for Suez zone and trains staff of Egypt's General Authority for Free Zones and Investments (GAFI).

2007   November. TEDA's proposed Suez Economic and Trade Cooperation Zone won the Chinese MOFCOM tender.

2008   July. Egypt TEDA established by TEDA (75 percent), ECCI (20 percent), and Suez International (5 percent) to develop the industrial park over three 3-year phases.

2008   October. China-Africa Development Fund signed an agreement to invest in TEDA's Suez Economic and Trade Cooperation Zone. They set up a new holding company with TEDA (on a 60%/40% ownership basis). This new company now holds the 75 percent of shares originally held by TEDA.

(continued next page)

Box 4.1 *(continued)*

2009   March. Chinese-Egypt TEDA wins Egyptian tender for SEZ development in North-West Suez.

2009   July 17. TEDA and Egyptian government sign contract to develop part of Sector 3 in North-West Suez as an SEZ. TEDA will invest US$280 million for infrastructure within zone.

2009   November. Chinese and Egyptian premiers presided at the opening ceremony of the North-West Suez Special Economic Zone in Sector 3.

Source: Authors.

established on a cluster model. Currently plans exist for four clusters: textile and garments, petroleum equipment, automobile assembly, and electrical equipment. In the second phase, electronics and heavy industries may be added (Interview, Vice Director of the Suez TEDA Zone, 2009).[5] As of July 2009, 16 enterprises already had moved into the first one square kilometer start-up zone. This start-up phase is planned to conclude around 2011, when the zone aims to have around 50 companies. Chinese companies with high energy consumption and high labor intensity are especially encouraged to invest in this zone.

In March 2009, TEDA won an international Egyptian tender, competing against 29 other companies for the right to develop Egypt's first "Chinese-style" SEZ ("Chinese-style" means that part of the zone will be developed for residential use). Phase I of the SEZ is located in an undeveloped portion of Sector 3 of the North-West Economic Zone. It will develop approximately 6 square kilometers (600 hectares) out of the available area of 20.4 square kilometers, adjacent to TEDA's existing Sector 3 industrial development. TEDA's investment in infrastructure and basic construction was expected to amount to between US$200 million and US$280 million.

Ethiopia Eastern Industrial Park. The Ethiopia Eastern Industrial Park is located 30 kilometers from Addis Abba. It originally was formed by two private Chinese steel product makers: Yonggang Group and Qiyuan Group from Zhangjiagang city. Qiyuan initiated the idea of building an industrial zone in Ethiopia and the participation of Yonggang, a much larger conglomerate, guaranteed financing so that it won the second MOFCOM bidding in 2007. Later, two additional Zhangjiagang companies, Jianglian and Yangyang Asset Management, joined the project.

Zhangjiagang Free Trade Zone was brought in as a technical partner, but not as a shareholder. Because of financial difficulties, however, Yonggang left the project early in 2009 and the smaller company, Qiyuan, has become the major shareholder and executor (Interview, Eastern Industrial Park Management, 2009). Originally, the park planned to attract 80 projects in five years and create 10,000 to 20,000 jobs for Ethiopians. This plan will be subject to substantial revision after the capital restructuring.

Because of the Chinese partners' financial difficulties (related to the global economic crisis), the area of the zone has been reduced from 5 to 2 square kilometers (500 to 200 hectares) and the investment from renminbi (RMB) 1 billion (US$146 million) to RMB 690 million (US$101 million). The start-up area is 100 hectares and is expected to cost US$22 million to launch. It currently is under construction, with an expected completion date of 2010. The zone developers still are negotiating with China Eximbank for loan finance (*Foreign Trade Information and Survey Newsletter* 2009), while CADF is also studying the feasibility of equity participation. Meanwhile, the first project in the zone, a cement plant, began production in 2010. Eleven enterprises with US$91 million total investment have signed letters of intent to move in—these enterprises cover such industries as construction materials, steel products (plates and pipes), home appliances, garment, leather processing, and automobile assembly.

Mauritius Jinfei Economic and Trade Cooperation Zone. JinFei Economic and Trade Cooperation Zone is located in Riche Terre, an undeveloped area 3 kilometers northwest of Port Louis, near the Free Port. The sole original developer was the Shanxi province Tianli Group, a provincial SOE active in trade, construction, real estate, and textiles. Tianli arrived in Mauritius in 2001, establishing a state-of-the-art spinning mill, which since has expanded several times. Tianli's plant supplies much of the demand for cotton and synthetic thread in the Mauritius textile industry, as well as exports to other countries.

Tianli's proposal for an overseas zone was one of the winners of the first MOFCOM tender in 2006. Securing land and resettling farmers caused delays, however, and the zone ran into further difficulties after the developer was hit by the global economic slowdown. The Chinese central government then instructed Shanxi province to coordinate capital restructuring of the Tianli zone. Two much bigger partners, Shanxi Coking Coal Group and Taiyuan Iron and Steel Company, joined the team. CADF also invested in the zone. Construction finally began on September 16, 2009.

The zone has an area of 211 hectares; the first development phase is on 70 hectares (0.7 square kilometers) with an expected investment of US$220 million. On completion in early 2012, the zone is expected to provide a manufacturing and service base for Chinese enterprises doing business in Africa. A second phase, targeted for 2016, aims to focus on solar energy, pharmaceuticals, medical equipment, and processing of seafood and steel products, as well as housing, hotels, and real estate. If fully implemented, the total project is estimated to cost US$720 million and hopes to create from 30,000 to 42,000 jobs.

Nigeria Lekki Free Trade Zone. The Lekki Free Trade Zone (LFTZ) is located 60 kilometers east of Lagos alongside a new planned deepwater port. The project is a joint venture between a consortium of four Chinese companies and Nigerian interests, including the Lagos state government. The government of Lagos state provided 165 square kilometers (16,500 hectares) of land—of which 30 square kilometers (3,000 hectares) has been officially transferred to the joint venture so far—and the right to a 50-year franchise. CADF also will provide equity finance, and a proposal to include CADF on the board of directors still is under negotiation.

The project was initiated in 2003 by China Civil Engineering Construction Corp. (CCECC), which has been operating in Nigeria for more than a decade. In March 2006, a Chinese consortium, CCECC-Beiya ("Beyond"), was set up in Beijing. In May 2006, the consortium partnered with Nigerians to establish the LFTZ Development Co. In November 2007, the Lekki zone won support in the second MOFCOM tender.

The development of the initial 3,000 hectares is divided into three phases. The first phase (1,000 hectares) is the official China-Nigeria Economic and Trade Cooperation Zone. Construction on these 1,000 hectares (designed to support 200 companies) began in October 2007. An investment of approximately US$267 million is planned for the first three years and the total investment is estimated around US$369 million. The zone will be divided into six sections: (1) transportation equipment, (2) textile and light industry, (3) home appliances and communication, (4) warehousing, (5) export processing, and (6) living and business. According to an interview with a Beijing representative of CCECC-Beiya (2009), this first phase will serve only or mainly Chinese companies.

Sources from the Nigerian partner, however, indicate that the zone is open to all investors, and the list of investors that have signed MOUs includes mainly non-Chinese companies. An initial group of companies (all Chinese) was expected to begin construction in March 2009. In interviews management indicated this was expected to be delayed until early 2010; however, this timeline has also slipped.

Nigeria Ogun-Guangdong Free Trade Zone. Nigeria Ogun-Guangdong Free Trade Zone is located in the Igbessa region of Ogun state, 30 kilometers from Lagos International Airport. Its shareholders include Guangdong Xinguang International Group, China-Africa Investment Ltd., Chinese CCNC Group, and the Ogun state government. The project originated from a 2004 study of South China University of Technology on the feasibility of setting up a Guangdong economic trade cooperation zone in Nigeria. This report was used for the successful bid by Xinguang International Group in the first MOFCOM tender in 2006. The project originally was sited in Imo state, but the developers apparently ran into high administration fees imposed by the state government, experienced a general climate of insecurity, and relocated to Ogun state (Soriwei 2008). This delayed the project, and construction began in Ogun only in the first half of 2009. By July 2009, several Chinese enterprises had begun to build staff housing.

The zone has a total area of 100 square kilometers, which will be developed in two phases. Phase I utilizes 20 square kilometers (2,000 hectares) with an estimated investment of US$500 million; within this, the start-up zone will be developed on 250 hectares, with an investment of US$220 million. The zone will focus primarily on light manufacturing, including construction materials and ceramics, ironware, furniture, wood processing, medicine, small home appliances, computers, lighting, and paper. A high-tech agricultural demonstration park may be added in the future. The developers aim to attract more than 100 enterprises to the zone within five years, and 700–800 companies within 10 years. As of the middle of 2010, 36 companies had registered to invest in the zone; six had begun construction.

Algeria-China Jiangling Free Trade Zone. Algeria-China Jiangling Free Trade Zone in Algeria will be developed by Jiangling Automobile Group from Nanchang, Jiangxu province and Zhongding International Group (there is no local partner at present). Jiangling Automobile, one of China's flagship companies, has more than 40 sales agents in Algeria and, by 2007, had taken one-third of Algeria's automobile market. Zhongding International Group is the arm for overseas construction and engineering of Pingxiang Coal Group (PKCC). PKCC has been operating in Algeria for more than 17 years and contracted dozens of medium and large projects there. Responding to MOFCOM's call for applications, the Jiangxi provincial government coordinated an effort to link PKCC and Jiangling Automobile Group, both based in Jiangxi, to establish a platform for the enterprises of Jiangxi province to go global. They won in the second MOFCOM bidding round in 2007.

The Algeria zone was projected to have a total investment of US$556 million and a land area of 500 hectares, with a first development phase on 120 hectares. It planned to attract 30–50 Chinese enterprises into an industrial park focusing on automobiles and construction materials. In March 2008, Zhongding International and Jiangling sent a combined team to Algeria for preparation. The zone has been in limbo since May 2008. Legislative reforms in Algeria's investment regime, passed in early 2009, require foreign investors to form joint ventures with Algerian partners as majority shareholders).[6] This may not be acceptable to the Chinese developers. Negotiations with the Algerian government were still ongoing as of November 2009 (Interview, Ministry of Commerce Official, Bejing, China, November 25, 2009).

China's Overseas Zones: Mechanisms

The Chinese government built on earlier experiences working with Chinese companies to establish Investment, Trade, and Development Promotion Centers in Africa and elsewhere, beginning in the mid-1990s, and studied experiences such as TEDA's in Egypt. Officials also considered China's past difficulties in ensuring that development projects established in Africa would be sustainable once Chinese involvement ended. This dictated a new model of engagement,[7] in which the Chinese government gave Chinese enterprises incentives to build and operate the zones.

Chinese enterprises take the lead in proposing and developing the zones for profit, but they compete for subsidies and support from the Chinese government. They propose the location, invest their own capital, negotiate with the host government, and compete with other Chinese companies for support through an open tender system. Once the zones are developed, the enterprises will rent space and offer services to other companies, replicating the model developed earlier in China's overseas

Investment, Trade, and Development Promotion Centers. As with many Chinese policy innovations, the zones are treated as an experiment, with a variety of approaches encouraged. The results of the first two sets of pilot projects (i.e., those projects approved during the two MOFCOM tender calls; see next subsection, "The tender process in China") will be examined for lessons learned before the effort is scaled up.

The Tender Process in China

After developing guidelines for the tendering process, China's MOFCOM asked its branch offices in the provinces and municipalities to promote the idea and the guidelines among enterprises in their region, and help them to apply. Two rounds of tenders were held, in 2006 and 2007, after which the government paused to see the initial results of the pilot projects. Although MOFCOM was primarily concerned with the potential for the projects to succeed as businesses, the Ministry of Foreign Affairs also had to provide a political sign-off on the projects, as they were to receive official government subsidies. There does not seem to have been any specific strategy for locating the zones in particular countries and, indeed, two separate proposals were funded for projects in Nigeria, one of Africa's largest markets. As a counter example, the Tanzanian government was interested in having a zone, and political ties between Tanzania and China are close, but no Chinese company was interested in proposing a zone in Tanzania (Interview, Dar es Salaam, 2008; Interview, Ministry of Commerce Official Beijing, China, 2009).

More than 60 companies submitted expressions of interest in the first tender round held in 2006. About half of these companies were invited to submit formal proposals, documenting the market potential and investment environment, and providing written evidence of support from the host country. Twelve companies were invited to Beijing as finalists to appear before a panel of independent outside experts (officials from Chinese special zones and university professors). Eight were selected, with the major criteria being the proposal (including the market potential, investment environment, and support from the host government), the financing capacity of the developer, and the developer's proven capacity to implement a major construction engineering project (Interview, Ministry of Commerce, 2009).

Based on lessons from the first tender round, the government added new requirements in the second round in 2007. The most important requirement was a stipulation that companies proposing zones for support needed to demonstrate an annual turnover of RMB 15 billion (about US$2 billion) for at least the two previous years. This was an effort to ensure that companies would have the resources to successfully finance the development of the zones, with the Chinese government playing only a supportive role. More than 50 companies applied in the second round, 20 of which were invited to submit formal proposals, with 11 proposals finally selected. At least two of the losing proposals were located in Africa, including the Guoji Industrial Zone in Sierra Leone, and the Nigerian industrial estate proposed by Ningbo CSI (Zhongce) Power and Machinery Group and Nigeria Lishi Group.

Chinese Government: Mechanisms of Support

In addition to the general going global policies in support of Chinese overseas investment, MOFCOM assists companies with winning proposals in a number of ways. Winning companies receive RMB 200 to 300 million (US$29 to US$44 million) in grants and long-term loans of up to RMB 2 billion (US$294 million). Subsidies can cover up to 30 percent of specific costs of zone development for preconstruction (feasibility studies, visits for planning and negotiating, securing land, the costs of preparing a bid) and actual implementation (the purchase or rent of land, factory or office space, legal and notary fees, customs, and insurance) through MOFCOM's Trade and Economic Cooperation Zone Development Fund. These costs can be retroactive to January 1, 2004, for preconstruction and January 1, 2006, for implementation.

Chinese enterprises moving into the zones are eligible for a number of incentives. First, they can be reimbursed for up to half of their moving expenses. They receive export and income tax rebates or reductions on the materials sent for construction and get easier access to foreign exchange in China's strict capital control system. They also can apply to a second MOFCOM fund, the Special Fund for Economic and Technological Cooperation, to receive a rebate on up to 100 percent of the interest paid on Chinese bank loans, a benefit good for five years. In addition, the stamp of approval from the government is expected to help Chinese policy banks (China Development Bank or China Eximbank) or funds like CADF look more favorably on companies' applications for low-cost finance or equity participation. For example, China Development Bank established a dedicated Zambia team to provide funding support for the Zambia zone and NFC African Mining activities in Zambia. Finally, Chinese embassies provide diplomatic support in negotiations with the host government over land, tax incentives, or work permits.

Some provinces and municipalities have provided additional funds for these overseas zones.[8] For example, Jiangsu province and Suzhou municipality have awarded the Ethiopian Eastern Zone more than RMB 100 million (US$14.6 million). In the Egypt zone, the government of Tianjin has promised to provide a subsidy of 5 percent of the actual investment amount, pay the utility costs (rent, gas, water, and electricity) for service enterprises in the zone, and provide full foreign investment insurance and overseas personal accident insurance for three years. The Tianjin government has given RMB 10,000 (US$1,470) for every Chinese employee in the zone as a food subsidy in the first year.

SEZs, industrial parks, and science and technology zones in China usually are managed by special authorities, which often are subsidiaries of provincial or local governments. Some of these authorities have established investment companies to explore opportunities overseas. At least three of these companies are among the firms and consortia involved in the winning bids for the zones in Africa. These include TEDA, the largest multi-industry, economic-technology development area in China, which is involved in Egypt's Suez zone; Nanjing Jiangning Development Zone, one of China's first national-level high-tech development zones, which is a minority partner in the Chinese consortium leading the development of the Lekki project in Nigeria; and Zhangjiagang Free Trade Zone, a satellite city and EPZ in Suzhou municipality, which is a technical advisor to the Eastern Zone in Ethiopia.

Strategy and Financial Commitments: Local Partners, Other Investors, and Incentives

The overseas economic zones have a variety of models with regard to local partners; level of financial commitments; managerial, development, and marketing roles; and openness to non-Chinese companies (local African companies and other FDI). The Chinese companies developing these zones include national and provincial SOEs, and also include some private firms (*minying*). The majority of the companies winning bids already were operating businesses in the respective countries for some time, at least a decade, in many instances. Ethiopia and Nigeria-Ogun are exceptions, and, in Algeria, Jiangling had been involved only in exports of its vehicles but had developed relationships with a network of agents.

The first overseas zone established under the new MOFCOM program was in Pakistan. A large Chinese appliance company, Haier, had earlier constructed an industrial park near Lahore with a Pakistani company,

Table 4.1 Structure of Investment in China-Africa SEZs

Zone (country)	Model	Details/Comments
Jiangling (Algeria)	100% Chinese	• Jiangling Automobile • Zhongding International (construction)
Suez (Egypt)	JV (75%+ Chinese)	• Tianjin TEDA (45%) • CADF (30%) • ECCI, formed in May 1998 by TEDA, Egyptian banks and other interests, and the Suez Canal Authority (20%) • Tianjin Suez International Cooperation Co. (5%)[1]
Eastern (Ethiopia)	100% Chinese	• Qiyuan Group (steel) • Jianglian and Yangyang Asset Management
JinFei (Mauritius)	100% Chinese	• Three partners: Taiyuan Iron and Steel Company (50%); Shanxi Coking Coal Group (30%); Tianli Group (20%) • CADF recently announced it would become an equity partner
Lekki (Nigeria)	JV (60% Chinese; 40% local) using special purpose vehicle: Lekki Free Zone Development Co. Ltd.[2]	• Chinese partners: CCECC-Beiya consortium (four partners); in 2009 CADF joined as an equity partner • Nigerian partners: Lagos state (20%): Lekki Worldwide Investments Limited (20%); Note that Lekki Worldwide Investments Limited is an investment company also owned largely by the Lagos state

		• Lagos state received its shares in return for provision of land and 50-year franchise to operate the zone; it is expected to contribute US$67 million to construction costs
		• The Chinese consortium is to invest US$200 million
		• Negotiations with communities affected by the project resulted in an agreement to transfer 5 percent of the shares of the Nigerian consortium (i.e., 2% of total project shares) to local communities, making them a stakeholder in the success of the project[3]
Ogun (Nigeria)	JV (82% Chinese; 18% local)	• Chinese consortium based in Guangdong
		• Nigerian share owned by state government—provided land and 100-year concession in return for shares[4]
Chambishi (Zambia)	JV (95%+ Chinese)	• CNMC (95%) has provided all the capital
		• NFC African Mining PLC (15%) is a JV between CNMC (85%) and Zambia Consolidated Copper Mines Ltd., a Zambian government-owned holding company (15%)

Source: Authors' research.

Note: CADF = China-Africa Development Fund; CCECC = China Civil Engineering Construction Corp.; CNMC = China Nonferrous Mining Co.; Egypt-China Corporation for Investment = ECCI; JV = joint venture; TEDA = Tianjin Economic-Technological Development Area.

1. Interview, Vice Director of Suez TEDA Zone, Suez City, Egypt, June 9, 2009.

2. CCECC-Beiya (Beyond) was an entity formed by four Chinese companies: China Railway Construction Corp. with 35 percent share, Nanjing Beyond Investment Ltd. with 35 percent, Nanjing Jiangning Economic and Technical Development Co. with 15 percent, and CCECC with 15 percent. In 2009, when the CADF joined the project, the ratios in the consortium shifted to China Railway Construction Corporation Limited (35 percent), CADF (20 percent), CCECC (15 percent), Nanjing Jiangning Economic and Technological Development Corporation (15 percent), and Nanjing North Asia Investment Co., Ltd. (15 percent, "Beyond/Beiya" consortium). Forty percent of Lekki Worldwide Investments is owned by LSDPC, the Lagos State Government Development Corporation, and 40 percent is owned by Ibile Holdings, the investment company of Lagos State. The proportions were confirmed in a telephone interview with the Lekki Chinese Consortium Office (2009).

3. Interview, Lekki Worldwide Investments, Lagos, December 14 and 16, 2009.

4. Mthembu-Salter (2009), 22.

Panapak Electronics, the distributor of Panasonic electronic products. In 2006, Haier proposed to establish the China Pakistan Enterprise Zone, an overseas trade and economic cooperation zone, and along with Ruba General Trading Company, became the first overseas economic zone to be launched. The Haier-Ruba zone ran into problems with the acquisition of land, however. According to some sources, Haier-Ruba insisted that land for the project be provided without cost, or with heavy subsidies, while the local government resisted this demand. In Africa, the partnerships and policies for the zones vary. Some are 100 percent Chinese owned, and others are African-Chinese joint ventures, usually with host governments as minority partners. In fact, the African private sector has no investment in these zones.

The Chinese government initiated the concept of overseas zones and established a framework for support for Chinese companies on an experimental basis. MOFCOM has had a role in negotiating double-taxation treaties and general investment protection treaties with host governments, but several of the zones have been established in countries in which there is no double-taxation agreement (e.g., Ethiopia and Zambia) or no investment protection agreement (e.g., Algeria, Mauritius, Nigeria, and Zambia). MOFCOM has stepped in to help Chinese companies in their negotiations, particularly when by stepping in, they were able to assure host governments that companies did have Chinese government support in their plans. From all accounts, however, the Chinese government has taken a hands-off attitude toward African policies on these zones. The Chinese government does not impose conditionality on host governments in return for investment in these zones, which is in keeping with long-standing Chinese policies that regard conditionality as interference in the internal affairs of another government. Chinese companies take the lead in negotiations with host governments over particular incentives.

Incentive structures for the Chinese invested zones appear to take no standard form and are dependent on individual negotiations and existing laws in each country. In most cases, the negotiation does not appear to be around tax and other fiscal incentives, but more around land values and pricing (Interview, Lekki Worldwide Investments, December 14, 2009), and the host partner's commitment to infrastructure provision. For the most part, the projects are governed by existing SEZ legislation in the host country and thus conform to the standard set of incentives offered through these regimes. One exception is Mauritius, where special incentives were negotiated to attract the Tianli investment, but at the request of Tianli, the agreement remains a secret (this is a bone of contention in democratic Mauritius). Several incentives have come to light: the Mauritian government agreed to supply land at a favorable rent, with a 99-year lease; investors meeting certain requirements could obtain Mauritian passports, whereas usually the policy is to allow only for permanent residence; investors apparently were allowed licenses to carry out banking and lottery businesses; and, although Mauritius has long used laborers from China (and elsewhere in Asia), the Jinfei Zone apparently has been given flexible permission to employ a high percentage of Chinese workers.

Development and Management: Division of Responsibilities

In China, most zones have infrastructure provided by various branches of the Chinese government. In some cases, such as the Qingdao Zone, foreign donors (Japan Overseas Economic Cooperation Fund) provided development assistance loans for some of the infrastructure (port, highway, and water supply) in the zone areas. In Africa, most of the development responsibilities inside the zones are carried out by the Chinese developers, with African governments responsible for providing infrastructure outside the zones, but there are exceptions (see below). In all cases, the master plans and development strategies for the zones are provided by the Chinese partner. The Tianli Group hired a Shanghai firm to work on the concept for the zone in Mauritius; CCECC-Beiya hired Shenzhen Institute of Planning and Design (Shenzhen Guihua Sheji Yuan) to plan the Lekki Zone in Nigeria; and, in Zambia, CNMC brought in the China Association of Development Zones. Consortium partner Jiangning also held an evaluation meeting in China, bringing in experts and consultants from Nanjing University, Southeast University, and Nanjing Planning and Design Institute to advise and comment on the security, transportation, layout, and other aspects of the initial zone design.

Construction responsibilities usually are shared between the Chinese and African partners, with the Chinese consortiums handling the on-site infrastructure. In Mauritius, for example, Tianli was expected to contribute US$3.3 million for external infrastructure, while the government of Mauritius invested US$16 million to enlarge a reservoir and extend water lines to the JinFei Zone, and US$5.6 million to build a new link road and bring wastewater, electricity, and telecoms to the project site.[9] In Nigeria's Lekki project, the joint venture consortium is responsible for building a gas-fired power plant, water, and wastewater treatment plants, as well as communication switching stations. The Lagos state government is responsible for off-site access roads. In Zambia, however, the government announced in 2010 that it had budgeted US$4.2 million for its share of infrastructure required for the Lusaka subzone.[10]

In terms of operations and management, Chinese companies tend to handle the day-to-day management, but administration takes place in several layers. For example, Egypt has an informal joint China-Egypt Task Force for the Suez Economic Zone addressing high-level problems; an Egyptian SEZ Authority for the zone, which operates under the prime minister and which has its own board of directors; a licensed joint-venture Main Development Company (MDC) with authority to develop the zone; and a development company (Egypt TEDA) that executes what has been licensed to the MDC (Government of Egypt 2002, 2). Ethiopia also has a layered structure, with (1) a bilateral coordination committee between the Chinese and Ethiopian governments; (2) the Ethiopian management and service agency of the industrial park, which will regulate the zone; and (3) the 100 percent Chinese-owned Eastern Industrial Park Ltd. Co., which will invest in and operate the park.

The Chinese developers often market the zone to Chinese companies (although their websites usually are bilingual English and Chinese). Their African counterparts, particularly state investment agencies, market it to local firms and other international firms. For example, in Nigeria, Lekki Worldwide Investments Ltd. has a website and is actively marketing the LFTZ, and the Chinese consortium has a separate website and has held a number of marketing events in China. In Mauritius, marketing is managed jointly by the Mauritius Board of Investment and Tianli. The most comprehensive approach can be found in Egypt. Tianjin municipality formed a leadership panel for the Egyptian Suez Economic and Trade Cooperation Zone. Coordinated by this panel, the Tianjin municipal State-owned Assets Supervision and Administration Commission promotes SOEs to invest in the zone, the Science and Technology Committee encourages technology enterprises, and the Agriculture Committee and the Construction Committee promote investment by agricultural enterprises and construction materials firms. TEDA also has formed the China-Egypt Commercial Association in Suez, organizing market information seminars, participation in large-scale trade fairs, and so on. TEDA has produced promotional materials both in Chinese and in Chinese and English. At the same time, Egypt's government agency, GAFI, does some marketing of the zone through its general promotional materials for investment in Egypt, and the General Authority for the Economic Zone North-West Gulf of Suez also markets the SEZ.

Chinese Enterprises and Chinese Labor

The Chinese developers appear to be open to investment from other foreign firms as well as local firms, although most are aiming for a majority of Chinese investors. In most cases, the expectation (from both parties) is clear that the Chinese partners will bring in a substantial Chinese investment. MOFCOM insists that because of the subsidies coming from China, the subsidized cooperation zones primarily must serve Chinese enterprises. Although no explicit limit is stated, MOFCOM hopes that Chinese companies can make up 70 to 80 percent of the enterprises in the cooperation zones. In some zones, however, they also have set specific, non-Chinese foreign investment targets.

- *Nigeria (Ogun):* The six companies that have started construction in Ogun, and indeed all of the 36 companies that have registered to invest, are from China (specifically, Guangdong). Initially, the plan was to have a mix of half SOEs and half private companies; this target was later reduced to 30 percent SOEs. In reality, all the existing companies that have begun construction are private companies.
- *Zambia:* Zambia's MFEZ regulations, which apply to the Chambishi Zone, require a minimum investment of US$500,000 to be able to take advantage of government incentives, but Chambishi does not prohibit Zambian firms or other foreign investors. Zone developers aim to have 40 Chinese companies and at least 10 from other countries by 2011, and they have developed bilingual promotional materials. According to Felix Mutati, Zambian minister of commerce, trade and industry, the Zambian government initially wished for the zone to be solely Chinese, but the Chinese wanted the zone to remain open to other investors. That said, at present, only Chinese investors have committed to open factories in the zone.
- *Mauritius:* Local investors are not allowed in the zone, at least in the first phase. This requirement, the only one of its type among the Chinese zones, was set by the Mauritian government, not the Chinese.[11] Non-Chinese foreign investors are specifically welcome, however.

Finally, responding to concerns about Chinese incentives being limited to Chinese companies, the Chinese government announced in November

2009 that it would establish two new programs. First, as part of the Action Plan for 2010–2012, the Chinese would assist African SMEs to invest in the zones. Second, a fund of US$1 billion will be set up for African SMEs. It is not yet clear how they will be carried out.

The zones vary with regard to the regime for Chinese labor during construction and operating phases. Most of the zones for which information exists state that local laws on the use of expatriate labor apply. Because only two of the zones have begun to operate (Egypt and Zambia), it is not possible to determine the degree to which this is actually the case. In these two zones, the workforce of the companies operating in the zones is primarily local; however, it does appear that a relatively large percentage of Chinese are employed during the construction and start-up phases in most of the projects. In Egypt, there is a clear national regime for foreign labor: one foreign employee is allowed for every nine Egyptians employed. The first stage of the TEDA zone has more than 1,800 local workers and (an informal estimate) about 80 Chinese staff, putting the share of Chinese workers at below 5 percent. The general contractor for the zone is an Egyptian company and some of the construction work was subcontracted to local Egyptian companies. In Zambia's MFEZ, approximately 400 Chinese and 500 Zambians were employed during the early phase of construction, machinery installation, and training, putting the Chinese share of employment at 45 percent. At present, with the installation and commissioning of specialized machinery at many of the factories, the percentage of Chinese employees is in flux. In the Chambishi Zone as a whole (including the mines), in late 2009, there were approximately 700 Chinese and 3,300 Zambians (Haglund 2009). CNMC's already commissioned factories have an average of two Chinese to every eight Zambians (25 percent Chinese workforce).

Information on the use of local and Chinese labor in other zones is patchy and is available only for the construction phase. According to Chinese sources, the first phase of construction of the Lekki Zone initially employed more than 50 engineers from China and 100 Nigerian workers. Chinese partners state that the project currently has a ratio of 20 Chinese to 80 Nigerians.[12] Nigerian officials confirm that informal agreements have increased the number of Nigerians employed, particularly from the project-affected community.[13] In Mauritius, the construction phase of JinFei began only in September 2009, so it is early to assess the situation. Overall, Mauritius has the most open approach to Chinese workers among the six countries. During the first phase of construction, 60–65 percent of the workers reportedly have been Chinese (Minister of Finance cited in "Zone Économique JinFei: Ce Que Vous Devez Savoir" 2009, 8). The zone was at first expected to use 8,000 Chinese contract workers at full development, while creating 5,000 local jobs (and another 2,500 indirect jobs). Later revisions of the plan predicted the creation of 34,000 jobs, with "more than half" expected to be local, although the actual expected numbers have been much debated in the media. Foreign workers have long been a staple of the island's manufacturing and construction industries. Concerns have been raised in Mauritius, however, about the sheer number of Chinese expected as a result of this project.

Progress, Challenges, and Potential

The Experience to Date and Key Challenges

China's initiative to develop SEZs in Sub-Saharan Africa is still in its early stages. Of the five zones, only the Chambishi Zone in Zambia is operating—the SEZs in Nigeria (LFTZ and Ogun Guangdong Free Trade·Zone) and Mauritius are in relatively advanced stages of construction, and the Eastern Zone in Ethiopia began construction in 2010. To date, some high-level knowledge sharing and training of local managers has taken place, but local employment, supply chain linkages, and technology transfer remain limited. The most advanced zone (Chambishi in Zambia) had, as of November 2009, attracted 11 companies and US$760 million in investment, with five additional companies expected in 2010. The zone employs about 4,000 workers (80 percent of whom are local). However, most of the 11 companies invested to date are subsidiaries of the CNMC developer and were present in 2006. Moreover, of the 4,000 workers employed, only 600 are in the zone, with the majority working in the mines or at other CNMC subsidiaries.[14]

All the zones have attracted interest from a number of (mainly Chinese) enterprises. Chinese companies, especially those new to Africa, appreciate the "feels-like-home" environment, convenient services, information network, and proven credibility. The expectation is that enterprises within a value chain will cluster together in a planned zone and increase their competitiveness. Furthermore, these zones are widely publicized and promoted in China. Embassies and provincial governments recommend the zones to companies planning to invest in Africa. Tax incentives and facilities are an extra bonus.

Yet, despite many expressions of interest, most of the zones have been slow to fill up with companies. It is still early in a process that may take

10 years or more, but several factors may explain the slow start. One is the global economic crisis and, perhaps more broadly, challenges of obtaining financing. The developers of the zones in Ethiopia and Mauritius encountered serious problems at home, which were related to the financial crisis. These problems required substantial modification of their plans. Both developers, however, have begun construction. Likewise, the main company developing the Ogun Zone, Xinguang International, has run into financial constraints at home, slowing progress on the zone.

The (in)experience of some of the developers has been a contributing cause of uneven progress. The Zambia Chambishi Zone already had a copper mine, copper smelters, sulfuric acid plant, and foundry before 2006. In Egypt, TEDA has been developing an experimental zone for nearly 10 years and knew the market and environment. For both, the inclusion into the MOFCOM program simply facilitated their expansion. On the contrary, developers for the Ethiopia and Algeria zones had no experience investing in those countries, and their plans were possibly less realistic. In Ethiopia at least, tested by the economic crisis, revised plans now account for such factors as the exchange rate, the need to plan for foreign exchange shortages, and, relatedly, risk diversification. Whereas the zone initially was going to focus in part on construction materials and the production of steel, the developers may add nonferrous metal mining to generate foreign exchange and diversify risks.

Another problem in some zones has been the failure to deliver a world-class investment environment. For example, in Egypt during the first years of the TEDA participation, a gap existed between the promised services, facilities, and other benefits and the reality of what was offered. Over time, the Egyptian government was able to fulfill most of its promises, but enterprises, understandably, do not want their investments to rest on promises. Egypt still has not been able to ensure a permanent supply of adequate water to the Suez Zone, for example. The greater Lekki peninsula is slated to get a new airport and port, the latter of which is critical to the competitive offering of the LFTZ, but progress has been slow.

Finally, several zones are located at some distance from a large city. Enterprises in the zones sometimes find it difficult to employ qualified workers and arrange their daily commute. Chinese promotional activities so far mainly target Chinese companies, often companies in their own province, which limits the sources of possible investment and can hamper the benefits clustering provides for the transfer of technology between firms (local personnel still can be a vehicle for transfer, however, if hired at a high enough skill level, which is another challenge).

Although it is premature to draw any conclusions, it is clear that while some positive progress is evident, its pace is slow, and the challenges that have arisen suggest that success is by no means guaranteed. Indeed, these projects not only face many of the typical difficulties that afflict large infrastructure projects, particularly in Africa, but additional issues of cross-cultural communication, governance, political factors, and power relations (see box 4.2 for an example of the challenges faced in one project).

Box 4.2

Challenges in the Lekki Free Zone in Nigeria

Nigeria's Lekki Free Trade Zone (LFTZ) is perhaps illustrative of some of the challenges facing both sets of partners in executing the joint venture SEZs in Africa. The project has been under planning since 2003. Although it has made significant progress, the development path of the project has faced many obstacles along the way. Among them are the following:

- *Financing constraints and partnership disputes:* Construction was delayed for a period because of financial constraints on the part of the Chinese consortium; this was apparently linked to a dispute over partnership terms within the Chinese consortium and a subsequent restructuring of the consortium.
- *Miscommunications over terms of partnership:* Nigerian partners expected the Chinese consortium to deliver their share of investment in capital, whereas the Chinese partners expected to deliver it in-kind through infrastructure development. In addition, there have been concerns from the Chinese partners on infrastructure responsibilities of the Nigerian partners (e.g., access to the gas for the power plant). Chinese partners have raised concerns over the Nigerian partners' potential to ensure that the enabling policies critical to the success of the zone actually will be implemented by the Nigerian federal authorities.
- *Local community disputes:* Local communities around the project protested over resettlement terms, the construction of utilities lines through their communities, as well as the employment of Chinese workers for construction. This caused project delays and resulted in transferring 5 percent of the shares of the Nigerian partner to the local community. In addition, negotiations resulted in increasing employment opportunities for workers from local communities.

Source: Authors.

On the basis of their experience at home, Chinese developers expect host governments to support zone development actively; instead, they are finding in some projects (e.g., Ethiopia) that governments allocate land to developers and do little else. Developers have been frustrated by the lack of progress or poor quality of infrastructure provided by some local governments outside the zones. In addition, many of the projects have faced difficulties related to land acquisition and compensation. Although these issues normally have been the responsibility of host governments, they have contributed to project delays and friction with the local communities (e.g., Lekki). Finally, although the political situation in the countries hosting zones generally is stable, abrupt policy changes and conspicuous gaps between de jure policy and de facto implementation has been problematic. Chinese companies have found that promises of services like "one-stop shops" fail to materialize (e.g., in Ethiopia). Even when express registration of investments has been set up, obtaining licenses and work permits has caused delays (e.g., Nigeria, Zambia).

African governments and civil societies have raised concerns on a number of levels. One of the biggest issues relates to lack of transparency and poor communication. Although governments are privy to the contracts signed for these zones, in most cases, they have not been published. This not only is problematic for civil society but also contributes to misunderstandings among the partners (see box 4.1). Some of these problems relate to language—for example, at one of the zones, African officials reported that relations improved when their Chinese partners brought in a couple of high-level officials who were fluent in English. Some African officials also worry that Chinese companies may use the zones to bring in Chinese goods for reexport with African labels into areas where African exports receive special incentives, as well as to enter local markets without paying duties, as occurred in Sierra Leone. The use of Chinese rather than local materials and labor has been a concern in certain projects (e.g., Mauritius). Chinese nationals tend to take most of the management and technical positions, at least in the initial project stages. For unskilled jobs, concerns about wages and working conditions have been raised, although at this early stage of development most of these concerns are still theoretical. Finally, there are concerns that the zones will become Chinese enclaves, unconnected with the rest of the domestic economy. Although all the zones are open to any foreign and (with the exception of the Mauritius Zone) domestic investors and no explicit preferential treatment is given to Chinese investors, the reality to date in most of the zones is that investor interest has come primarily from Chinese companies. Thus, in the absence of proactive efforts to promote integration, Chinese enclave zones are a real risk.

Despite these risks and the challenges experienced to date, these zones have the potential to deliver benefits to both parties. Benefits for African economies should include those associated with foreign investment more generally: employment, transfer of more advanced technologies, spin-offs to local firms and foreign exchange earnings from exports. The more African firms invest in the zones, the greater the opportunity for technology transfers and spin-offs, although technical skills also can be taught on the job to African employees of Chinese firms. Furthermore, the zones should contribute to the government revenue, at least moderately. For Chinese enterprises, benefits include the reduction in transport costs from being closer to African or European markets, lower labor costs in some cases, cluster economies, as well as the discussed incentives. Chinese zone developers expect to profit from the increased value of the land, fees, and rents. Some (Lekki, Mauritius) have planned extensive residential, commercial, and entertainment areas, making the zones multiuse.

Maximizing Benefits

The partnership to develop SEZs is part of a long-term process of strategic engagement between China and Africa. It offers a significant opportunity to contribute to job creation, industrialization, and poverty reduction in the region. To fulfill this potential, however, the projects must be successful from a business, social, and environmental perspective. This will require a partnership framework that includes the following elements:

- *High-level commitment and active engagement from host governments*: As noted, China learned many aspects of SEZ management through building zones with overseas partners. These lessons were widely applied throughout China's SEZs and have become common practice. African governments have been less strategic at managing the projects as learning experiences. Few participate actively in the management of the projects or have set up specific programs aimed at developing SEZ expertise over the long term. Assigning specific individuals, preferably Mandarin-speaking, to work with Chinese development teams can help, as can high-level participation on boards.
- *Ensuring the provision of quality off-site infrastructure*: Worldwide, getting zones off the ground has proven difficult in part because of

infrastructure inadequacies (power, roads, water, sanitation). PPPs or other models, such as independent power producers, are options that can accelerate this development, bringing employment and other benefits online earlier. Involving the local private sector, in addition to Chinese investors, will be critical.

- *Communicating and enforcing standards*: Local job creation, environmental sustainability, and labor standards all depend on African governments enforcing existing standards and regulations. It may help to have these translated into Mandarin, as Mozambique has done for labor regulations.
- *Implementing programs to promote domestic market linkages*: African countries will not profit from the dynamic benefits of SEZs without ensuring closer links between the (mostly Chinese) foreign investors in the zones and the domestic private sector. Supplier development programs and initiatives to facilitate local companies to set up inside the zones can play an important role in creating these linkages. The recently announced funding from the Chinese government to support African SMEs and plans to assist these SMEs to invest in the zones could provide a foundation to improve linkages.
- *Transparency and community relations*: When contracts and agreements for these important zones are not made public, suspicion can fester. For the zones to be sustainable, they need to have buy-in from local communities who understand the nature of the agreements. The agreement in the Lekki project for example, where 5 percent of the shares of the Nigerian consortium were transferred to local communities, may be one way of addressing some of these concerns.

Appendix 4.A. China's Official Overseas Economic and Trade Cooperation Zones

Country	Zone
2006 Tender	
1. Pakistan	Haier-Ruba Home Appliance Industrial Zone
2. Zambia	Chambishi Nonferrous Metal Mining Group Industrial Park
3. Thailand	Luoyong Industrial Zone
4. Cambodia	Taihu International Economic Cooperation Zone, Sihanouk Harbour
5. Nigeria	Guangdong Ogun Economic and Trade Cooperation Zone
6. Mauritius	Tianli (now JinFei) Economic and Trade Cooperation Zone

(continued next page)

Country	Zone
7. Russian Federation	St. Peterburg Baltic Economic and Trade Cooperation Zone
8. Russian Federation	Ussuriysk Economic and Trade Cooperation Zone
2007 Tender	
9. Republica Bolivariana de Venezuela	Lacua Tech and Industrial Trade Zone
10. Nigeria	Lekki Free Trade Zone
11. Vietnam	Chinese (Shenzhen) Economic and Trade Cooperation Zone
12. Vietnam	Longjiang Economic and Trade Cooperation Zone
13. Mexico	Ningbo Geely Industrial Economic and Trade Cooperation Zone
14. Ethiopia	Eastern/Orient Industrial Park, Jiangsu Qiyaan Investment Group
15. Arab Republic of Egypt	Tianjin TEDA Suez Economic and Trade Cooperation Zone
16. Algeria	Chinese Jiangling Economic and Trade Cooperation Zone
17. Republic of Korea	Chinese Industrial Zone
18. Indonesia	Chinese Guangxi Economic and Trade Cooperation Zone
19. Russian Federation	Tomsk Siberia Industrial and Trade Cooperation Zone

Source: Brautigam 2009, 315–16.

Notes

1. Some of this information has been published in Deborah Brautigam, *The Dragon's Gift* (Oxford University Press, 2009).

2. China introduced a new tax regime in 2008 that essentially did away with the tax holidays that previously were offered in the SEZs and harmonized the tax structures between SEZ and domestic firms. This new regime is in compliance with the WTO.

3. As China prepared to join the WTO, policy makers sought ways to assist Chinese firms to face the increased competition and inevitable restructuring that trade liberalization would bring. Helping mature "sunset" industries to move offshore, where they could be closer to their markets or raw materials, would reduce costs and increase competitiveness. For example, Chinese companies with high energy consumption and high labor intensity are especially encouraged to invest in the Egypt zone (see Suez.TJCOC.gov.cn (2008)).

4. "Jiangxi Province plans to invest RMB 3.8 billion in Algeria" (2008).

5. The difference between the 19 zones chosen by tender, and the public goal of 10, allows for a comfortable margin. The Chinese government would prefer to overshoot its goals, rather than come up short. In Africa, for example, the official goal was announced in November 2006 as "three to five" zones by 2009. Seven actually were approved, and six were announced as under way in November 2009 at the FOCAC meeting in Egypt.

6. "Aerjiliya Xincuoshi jiang dui Woqiye Chukou he Touzi Chansheng Yingxiang" (2009).

7. This is discussed further in Brautigam (2009).

8. "Dongfang Gongyeyuan, Kaipi Feizhou Taojinlu" (2008); "Suyishi Jingwai Jingmao Hezuoqu 10 yue Jiepai" (2008).

9. "JinFei Project—Infrastructure Works, Terms and Conditions of Agreement" (2009).

10. "Government allocates K 20 billion for Lusaka South Multi Facility Economic Zone" (2009).

11. The government wanted the special incentives for the zone to be used to attract additional new investors from overseas, and not investors already present in Mauritius (Interview, Minister of Finance, 2008).

12. Interview, Lekki Zone Representative (2009); "Weida de Kaituo – Laiji Zimaoqu Jianshe Jishi" (2008).

13. Nigerians reported that they had asked the Chinese to send some of their construction workforce of about 200 back to China and hire Nigerians. One researcher reported that an agreement negotiated between the two sides calls for at least 40 percent of the workforce to be Nigerian. However, Nigerian officials we spoke with denied that this was the case (Mthembu-Salter 2009, 3; interview, Lekki Worldwide Investment officials, December 14, 2009 and December 16, 2009).

14. The mining activities and the CNMC subsidiaries are not technically considered part of the zone.

References

"Aerjiliya Xincuoshi jiang dui Woqiye Chukou he Touzi Chansheng Yingxiang" [Algeria New Measures in Trade and Investment Will Affect Export and Investment of Chinese Enterprises]. 2009, March 17. Commercial Office of Chinese Embassy in Algeria. Available at http://dz.mofcom.gov.cn/aarticle/jmxw/200903/20090306105852.html (accessed November 3, 2009).

Brautigam, Deborah. 2009. *The Dragon's Gift: The Real Story of China in Africa.* Oxford: Oxford University Press.

CCECC-Beyond. 2008. Gongsi Xinwen [Corporation News]. Available at http://www.cceccbeyond.com.cn/news-show.asp?ID=279 (accessed December 14, 2009).

"Dongfang Gongyeyuan, Kaipi Feizhou Taojinlu" [Oriental Industrial Park, Paving Gold Path in Africa]. 2008, February 25. *Zhangjianggang Daily.* Available at http://www.zjgxw.cn/html/tebieguanzhu/20080225/63110.html (accessed December 14, 2009).

Foreign Trade Information and Survey Newsletter. 2009. Suzhou Municipality Foreign Trade Administration, no. 38 (July 21).

"Government Allocates K 20 Billion for Lusaka South Multi Facility Economic Zone." 2009. *Lusaka Times,* October 10.

Government of Egypt. 2002. "Law of Economic Zones of a Special Nature." Available at http://suez.tjcoc.gov.cn/news_display.asp?id=106&iid=%BA%CF %D7%F7%C7%F8%B6%AF%CC%AC (accessed December 14, 2009).

Haglund, Dan. 2009. E-mail communication, December 10. Bath, UK: University of Bath.

"Jiangxi Nizai Aerjiliya jianli Hezuoqu" [Jiangxi Plans to Establish Cooperation Zone in Algeria]. 2007, September 4. International Online. Available at http:// gb.cri.cn/14714/2007/09/04/2925@1745553.htm (accessed November 3, 2009).

"Jiangxi Province Plans to Invest RMB 3.8 billion in Algeria." 2008. *China Knowledge,* May 5.

"JinFei Project—Infrastructure Works, Terms & Conditions of Agreement." 2009. Republic of Mauritius, Parliamentary Debates No. 25, October 20.

Mthembu-Salter, Gregory. 2009. "Elephants, Ants and Superpowers: Nigeria's Relations with China." South Africa Institute of International Affairs, China in Africa Project, Occasional Paper No. 42.

Mthembu-Salter, Gregory. 2009. "Chinese Investment in African Free Trade Zones: Nigeria." South Africa Institute of International Affairs, China in Africa Project, Policy Briefing No. 10.

NBFET.gov.cn. 2009. Laiji Ziyou Maoyiqu-Zhongni Jingmao Hezuoqu Jianjie [Lekki Free Trade Zone – profile of Sino-Nigeria Economic Cooperation Zone]. Available at http://www.nbfet.gov.cn/index.php/default/view/ id/14385/sub/1 (accessed November 12, 2009).

Soriwei, Fidelis. 2008. "How Imo Lost Free Trade Zone to Ogun," January 7. Available at http://www.stocknewsline.com/regions/africa/how-imo-lost-free-trade-zone-to-ogun/ (accessed December 13, 2009).

Suez.TJCOC.gov.cn. 2008. Hezuoqu Dongtai [Latest Activities of the Economic Cooperation Zone]. Available at http://suez.tjcoc.gov.cn/news_ display.asp?id=54&iid=%BA%CF%D7%F7%C7%F8%B6%AF%CC%AC (accessed December 14, 2009).

"Suyishi Jingwai Jingmao Hezuoqu 10 yue Jiepai" [Suez Overseas Econ & Trade Cooperation Zone Opening in October]. 2008, February 23. *Jingji Cankao Daily.* Available at http://invest.people.com.cn/GB/75571/105500/8852019 .html (accessed December 14, 2009).

"Weida de Kaituo – Laiji Zimaoqu Jianshe Jishi" [Great Exploration – Reporting the construction of Lekki Free Trade Zone]. 2008, September 12. Lekki Free

Trade Zone. Available at http://lekki.jndz.gov.cn/Lekki_News_Show_55 .html, 2008.9.12 (accessed December 14, 2009).

"Zone Économique JinFei: Ce Que Vous Devez Savoir." 2009. *L'Express Dimanche*, September 20, p. 8.

Interviews

Interview, Beijing Representative of CCECC-Beiya, Beijing, China, November 27, 2009.

Interview, Dar es Salaam, January 2008.

Interview, Lekki Chinese Consortium Office, Beijing, December 14, 2009.

Interview, Lekki Zone Representative, Beijing, November 27, 2009.

Interview, Lekki Worldwide Investments, Lagos, December 14 and 16, 2009.

Interview, Lekki Worldwide Investments, Lagos, Nigeria, December 14, 2009.

Interview, Lekki Worldwide Investment Officials, Lagos, Nigeria, December 14 and 16, 2009.

Interview, Ministry of Commerce Officials, Beijing, China, November 25, 2009.

Interview, Minister of Finance, Port Louis, Mauritius, July 2008.

Interviews, Oriental Industrial Park Management, Addis Ababa, Ethiopia, June 15, 2009.

Interview, Vice Director of the Suez Teda Zone, Suez City, Egypt, June 9, 2009.

CHAPTER 5

Partnership Arrangements in the China-Singapore (Suzhou) Industrial Park: Lessons for Joint Economic Zone Development

Min Zhao and Thomas Farole

Background

SEZs were established in China in the early 1980s as "demonstration areas" to test policy reforms aimed at economic liberalization and to attract foreign investment. SEZs have had a transformational effect in building a competitive manufacturing sector in China and catalyzing its economic development. They have played a significant role as a laboratory for economic reforms in the country and have been a major source of technological learning to enable upgrading by local firms. During the development of the SEZ program, the Chinese government made an explicit effort to partner with foreign entities to learn about setting up and managing modern industrial parks. One example of this approach was the China-Singapore Suzhou Industrial Park, a modern industrial township developed in the early 1990s. Although it faced many difficulties in its early years, it has emerged as a major success, attracting US$17 billion in FDI and supporting more than 500,000 jobs.

Governments throughout the world, particularly in developing countries, are keen to develop SEZ programs to support diversification, attract investment, create employment, and benefit from skills and technology transfer. Many of these governments are turning to foreign partners, including China, Malaysia, and Singapore, that can bring not only investment but also substantial expertise and experience in establishing and running SEZs. China's own experience in making use of foreign expertise through joint venture partnerships suggests that this approach may offer significant potential for developing-country governments not only to attract investment and international-standard infrastructure, but also, and perhaps most important, to learn about how to plan, develop, and manage large economic zone projects.

This chapter highlights the case example of China-Singapore Suzhou Industrial Park (SIP) as a lesson for how governments and SEZ investors in developing countries can maximize the benefits of partnership arrangements in their zone programs.

Introduction to Suzhou Industrial Park

SIP is a "new township" located in East Suzhou, a major industrial city approximately 80 kilometers from the commercial center and port facilities at Shanghai. Launched in 1994, SIP now hosts six functioning areas:

- Jinji Lake-Rim Central Business District (CBD)
- DuShu Lake Innovation District of Science and Technology (11 square kilometers)
- Eastern High-Tech Industrial Area
- Integrated Free Trade Zone (5.28 square kilometers)
- SIP Ecological Science Hub (4 square kilometers)
- Yangcheng Lake Tourism Resort

Of the six functioning areas, Jinji Lake-Rim CBD, Eastern High-Tech Industrial Area, and the Integrated Free Trade Zone are located in the 80-square-kilometer (8,000-hectare) China-Singapore cooperative zone, which covers just over one-fourth of SIP's total land area. SIP Ecological Science Hub is outside of the core zone, but it was developed by the joint venture development company China-Singapore Suzhou Industrial Park Development Co., Ltd. (CSSD) in 2007.

By the end of June 2008, SIP had attracted around 3,300 foreign enterprises, including 82 Fortune 500 MNCs with a cumulative contractual foreign investment of US$34 billion, and domestic companies with total contractual investment of RMB 130 billion (US$19 billion). In 2008, exports from the zone grew to more than US$30 billion. There has been rapid clustering of industries in information and communications technologies (ICT), thin-film transistor and liquid crystal display screens, and automotive and aeronautical parts, and recently, the zone has shown rapid emergence of high-end sectors, including software, outsourcing services, and pharmaceuticals.

SIP has become a major driving force of the Suzhou economy, achieving an annual average economic growth of 30 percent since its launch (see table 5.1). With around only 4 percent of the total land and population, and 7 percent of the industrial electricity, SIP contributes about 15 percent of Suzhou's GDP and 30 percent of its trade. By the end of 2008, SIP accommodated 600,000 residents and supported more than 500,000 jobs. More notable, SIP has built a reputation as one of the most business-friendly, residential-friendly, and environment-friendly industrial parks in China. SIP ranks the second best in terms of investment climate among 57 national-level industrial parks in China, according to the Ministry of Commerce. It ranks highest in infrastructure, human resources, and social responsibility, and it ranks second in economic strength, environment protection, and technology innovation (China Economic Development Zone Association 2008).

The success of SIP has built considerable mind share among the Chinese officials and a "Singapore" brand name that Singapore companies can leverage, especially in the area of township development and urban

Table 5.1   SIP Key Statistics

Foreign companies	3,300
Investment:	US$34 billion (25%)
– Foreign (Share of Suzhou FDI)	RMB 130 billion (US$19 billion)
– Domestic	
Employment (end 2008)	500,000
Exports (GDP) (2008)	US$ 31 billion
– Share of Suzhou Exports	~30% (share of total trade)
Output (GDP) (2008)	RMB 100 billion (US$14.6 billion)
– Share of Suzhou GDP	15%
Average annual growth (1994–2008)	30%
Taxes generated (2008)	RMB 9.5 billion (US$1.4 billion)
– Share of Suzhou revenue	15%

Source: Suzhou Industrial Park.
Note: GDP = gross domestic product; FDI = foreign direct investment.
For more detailed annual statistics, see appendix 5.A.

solutions throughout China. It also brought a good financial return to its investors. Although the project incurred significant losses in its initial years, CSSD reached cumulative profitability in 2003 and has been profitable every year since. Reported profits in 2007 were RMB 360 million (US$52.7 million). For an overview of key milestones in SIP's development from 1994 through 2009, see appendix 5.B.

The Strategy of the Chinese and Singaporean Governments

The SIP was launched on February 26, 1994, when Chinese Vice Premier Li Lanqing and Singapore Senior Minister Lee Kuan Yew signed the *Agreement on the Joint Development of Suzhou Industrial Park* in Beijing. On the same day, both parties also signed the *General Agreement on Suzhou Industrial Park*, which laid a foundation for the establishment of the CSSD. From the outset, SIP was viewed a flagship project in economic cooperation between China and Singapore and commanded high-level political attention. Indeed, SIP played an important strategic role both for the Chinese and the Singaporean governments.

For China, SIP was established against the context of the transition from a planned, closed, mainly agricultural economy to a global, industrial, market economy. Following Deng Xiaoping's now famous southern tour in 1992, the 14th National Congress of the Communist Party adopted the goal of establishing a socialist market economy and accelerating the pace of opening up. Faced with the task of learning how to manage in a market economy, senior leaders were inspired by the economic miracle achieved by Singapore in the 30 years after its independence. As Deng Xiaoping laid out in 1992, "Singapore enjoys good social order and is well managed. We should tap on their experience, and learn how to manage better than them" (Deng 2004). That year, more than 400 Chinese officials visited Singapore to study how the country achieved progressive economic success while maintaining social order. Because China already was experimenting with large-scale industrial zones, Singapore's successful experience in developing such zones was of great interest.

For Singapore, SIP offered opportunities on both economic and political grounds. At the same time China launched its first stages of market-oriented reform, Singapore was moving to a new phase of its development. With the economy expanding, finding space for new industries became a significant challenge. At the beginning of the 1990s, the government of Singapore launched the Regional Industrial Parks Initiative, one of several thrusts within its broad "regionalization strategy." The aim of the initiative was "to generate an external stream of revenue that would supplement Singapore's domestic economy" (Pereira 2007; Perry and Yeoh 2000). SIP was an important vehicle to demonstrate that the Singapore model of industrial parks could be transferrable (Inkepen and Pien 2006), thus opening up a potential new industry for the country, delinked from the physical constraints of its small market. Politically, SIP provided Singapore with the opportunity to better understand an emerging China, and to deepen relations with the country, through the various platforms set up for interaction between both leaders and officials. To achieve these aims, Singapore was particularly keen to work not just on a project *with* China but *in* China. For this, SIP fit the bill perfectly. The project allowed Singapore to share its development lessons comprehensively, including how to plan, implement, and administer an entire integrated development with industrial, housing, commercial, and recreational components in "the Singapore way." Although Singapore invested in other industrial parks in the region, the economic and political importance of China gave this project a high profile and strong government involvement.

Jointly, a key objective of SIP was that Singapore would share its knowledge of efficient economic management and public administration experience with its Chinese partner so that the latter could formulate pro-business policies in SIP and could govern with transparency and efficiency. With a benign business environment and good infrastructure, SIP was expected to be competitive in attracting investment and generating positive return to developers. But beyond this, both Singapore and China's leaders had a larger vision for SIP to be a model of reform and innovation for other parts of China.

Partnership Structure

SIP was established with a multilevel governance structure, as illustrated in figure 5.1. Overall governance of SIP is the responsibility of the China-Singapore Joint Steering Council (JSC). The JSC was designed to meet relatively infrequently (every 12–18 months) to review the progress, resolve major implementation issues, and set future development goals. The JSC is cochaired by the Chinese vice premier and the Singapore deputy prime minister and includes ministerial chiefs of the two countries, senior officials of Jiangsu provincial and Suzhou municipal governments, and the head of Jurong Town Corporation (JTC). At a more operational level, the Joint Working Committee, which was more active

Figure 5.1   Governance Structure of SIP

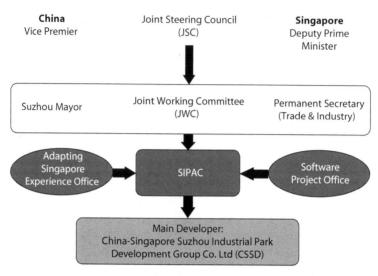

Sources: http://www.cssd.com.cn/chinese/yqjj.shtml, 2009.
Note: SIPAC = Suzhou Industrial Park Administrative Committee.

during the start-up phase of the SIP, is cochaired by the mayor of Suzhou and Singapore Ministry of Trade and Industry permanent secretary.

The Suzhou Industrial Park Administrative Committee (SIPAC) was empowered by the Suzhou municipal government as an independent local government authority to oversee SIP, which covers a total jurisdiction of 288 square kilometers (of which 80 square kilometers belongs to the China-Singapore cooperative zone[1]). The remaining area belongs to three counties—Loufeng, Weiting, and Shengpu.[2] SIPAC was granted high autonomy in policy making and law enforcement. Currently, SIPAC is also primary land developer of SIP.[3]

CSSD was initially the main land developer and still is a major real estate developer and industrial property agent of SIP. CSSD is a joint venture between China Suzhou Industrial Park Co., Ltd. (the Chinese consortium) and Singapore-Suzhou Township Development Co., Ltd. (the Singaporean consortium). The Chinese consortium is made up of several large Chinese SOEs at national, provincial, and municipal levels. The Singaporean consortium was composed of 24 companies, of which 10 are government-linked companies and statutory boards with total share of about 42 percent of the Singaporean consortium (*Straits Times*, January 15, 1998). From 1994 through 2000, CSSD was controlled 65 percent by the Singaporean consortium and 35 percent by the Chinese consortium. But based on an agreement made in 1999, the equity stake of the two consortia was flipped on January 1, 2001. Along with this, corporate control and management responsibility also shifted from the Singaporean side to the Chinese side. As of August 2005, CSSD attracted three more minority shareholders, which took a 20 percent share, diluting the Chinese and Singaporean consortia to 52 percent and 28 percent, respectively. The current structure of CSSD is shown in figure 5.2.

Currently, CSSD has formed the four core businesses, namely, primary land development, real estate development, public utilities, and multiservices. The primary land development is represented by the development of SIP Ecological Science Hub. The real estate development includes the industrial properties developed by CSSD headquarter and the residential properties developed by CS-SIP Land Corporate. The public utilities mainly refer to the water, power, and gas operated by CS-SIP Public Utilities Development Group Corporate. And the multiservices mainly include investment promotion, infrastructure development, international education and property management, and so on.

The Knowledge-Sharing Process

Singapore not only provided initial capital for zone development and designed a high-standard land-use plan, but also played a critical role in facilitating improved governance and, perhaps most important, in transferring wide-ranging technical knowledge of industrial-city planning and management. In all of this, the government of Singapore played a critical lead role.

First, Singapore provided substantial initial investment capital, risk sharing, and investment promotion, in particular, in the early phase of development. In addition to its equity share in CSSD, Singapore government-linked companies also have stakes in other joint venture companies in SIP: total investments by statutory boards and government-linked companies to SIP came to more than US$120 million by the end of 1997 (*Straits Times*, January 15, 1998).[4]

To attract MNCs to locate their high value added operations in SIP, the Singapore Economic Development Board (EDB), the lead government agency to attract foreign investment, was brought in to share their knowledge with SIP officials on investment promotion in the initial stage of SIP implementation. EDB's overseas centers also assisted with SIP's investment promotion initiatives in the start-up years and even introduced to CSSP some investors who intended to invest in Singapore. At a time

Figure 5.2   Current Ownership Structure of CSSD

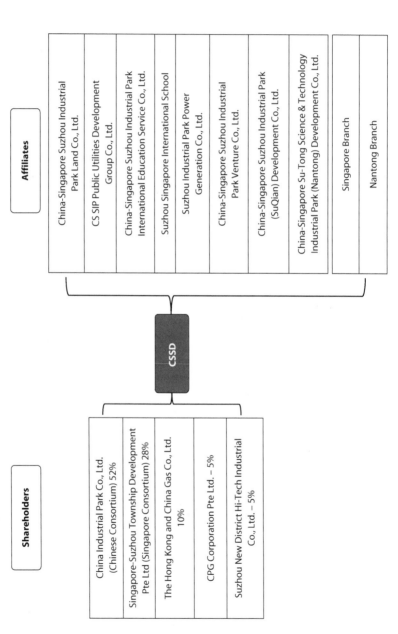

Shareholders

- China Industrial Park Co., Ltd. (Chinese Consortium) 52%
- Singapore-Suzhou Township Development Pte Ltd (Singapore Consortium) 28%
- The Hong Kong and China Gas Co., Ltd. 10%
- CPG Corporation Pte Ltd. – 5%
- Suzhou New District Hi-Tech Industrial Co., Ltd. – 5%

CSSD

Affiliates

- China-Singapore Suzhou Industrial Park Land Co., Ltd.
- CS SIP Public Utilities Development Group Co., Ltd.
- China-Singapore Suzhou Industrial Park International Education Service Co., Ltd.
- Suzhou Singapore International School
- Suzhou Industrial Park Power Generation Co., Ltd.
- China-Singapore Suzhou Industrial Park Venture Co., Ltd.
- China-Singapore Suzhou Industrial Park (SuQian) Development Co., Ltd.
- China-Singapore Su-Tong Science & Technology Industrial Park (Nantong) Development Co., Ltd.

- Singapore Branch
- Nantong Branch

Source: http://www.cssd.com.cn/chinese/yqjj.shtml, 2009.
Note: CSSD = China-Singapore Suzhou Industrial Park Development Co., Ltd.

when foreign investors were skeptical about China's business environment, the partnership with Singapore provided foreign investors with confidence to invest in SIP.

The most important contribution of the partnership arrangement in SIP has been in the area of knowledge transfer. Indeed, a formal knowledge transfer scheme and institutional structure was built into the partnership agreement. The Chinese side established an Adapting Singapore Experience Office under the SIPAC, and the Singapore side set up a counterpart—the Software Project Office (SPO)[5] affiliated with the JTC. These two agencies meet quarterly in SIP to review the software transfer program. In the early years when SIP was putting in place the basic infrastructure, software transfer focused on such topics as Township Development, Urban Planning, and Public Works Management. With SIP moving into higher value added industries in recent years, such as high-tech manufacturing, R&D, and modern services, software transfer has kept pace with these changes to include such topics as the following:

- Eco-Friendly Industrial Park Development
- Science and Technology Development
- Talent Management
- Development of the Business Process Outsourcing (BPO) Industry

Since SIP's inception, more than 2,000 Chinese officials have attended training conducted by the Singapore SPO.

To ensure the effectiveness of the knowledge transfer, officials that attended training were required to report what they had learned. Additionally, they drafted laws and regulations by adapting Singapore practice to local conditions. So far, more than 100 regulations have been enacted by adapting Singapore practice. Meanwhile, knowledge transfer was reinforced through staff exchange. SIPAC sent staff to their Singaporean counterpart and Singapore also sent staff to SIPAC and CSSD to work for short-term periods. The rotation period was often three months. These rotations helped SIPAC and Suzhou municipality to build up public management capacity, as SIP strived to become a service-oriented, transparent government providing full-day, complete process, and all-round services to investors and residents.

In the process of SIP development, the Chinese side also learned by doing. One example that received great recognition was urban planning. Right before the construction of SIP and with the strong emphasis of Singaporean side, experts from both China and Singapore drafted a sophisticated urban plan, which Chinese officials marked as far-sighted. The plan included not only a general framework and detailed master plan, laying out land by industry, trade, living, and other town functions, but also set up more than 300 professional plans. This plan helped to build a philosophy among Chinese officials of (1) planning before construction and (2) constructing underground works before works above ground. Meanwhile, the partnership arrangement also strengthened governance, including a law enforcement management system.

SIP has strictly followed the plan over the 15 years since it was drafted. At the time, this was rare. Such a philosophy now has been widely expanded among industrial parks in China. Many new industrial parks invited Singaporean companies to design their land plans. SIP has become a model of change and innovation for other parts of China. It is estimated that more than 20,000 officials from all over China make learning visits to SIP each year. Singapore also has been asked by various Chinese cities and provinces to share their experiences, given the attention generated by SIP's success. CSSD is now beginning to leverage its expertise within China; it recently began the development of a 10-square-kilometer industrial park project in Suqian, in northern Jiangsu Province. CSSD also ventured to neighboring Nantong to develop a 40-square-kilometer Suzhou-Nantong High-Tech Park in a joint venture with the Nantong government.

Challenges to the Partnership

Although the partnership arrangement brought many benefits to the project, it also brought difficulties that might not exist, or at least would be less complex, in a typical government-run project. Having the majority stake in the initial project stages was critical to enable the Singaporean consortium to drive the project forward, but it also created its own set of problems, in particular, the misaligned incentives of some of the key Chinese stakeholders. The Singaporean partners focused on using SIP as a platform to transfer developmental experience, and so put emphasis on knowledge transfer and urban planning. They intended to build SIP infrastructure to international standards, which implied high development costs. By the end of 2000, infrastructure investment in the 9 square kilometers developed at SIP totaled RMB 7.8 billion (US$1.14 billion), whereas in the other four state-level development zones in Suzhou, 50 square kilometers were developed with an investment of only RMB 6.9 billion (US$1.01 billion) (*Suzhou Statistical Yearbook*, various years)—

that is, infrastructure investment in SIP was six times more intensive (expensive) than in the other parts of the zone. As a result, the land was expected to be sold or rented at a rate high enough to recover this development cost.

For local government, which had only a minor share of the project, the incentives were quite different. They cared less about commercial returns and more about the social and economic returns, including job creation, GDP, and perhaps most important, tax revenue. In China, local government is responsible for the provision of most public goods and services, and its main source of revenue is the value added tax paid by industrial firms. Thus, the incentive for local government is to attract as many industrial investors as possible, as quickly as possible. Land rents and prices that are too high to attract industrial investors result in less tax revenue and fewer jobs. Thus, there was a clear misalignment of incentives between the Singaporean majority stakeholders and the local government. This misalignment was exacerbated by the fact that the central government made a commitment in the initial project agreement to allow SIP to keep all tax revenues generated in the zone. Thus, local government had no incentive to invest in the critical connecting infrastructure to SIP.

Perhaps the biggest source of difficulty in the partnership was the fierce competition that arose in neighboring industrial parks. Before the launch of SIP in 1994, Suzhou Administration already had four state-level economic development zones—Suzhou New and Hi-Tech Development Zone (located west of the old Suzhou city),[6] Kunshan Economic and Technological Development Zone (just 30 kilometers away from SIP), Zhangjiagang Bonded Area, and Suzhou Taihu National Tourism and Vacation Zone, as well as numerous provincial-level zones. Except for the latter of these, all the zones targeted industrial investors. As the other industrial parks were all government sponsored, land developers in those industrial parks usually were SOEs. Their interests naturally were aligned much more closely with local governments. Attracting investors, rather than short- or medium-term commercial returns, was tops on their agenda. Industrial land therefore was rented to industrial investors at a subsidized rate, creating serious competition for SIP and making it almost impossible to maintain rents at levels that could deliver a commercial return.

Moreover, free-riding could hardly be avoided. As SIP is an open area, roads built inside or connecting to SIP also could be used outside of SIP, including in adjacent industrial zones. At the time SIP was attracting interested investors with the help of Singapore's promotion, other industrial parks and neighborhood villages and towns were watching and learning from SIP, recruiting staff who received on-the-job training in SIP, and even lobbying investors who initially were attracted by SIP. Competition with the Suzhou New and High-Tech Development Zone drew the most attention and criticism from Singapore partners in late 1990s.

Despite excellent infrastructure and governance, SIP had little competitive advantage relative to other industrial parks in Suzhou during its initial years, partly because its world-class approach may have been too far ahead of the market at the time. Heavy infrastructure investment, misaligned incentives, and the decline in FDI resulting from the Asian financial crisis in the late 1990s resulted in huge losses for CSSD in the early years. From 1994 to 2001, the total cumulative losses for CSSD totaled US$77 million. By 1999 (the fifth anniversary of SIP), with the foundation of SIP firmly laid and the knowledge transfer process in an advanced stage, the Singapore consortium reviewed its position and decided to relinquish majority shareholding to the Chinese partners in 2001 to better align the incentives and encourage the local officials to focus on the long-term development of SIP. Management responsibility for CSSD was also transferred to a Chinese partner as of January 1, 2001.

Since the time of the shift in ownership control, SIP has emerged as a major success. However, interviews with Chinese officials from SIPAC attribute the change in fortunes at SIP after 2000 mainly to the change in the macroeconomic context rather than anything related to the management or ownership structure of the project. From around 2000, China experienced a wave of industrial relocation of MNCs; in addition, the Chinese ecotnomy recovered from Asian financial crisis. Both trends were accelerated further with China's accession to WTO. Indeed, from 2000 to 2007, FDI to China grew much more rapidly than in from 1995 to 2000 (see table 5.2). SIP attracted FDI at more than double the national rate, but this was from a small base. Similarly, exports also boomed during this period: China's nationwide exports increased 3.9 times, while Suzhou's

Table 5.2   FDI Utilized, US$ Billion

	1995	2000	2007	CAGR '95–00	CAGR '00–07
SIP	0.41	0.52	1.76	4.9%	19.0%
Suzhou	2.32	2.88	7.16	4.4%	13.9%
China	37.5	40.7	74.7	1.7%	9.1%

Source: SIP Statistical Office, 2009; Suzhou Statistical Bureau, 1995–2008; and authors' calculations.

exports increased 10.3 times and SIP's exports increased by 17.9 times, although again from a low base (*China Statistical Bureau* 2008; SIP Statistical Office 2009; *Suzhou Statistical Bureau* various years).

Overcoming Partnership Challenges and Implementing Innovations

It is perhaps unsurprising that the early implementation of SIP encountered significant teething problems. An ambitious project such as SIP required a considerable shift in mind-set and an alignment of expectations and objectives of all major stakeholders. Despite similarity in language and culture, Singapore and China have two different administrative systems and corporate cultures. The key to SIP success was the fundamental resolution by both governments to make SIP a win-win project, and their willingness to evolve the business model to address operational problems, without compromising the emphasis on the softer aspects of developmental planning and a pro-business environment.

Over the past 15 years, partnership arrangements evolved to overcome or mitigate difficulties. The key change was to align the interests of all stakeholders. Tax revenues (VAT) generated from SIP, which were allowed to be kept in SIP at the inception, are now shared between central government, Jiangsu provincial government, Suzhou municipal government, and SIPAC: the central government gets 75 percent, Jiangsu provincial government gets 12.5 percent, Suzhou municipal government gets 10 percent, and SIPAC keeps only 2.5 percent. The main tax revenue source for SIPAC is corporate and personal income tax, 60 percent of which is retained; SIPAC also is allowed to keep all revenues from land sales. Original residents of cooperative areas (farmers) were relocated to the other towns in SIP, but are under the governance and support of SIPAC. These original residents are compensated by SIPAC with residences and monthly allowances. Suzhou New and High-Tech Development Zone, a major competitor of SIP, took 5 percent of the CSSD stake in 2005. Thus, all stakeholders are now able to benefit in one way or another from the development of SIP. Meanwhile, the role of SIPAC has been strengthened and the head of SIPAC was granted the rank of vice mayor. The head of each department in SIPAC now enjoys rank of director, the same level as their counterparts in Suzhou municipal government.

As a result of the realigned incentives, SIPAC has emerged as a de facto main land developer. An Investment Promotion Office was established, and SIPAC has put substantial resources into attracting both domestic and foreign investors. Industrial land and factories were rented at a competitive market rate, while commercial and residential land was auctioned. Revenues from land sales were used to finance infrastructure investment. Several state-owned corporations under the supervision of SIPAC were established following the model of Temasek—some join CSSD in land development and some manage state-owned properties. The participation of these SOEs accelerated the pace of SIP development. Although CSSD still plays an active role in the industrial land development, it also has expanded its business areas to residential and commercial estate development, property management, and the provision of other services.

The success of the partnership also can be attributed to the high-level leadership attention accorded to the project by China and Singapore. The Singapore government invested substantial resources into making the project a success. In addition to committing many of its best officials to spearhead the project,[7] many Singapore government ministries and agencies in charge of such areas as urban planning, water treatment, community infrastructure, and social security actively provided knowledge transfer to SIP officials, a commitment that continues into 2011.

The strong support from China's central government extends to the many policy incentives granted to SIP, which further sharpened SIP's competitive edge. SIP was awarded the same status as China's five SEZs and Shanghai's Pudong New District at its inception in 1994. In addition to the preferential policies enjoyed by the SEZs and Pudong, SIP also enjoyed many other privileges of its own as a unique Singapore-China cooperation project. For example, at the project's inception in 1994, the corporate tax in SIP was reduced to 15 percent from the usual 30 percent for most parts of China. The local authority, SIPAC, also was authorized to approve investments of any size with no upper limit on the total amount of investment in SIP.[8] Adopting Singapore's experience of the Central Provident Fund system, SIP developed the SIP Provident Fund System (SPF), the only such regional scheme in China and perhaps the most important preferential incentive offered at SIP. Based on prepayment accumulation and personal account deposit, the system covers social security items, such as pension, medical care insurance, unemployment insurance, employment injury insurance, maternity insurance, and a housing fund. The contributions from enterprises or individuals to SPF all go to a personal account and can be moved when employees leave SIP. In contrast, the contribution from enterprises to pension funds is put into a pool and is not portable when employees move to other provinces or cities. This SPF model lowers the cost to employers by up to 60 percent of wage costs for a typical low-skilled worker versus the cost to provide the same income, including pension, in a personal account. Thus, it helps enterprises not only to lower labor costs but also to retain talent.

In addition to preferential tax policies, the government has supported the zone by streamlining regulatory and approval procedures for firms operating in the zone. With the support of the central government, SIP made many innovations in public administration by adapting the Singaporean experience. In January 1995, 19 departments, including the Special Economic Zones Office of the State Council, set up on-site offices in SIP to facilitate licensing, regulatory, and operating administration for SIP-based firms. Since 2002, this one-stop service center has been empowered by SIPAC to operate as a fully authorized, independent government department since 2002.

Perhaps the most prominent feature of government support has been the continued streamlining of customs procedures and port handling, which have been adapted and upgraded to help SIP overcome its natural disadvantage of being landlocked. From SIP's inception in 1994, a Customs Sub-Administration was planned; it was launched formally in 1999 (box 5.1 lists major milestones of its development). SIP now operates as a virtual port, and it is allowed to handle customs clearance of exports and imports directly. Firms in SIP enjoy an efficient "green lane" and independent customs supervision, which has run 24 hours a day, seven days a week since 2003. An Integrated Free Trade Zone (IFTZ) was founded in SIP in 2008, by integrating two processing trade zones, one bonded logistic center and one customs checkpoint.[9] The IFTZ now serves as a platform to promote the development of the BPO industry in SIP. Some multinational corporations, including Fairchild Semiconductor Inc., Samsung, and Chi Mei Optoelectronics, already have established or are planning to establish their distribution centers in the IFTZ. Thus, an international logistics and distribution base is gradually taking shape.

Conclusion

As developing-country governments engage with China and other foreign partners in large economic zone development projects, the experience of China's partnership with Singapore for SIP reveals a number of valuable lessons. These are summarized in three main categories: (1) partnership structure and governance; (2) planning, development, and operations; and, possibly of most importance, (3) learning and knowledge sharing.

Box 5.1

SIP Free Trade Zone Development

1994 (August): An office was set up to make preparation for the establishment of SIP Subadministration of Customs.

1995 (August): Custom's Regulation on Supervision over Exports and Imports in SIP was enacted.

1997: SIP Weiting Customs Supervision Station was founded and became one of the first three express inland ports in China.

1998 (September): The second-class land port was opened in SIP.

1999 (May): SIP Subadministration of Customs was formally in operation.

2001 (January): SIP bonded zone for export processing (EPZ) was in operation. Customs adopted an electronic customs declaration and supervision system to manage enterprises in EPZ, where the Electronic Data Interchange system replaces the use of the Processing Trade Logbook and Bank Deposit Account System. Enterprises located in EPZ can enjoy additional preferential policies, including duty exemption for construction materials, equipment, packing materials, consumable materials, and a rational amount of office appliances. Other preferential policies include exemption from value added tax on products produced in EPZ and exemption from tariff quota and license control for cargos into and out of EPZ to and from overseas (excluding restricted items), and a tax rebate on Chinese-made raw materials, parts and components, packing materials, and construction materials entering into EPZ.

2002: With the approval of State General Administration of Customs, the first air-land transfer mode was introduced, making SIP a virtual airport. With the Air-Land Transshipment Model, supervised warehouses of the Shanghai Airport are extended directly to SIP, making import and export declaration possible at the local customs—SIP Customs. This function realizes a one-stop service for declaration, inspection, and dispatch, and it offers flexibility in the arrival, declaration, inspection, and clearance of goods. The time required for getting through customs procedures was greatly reduced from one to two days to seven to eight hours, making it possible for local IT companies to control their production cycle within five days.

(continued next page)

Box 5.1 *(continued)*

2003: SIP Subadministration of Customs provides all-day services—24 hours a day, seven days a week.

2004: SIP Bonded Logistics Center (Type B) with a total planned area of three square kilometers was founded. The Type B Bonded Logistics Center has the functions of a "free trade port." All imported goods entering the logistics park enjoy "bonded" status. Goods entering the logistics park from within China can be regarded as an export and enjoy a tax rebate.

2007: With the operation of a new land-air transfer mode, the virtual airport finally realized the two-way direct transportation. This made SIP a unique virtual port in China combining ocean, air, and land shipment, and allowed SIP to handle customs declaration, inspection, and clearance of exports and imports directly.

2008 (January): The SIP IFTZ (China's first) was in operation by integrating the existing two EPZs, the Customs Bonded Logistic Center and Weiting Customs Checkpoint. Within the planned area of 5.28 square kilometers, the IFTZ has the functions of bonded logistics, bonded processing, international trade, and port operation. Incoming foreign goods are under duty bond, incoming domestic goods enjoy export duty refund, and all transactions of goods within the area are exempted from VAT levies. Customs set up a dedicated office in the zone.

Source: Authors.

Partnership Structure and Governance

- *Ensuring active political commitment at the highest level:* One key to success was the strong resolution of both Chinese and Singaporean governments to make SIP a win-win success. Top-level political commitment is demonstrated by the profile of the board of the project's joint steering committee, which is cochaired by the Chinese vice premier and the Singapore deputy prime minister and includes ministerial chiefs of both countries. Singapore also has put senior ministers in charge of different aspects of the knowledge exchange program. This political commitment helped to overcome many of the problems faced in the early days of the partnership, ensuring that both parties had an active interest in finding ways to make things work.

- *Aligning incentives among key partners:* The main challenges to the partnership arose in part because of the difficult balance of meeting both commercial and political objectives. For these high-profile projects, both objectives are critical. In the initial structure of the partnership arrangement, however, incentives were not properly aligned to address this balance. Although the flip in ownership and control of the project was the high-profile part of the realignment of incentives, a number of other important actions were taken to ensure that all stakeholders involved had the incentive to work toward common goals.

- *Establishing a strong institutional structure for project governance:* The partnership developed a strong, multitiered governance structure for SIP, consisting of three elements: (1) a steering committee that functions as a platform of policy dialogue, coordination of policies among all government departments, and problem resolution when needed; (2) an empowered local authority who performs the government role and whose interest is closely aligned with the zone development; and (3) a joint venture development entity, invested by both parties so that both sides will share cost, risk, and return from zone development.

- *Planning for local phase-in:* Although having the Singaporean partner control the project at the outset was practical, as the Chinese partner built its technical capacity, a phase-in of local management control was practical, both politically and commercially.

- *Recognizing the importance of flexibility:* Given the long-term nature of these projects, and the large sunk costs to get them started, it is critical that partners show a willingness to evolve the business model as necessary. China and Singapore both proved to be highly practical in their approach to resolving the significant early stage challenges of the project.

- *Building mutual respect and recognizing capabilities and constraints:* On the one hand, the host side should be flexible and ready to build a business-friendly investment environment in an innovative and pragmatic manner, and should provide the needed support to make zone development sustainable and profitable. On the other hand, the investor should respect the constraints that the host government faces and should take advantage of the local knowledge of its counterpart. SIP suffered at first because of the failure of both parties to fully appreciate this necessity.

Development and Operations

- *Complementing physical development with policy reform to generate a business-conducive environment*: In the context of building economic zones, streamlining customs procedures and reducing the time and cost of documentation, transit, port handling, and customs procedures would be of the highest priority. The more efficient government services the host government provides and the better investment environment, the fewer tax incentives are needed to make the zone development sustainable. In this respect, SIP established a comprehensive one-stop service with a strong mandate (including devolved decision-making authority). Efficient, on-site customs service was a fundamental component of the zone offering. Officials not only established a dedicated customs subadministration (and gave it a strong mandate) but also continued to evolve and expand the services available, eventually leading to the establishment of an integrated free trade zone within SIP. Finally, innovations in other aspects of administration and regulations, most notably the SPF, created important sources of competitive advantage for SIP.

- *Shifting the mind-set from "hardware" to "software"*: Although the Chinese local partners largely were focused in the beginning on infrastructure (as tangible evidence of "success"), the Singaporean partners placed great emphasis on the importance of "software" or knowledge, whose results were not immediate but were critical to the sustainability of the project. Facilitating this shift in mind-set is a difficult challenge, practically and politically, and is aided strongly by a robust program of knowledge sharing.

Learning and Knowledge Sharing

- *Ensuring a strong, two-way institutionalized commitment to learning*: Knowledge sharing was fundamental to the partnership from the beginning. Critically, this was one of the main objectives of both the host government and the investor. Moreover, it went well beyond platitudes to clear, active commitment. On the Singaporean side, this was evidenced by putting senior officials in charge of various parts of the "software transfer" program over the years. On the Chinese side, the government not only put many officials through the training programs, but also required those officials to demonstrate their acquired knowledge on the job.

- *Making use of practical exchanges:* Formal training also has been embedded at SIP through a long-running program of staff exchanges between the partners.

- *Establishing a formal institutional structure to promote the learning program:* A formal program was put in place at the start, with both partners setting up counterpart offices (China's Adapting Singapore Experience Office and Singapore's SPO) designed to plan and oversee the process of knowledge exchange.

- *Taking a comprehensive approach to the curriculum, with an evolving focus over time:* The knowledge-sharing program designed for the partnership covered almost all important aspects of zone planning and implementation, and public services delivery. Moreover, as the focus of SIP evolved over time, so too did the training needs. And the curriculum was adapted to meet these needs, bringing in new subjects, such as environmentally friendly part development and BPO sector development.

Appendix 5.A Selected Indicators: Developments at SIP, 1994–2008

	Units	1994	1995	1996	1997	1998	1999	2000	2001	2002	2003	2004	2005	2006	2007	2008
Employment within Sino-Singapore Cooperation Area												208,291	334,829	422,476	501,961	
FDI utilized	billion US$	0.1	0.2	0.4	0.7	1.2	0.8	0.6	0.5	0.9	1.2	1.8	1.6	1.6	1.8	1.8
within Sino-Singapore Cooperation Area		0.1	0.2	0.4	0.7	1.2	0.8	0.6	0.4	0.7	0.7	1.0	1.2	1.0	1.1	
Investment within Sino-Singapore Cooperation Area	million RMB	252	1,402	2,380	1,093	985	890	1,008	3,788	4,836	5,827	10,078	7,748	7,512	9,534	
		234	1,338	2,352	1,039	866	748	674	3,083	3,228	3,315	5,818	4,195	3,855	5,538	
Fixed asset investment	billion RMB	0.7	1.2	4.6	6.8	11.7	8.8	5.4	6.2	10.4	20.3	28.2	35.7	39.5	41.6	
Industry		0.1	0.2	2.5	4.5	8.5	6.4	3.2	3.6	5.0	10.0	12.9	15.3	16.8	17.0	
Infrastructure		0.5	0.5	1.7	1.4	2.3	1.3	1.2	1.5	3.2	5.7	5.8	5.9	7.7	5.3	
Real estate		—	0.4	0.3	0.6	0.4	0.5	0.6	0.8	1.8	2.8	6.2	10.0	11.0	12.5	
Public utilities		—	—	0.1	0.2	0.4	0.4	0.2	0.2	0.4	1.6	2.8	3.7	3.7	6.5	
Other		0.1	0.2	0.1	0.1	0.1	0.1	0.2	0.1	0.0	0.2	0.6	0.9	0.3	0.4	
Gross domestic product	billion RMB	1.1	1.4	2.0	3.3	5.0	7.4	13.0	18.0	25.2	36.5	50.3	58.1	68.0	83.6	100.2
Local budgetary revenue	billion RMB	0.0	0.1	0.1	0.2	0.2	0.4	0.8	1.2	1.4	2.1	2.9	4.2	5.3	7.6	9.5
as percentage of GDP	%	1.9	3.7	4.2	4.6	4.5	4.9	6.0	6.8	5.5	5.6	5.8	7.2	7.7	9.1	
Local budgetary expenditure	billion RMB	0.0	0.0	0.1	0.2	0.2	0.4	0.8	1.1	1.4	1.9	2.5	4.3	4.8	5.7	
as percentage of GDP	%	2.5	3.5	3.8	4.8	4.9	5.3	5.8	6.0	5.5	5.3	5.0	7.5	7.1	6.9	
Exports	billion US$	—	0.0	0.1	0.2	0.3	0.6	1.5	1.7	2.6	6.0	11.9	19.2	25.0	28.5	31.1
Imports	billion US$	—	0.0	0.3	0.5	1.1	0.9	2.0	2.1	3.2	8.4	16.3	21.3	25.0	28.4	31.4

Source: www.sipac.gov.cn 2009.

Note: FDI = foreign direct investment; GDP = gross domestic product; RMB = renminbi; — = no data.

Appendix 5.B   SIP Timeline and Major Milestones

1994 On February 26, the representatives from the governments of China and Singapore signed the Agreement on Joint Development of Suzhou Industrial Park.

"Suzhou Industrial Park Development Co., Ltd.", invested in by Suzhou Industrial Park Co., Ltd. (Chinese Consortium) and Singapore-Suzhou Township Development Pte. Ltd. (Singapore Consortium), was approved to establish in mid-1994. The total amount of investment was US$100 million. The registered capital was US$50 million, in which Singapore consortium invested US$32.50 million that accounted for 65 percent and China consortium invested US$17.50 million that accounted for 35 percent.

On September 2, Jiangsu Provincial Government issued a notification on accelerating SIP construction, asking all government departments to put SIP development at the top of their work agenda and give full support.

In November, the company changed its name to "China-Singapore Suzhou Industrial Park Development Co., Ltd."

October 12, an office was established to prepare for the establishment of SIP Subadministration of Customs.

On November 18, the master land plan for phase 1 was approved.

1995 On January 5, 19 departments, including SEZs Office of State Council, set up on-site offices in SIP.

On February 21, Suzhou Industrial Park Administration Commission (SIPAC) was established.

On August 1, the Customs Regulation on Supervision over Exports and Imports in SIP was enacted.

On December 27, SIP was granted preferential treatment of Special Economic Zones in terms of import tariffs.

CSSD increased the total amount of investment from US$100 million to US$150 million.

(continued next page)

1996   CSSD company increased the total amount of investment to US$300 million and increased the registered capital to US$100 million. The shareholding structure remained unchanged.

On October 12, the Steering Committee announced that the phase 1 of 8 square kilometers were to be completed by end of 1997.

1997   On March 16, Suzhou municipal government approved the Provision on SIP Provident Funds Management.

1998   On September 1, the second-class land port was opened in SIP.

1999   On January 1, SIP Local Tax Administration was established.

On May 12, SIP Subadministration of Customs was formally in operation.

On June 28, China and Singapore signed a Memorandum of Understanding on the Development of SIP. It states that Chinese and Singaporean consortium would flip its stake on January 1, 2001. After the adjustment, the major responsibility of management of CSSD would be transferred from the Singaporean side to the Chinese side.

2000   On September 5, Suzhou municipal government called for mobilizing all resources and pushing forward the development construction of SIP.

2001   In line with the spirit of the Memorandum of Understanding on the Development of SIP reached on June 28, CSSD adjusted the investment proportion of China and Singapore on January 1, 2001. The investment proportion of Chinese consortium was adjusted from 35 percent to 65 percent, and that of the Singapore consortium was adjusted from 65 percent to 35 percent. After the adjustment, the Chinese side took over the major responsibility for management.

January 10, SIP bonded zone for export processing was in operation.

March 23, Suzhou municipal government launched the development of phase 2 and phase 3 of SIP.

On October 28, the state-owned land-use right was auctioned for the first time.

(continued next page)

2002   CSSD completed the capital enlargement and injection in August 2005. The registered capital was increased to US$125 million. Three new shareholders were attracted: Hong Kong and China Gas Investment Ltd., CPG Corporation Pte. Ltd., and Suzhou New District Hi-Tech Industrial Co., Ltd.

2003   On December 9, SIP Intelligent Property Right Protection Center was in operation.

On March 31, SIP People's Court and People's Procuratorate were in operation.

2007   In April, SIP became a pilot of National High and New Technology Zone.

In May, SIP became a demonstration zone for service outsourcing.

2008   On January 15, the SIP Integrated Free Trade Zone (the first one in China) was in operation and customs set up an office in the zone.
On June 29, CSSD joint stock company founding meeting was held and the joint stock company was established on June 30.

Source: Authors.

Notes

1. This is equivalent to more than one-tenth of the total land area of Singapore.

2. The initial cooperation area was 70 square kilometers and there were five townships at the outset of SIP. Later the cooperation area was expanded to 80 square kilometers and the five townships were combined into three townships.

3. The 80-square-kilometer Cooperative Zone was designed to met the standard of "Nine Utilities and Leveled Land" (the nine utilities being Roads, Power Supply, Water Supply, Gas Supply, Steam Supply, Sewage System, Storm Water Drainage, Telecommunication, Cable Television), meaning it was fully prepared and serviced, ready for development of operating infrastructure.

4. Xinsu Industrial Development was set up to develop and operate ready-built factories in the park. These are Temasek Holdings (US$4.14 million), JTC International (US$16.54 million), Keppel Land (US$10.33 million), and Sembawang Industrial (US$10.33 million). Three companies have additional stakes in Gasin (Suzhou) Property Development Co. Ltd., a company set up to develop residential property in the SIP: Temasek Holdings (US$4.23

million), JTC International (US$4.23 million), and Keppel Land (US$5.29 million).

5. "Software" in this context refers to knowledge—the term is intended to contrast with the "hardware" of infrastructure, which is at the core of the commercial partnership.

6. This site initially was offered to Singapore for development of SIP.

7. For instance, current Minister (Prime Minister's Office) Lim Swee Say was the first director of the Singapore SPO, and former Minister of State for Trade and Industry Chan Soo Sen was the first chief executive officer of the joint venture CSSD.

8. SIP's approval limit subsequently was capped in a State Council decree issued in 2002, but the approval limit has since increased.

9. After the success of the scheme in SIP, it has since been extended to 20 other cities.

References

China Economic Development Zone Association. 2008. *China Development Zones Yearbook*. Beijing: China Financial & Economic Publishing House.

China Statistical Bureau. 1992–2009. *China Statistical Yearbook*. Beijing: China Statistic Press.

Deng, X. 2004. *Selected Works of Deng Xiaoping, Volume 3*. Beijing: People's Press.

Inkepen, A., and W. Pien. 2006. "An Examination of Collaboration and Knowledge Transfer: China-Singapore Suzhou Industrial Park." *Journal of Management Studies* 43 (4): 779–811.

Pereira, A. 2007. "Transnational State Entrepreneurship? Assessing Singapore's Suzhou Industrial Park Project (1994–2004). *Asia Pacific Viewpoint* 48 (3): 287–98.

Perry, M., and C. Yeoh. 2000. "Singapore's Overseas Industrial Parks." *Regional Studies* 34 (2): 199–206.

Singapore Ministry of Trade and Industry. 2010. "Reply to World Bank on China-Singapore Suzhou Industrial Park." Background note.

Singapore *Straits Times*, January 15, 1998. "Suzhou Park problems can be overcome." http://www.singapore-window.org/80115st1.htm.

Suzhou Statistical Bureau. 1995–2009. *Suzhou Statistical Yearbook*. Beijing: China Statistical Press.

CHAPTER 6

SEZs in the Context of Regional Integration: Creating Synergies for Trade and Investment

Naoko Koyama

Introduction

Paralleling the rapid development of SEZs in recent decades has been the development of regional trade agreements (RTAs)[1] to promote trade and economic integration. As of February 2010, a total of 457 RTAs have been notified to the WTO, out of which 266 are already in force. These numbers are expected to continue to rise.

SEZs and RTAs are policy tools that promote trade and investment of countries and regions. When successful, SEZs generate significant local employment, increase exports, and accelerate economic growth. Meanwhile, successful RTAs contribute to increased trade among member countries and promote regional integration more broadly. When the two initiatives exist simultaneously, they have the potential to generate significant synergies. Specifically, by lowering barriers to regional trade and facilitating the potential for realizing scale economies in regional production, RTAs stimulate investment by both domestic and foreign firms. By providing serviced land, infrastructure, and an improved regulatory environment, SEZs lower the cost and risk to firms in undertaking such investments. In addition, the growth of intraregional trade may create opportunities for specialized zones, for example, focusing on logistics or cross-border trade.

Although SEZs have the potential to facilitate regional synergies, RTAs often face challenges in incorporating SEZs into their regulatory frameworks. This is particularly true in the case of traditional EPZs. This challenge stems from the fact that although RTAs represent bilateral or multilateral instruments, SEZs are, in all cases to date, instruments by which an individual country promotes investment and exports, the former potentially in competition with their RTA partners. In particular, when SEZ programs provide enterprises with tariff-related incentives, they trigger various issues in the context of RTAs. For example, they may create an incentive for "tariff-jumping"—that is, when a foreign firm decides to jump over the tariff wall to avoid trade costs (tariffs). This tariff-jumping might happen through investment of a physical presence in a member country (the traditional definition of tariff-jumping), although in this case, the investment would be in an SEZ and not necessarily within the member country's customs territory. But it also might happen without any physical presence at all, by using the SEZ as a bulwark to enter the customs territory. Specifically, because many SEZs allow duty-free entrance of inputs imported from outside of a territory, foreign (extra-RTA) goods could potentially enter the RTA free of duty through an SEZ, and then leak into the customs territory of other RTA member states. If a newly established RTA disallows exports from a member country's SEZ to the territory of other RTA member countries, however, the operation of existing SEZ investors may be affected substantially. Consequently, this may necessitate a reform of SEZ programs in member countries to prevent a large loss of investment. Furthermore, excluding SEZ investors from taking advantage of the RTA prevents member countries from realizing the full potential of these two trade and investment-generating instruments and achieving effective regional integration. To leverage fully both of these policy tools, RTA member countries need to take a collaborative approach to harmonize their SEZ programs.

Despite the growing significance of both SEZs and RTAs, research on the connection between these two instruments of trade and investment has been limited. In practice, most RTAs take measures to prevent tariff-jumping through SEZs. Yet, few efforts have been made to harmonize SEZ programs across member countries in some RTAs. Such collaboration could generate considerable benefits by creating synergy between

SEZ and RTA and by acting as a step toward greater economic integration. This chapter aims to fill part of the research gap. In particular, the objectives of this chapter are (1) to discuss the implication of RTAs on SEZs and review experiences in various RTAs, including country-specific cases; and (2) to outline the potential opportunities that a harmonized approach toward SEZ initiatives might generate.

In the above framework, this chapter first reviews briefly the role, trend, and impact of RTAs, with particular attention to those of Sub-Saharan Africa. Then, after laying out various types of issues arising from overlap of RTAs and SEZs with preferential tariff treatment, it reviews how RTAs have been managing these issues and draws lessons from case examples. Finally, it discusses how harmonizing SEZ programs, including but not limited to duty-free imports and fiscal incentives, within RTA member countries can help realize synergies between the two policy instruments and contribute to greater trade and investment generation and deeper economic integration.

Regional Trade Agreements

Introduction to RTAs

RTAs promote the expansion of trade between or among member countries by offering preferential access to certain products through the reduction (but not necessarily elimination) of tariffs. Under the WTO and General Agreement on Tariffs and Trade (GATT) principles of MFN treatment, any arrangements to offer zero or low rates of tariffs between two members would automatically require an extension of this treatment to all WTO members. GATT article XXIV, however, allows for a deviation from MFN principles, in the form of "regional trade agreements" (WTO 2009).

RTAs offer both static and dynamic benefits to member countries. At the firm level, by removing or reducing trade barriers, RTAs lower the cost of exporting or (in the case of a free trade agreement) essentially expand the size of the "domestic market." They also provide export-oriented producers with access to lower cost and possibly higher quality inputs than might have been available in the domestic market (or through imports from alternative sources). At the level of the wider economy, RTAs facilitate industrial restructuring, resulting in higher scale, more specialized, and competitive producers. The procompetitive effect of reducing barriers to cross-border trade and investment results in the least productive firms exiting the market, merging with or being acquired by larger or more productive firms, and contributing in time to greater production scale and lower costs, with competition ensuring that the savings are passed on in the form of lower prices (Baldwin, forthcoming). From the perspective of economic development, RTAs can facilitate industrialization and specialization. In small markets (as is the case in many countries of Sub-Saharan Africa), the requirement for firms to cover their fixed costs places strict limits on the degree of specialization that is possible. By expanding the scale of the accessible market, RTAs therefore enable local firms to specialize while maintaining sufficient economies of scale. Specialization then becomes another source of competitiveness—a virtuous circle is created.

For firms, one of the most fundamental implications of RTAs is that they turn regional export markets into "virtual" domestic markets. Although this creates significant opportunities, for firms that are based inside SEZs (particularly those inside traditional EPZs that combine duty-free import and fiscal incentives with restrictions on sales to the domestic market), it may also mean a loss of their privileged position in selling to regional markets vis-à-vis firms based outside the zones. Unlike SEZs, which have historically targeted foreign investors,[2] RTAs benefit businesses regardless of the source of capital. As discussed, RTAs should facilitate the ability of local firms to exploit economies of scale, specialize and become more sophisticated, and start exporting in the regional market. It is this balance between foreign and local investors and exporters that creates the tension in the relationship between SEZs and RTAs.

Trends in Development of RTAs

Although more countries join the WTO, the creation of RTAs also has been increasing at an accelerating speed, as illustrated in figure 6.1. In 2009, the number of RTAs notified to the WTO reached its historical record of 37 cases. As of February 2010, 457 cumulative cases have been notified, of which 266 are in force. These include bilateral and multilateral reciprocal preferential trade agreements, including free trade agreements (FTAs), customs unions, partial scope agreements, and economic integration agreements. Among these, FTAs account for the majority.

Should the Doha Round ever reach successful completion, it should be expected to curtail the need for RTAs. Yet, many analysts predict that the number of RTAs will continue to grow, at least in the short term. One reason is that some agreements already are signed or under negotiation and will come in effect soon. But it can also be attributed to the

Figure 6.1 Total Notifications Received by Year, 1948–2009

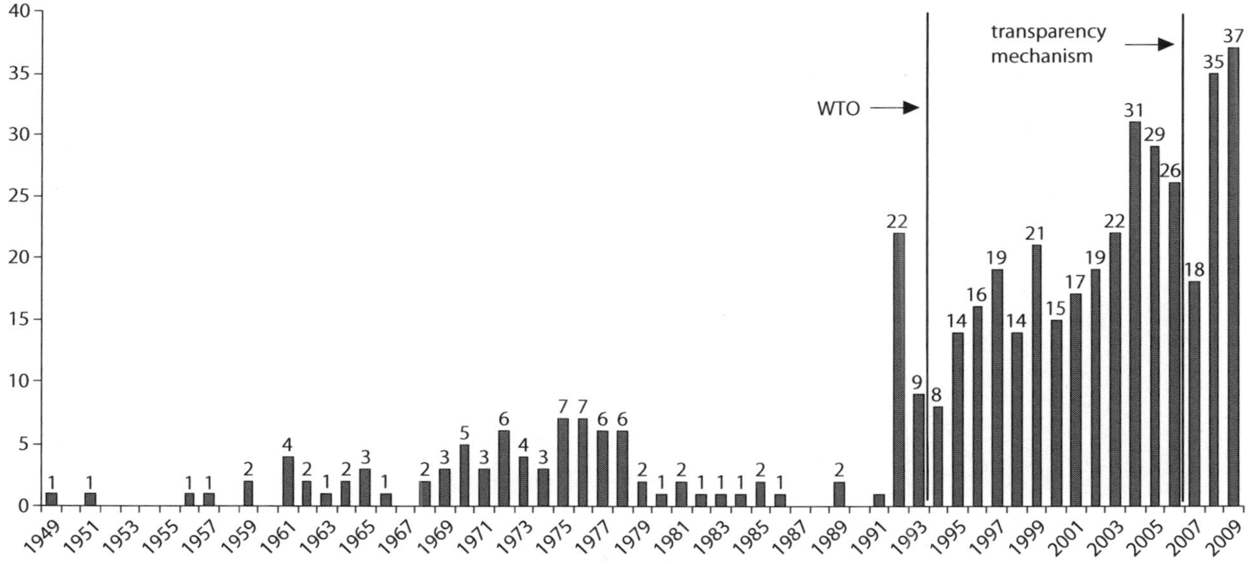

Source: WTO Secretariat (2010).

RTAs' capacity to address multiple dimensions of economic and other regional concerns that cannot be covered within the WTO framework. Many countries are members of more than one RTA, some RTAs are subgroups of larger groups, and many regional trade blocs negotiate a further RTA or Economic Partnership Agreement with another regional bloc. All of these aim for greater regional integration. Yet, they also add complexity to trade relationships, as each RTA tends to have its own set of rules and regulations, which may create contradictions and complexities in managing overlapping relationships. In the case of SEZs, for example, it may be that different trade agreements specify a different treatment of SEZs.

Sub-Saharan Africa is not an exception in this regard. Figure 6.2 exhibits the current landscape of RTAs in Africa and Middle East.

Figure 6.2   Network of Plurilateral Groupings in Africa and Middle East

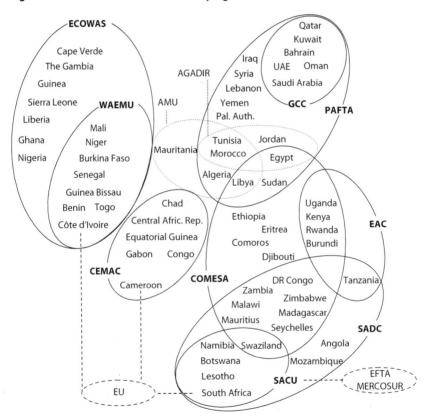

Source: Acharya, Crawford, Maliszewska, and Renard (2011).

A decomposition of RTA participants by the level of economic development reveals another interesting trend. Increasing numbers of newly signed RTAs involve both industrial and developing countries, with RTAs among industrial countries growing almost fourfold between 2005 and 2009. RTAs involving both industrial and developing countries account for more than two-thirds of the cumulative number of RTAs under negotiation and signed as of February 2010.

Increasing numbers of RTAs, especially since the early 2000s, go beyond the simple agreements on trade. They include rules and measures to create harmonized frameworks of various cross-border policies among participating members. Such rules and measures typically relate to customs administration, intellectual property, competition policy, technical barriers to trade, sanitary and phytosanitary agreements, government procurement, and investment. In this context, policies regarding SEZs are also referred to in several agreements, including the East African Community (EAC) and the Common Market for Eastern and Southern Africa (COMESA).

The Performance of RTAs

The primary, short-term objective of RTAs is to increase trade and investment as a result of providing access to a larger market. But given that many countries participate in various RTAs with different degrees of liberalization, they may create additional complexity and, ironically, may adversely affect trade relations.

The performance of RTAs in promoting trade has varied around the world. Several RTAs signed in the 1990s appear to have contributed to significant growth in intraregional trade, including the European Economic Community, the Association of Southeast Nations (ASEAN) Free Trade Area (AFTA), the Andean Community, and the South Asian Free Trade Agreement (SAFTA). All of the member countries experienced an increased share of intra-RTA trade to total trade following the trade liberalization in the region. But other RTAs, including the European Free Trade Association (EFTA) and the Central American Common Market (CACM), actually experienced a stagnant or declining share of intra-RTA trade after the implementation of the agreement. Finally, in some RTAs, significant growth in trade in the initial years following the agreement later gave way to declining trade after a certain period. These include NAFTA, the Gulf Cooperation Council (GCC), the Closer Economic Relations Agreement between Australia and New Zealand, and the Economic and Monetary Community of

Central Africa (CEMAC). The evolution of the intra-RTA trade is illustrated in figure 6.3, along with the indications of RTA implementation and enlargement. When assessed in terms of intratrade's contribution to GDP, however, the results have been promising for most RTAs. Except in EFTA, all of the major RTAs experienced growth in the ratio of intra-RTA trade (export and import) to GDP since 1980s (Acharya, Crawford, Maliszewska, and Renard 2011).

Various factors determine the effectiveness of RTAs. Coverage and the degree of liberalization in the agreement appear to be among the most important. In addition, many successful RTAs go beyond simple agreements on tariffs and address comprehensive trade facilitation measures, such as harmonized procedures and rules on behind-border procedures, investment, and intellectual property rights. Also, RTAs appear to be likely to yield a greater result when they are designed to align with overall economic reforms of member countries. RTAs that fail to get implemented fully tend to be less successful, as do those with overlapping rules of origin and tariff schedules, which complicate trade relations and prevent member countries from integrating into global value chains. These findings on RTA success factors suggest an important implication for SEZ programs—that is, that harmonization and simplification of SEZ programs likely is crucial in the context of RTAs.

Implication of RTAS for SEZs

RTAs have, by and large, been successful in promoting trade among members, but the existence of SEZs in countries within RTAs sometimes has been problematic. This section will first discuss the reasons why SEZs and RTAs can sit uneasily together. It then reviews how RTAs, particularly those in Africa, have responded to these issues. Although SEZs vary significantly in objectives, form, and function, those that are most problematic in the context of RTAs are those that provide preferential tariff treatment based on export performance. This is most commonly the case in traditional EPZs.

Why is it an Issue?

The issues arising from the coexistence of RTAs and SEZs relate to trade triangulation, competitiveness of local producers, promotion of regional economic integration, and competitive positioning. This section discusses each of these in turn.[3]

Figure 6.3   Evolution of the Share of Intra-PTA Imports in Total Imports, 1970–2008

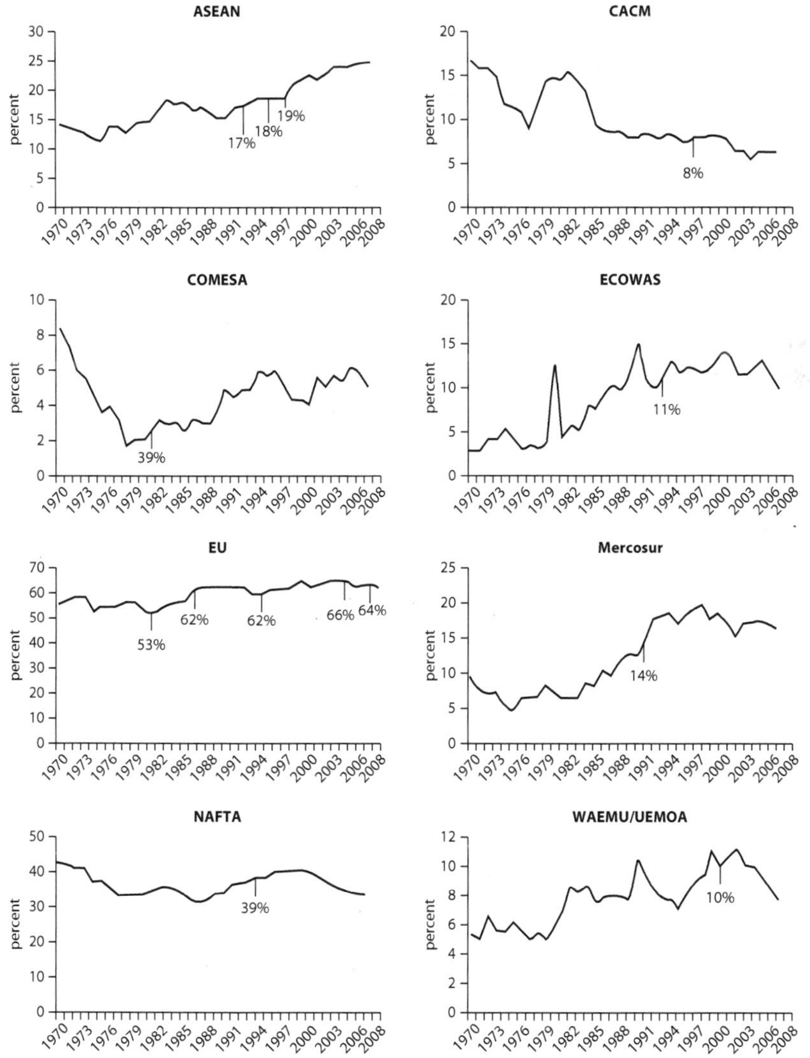

Source: Acharya, Crawford, Maliszewska, and Renard (2011).
Note: ASEAN = Association of Southeast Asian Nations; CACM = Central American Common Market; COMESA = Common Market for Eastern and Southern Africa; ECOWAS= Economic Community of West African States; EU= European Union; Mercosur = Southern Cone Common Market (*Mercado Commún del Sur*); NAFTA = North American Free Trade Agreement; WAEMU/UEMOA= West African Economic and Monetary Union (*Union Économique et Moné-taire Ouest-Africaine*). The marked point (with percentage noted) in each panel indicates the date of entry into force of the agreement (or enlargements, in the case of the EU) .

Trade triangulation. The primary concern for RTA members regarding SEZs is the potential for trade triangulation. If a product processed under a preferential duty scheme of an SEZ is allowed to enter into the customs territory of an RTA member as an originating product, it opens the possibility that any product not originating in an RTA may enter the RTA free of duties through the SEZ. This could happen, for example, if a product from Country A was shipped into a firm located in an SEZ in Country B and subsequently was relabeled as "Made in Country B" or received a certificate of origin from Country B. In that case, the product could enter the customs territory of Country B's RTA (and therefore the markets of all other countries in the RTA) with little to no value added within the RTA. This would infringe on the tariff collection policies of RTA members and potentially could erode the RTA's bloc against extraterritory countries.[4]

From the perspective of RTA member governments, a second problem with trade triangulation is that it has the potential to undermine FDI opportunities in the territory. If an RTA prohibits the duty-free entry of SEZ-processed products, foreign suppliers of inputs to SEZ operators may consider setting up an operation in the territory so that their customers and thus themselves can take advantage of the expanded market access resulting from the RTA. But when duty-free entry is possible through an SEZ, foreign suppliers may have less incentive to invest in a new operation in the territory.

Competitiveness of local producers. A producer operating under an SEZ program typically benefits from preferential duty schemes, including but not limited to drawbacks and suspensions of duties on imported equipment and inputs. A local producer who pays full import duties on imported equipment and inputs will therefore be at a disadvantage against an SEZ operator if products processed under the SEZ program can enter the RTA's local market as originating products. In addition, the financial incentives that may be available to SEZ-based producers (again, particularly those based in traditional EPZs) often go beyond those related to import duties. In many cases, these incentives are granted partial or total exemption of direct and indirect taxes temporarily or permanently, often on the condition that their export performance meets a required threshold. Such special incentives for SEZ operators also put local non-SEZ producers at a disadvantage if products from the SEZs are allowed to enter local markets free of duty.[5]

Promotion of regional economic integration. Placing local suppliers at a disadvantage against SEZ-based operators also may pose a threat to the effectiveness of the RTA in promoting one of its primary objectives—i.e., regional economic integration—by hindering interindustrial integration across member countries. If SEZ-based operators, including those engaged in trading of foreign equipment and inputs, are allowed to sell their products to local producers in RTA member countries, they risk crowding out immature local suppliers.[6] Thus, local producers, even with greater access to suppliers in another member country of the RTA, may choose to purchase foreign inputs through SEZ-based operators, who may be able to offer both a cost and a quality advantage. On the one hand, this should improve the competitiveness of local producers (through their access to higher quality, lower cost inputs) at least in the short term; on the other hand, it may curtail the effectiveness of the RTA in nurturing local suppliers and promoting local vertical industrial linkages.

Competitive positioning of the SEZ. The flip side to promoting regional integration is that firms based inside the SEZs may suffer a deterioration of the relative advantages they enjoyed before the RTA. Specifically, as many of the fiscal benefits provided in traditional EPZs are linked directly to exports (or at least dependent on the firm serving export markets), the RTA essentially turns what were regional export markets for these firms into "domestic markets." This not only puts these firms on a more level playing field in terms of market access versus non-zone-based firms, but also may have implications for zone-based firms to maintain the export requirements on which their incentives are based. The implication is that this market access potentially reduces some of the advantages of being based in the SEZs, and thus has implications not only for the zone-based firms but also for existing zone developers and managers (which, in many countries, is the government).

The Response of RTAs to Tariff-Related Issues

RTAs have taken various approaches in response to the problematic issues of SEZs. In particular, most RTAs have implemented a system to avoid strict duty-free entry of products processed under SEZ schemes, although the degree of stringency varies from one RTA to another. This section explores the main approaches taken by RTAs in controlling the entry of SEZ-processed products into the RTA territory. It then reviews some cases in which RTAs responded to the needs of particular countries, as well as cases in which RTA member countries reacted to an RTA's policy on SEZs.

Major approaches. Most RTAs take measures to prevent the products processed in SEZ from freely entering into the territory, but how they achieve this and how restrictive they are varies widely. Most RTAs do so either by establishing a special rule on the treatment of products processed in SEZs of RTA member countries or by applying rules of origin that are generally applicable to products processed anywhere in the RTA.

Special clause for SEZ-processed products. Many RTAs set out a special clause to stipulate how the goods from SEZs in member countries should be treated in the context of the RTA. Examples include the EAC customs union and the West African Economic and Monetary Union (WAEMU, or UEMOA from its French name). Many of these RTAs establish an article to address specifically the entry of SEZ-processed products into the principal protocol of trade or an additional protocol, although some unions set a rule in the annexes of the trade agreement. The most stringent rule takes the form of complete prohibition of the entry of products processed under SEZ programs into the RTA territory. NAFTA is the only major RTA that applies such stringent rules—this agreement was implemented over a seven-year transitional period through 2001.

All other RTAs reviewed in this study that include a special clause on SEZ-processed products stipulate that such products may not benefit from the status as an originating product. Unlike rules of origin, this rule usually applies regardless of the level of local content of products. There are some variations in how RTAs define the products subject to the special clause. Some RTAs refer to goods processed in SEZs, whereas others describe these goods as goods processed under special tariff regimes. None of the RTAs reviewed in this study refers to whether the MFN status would apply to SEZ-processed products that cannot benefit from the status as an originating product. Yet, in practice, these products that do not carry a certificate of origin are subject to normal tariff schedules.

Many RTAs, although not all, set up exceptions to this rule in various dimensions. For example, some RTAs accept products processed in SEZs as originating products if import duties are paid on the inputs of these products. In Africa, WAEMU adopts this type of exception rule. WAEMU also has a unique exception rule that SEZ-processed products can be granted the status as an originating product if the import duties applied on their inputs are greater than those that would be applied on finished goods. Another type of exception, such as that in the RTA agreement between Central America and the Dominican Republic, allows for the entry of SEZ-processed products under the same terms as the host country if the SEZ allows the entry of such products into their own domestic market.

Rules of origin. Many RTAs that do not establish a specific clause for the treatment of products from SEZs simply apply rules of origin. Rules of origin is a standard and widely used method of avoiding trade deflection or tariff-jumping in cases in which a product enters into the trade area through a low or no-tariff member country to exploit the duty-free nature of the RTA. To some extent, rules of origin can restrict the entrance of SEZ-processed products because SEZ operators generally have a relatively high import ratio and thus may not meet the rules-of-origin requirement. Yet, when the local content requirement is sufficiently low, SEZ operators still can benefit from both duty-free import (SEZ) and duty-free access to a greater market (RTA). For example, COMESA applies relatively loose rules of origin and it allows up to 60 percent of extraterritory inputs.[7] Under such a generous rule, many SEZ operators may be able to take advantage of both SEZ and RTA, placing local producers at disadvantage.[8] Conversely, stringent rules of origin, such as those proposed at the Southern African Development Community (SADC) Free Trade Area, also can be problematic. When rules are too strict, local producers are at a competitive disadvantage against foreign producers because they are forced to purchase costly local inputs. In an extreme case, foreign producers may be able to sell products at a cheaper price than an RTA's local producers, especially when external tariff rates for finished goods are not so high (Flatters 2002).

No rule. Among those RTAs reviewed in this study, a few have neither a special clause on SEZ-processed goods nor rules of origin. In most RTAs, however, the SEZ issue has been raised as a concern. In such cases, either a special clause or rules of origin or both are being discussed. These include the agreement between Dominican Republic and the Caribbean Community, in which case a special agreement on the treatment of products from free zones has been proposed. The proposed arrangements include (1) products from SEZs must not enjoy additional advantages to those they now enjoy in the different customs territories, and (2) they must enjoy no less favorable treatment than what they now enjoy in reciprocal trade (Granados 2003).

Figure 6.4 summarizes the classification of various tariff-related measures taken by RTAs discussed above. Appendix 6.B contains a list of how various RTAs treat SEZ-processed goods.

Figure 6.4 Classification of Various Tariff-Related Measures by RTA

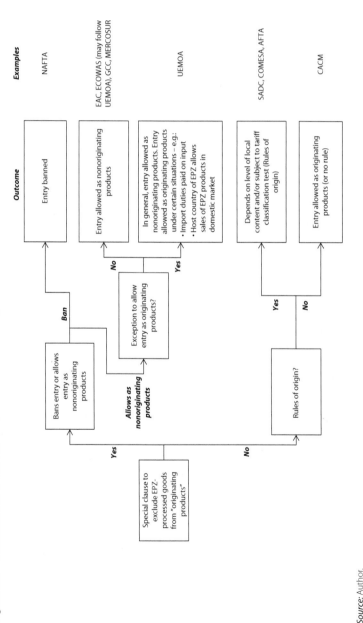

Source: Author.

Note: AFTA = ASEAN Free Trade Area; CACM = Central American Common Market; COMESA = Common Market for Eastern and Southern Africa; EAC = East African Community; ECOWAS = Economic Community of West African States; GCC = ; Mercosur = Southern Common Market; NAFTA = North American Free Trade Agreement; SADC = Southern African Development Community; UEMOA = West African Economic and Monetary Union.

Country- and Region-Specific Cases

In some cases, the incompatibility of a country's existing SEZ program with the rules under a newly established RTA constitutes a significant impediment to the country's trade and investment potential. The responses of countries and of trade blocs to these challenges have varied considerably, depending on factors such as the region, government's leadership, and the importance of intra-RTA trade for existing SEZ operators. In some countries, such as Mexico under NAFTA, governments modified their zone policy to overcome such challenges and grandfathered in existing investors. In other countries, such as Uruguay under the Southern Common Market (Mercosur), in the absence of any significant government policy initiatives to redress the challenges, industries evolved to adjust themselves to the new environment. In some cases, an RTA has allowed for temporary exceptions to consider country-specific circumstances (e.g., SADC). Following is a brief review of some of these country- or region-specific cases.

Mexico. NAFTA, which came into force in January 1994, set a strict prohibition on the entry of goods processed under SEZ schemes, within a seven-year transitional period. At this same time, Mexico's exports from the *maquila* program had increased substantially, reaching 41 percent of the country's total exports and accounting for 1.3 million jobs by 1998. With most products from *maquila* exported to the United States, it was critical for the Mexican government to find a solution to comply with the NAFTA requirement without dampening fast-growing industries. As a part of the policy response, Mexico established the Sectoral Promotion Program. This program grants registered companies MFN tariff preferences, which are 5 percent or less in most cases, on more than 5,000 inputs used in production. Companies engaged in specified industries[9] are eligible to register for and benefit from this program. Critically, this preferential tariff treatment is not contingent on export performance, and it applies equally to exporters and to companies who sell to the domestic market, thus ensuring that it is in compliance with NAFTA. This is a successful case in which a country managed to comply with an RTA's stringent rule on export-based special incentives by shifting from an export-oriented program to a sector-focused one (Granados 2003).

Uruguay. Facing a similar challenge with its participation in Mercosur, in 1994, Uruguay had little scope to restructure its incentives regime. Under Mercosur's Decision 8, goods processed or entered into SEZs are treated as extraterritory products and thus are subject to external tariffs and are not granted certificates of origin. Although a transitional period was allowed for the Manaos free zone in Brazil and the Tierra del Fuego free zone in Argentina (because of their location in "lagging" peripheral regions), Uruguay could not secure such an exemption for its SEZs. The Uruguayan government did not take a particular initiative to mitigate the impact of Decision 8 on existing SEZ operators. Thus, SEZ operators were forced to adapt to new rules and find a way to survive. Within a few years, the nature of activities in the SEZ had changed considerably, refocusing toward the changing comparative advantage of Uruguay within the region. Specifically, firms began focusing on offshoring (including financial services) and logistics activities, positioning the zone as a gateway into Mercosur for firms based outside of the regional bloc. By 2005, only 27 percent of exports from SEZ operators in Uruguay were destined to Mercosur. This shift was supported by a later government policy, which responded to the evolution of SEZ activities by endorsing a tax reform to allow all types of offshore activities in SEZ and by granting some incentives, including the elimination of accounting requirements for companies whose assets are all offshore (Granados 2003; Malaver 2009). Thus, despite a pessimistic prospect of SEZ continuity after the launch of Mercosur, SEZ operators in Uruguay adapted to the new environment and some of them now generate high incomes. Yet, unlike the Mexican case, its development is parallel to the regional integration under Mercosur, and no synergy exists between the RTA and SEZ programs.

Kenya. The EAC customs union, which came into effect in 2005, clearly excludes SEZ-processed goods from benefiting from the status as originating products. Among five member countries, only Kenya had the potential to be affected immediately, because it is the only country that had established a sizable SEZ program at the signing of the customs union. Most current users of SEZs are not affected by Kenya's integration into EAC customs union either, because their major export destinations are outside of the EAC (mainly to the United States and Europe). Thus, Kenya's SEZ program has not been forced to address reform, so far. However, there is no guarantee that the impact will remain limited in the future. Kenya's full integration to EAC customs union is likely to change the economic rationale of potential investors, leading to more investments targeting the large EAC market. Indeed, some investors in the SEZs are already requesting Kenyan authority to loosen the current rule that requires all SEZ firms to export at least 80 percent of their output and allow them to sell more to the EAC market (Manchanda 2010). The current request does not relate to the treatment of tariffs on finished goods entering into EAC territory, but rather to the minimum export requirement to reside in SEZ areas. However, once the SEZ tenants are allowed to sell more to EAC territory, the question of the tariff on the goods processed in the SEZ will undoubtedly arise as an issue among EAC member countries.[10]

SADC. Although SADC does not set specific rules governing the entry of SEZ-processed goods, it has proposed restrictive rules of origin, requiring high local content for any import into the RTA territory to take advantage of duty-free access. At the same time, however, some exceptions are granted to accommodate the circumstances of member countries and sectors. In particular, it allowed temporary special arrangements for textiles and garments exports from Malawi, Mozambique, Tanzania, and Zambia to the partner countries of the Southern African Customs Union (SACU) (Botswana, Lesotho, Namibia, South Africa, and Swaziland). This special arrangement, which expired in 2009, enabled the manufacturers in the four countries to continue procuring fabrics from outside SADC for duty-free sales to SADC, during which time the countries were expected to develop their local fabric-producing capacity. This arrangement included all textiles and garments produced in SEZs. It provides an example in which an RTA flexibly adjusted its rules considering the significance of the industry—in this case, textiles and garments—for some member countries as well as the volume of its trade within the region. Although the policy does not focus specifically on SEZs, a similar approach could be taken, by which an RTA establishes a special arrangement for SEZ-processed goods. This approach could be especially helpful when a practical approach is necessary to allow member countries time to adjust their national policies and to enable existing investors to restructure their business under the new RTA context.

Harmonization of SEZs: Beyond Tariff Issues

The previous section discussed how RTAs take various measures to control the entry of the goods processed in SEZs. Yet, this approach merely constitutes a passive response to the issues arising from the overlap of SEZ and RTA. It addresses potential risks caused by the SEZs, but it misses out on the potential to develop synergies between the SEZ and RTA instruments, specifically to enable SEZs to leverage and promote regional integration under the context of RTAs. In practice, few RTAs have made efforts toward harmonization of SEZ programs among member countries, although some discussions and initiatives have been launched, for example, by EAC and COMESA.

In several potential areas, however, the complementarities between SEZ and RTA could be better exploited, including the following:

- Harmonizing regulations
- Taking collective action to lower or remove financial incentives (e.g., general investment incentives)
- Establishing strategic frameworks as a region, such as the following:
  - Joint marketing of region as investment destination
  - Creation of industrial linkages among SEZs in RTA
  - Specialization of SEZs based on comparative advantage relative to other members in RTA

This section explores the opportunities that harmonized SEZ programs might generate for RTA member countries and the challenges in doing so. The discussion in this section is most relevant for RTAs within the context of regional integration agreements; it will be less relevant for bilateral or multilateral trade agreements that have no integration component or that involve countries that are not proximate.

Regulatory Framework

Having simple, straightforward regulations helps a country to promote investment by lowering investors' costs of search and compliance. The same logic applies to the SEZ-related regulations within an RTA. When investors consider exploring a new market or opening a new production site, they will research and compare the investment-related laws, including SEZ regulations across all potential locations in a chosen region. They are likely to assess various factors, including the existence and details of the SEZ law, the requirements for establishing operations in the zone, the fiscal and nonfiscal incentives available, how application and registration processes are managed, and whether a competent zone authority has been established. Having clear SEZ rules and consistent definitions of terminologies across member countries reduces the search costs for investors, allowing them to focus more on strategic factors, such as target customer base, suppliers, distribution network, and so on. More attractive regulations, infrastructure, or incentives may help a country to win an investment over its neighbors, but harmonized SEZ regulations across an RTA may be a powerful tool through which to compete against other regions to ensure that an investment comes into the RTA. Perhaps most important, such a harmonized approach then allows SEZs in each member country to compete for an incoming investment based on their own sources of comparative advantage.

Coordination among member countries on regulations yields another benefit, especially to the government whose credibility is perceived as questionable by investors. By binding together within the RTA, governments are less likely to change their regulations, as the cost of deviating from the RTA agreement may be higher than the benefits that would accrue from altering an individual regulation. This provides predictability to investors, which is critical to building a long-term, sustainable business base in the country.

Harmonizing regulations is, of course, more easily said than done. Each country inevitably will have its own agenda. Even when some member countries are ready to simplify and harmonize the regional rules, others, especially those that are economically lagging, may see offering more favorable or liberal SEZ rules as a potential means of attracting investment and "catching up" to their neighbors. Also, each country has a different level of political and administrative capacity. Thus, it takes a long time for all parties to agree. One potential solution is to set a transitional period to allow each member to discuss the changes and their implications with existing investors, and adjust their national SEZ policies. Such efforts will not only help establish integrated SEZ rules but will also be a step toward harmonizing the overall investment laws among RTA member countries. Finally, countries without experience with SEZs can leverage the experiences of more advanced neighbors by consolidating their programs, although the caveat remains that the existing SEZ programs of advanced neighbors may not necessarily represent "best practice."

Financial Incentives

Different structures and levels of financial incentives among SEZs of member countries pose further problems than simply adding search costs for investors. First, differences often involve export-performance-based conditions, which usually are incompatible with the RTA framework and with the WTO rules. Second, when member countries compete for investment by offering ever-greater financial incentives, they risk eroding their tax bases without necessarily attracting more investment than they otherwise would—in effect, transferring rents directly to (usually multinational) investors.

Among various incentives, export-based incentives, a form of incentives that most SEZs employ, are particularly problematic. As is clear from the discussion in the previous section, export-based tariff-related incentives prevent member countries from taking full advantage of potential synergies between RTA and SEZ programs. Such incentives motivate member countries to rule out the possibility of SEZ-processed products enjoying RTA benefits or, in extreme cases, they prohibit the entrance of such goods into the RTA territory altogether to prevent tariff-jumping.

As is the case with regulatory harmonization, removing or unifying financial incentives among member countries takes time, especially if some member countries have established SEZ programs in which many investors are already granted with permanent exemption or reduction of tariffs or other taxes. Even if a country currently does not have financial incentives for SEZ operators, it may feel pressure from potential and existing investors to establish one, particularly if many of its neighbors have them. Yet, the advantage of investment promotion through financial incentives should be balanced with the potential loss of a tax base as well as lost opportunities from synergies with RTAs. Also, by aligning the factors that are most evident and most frequently exposed to comparison (i.e., quantifiable financial incentives), member countries can establish a foundation on which they can move forward to discuss strategic development and integration on equitable terms. To remove the most problematic form of financial incentives based on export performance, countries can learn from Mexico, which managed the participation in NAFTA by shifting incentive programs away from export-based ones to those based on other type of performances, such as investment amount or employment generation.

Strategic Framework

Ideally, an RTA would establish an integrated strategic framework for SEZ programs of member countries, not only establishing rules of the game with respect to financial incentives, but more broadly, enabling them to complement each other's resources and capacities and cooperate to achieve shared goals.

An integrated strategic framework can take several forms. One such form is to develop regional manufacturing or service linkages, using the

SEZs as hubs. By combining and coordinating efforts to strategically foster SEZ-based clusters that take advantage of complementary endowments of different member countries, member countries can help sectors leverage SEZ infrastructure and RTA depth to overcome limitations of scale and specialization. This might facilitate improved backward linkages in critical sectors like garments. Such integration of regional value chains within SEZs might also represent an important test case toward deeper regional economic integration.

Furthermore, in parallel to the "soft" elements of regional integration, such as trade agreements, many developing countries and their donors are placing vast resources on transportation infrastructure to connect regional producers to markets. Developing these regional industrial linkages through SEZs also makes sense in this context, if countries wish to leverage the improved transport corridors that allow smoother and more cost-effective logistics within the region.

Cooperation on strategic framework can also take the form of cobranding and comarketing of SEZs in the region. Members of an RTA typically promote investment by advertising the potential to access the wide regional market. In this context, it would be natural (and certainly cost-effective, particularly for small countries with limited investment promotion budgets) also to consider advertising the region's SEZs collectively as investment destinations.

Again, this is more easily said than done. On the one hand, SEZ programs are meant to be the pilot test for investment promotion policies for countries with limited resources and are intended to generate quick successes. On the other hand, coordinating among countries takes time. Therefore, how to handle the balance between quick wins and long-term strategy and how to handle the transition from a stand-alone policy to a regional policy are critical issues when considering the harmonization of SEZ strategic frameworks.

Cases of SEZ Harmonization
While regional harmonization of SEZ policy remains in its infancy, following are brief descriptions of two regions—in Southeast Asia and in East Africa—in which some initiatives have been taken.

Growth triangles in Asia. In 1993, Indonesia, Malaysia, and Thailand launched the subregional growth triangle—the "transnational export processing zone"—to accelerate their subregion's economic growth and industrial transformation. As growth triangles create greater economies of scale and allow firms to exploit complementarities and comparative advantages of member countries in various production factors, such as natural resources, low labor costs, and technology, they may offer greater potential to attract investments than standalone SEZ programs. In addition to the coordinated investment in infrastructure and human resources, the governments of these three countries are trying to harmonize regulations governing investment, tax, land, labor and immigration, and customs to market this subregion effectively to investors. This growth triangle is fostering economic expansion of participating regions through industrial linkages and by positioning the area as an integrated manufacturing base of various high value-added products. These linkages have contributed to developing advanced manufacturing as well as R&D capacity across the region. Many other subregions followed similar triangle initiatives, including the growth triangle between Singapore, Johor in Malaysia, and Riau Island in Indonesia.[11]

Harmonization of export processing zones programs in EAC. As a rare example, the EAC customs union formed an extensive annex to establish a common regulatory framework on EPZ in the member countries. As Article 2 of the regulations state, they were created to ensure that the process regarding EPZ is "transparent, accountable, fair and predictable." They first define the terminologies related to EPZs, including "EPZ" itself, "export," and "duties and taxes," so that these words are used consistently by all member countries. They also set out permitted activities in EPZs, define the establishment and function of competent authorities, stipulate how EPZ-processed goods are treated when entering into the territory, and identify how complaints are to be resolved.

The Investment Climate Advisory Services (CIC) of the World Bank Group is engaged by a multidonor facility to work with EAC to promote its regional trade in the region, and part of its work covers the advisory for SEZ programs. As of April 2009, CIC's global SEZ team assessed the current SEZ programs in the region and made preliminary recommendations on harmonization to the EAC and host governments. In terms of spatial mapping, most of the region's zones are located close to the major transport corridors. Given the considerable upgrading of these infrastructure networks that facilitates smooth and cost-effective transport among SEZs, the CIC team suggested that the EAC countries consider developing regional linkages, because current manufacturers in SEZs have limited transactions among them and their capacity for specialization is limited. Other recommendations include jointly marketing SEZs for priority sectors such as ICT considering the importance of sectors for all member countries as well as the small size and resources of each country. These are preliminary recommendations, and EAC member countries have not yet taken any significant steps to implement them. Yet, these countries have made first steps to unify the regulatory framework and establish competent authorities that will have similar powers across member countries. How effectively the EAC member states build on this common ground and integrate their SEZ program is likely to play an important role in their ability to take full advantage of the customs union and transport facilities to achieve greater regional integration, more effective trade and investment, and, ultimately, more rapid and sustainable growth.

Conclusion

When a country participates in an RTA, export-based preferential tariff treatment (a typical incentive granted under SEZ programs) poses problems such as tariff-jumping and raises concerns over local business competitiveness. Because such preferential treatment tends to be granted for a certain period of time, these incentives cannot be removed immediately. Therefore, preventing duty-free entrance of SEZ-processed goods is probably a necessary measure as an immediate response to protect the effectiveness of an RTA. Although it may be a best available temporary measure at the introduction of a RTA, more creative solutions may be appropriate in the longer term to avoid creating a mutually exclusive system between these two instruments of trade and investment: RTAs and SEZs. It would also be worthwhile for RTAs to consider options to provide exceptional treatment or a transitional period under special circumstances to allow a smoother transition to greater integration, as the case examples from NAFTA and SACU illustrated.

In addition to passive responses to these issues rising from RTAs and SEZs, RTA member countries should move forward to consider harmonization of SEZ programs to further promote regional integration. Traditionally, SEZ have been employed as a country-specific policy instrument. Therefore, coordinating among member countries on regulatory framework, financial incentives, and strategic framework of SEZ program can be a challenging and time-consuming task. Such collective efforts have the potential not only to yield the short-term benefits in the form of trade and investment, but also to build collaboration toward deeper regional economic integration.

Appendix 6.A Regulations and Handbooks of Regional Trade Agreements

ASEAN Free Trade Area (AFTA)

- ASEAN Trade in Goods Agreement, Cha-am, Thailand, February 26, 2009
- Annexes of the ASEAN Trade in Goods Agreement, Cha-am, Thailand, February 26, 2009
- Protocol to Amend the Agreement on ASEAN Preferential Trading Arrangement, Bangkok, December 15, 1995
- Agreement on the Common Effective Preferential Tariff Scheme for the ASEAN Free Trade Area, Singapore, January 28, 1992

Common Market for Eastern and Southern Africa (COMESA)

- COMESA Treaty
- Protocol on the rules of origin for products to be traded between the member states of the COMESA

East African Community (EAC)

- The EAC Customs Union Regulations, Annex VII on Export Processing Zones

Economic Community of West African States (ECOWAS)

- Treaty of the ECOWAS
- Protocol relating to the definition of the concept of products originating from member states of the ECOWAS

Gulf Cooperation Council (GCC)

- The Customs Union of the GCC Member States, January 2003

Southern African Development Community (SADC)

- SADC FTA Handbook 2008
- Protocol on Trade

West African Economic and Monetary Union (WAEMU, also UEMOA)

- Acte additionnel n° 04/96 / 1996
- Protocole additionnel n° III/ 2001
- Protocole additionnel n°I/2009

Appendix 6.B Summary of Tariff-Related Measures Taken by Regional Trade Agreements for Special Economic Zone–Processed Goods

Agreement	Treatment (Summary)	Source	Treatment	Definition of products subject to the rule
Agreements in Africa				
Common Market for Eastern and Southern Africa (COMESA)	Rules of origin	Protocol on the rules of origin for products to be traded between the member states of the COMESA	Rules of origin apply: imported inputs less than 60 percent; production value added at least 35 percent; or goods transformed into another tariff heading. Goods of particular importance have lower requirements.	n.a.
East African Community (EAC)	Special regulations on SEZ-processed goods	The EAC Customs Union Regulations, Annex VII on Export Processing Zones	Will be treated as goods imported into the customs territory of RTA.	Goods which are brought out of an export processing zone and taken into any part of the customs territory for use in the customs territory, or services provided from an export processing zone to any part of the customs territory
Economic Community of West African States (ECOWAS)	Special regulations on SEZ-processed goods	Article 7 of Protocol relating to the definition of the concept of products originating from member states of the ECOWAS	Shall not be considered as originating products.	Goods transformed within the framework of economic or suspensive customs regimes or certain special regimes involving the suspension or partial or total exemption from customs duties on inputs

(continued next page)

Appendix 6.B *continued*

Agreement	Treatment (Summary)	Source	Treatment	Definition of products subject to the rule
Southern African Development Community (SADC)	Rules of origin	SADC FTA Handbook and Annex I of Protocol on Trade (Concerning The Rules Of Origin For Products To Be Traded Between The Member States Of The SADC)	Unless wholly produced/obtained, two tests apply: limited import test (threshold varies by product) and HS tariff classification test. Special arrangement for textiles and garments exports of Malawi, Mozambique, Tanzania, and Zambia to South Africa and to the Southern African Customs Union.	n.a.
West African Economic and Monetary Union (WAEMU, UEMOA)	Special regulations on SEZ-processed goods	Article 8 of Additional Protocol on Trade (Revised in Additional Protocol N.1/2009.)	Cannot benefit the status of originating products. Exceptions are: when taxes on utilized materials are paid and for manufactured products for which the inputs are taxed higher than finished products.	Goods transformed under special regime that partially or totally suspend or exempt import duty on inputs, goods transformed under economic or suspensive customs regime

Agreements in Southeast Asia (cited in this chapter)

Agreement	Treatment (Summary)	Source	Treatment	Definition of products subject to the rule
ASEAN Free Trade Area (AFTA)	Rules of origin	Rules of Origin for the Agreement on the Common Effective Preferential Tariff Scheme	Rules of origin apply: local content must be at least 40 percent or goods transformed into another tariff classification at four-digit level. Exceptions exist.	n.a.

Other Agreements (cited in this chapter)

Gulf Cooperation Council (GCC)	Special regulations on SEZ-processed goods	Article 4 of Principles of the Customs Union in the Customs Union of the GCC Member States January 2003	Shall be treated as imports from non-GCC member states, and shall be subject to customs duties once taken out from the free zones.	Foreign goods imported from the free zones within the GCC states
Southern Cone Common Market (Mercosur)	Special regulations on SEZ-processed goods	Resolution CMC/DEC N8/94	These goods are subject to the payment of the common external tariff or the national customs tariff as the case may be.	Goods under the regimes of free trade zones, industrial zones, export processing zones and special customs areas
North American Free Trade Agreement (NAFTA)	Special regulations on SEZ-processed goods	Article 303 and its annex	After the transitional period, paid duties cannot be refunded and customs duties on goods for export, or that are to be included in other goods for export, or substituted for other goods for export to the territory of another member of the agreement, cannot be reduced or exempted, in an amount that exceeds the lesser between the total amount of customs tariffs paid or levied on imports of the good to its territory, and the total amount of customs tariffs paid to the other member with respect to the good that is later exported to the territory of that other member.	Refers to goods processed under programs of duty drawback and deferral

Source: Author, based on review of regional trade agreements.

Notes

1. Multiple variants of regional trade agreements and terminologies are not always used consistently by different institutions and researchers. This report uses the generic term of "regional trade agreement" to refer to all reciprocal preferential agreements, including free trade agreements, customs unions, partial scope agreements, and economic integration agreements. For more detail, refer to Acharya, Crawford, Maliszewska, and Renard (forthcoming).

2. Some SEZs, normally traditional EPZs, target foreign investors explicitly by setting the eligibility criteria of foreign capital. Others do not limit the zones to foreign investors, but other eligibility criterion often become too high a hurdle for domestic investors, especially those with limited capital. More recently established zones, particularly those under the more modern SEZ models, encourage domestic as well as foreign investment.

3. Most of the discussion in this section is drawn from Granados (2003).

4. Although erosion of the bloc constitutes one of the major reasons why RTAs takes measures against allowing the duty-free entry of SEZ-processed goods, a liberal trade policy would argue against any bloc attempting to raise trade barriers against countries outside the bloc. Such a barrier typically would lead to trade diversion and goes against the principles of "open regionalism."

5. WTO prohibits subsidies and other financial incentives that are conditional on export performance. Therefore, various schemes of SEZs also raise an issue for WTO accession and compliance. This chapter focuses on the discussion of SEZs and RTAs and leaves the discussion of WTO compatibility to other literatures.

6. Indeed, this "infant industry argument" is one of the primary contentions of many countries for maintaining tariffs on foreign producers. This is a controversial argument, which various empirical research has both refuted and supported.

7. Although 60 percent is the general rule, the actual rule is more complex and depends on product categories.

8. Taking advantage of COMESA's rules of origin, South African juice makers process and package South African juice concentrate in a free zone in Mauritius for sale in the COMESA market. See box 4 of Flatters (2002). The example is cited as a successful case of investment generation through a lower requirement of local content. Yet, at the same time, this practice may be placing local juice producers at disadvantage.

9. Eligible industries include electrical, electronic, furniture, toys and sporting goods, footwear, mining and metallurgy, capital goods, photographic, agricultural machinery, various industries, chemicals, rubber and plastics, iron and steel, medicines and medical equipment, transport, automotive and vehicle

parts, paper and cardboard, leather and hides, textiles and clothing, chocolates and confectionary, and coffee.

10. While it is considered in practice that 80 percent minimum export requirement may apply to SEZ operators, technically, it may not be the case when the EAC agreements are analyzed. Whereas the EAC Customs Protocol stipulates that an 80 percent minimum export requirement applies to any "export promotion scheme," that is, economic benefit contingent on export performance, it is not clear whether this rule applies to SEZs. First, the extraterritoriality of SEZs may make the export promotion argument irrelevant for SEZs. Second, analysis of the agreements, particularly Part G of the EAC Customs Protocol, reveals that free ports and other special economic arrangement do not constitute an "export promotion scheme."

11. See Landingin and Wadley (2005) and Australia Department of Foreign Affairs and Trade (2005) for more examples of Asian growth triangles.

References

Acharya, Rohini, Jo-Ann Crawford, Maryla Maliszewska, and Christelle Renard. 2011. "Landscape." In *Handbook on Preferential Trade Agreements*, edited by J. P. Chauffour and J. C. Maur. Washington, DC: World Bank.

Australia Department of Foreign Affairs and Trade. 1995. *Growth Triangles of South East Asia*. Canberra: Australian Government Publishing Service.

Baldwin, Richard. Forthcoming. "Economics." In *Handbook on Preferential Trade Agreements*, edited by J. P. Chauffour, and J. C. Maur. Washington, DC: World Bank.

FIAS (Foreign Investment Advisory Service). 2008. *Special Economic Zones: Performance, Lessons Learned, and Implications for Zone Development*. Washington, DC: FIAS, the World Bank Group.

Flatters, Frank. 2002. "The SADC Trade Protocol: Outstanding Issues on Rules of Origin." Updated version of background paper prepared for the Second SADC Roundtable on Rules of Origin, held in Gaborone, Botswana, October 24–26, 2001. Available at http://qed.econ.queensu.ca/pub/faculty/flatters/writings/ff_sadc_roo_tnf.pdf. Accessed April 2010.

Granados, Jaime. 2003. "Export Processing Zones and Other Special Regimes in the Context of Multilateral and Regional Trade Negotiations." Inter-American Development Bank. Available at http://www.iadb.org/intal/intalcdi/PE/2007/00739.pdf. (Accessed April 2010).

Landingin, Nathaniel, and David Wadley. 2005. "Export Processing Zones and Growth Triangle Development: The Case of the BIMP-EAGA, Southeast Asia." *Journal of International Development* 17: 67–96.

Malaver, Yeny. 2009. "Mercosur and Its Effects to Special Economic Zones.". Mimeo. Investment Climate Department. Washington, DC: World Bank.

Manchanda, Sumit. Interview. Investment Climate Advisory Services. Washington, DC: World Bank Group.

WTO (World Trade Organization). 2009. *Multilateralizing Regionalism: Challenges for the Global Trading System*, edited by R. Baldwin and P. Low. Geneva: World Trade Organization.

PART II

Moving from Static to Dynamic Gains: Can SEZs Deliver Structural Change?

CHAPTER 7

When Trade Preferences and Tax Breaks Are No Longer Enough: The Challenge of Adjustment in the Dominican Republic's Free Zones

Jean-Marie Burgaud and Thomas Farole

Introduction

One of the original pioneers of free zones (FZs), the Dominican Republic is probably the Western Hemisphere's most widely recognized success story in the literature on free zones. Indeed, few other countries worldwide have used the free zones program as effectively as an engine of diversification and growth. Fueled by the offshoring of the U.S. textile and garment industry (see box 7.1) and supported by preferential trade agreements and a favorable exchange rate policy, the FZs were principally responsible for the Dominican Republic's shift away from a commodity-oriented economy, with the manufacturing sector growing from just 18 percent of GDP in the 1970s to 30 percent by the 2000s. GDP growth in the Dominican Republic has far exceeded the regional and global average in every decade since FZs were established. At its peak in 2003, FZ companies accounted for 7.5 percent of total GDP in the country.

Box 7.1

The Apparel Sector in the Dominican Republic

Since almost the start of the FZ program, and until the recent crisis, apparel was the star of Dominican Republic's FZ, to the extent that it gave birth to several leading companies in the region. Bratex International, created in 1988, became the largest exporter of brassieres in Latin America and the Caribbean. The company, created in 1988, developed its own patent for a model of brassiere, which required special equipment for its production, and reached an agreement with DuPont for its commercialization. Interamericana Products International, started in 1985, developed to become a full-package service provider by 1995. The company grew to include Claiborne, Lee, Levi's, and Eddie Bauer among its clients. Finally, Grupo M became the largest apparel manufacturer in the Caribbean, employing up to 14,000 workers in the Santiago FZ and in the Dominican Republic. The company now employs only 4,000 in the Dominican Republic, but another 4,000 in a FZ the group created in Haiti (see box 7.3).

At its height, Dominican Republic's FZs had about 5 percent market share in the United States. However, this has now fallen to around 2 percent. According to U.S. trade statistics (see http://otexa.ita.doc.gov/msr/catV1.htm), U.S. imports of Dominican apparel fell by 28 percent during the first eight months of 2009, compared with same period of previous year—more than twice the rate of decline for U.S. imports overall and higher than the declines experienced by regional competitors such as Nicaragua (11 percent), El Salvador (18 percent), Honduras (22 percent), and Guatemala (26 percent), all of which offer lower labor costs than the Dominican Republic.[1]

Source: Authors.

After rapid growth in FDI and exports throughout the 1980s and most of the 1990s (FDI, for example, grew 37 percent per year between 1994 and 1999), over the past decade, the Dominican Republic has faced significant threats to their FZ-based economic model. Between 1999 and 2003, a rise in oil prices; global economic slowdown; the impact of September 11, 2001, on tourism; and the collapse of the second-largest Dominican private bank, *Baninter,* all contributed to slowing growth in the Dominican Republic economy. But for the FZ sector in particular, the end of the MFA and the growing dominance of Asian manufacturing threaten the future of the Dominican Republic's textile and garments-exporting sector, which is at the heart of the FZs. The program has stagnated since 2004 in terms of its value added, with its subsequent contribution to national GDP halving in only five years.

In response to this stagnation, the government has attempted some policy reforms in the FZ sector and given policy priority to wider economic competitiveness. Among other measures taken in recent years, customs procedures were streamlined, tariffs were reduced, import surcharges and export taxes were eliminated, and new legislation was adopted on government procurement, competition policy, and intellectual property rights. On the trade policy side, the Dominican Republic signed the FTA among the Dominican Republic, Central America, and the United States (DR-CAFTA) and the economic partnership agreement (EPA) between the European Union and the Caribbean Forum of African, Caribbean, and Pacific States.

It appears, however, that the malaise in the FZ sector has deepened through the recent global economic crisis. Since the beginning of 2009, exports have declined considerably. Although there is some evidence of slowly increasing diversification in manufacturing and a shift to more value added production activities as well as services in the FZs, many argue that the FZ program is principally to blame for the economy's overdependence on apparel manufacturing and its relative failure to adjust to changing comparative advantage. Indeed, the FZ's export-oriented growth model, which relied on cheap labor and trade preferences, was perhaps equipped to deliver jobs but not necessarily able to facilitate substantial poverty reduction or an evolutionary pattern of upgraded in the economy. Whether success will continue into the future, given the evidence of declining competitiveness in recent years, remains to be seen.

The Dominican Republic's experience highlights the limitations of FZ programs that rely on sources of competitiveness that are unlikely to remain sustainable—specifically, low wages, trade preferences, and fiscal incentives. Although these all may offer valuable advantage in the short term, the Dominican Republic (like many countries who have embarked on export processing zones) failed to build competitiveness in parallel, through investments in education and skills, and through integration of FZ firms with the local economy. This chapter discusses briefly the history and achievements of the FZ program in the Dominican Republic. It focuses on the challenges that the program faces in light of declining competitiveness in traditional labor-intensive garment production, the government and FZ industry's response, and the gaps in the long-term approach to these challenges.

Free Zones in the Dominican Republic

Like most countries in the region, the Dominican Republic followed import substitution policies from the 1960s, including protection of the domestic market and subsidies for domestic production. The economy remained highly specialized, based on primary agricultural products (e.g., sugar, bananas, and coffee) and mining. The launch of the Dominican Republic's first FZ in 1969 was not part of a policy initiative to move away from imports substitution toward export-oriented diversification, as was the case in many countries that later adopted SEZs. Rather, it was a private initiative—led by the Gulf and Western company—in a specific context (see box 7.2). In any case, this initiative demonstrated that the Dominican Republic could develop competitive assembly operations under an FZ regime. In the 1970s, the government followed suit, opening a public zone in San Pedro de Macoris, with the main objective of generating employment. The private sector in Santiago—the second-largest

---

Box 7.2

Gulf and Western Establishes the Dominican Republic's First FZ in 1969

The American conglomerate Gulf and Western purchased a sugar plantation and the Dominican Republic's largest existing sugar mill—the Central Romana (located in the town of La Romana in the southeast of the Dominican Republic)—in 1968. To avoid what they viewed as unsustainable wage demands by the workers in the mill, the company opened an industrial FZ nearby to provide wage-earning opportunities to the wives and families of those workers as well as to absorb labor that had been shed as part of their modernization of the mill. Gulf and Western lobbied the government in support of incentives, which were introduced into Law 299.[2] To kick-start the zone, Gulf and Western transferred some of their own U.S.-based manufacturing subsidiaries into it. A number of U.S. companies followed suit, setting up assembly plants in the La Romana Zone.

The results were impressive. Within a short period, the local economy experienced major growth in employment. The towns of San Pedro and Santiago, also dependent on agricultural products (sugar, coffee, and tobacco) began to lobby the government to establish their own FZs in the early 1970s. The government approved both of these requests and the groundwork was laid for the major expansion of the FZ program by the 1980s.

Source: Derived from Schrank (2008).

city in the Dominican Republic—also joined together to establish an FZ under the management of a nonprofit association.

But during these initial years, the free zones remained very much enclaves, from both a physical and a policy perspective. Partly as a result, growth of zones during the period 1969 to 1983 remained relatively slow. During those years, the four zones generated about 10,000 jobs, primarily in the garment activity. But following the debt crisis in the early 1980s, the Dominican Republic began to liberalize its economy and shifted toward the promotion of nontraditional exports. Along with the growth of the tourism sector, key to this economic restructuring was the expansion of the free trade zone program. FZ development accelerated during the second half of the 1980s, as the country became a favored location for relocating factories (particularly in the apparel sector) to serve the U.S. market, and FDI rapidly flowed into the country. This growth was driven by several factors, including the following:

- *Trade preferences*: The U.S. CBI introduced in 1984 provided duty-free access to the United States for about 3,000 products, including apparel.
- *Low wages*: Linked to trade preferences, a huge wage arbitrage opportunity existed between the United States and Dominican Republic in the 1980s. Hourly compensation for semiskilled workers in export-manufacturing sectors in the Dominican Republic was only 6 percent (US$0.79 per hour versus US$13.66 per hour) that of the United States in 1987 (Kaplinsky 1993). Even at this time, the Dominican Republic's wages were three times higher than in "low-wage Asia,"[3] which underscores the critical importance of trade preferences and of FZ incentives in the competitiveness of the Dominican Republic from the beginning. Special provisions inside the FZs facilitated the Dominican Republic's low-wage competitiveness. Although the FZ law states that the national labor law applies in FZs (including the requirement to make Social Security contributions), minimum wage[4] is lower in the FZs and profit-sharing (compulsory in the domestic market) is not required.
- *Competitive exchange rate*: A series of devaluations in the early 1980s, with a sharp devaluation in 1985 (resulting from floating the peso in relation in the dollar), depressed labor and other operating costs.
- *Fiscal incentives*: Within the FZ environment, foreign investors could access generous incentives, including exemptions on corporate income

tax, import duties, value added tax,[5] and property taxes. Tax exemptions are valid for a period of 15 years for location in most zones; a special exemption period of 20 years is offered for developers and companies in free zones located in provinces on the Haitian border. Both periods may be extended on a company-by-company basis, upon petition to *Consejo Nacional de Zonas Francas de Exportación* or National Free Zones Council (CNZFE). FZ companies are required to export at least 80 percent of their production, although this restriction can be lifted in cases in which the product is not manufactured domestically and if local inputs account for at least 25 percent of value.

Box 7.3

Profile of the Dominican Republic's Free Zones in 2010

As of the end of 2009, the Dominican Republic had 55 registered FZ industrial parks, 47 of which had active companies operating within them. The majority of these parks are clustered in two locations: outside the main city of Santo Domingo on the southern coast and outside the second-largest city, Santiago (de los Caballeros) in the Cibao Valley in the North-Central region.[6] Few zones are located in the western half of the island, despite the incentives available for establishing and locating in zones along the Haitian border.

Among the zones there are 31 private parks, 21 public parks, and 3 parks that are operated as PPPs or through registered charities. Most of the public parks are run by a government agency, the Center for Industrial Development and Competitiveness (*Proindustria*).[7] Some 456 firms were operating in these parks, and 110 single factory zones are registered across the country. Most of the parks are relatively small in size—indeed, the vast majority of the parks have a constructed area that is less than 5 hectares in size, with the largest park (Santiago) constructed on only 35 hectares (and only five other parks with more than 10 hectares). More than half the parks have less than 5 companies operating within them; only a handful have more than 10 companies.

A large majority of the companies operating in the FZs originate from the United States or the Dominican Republic. According to statistics from CNZFE, as of the end of 2008, 44 percent of zone companies were U.S. owned (and another 3 percent were from Puerto Rico), with 32 percent having domestic ownership. The next largest investors are from the Republic of Korea (14 firms or 2.7 percent of the total), Spain (12 firms), and Holland (11 firms).

Source: Authors.

Import duty is payable on all local sales; however, the valuation on which duty is payable excludes the value of local inputs.

- *Strong regulator*: The Dominican Republic's FZ program benefits from an effective regulator. The CNZFE was established in 1978. It reports directly to the presidency and is governed by a board of directors, which gives 50 percent representation and voting power to the private sector.

The FZs became the most dynamic engine of growth in the Dominican Republic's economy during the 1980s and 1990s. Between 1985 and 1989, the number of FZs more than tripled, from 6 to 19, the number of FZ companies rose from 146 to 220, and employment jumped from 36,000 to nearly 100,000. The program continued to expand during the 1990s, helped in part by the government enacting a comprehensive FZ law and regulations in 1990. By the end of the 1990s, the Dominican Republic had more than 50 operating industrial parks housing more than 500 companies. In addition, more than 100 single factory zones, known as *zonas francas especiales* (ZFEs) have been established since the 1990 law. The program reached its peak in terms of employment (195,000) in 2000; this was equivalent to up to 10 percent of the country's total employment.

In the past decade, however, the zones have faced major challenges (see figure 7.1) related to competitiveness in the core textile and apparel

Figure 7.1   Index of Growth (1995 = 100) in the Free Zone Program

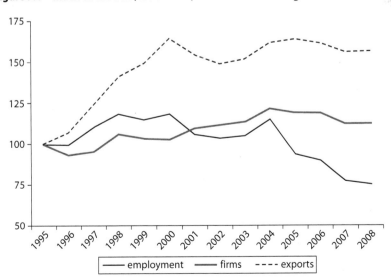

Source: Authors' calculations based on data from CNZFE.

sector, which is maturing and no longer a particularly low-cost production base for the U.S. market. Declining performance of the apparel sector began in 2001, with increasing competition from companies established in Central American FZs, which has gathered pace since the MFA ended in 2005, and with subsequent competition from Asia.

Employment in the FZs has declined some 35 percent since 2000. Yet despite this, exports have remained steady, as the result of some diversification in the FZ program over recent years. Less than one-third of FZ companies in the Dominican Republic now manufacture textiles and garments; other key manufacturing now includes shoes, leather goods, cigars, jewelry, pharmaceutical products, and electronic parts. Potentially more important has been the limited, but evident, growth in service activities within the FZs, including trading, call centers, and data processing.

Since 2009, however, the FZ program has experienced absolute decline across all sectors. According to the president of the Dominican Association of Free Zones (ADOZONA), the number of operating firms will decline to below 500 and more than 8,000 jobs were lost in the FZs during the first quarter of 2009 alone. The decline in exports is even steeper, at more than 20 percent annualized. Although this decrease is driven by the global economic crisis, it highlights more fundamental competitiveness issues that will remain a major challenge to the sustainability of the program into the future.

Performance and the Challenge of Adjustment

As discussed earlier in this case study, the FZ program in the Dominican Republic undoubtedly has had a major impact on the growth and development of the economy since its inception (see figure 7.2). Since 2000, the FZ program has made a contribution of around US$1 billion in foreign exchange. It has been chiefly responsible for diversifying and industrializing the economy, has contributed substantially to employment, and has been the main source of productivity growth in the economy. On the other hand, on virtually all measures, the FZs program is in stagnation or decline, and this is contributing to a significant slowdown in the Dominican Republic's overall economy.

The following sections provide a brief summary of performance and challenges against key measures of investment, exports, and employment.

Figure 7.2   Free Zone Value Added (US$m) and Contribution to GDP, 1995–2008

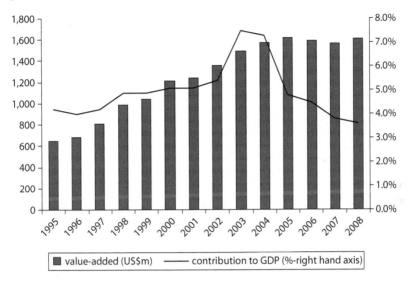

value-added (US$m)   ——— contribution to GDP (%-right hand axis)

Source: CNZFE (2009).

Investment. At the end of 2008, accumulated FDI in the FZs was US$2,611 million, 80 percent of which was made within free zone parks and 20 percent through single factory zones (called ZFEs in the Dominican Republic). This was equivalent to about 23 percent of the total FDI stock in the country at that time (CNZFE 2009). In 2002 and 2003, more than 90 percent of all FDI in the Dominican Republic went into the FZs (World Bank 2006). By the end of 2008, the main part of FDI in FZs was concentrated in textiles and garments (33 percent), which was followed by tobacco (19 percent). In terms of investment source, at the end of 2008, 46 percent of the FDI stock had its origin in the United States, followed by 26 percent from the Dominican Republic, 6 percent from the United Kingdom, and 5 percent each from Canada and Sweden. Although most of the initial investments in the FZs came from foreign companies, Dominican Republic domestic investors later became important sources of investment, mainly as subcontractors in the apparel sector as well as developers of industrial parks.

Between 1995 and 2004, the number of FZ industrial parks grew from 35 to more than 60. The number of companies operating in the FZs also grew by about 20 percent over this decade, reaching a high of 569 in 2004. After this time, both zones and firms began to decline, with at least 10 zones (most of them housing only one or two firms) closing since 2004.

Exports. Exports from the FZ program grew more than 10 percent annually between 1995 and 2000, reaching nearly US$4.8 billion. The contribution of the FZ program to total exports in Dominican Republic is one of the highest anywhere in the world. At its peak in 2001, the FZs accounted for 81 percent of national merchandise exports.[8] FZ exports have been stagnant since that time, however, actually declining by 2008 to US$4.5 billion. In parallel, the FZ contribution to total national exports has fallen sharply to 65 percent in 2008 (see figure 7.3).

Decomposing the FZ exports to isolate the impact of the all-important textile and apparel sector results in a striking picture. As shown in figure 7.4, which presents the relative growth of textile and nontextile sector exports from 1995 through 2008, the apparent flat trend in FZ exports masks a major underlying dichotomy. Textile and apparel exports began to decline from 2000, and the pace of collapse accelerated sharply after 2004. At the end of 2008, textile exports had declined 33 percent since 1995 and stood at less than half their 2000 peak. For a sector that was responsible for well over half of all FZ exports over the

Figure 7.3   Free Zone Exports (US$ million) and Share of National Exports

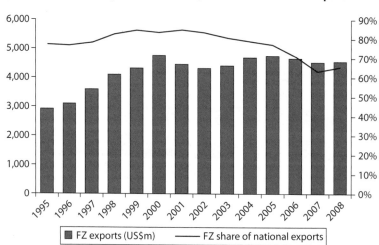

Source: CNZFE (2009).

Figure 7.4   Index of Free Zone Exports: Textile versus Nontextile (1995 = 100)

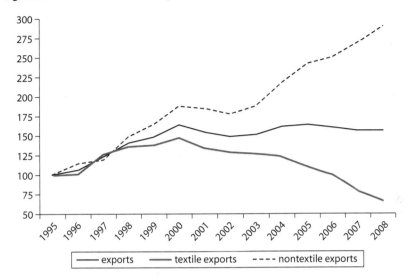

Source: Calculations based on data from CNZFE (2009).

past decade, this represented a massive shock to the program, and the economy more widely.

Figure 7.5 sets out clearly the level of decline in the Dominican Republic's position as a textile and apparel sector exporter to the United States. The first graph shows that exports of knitwear to the United States fell by more than half between 2004 and 2008, as the Dominican Republic was replaced mainly by Asian exporters, as well as Nicaragua. Although most other producers in the region also experienced declines, none was as deep as in the Dominican Republic. The graph on the right suggests that this pattern is deepening through the recent global crisis. The Dominican Republic not only experienced a much deeper decline in textiles and apparel exports to the United States in 2009 than most other countries, but it continued to face declining exports in 2010, whereas almost all other countries experienced considerable recovery.

The key question is whether the FZ program, which was heavily reliant on one sector (textiles and garments) and one market (the United States) can diversify and upgrade itself, in the face of commoditization and increasing competition in this sector. Figure 7.4 shows that nontextile exports have grown rather well, offsetting much of the decline in textile exports. What also is clear, however, is that the growth

Figure 7.5   Comparative Growth in U.S. Imports of Knitwear by Key Countries, 2004–08, and U.S. Imports of Apparel and Textiles by Key Country, 2009 and 2010

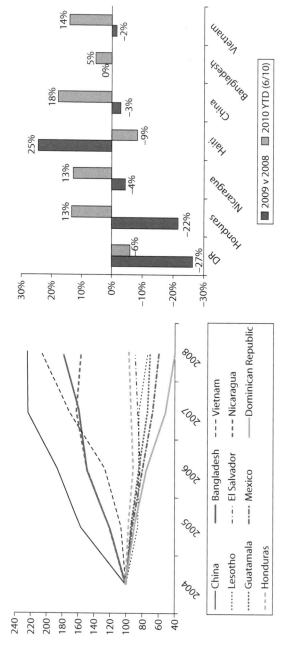

Source: U.S. Office of Textiles and Apparel (http://otexa.ita.doc.gov/msr/catV1.htm).

of nontextile activities may stem from the decline in exports, but it is doing little to absorb the workforce shed from the garment sector.

Employment. Figure 7.6 illustrates the growth in employment in the Dominican Republic FZs over the life of the program. Up until the early 1980s, employment was relatively modest. But from then it took off rapidly, growing at an average of more than 13 percent annually between 1985 and 2000, when it peaked at close to 200,000. It has since fallen rapidly, shedding more than 80,000 jobs. At its height, the FZ program was responsible for 10 percent of total employment in the country and 38 percent of manufacturing sector jobs, but the program has since declined to account for around 30 percent of total manufacturing employment.

It is worth noting that the large growth in employment until recent years came also in parallel with ongoing, robust growth in total factor productivity (TFP). FZ companies grew TFP 3.4 percent annually between 1975 and 2004, a level which is high by international standards and was five times greater than the growth achieved by Dominican Republic firms outside the free zones (World Bank 2006).

Other challenges to the FZ program. In parallel with the problem of structural adjustment, the FZ program also must cope with an additional factor that may limit its scope to react to the challenge—compatibility

Figure 7.6   Evolution of FZ Employment, 1969–2008

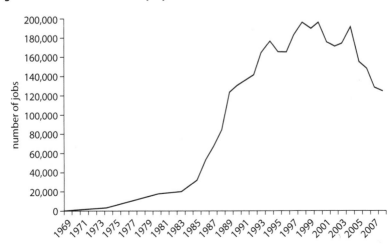

Source: CNZFE.

with the WTO. The tax exemptions that are at the heart of the FZ regime are not compatible with the Agreement on Subsidies and Countervailing Measures (SCM) signed under WTO. In 2002, the Dominican Republic notified the WTO of the subsidies and requested an extension of the transition period allowed by the agreement (WTO 2002). In September 2007, the Dominican Republic requested continuation of the extension relating to Law No. 8-90 (WTO 2007c; also see WTO 2007a, which contains an updating notification of subsidies under Law No. 8-90), in accordance with the procedure adopted by the General Council in favor of certain developing-country members (WTO 2007b). According to this procedure, the members concerned undertook to eliminate export subsidies by December 31, 2015, at the latest and to submit an action plan for this purpose in 2010. By amending the FZ Law and abolishing the local content requirements and restrictions on sales in the domestic market, as well as the 25 percent export performance requirements on several products, the Dominican Republic authorities believe that Law No. 56-07 represents a step forward in bringing domestic legislation in line with the SCM. Of course, much remains to be done to bring the program into compliance.

The Policy Response

The Dominican Republic government has taken some steps to respond to these challenges. These responses should help, but the balance of initiatives taken appear to be designed more to bolster the existing basis of competitiveness on which the current free zone industry is based, rather than to address the structural changes that are required. This may not be surprising, given the strength and organization of the FZ sector and their effectiveness in lobbying the government.

In an attempt to halt job losses in the FZ sector, the government offered in 2008 a temporary wage subsidy.[9] For the first nine months of 2008, the government offered FZ companies 2,000 pesos per worker per month (around US$65). This was equivalent to nearly 30 percent of the average salary of a low-skilled worker in the FZs. For the final three months of 2008, the subsidy was reduced to 1,200 pesos, after the country entered into a period of budgetary crisis. The subsidy, however, proved to be ineffective as companies realized it would be only temporary. ADOZONA (the sector's industry association) also has proposed to amend the FZ Law, introducing two additional incentives: (1) exonerating all FZ employees from income tax; and (2) exonerating the tax on dividends of FZ companies. The association also has proposed to reform the labor code to reduce severance compensation and therefore make firing much more economical for FZ companies. This measure is, however, unlikely to be adopted by the Dominican Republic Congress.

FZ companies that produce goods that are not produced by domestic companies in the Dominican Republic always have been able to sell 100 percent of their production in the domestic market, as long as the domestic value added is at least 25 percent. In recent years, the Dominican Republic took a number of additional initiatives to promote forward linkages. The most important was Law 56-07 (May 2007), which opened up the domestic market fully (100 percent) to FZ producers of key products, including textiles, clothing and accessories, hides and skins, and footwear and leather articles. The purpose of the amendment was to give an extra incentive to key sectors in which job losses have been heavy in recent years. Perhaps more important, it also extended the customs and fiscal benefits of FZs to domestic-based producers in these sectors.[10] The amendment also opened up the possibility of FZ companies that provide logistical services (e.g., consolidation and storage of goods) to import and sell goods in the domestic market, subject to authorization by the CNZFE and payment of the relevant duties. Despite these incentives, sales to the Dominican Republic remain insignificant for most FZ companies.

Private sector initiatives are attempting to address the challenge of competitiveness in the apparel sector. As the Dominican Republic benefited from a twin-plant scheme in the early days of its FZ program in the 1970s, some of its major companies now are extending a similar concept to integrate production with plants in Haiti (see box 7.4). This strategy combines Haiti's cheap labor with Dominican Republic assets (political stability, skilled labor, networks in established markets) and takes advantage of market access programs in the United States that allow cumulative value requirements between beneficiary countries.

Several public and private initiatives are attempting to address long-term structural upgrades in the FZ sector. For example, in 2009, ADOZONA managed to build a consensus within the sector and with the government for the creation of a Fund for the Promotion of Exports and Investment (Decree 244-09). This special fund was created by a decree and was intended to include contributions from both the government and the private sector. It is supposed to carry out international investment campaigns to promote investment in the FZ sector. As of September 2010, however, the corresponding decree has not yet been adopted, and the government has not budgeted any resources for the

Box 7.4

Grupo M Pioneered the Strategy of Production Sharing between FZs in the Dominican Republic and Haiti

Grupo M was created in 1986, became a conglomerate in 1993, and during the 1990s grew at around 12–15 percent per year for several years. With more than 14,000 workers, it became the largest apparel conglomerate in the region, with up to 24 different firms located in the Dominican Republic, Haiti, and the United States. In the early 2000s, its annual sales averaged US$200 million. It gained the confidence of some of the best-known brands, such as Polo, Ralph Lauren, Liz Claiborne, Tommy Hilfiger, Hugo Boss, Banana Republic, Timberland, and Nike. Grupo M also built joint ventures with main global suppliers of zippers, chemical producers, and other products, and began producing intermediate products such as yarn, certain fabrics, and labels. Like all companies in the Dominican Republic, however, it is struggling to survive in the face of rising competition from Asia.

In response to this challenge, Grupo M has pioneered the strategy of production sharing with Haiti. This strategy, sometimes referred to as "twin-planting," "production sharing," or "coproduction," involves sending the most labor-intensive operation (assembly) to Haiti and sending the products back to the Dominican Republic for finishing (washing and packaging) and export. This is being done in two factories in Haiti—one for Levi's jeans and another for Sara Lee T-shirts. Grupo M takes advantage of lower wages in Haiti and also of its status as an LDC country, which allows Haitian apparel to enter duty free into the United States, even when the fabric is not of U.S. origin. The advantage of purchasing fabrics in Asia rather than the regional market is significant, as the price differential can be as much as 30 percent.

The CODEVI FZ, where these activities are carried out, was created with the support of the IFC on the border with the Dominican Republic. CODEVI is a private zone owned and operated by Grupo M. After a number of problems in the starting stages, particularly related to labor difficulties, the project has expanded well over the past five years. More than 20 hectares of land have been developed, with more than 25,000 square meters of facilities in operation. Exports of the zone were expected reach US$120 m in 2009. The company already employs 4,000, and plans to create 5,000 more jobs in the next five years.

Source: Authors.

fund. ADOZONA is engaged in a campaign with the government with the objective to develop the "export culture"—specifically, it is aimed at education and convincing local businesses of the importance of export markets and export readiness. This activity is carried out under the umbrella of the recently created Presidential Table for the Promotion of Exports (Decree 174-09). Unfortunately, here again, in the absence of decree of application, the first meeting of the table is pending. An agreement between the national investment promotion agency and the national vocational training institute (INFOTEP) allocates 1 percent of each park's payroll for each park's training needs, which are defined by the users through the corresponding park association.

Current Situation and Conclusions

As discussed, textile exports, which accounted for about half of exports value and a greater share of employment, declined by more than 50 percent in the past five years alone. Yet, there is some evidence that the FZ sector has managed to attract new and competitive industries. In the past five years, exports of medical equipment and pharmaceuticals have increased two and a half times and electronics by 50 percent— these two sectors are now each responsible for almost as many exports as the textile and garments sector. Similarly, the jewelry and tobacco sectors, which grew at 54 percent and 44 percent over this period, respectively, are increasingly important to the Dominican Republic economy. The services sector is also becoming an important part of the FZs. The Dominican Republic's first call center (employing just 100 workers) was established only in 2006; by 2009, the sector now employed more than 5,000 employees. In parallel with the growth in these nontraditional sectors, the Dominican Republic has experienced a rapid growth in the value added share of exports. Although this figure stayed steady between 30 percent and 32 percent throughout the 1980s and 1990s, it began to rise at the end of the 1990s and neared 50 percent by 2005 (it has since fallen slightly to 44 percent). Within the textile and apparel sector, too, there is evidence of upgrading, with large firms like Grupo M and Bratex having developed full-package operations, including preproduction services and sourcing.

The financial crisis has caused a widespread and steep decline not only in textiles and apparel but also throughout all FZ manufacturing sectors. Exports of textiles and apparel declined by more than 25 percent in 2009, and an even faster decline has been experienced in jewelry

(–59 percent) and electronics (–51 percent).[11] This suggests that the problem is not simply one of the MFA phaseout or of the global economic crisis, but rather a more fundamental problem of competitiveness (and the limited scale of upgrading in the Dominican Republic's FZ sector).

The challenges being faced by the Dominican Republic highlight the classic problems of many export-processing programs worldwide. In addition to weak infrastructure, particularly the instability and cost of electrical power, the export sector faces structural challenges, including (1) an overreliance on trade preferences and narrow export markets; (2) poor linkages with the local economy, which prevent the program from facilitating dynamic gains that could contribute to economywide upgrade; (3) failing to recognize or act on the links between social upgrading and sustainability of the FZ program. Each of these challenges is summarized in the following sections.

Overreliance on Trade Preferences

Trade preferences have played a critical role in the development of the FZ program in the Dominican Republic. In 1984, the Dominican Republic became beneficiary of the CBI launched by the United States under the legislation of the CBI-II (Caribbean Basin Economic Recovery Expansion Act). This initiative granted the Dominican Republic duty-free access to the United States market for most products until 1990. Ten years later, in 1994, the United States and Canada signed the NAFTA. To offer the Caribbean countries similar trade benefits, the Caribbean Basin Trade Partnership Act offered these countries "textile parity" with NAFTA partners in 2000. The Dominican Republic also joined the CACM in 1998 by signing bilateral FTAs between each member. In May 2004, the United States signed CAFTA and, in August, DR-CAFTA, which entered into force in the Dominican Republic in March 2007. In textiles and garments, DR-CAFTA expanded the CBI legislation by eliminating duties on nearly all textiles and garment imports assembled from components made in DR-CAFTA countries and the United States. The Dominican Republic has had preferential access to the European market since the Lomé Convention of 1975 (now under the Cotonou Agreement), and consolidated in a two-way trade preference scheme in the EPA signed in 2009. Until recently, however, its focus has been almost exclusively on the U.S. market, a dependency that has been exposed as a significant vulnerability during the recent crisis.

Although trade preferences clearly have been critical in catalyzing the Dominican Republic's FZs, they also can be criticized for having contributed to complacency, both in terms of market focus and more broadly in terms of competitiveness. Although the textile and apparel sector remains relatively highly protected in many markets, the trend in tariff and quota protection has moved inevitably downward, even through the crisis. As such, the Dominican Republic's preferential advantage in market access continues to erode steadily. The shift in market share toward Asian manufacturers following the elimination of quotas at the expiration of the MFA (as shown in figure 7.5) is illustrative of the declining value of trade preferences in underpinning competitiveness in the FZ's traditional labor-intensive assembly operations. The cost of productivity gap is now too wide to be closed by the ever-diminishing scope of these preferences.

Failure to Integrate with the Local Economy

Despite many efforts made over the years, a critical failing of the Dominican Republic FZ program has been its inability to forge effective links between the FZ sector and the rest of the economy. This has been one of the main factors inhibiting the FZs from diversifying and upgrading. In terms of forward linkages, the FZ legislation is fairly conducive to supporting integration with the local market. FZ companies always have been free to export up to 20 percent of their production to the Dominican Republic domestic territory, provided they pay all relevant tariffs and taxes that imports from other countries incur. In addition, the import duty assessment on these exports does not take into account the value of any domestic components used and other value added (e.g., through labor, utilities, etc.). In 2008, however, only 12 FZ companies sold into the Dominican Republic market, making the Dominican Republic only the 13th most important market for FZ companies.[12]

The legislation is relatively favorable to supporting backward integration of FZs into the local economy. Suppliers from the domestic economy to FZ companies are exempt from import duties on the raw materials used in this production. This allows them to at least be on equal footing with competitors supplying the zones from outside the Dominican Republic. From the early days of the program, however, it was apparent that FZ companies imported virtually all their manufacturing inputs. The U.S. trade preference program for the apparel industry was designed to ensure that key inputs were sourced from the United States. Even after the CBI in 2000, which allowed apparel producers to use inputs from all countries within the Caribbean, linkages have remained low (even at a regional level). The lack of supply links went beyond textiles and extended to capital equipment and even basic packaging materials. In the apparel sector, local spending (encompassing material inputs, capital equipment, water, electricity, and statutory payments of Social Security and training) in the early 2000s accounted for only 1.5 percent of the export value of FZ companies (Sanchez-Ancochea 2006).

The Dominican Republic government, with the support of the U.S. Agency for International Development, set up a program in the 1990s to develop backward linkages with EPZs. Feasibility studies revealed abundant EPZ demand for textiles, precision plastic parts, metal stamping, machine shops, and tool, mold and die making. The program also revealed the main reasons why backward linkages failed to develop, including the following: (1) the capital or intermediate goods required by FZ producers frequently did not exist in the Dominican Republic; (2) some local manufacturers who did produce the goods required frequently had little interest in supplying FZs because they were satisfied with current operations and profitability levels of a protected local market; and, most important, (3) local producers generally failed to meet market standards for price, quality, and delivery terms. With the benefits of duty-free import and relatively low transport costs in and out of the Dominican Republic, FZ companies generally have little incentive to purchase local inputs.

In the absence of these linkages, however, FZ operators are losing out on significant potential to benefit from the development of dynamic local clusters of suppliers, customers, and supporting services. In successful FZ programs—for example, Malaysia and the Republic of Korea—the development of strong local clusters is acknowledged as making a significant contribution to the successful upgrading of FZ-based manufacturers by giving them access to competitively priced, world-class quality inputs.

Lack of Attention to Skills Development and Wider Social Upgrading

The FZs have been criticized for not having contributed significantly to the upgrading of the workforce, relying instead on low-skilled, low-wage workers, with little interest or incentive to move these workers upward. Although the FZ law states that the national labor law applies in FZs (including the requirement to make Social Security contributions), it does make some special provisions for wages in the zones. Specifically, minimum wage is lower in the FZs and profit-sharing (compulsory in the domestic market) is not required. In practice, wages in the FZs are, on average, significantly above the minimum wage: the average wage in 2008 for a laborer was around Dominican peso (RD$)7,000 monthly while the minimum wage was RD$4,900. However, wages in the FZs are consistently lower than for the Dominican Republic economy overall—more than 15 percent for male workers and more than 20 percent for female workers (World Bank 2006). This is, however, likely driven mainly by the low-skilled, labor-intensive nature of work in the FZs relative to the overall economy. In addition, for unskilled workers, real wages (in U.S. dollars) in the FZs has been largely stagnant over the past 15 years.

The FZ program does have close links with INFOTEP, and a formal training program is available for workers at FZ companies. According to data from CNZFE, in 2008, 25,555 workers were enrolled in INFOTEP training programs—this is equivalent to about 20 percent of all workers. The training is relatively limited in scope, however, and the average training time per participant was less than one hour.

Some of the blame for the poor skills development can be attributed to the FZ enterprises (and is linked to the issue of poor integration), although much of this failure derives from the wider policies of the Dominican Republic government, particularly its failure to invest in social spending (including education). In fact, the Dominican Republic has long had one of the lowest levels of government social spending in Latin America—for example in 2001, social spending was 7.6 percent of GDP in the Dominican Republic, in comparison to Costa Rica, which by that time had contributed 20 percent of its GDP toward social spending for several decades (Sanchez-Ancochea 2006).

Despite the skills problems, evidence from the structure of the FZ workforce suggests that there has been some relatively significant structural upgrading over the past decade. The share of skilled workers (technicians) rose from only 7 percent of the FZ workforce in 1998 to 12 percent in 2008. Meanwhile, the share of unskilled workers declined from 90 percent to 81 percent. Whether this change reflects active upskilling *within* the existing workforce or merely reflects the structural change of industries within the FZs (or more specifically, the decline in textiles) is unclear. Whatever the case, what is clear is that demand for skilled labor continues to rise in the FZs, even while unskilled labor has collapsed (down more than 40 percent in the past decade).

The role of the FZs as a significant source of job creation is likely to be limited in the future. Certainly, the traditional FZ strategy based primarily on proximity to the U.S. market, strong fiscal incentives, and cheap, low-skilled labor is proving to be unsustainable. Only the companies that build competitiveness on product quality and innovation are likely to remain competitive in the FZ sector in the years ahead. Achieving this competitiveness will require greater attention—by FZ firms, the FZ sector, and the government—to upgrading the skills and technology base of the country and to developing more sustainable sources of competitive advantage.

Notes

1. Exports from Costa Rica, whose wages are higher than those in the Dominican Republic, declined by an even more rapid 38 percent during this period.

2. This law, however, was not designed specifically to support the Gulf and Western investment. Rather, the law was really an import-substitution vehicle—it did not specifically define an FZ regime, rather it established the zero tax incentive package for companies who exported at least 80 percent of their production.

3. Average of Thailand, Sri Lanka, Philippines, China (World Bank 1988, cited in Kaplinsky 1993).

4. Most studies, however, have found that wages in the zones are, on average, well above the national minimum wage, particularly when overtime and productivity bonuses are included.

5. Value added tax known as *Impuesto de Transferencia a los Bienes* in the Dominican Republic.

6. The area around Santiago is the most important agricultural region in the Dominican Republic. The city has developed a major services economy, which is critical to provide the business services and support required by manufacturers in the free zones.

7. Two public parks that were created by the *Consejo Estatal del Azucar* (the state-owned sugar corporation) were transferred to a publicly owned bank, *Banco de Reservas*, under whose ownership they remain. The rest of the public parks are under the responsibility of Proindustria.

8. This excludes receipts from tourism.

9. See Decree No. 552-07, creating the Employment Protection and Creation Fund with the aim of preventing job losses in free zones, of October 8, 2007.

10. Including duty-free imports and exemption from corporate and value-added taxes.

11. Data on apparel and electronics are from the first half of 2009 only.

12. By contrast, 366 companies sold to the United States, 45 to Puerto Rico, 44 to Spain, 36 to Germany, and 27 to Haiti (CNZFE 2009).

References

CNZFE (*Consejo Nacional de Zonas Francas de Exportación*). 2009. Available at http://www.cnzfe.gob.do (accessed December 2009).

Kaplinsky, R. 1993. "Export Processing Zones in the Dominican Republic: Transforming Manufactures into Commodities." *World Development* 21 (11): 1851–65.

Sanchez-Ancochea, D. 2006. "Development Trajectories and New Comparative Advantages: Cost Rica and the Dominican Republic under Globalization." *World Development* 34 (6): 996–1015.

Schrank, A. 2008. "Export Processing Zones in the Dominican Republic: Schools or Stopgaps?" *World Development* 36 (8): 1381–97.

U.S. Office of Textiles and Apparel. 2009. *Major Shippers Report*. Available at http://otexa.ita.doc.gov (accessed December 2009).

World Bank. 2006. "Dominican Republic Country Economic Memorandum: The Foundations of Growth and Competitiveness," September. World Bank, Washington, DC.

WTO (World Trade Organization). 2002. Document G/SCM/N/74/DOM, January 8.

WTO. 2007a. Document G/SCM/N/160/DOM, July 5.

WTO. 2007b. Document WT/L/691, July 31.

WTO. 2007c. Document G/SCM/N/163/DOM, September 14.

CHAPTER 8

Fostering Innovation in Developing Economies through SEZs

Justine White

Introduction

Recognition is growing that technological innovation is central to economic growth and development both in high-income and developing countries (Aghion and Howitt 1998; Fagerberg, Srholec, and Verspagen 2009). Innovation should be understood as the implementation of new or improved products, processes, marketing, or organizational methods in business practices and workplace organization (OECD 2005). Importantly for developing countries, "new" is meant in a relative sense, insofar as innovation can be as much about applying existing global technologies that are new to the local context or bringing small improvements to existing technologies (incremental innovation) as it is about the creation of "new-to-the-world" innovations (radical innovations).

Against this backdrop, FDI, trade, and innovation are likely to be closely intertwined and mutually beneficial for development. Indeed, trade and FDI represent an opportunity for less developed economies to access high(er) technology goods and services, as well as to become familiar with innovative processes and demanding markets.

Since the 1990s, economic globalization (Bhagwati 2004) and, in particular, the lowering of transportation costs and the fragmentation of the production chain (Friedman 2005; Porter 1990; Saxenian 1999) have increased the opportunities for developing countries to receive FDI and increase trade. In parallel, the use of SEZs as a policy tool to attract FDI and promote trade has expanded rapidly, particularly in developing countries. The examples of some countries in East Asia have forcefully demonstrated the catalytic role that SEZs can play in diffusing technologies and stimulating innovation in the domestic economy, and in facilitating opportunities to climb up the value added chain. However, the failure of many SEZ programs in the developing world to go beyond basic, low-wage assembly activities suggests that the basic instrument of SEZs alone may not be sufficient to foster innovation. Beyond the core role of SEZs in fostering openness to trade and investment, further conditions are required, and these most likely extend beyond the spatial confines of the SEZs and into the wider domestic economy.

This chapter explores the possible preconditions and policy recommendations required for SEZs to support innovation in developing countries. First, it highlights the channels through which SEZs may positively influence innovation. Second, it underlines some policy initiatives and capabilities that seem to strongly condition the development of innovation through SEZs. Third, it advocates a step-by-step approach in designing SEZs, building on the example of successful experience in East Asian countries.

SEZs as an Instrument for Innovation

In developing countries, SEZs often are associated with low wages and low-skill production capabilities that typically are set up to build on the comparative advantage of cheap labor to expand the export base. Experience shows, however, that in addition to the direct economic benefits that can be derived from boosting trade, including employment generation and increasing exports, SEZs also can carry indirect economic benefits, which in turn can drive local innovation. Indeed, while attracting "content-rich" FDI and stimulating trade, SEZs tend to favor the acquisition of international knowledge and know-how, which are crucial to the development of innovation capabilities. Furthermore, the local interactions set in motion by SEZs appear particularly well-suited to innovation, which greatly benefits from local-level interactions.

In Addition to Boosting National Accounts, Foreign Investment, and Trade, SEZs Can Have More General Benefits for Development

From a host country's perspective, the benefits of SEZs can fall into two categories: (1) direct benefits, which straightforwardly and quantitatively affect current account and public finance developments, via export growth and foreign exchange earnings, FDI, and increased government revenue; and (2) indirect, or dynamic, benefits, which include skills upgrading of workforce and management, technology transfer, backward linkages with domestic firms, demonstration effect, export diversification, and knowledge of international markets. These effects are listed in table 8.1. The majority of these indirect benefits may crucially nurture ingredients that are needed for innovation in the context of development or economic catching-up.

According to modern innovation systems theory, innovation and technology development at the aggregate level are essentially the result of an interactive process involving a set of actors and institutions at the micro level, whose activities and interactions initiate, import, modify, and diffuse knowledge and new technologies (Freeman 1987). The key ingredients in this process include firms, human capital (thus skills), and technology or new knowledge, all of which can be stimulated by SEZ-linked interactions In this respect, successful SEZs are those that prove able to sustain development in the medium to long term while influencing production processes throughout the whole economy, beyond the positive impact derived from direct trade benefits (box 8.1).

Table 8.1   Direct and Indirect Benefits of SEZs

	Direct benefits	Indirect benefits
Balance of payments		
– Foreign exchange earnings		
– Export growth		
– FDI		
Public finance		
– Government revenue		
Organizational benefits		
– Testing field for wider economic reform		
– Demonstration effect		
– Export diversification		
Technological capabilities and know-how		
– Skills upgrading		
– Technology transfer		
– Enhancing trade efficiency of domestic firms		

Source: Author.
Note: FDI = foreign direct investment.

Box 8.1

The First Modern SEZ, Shannon, Ireland

Shannon, Ireland, as the most Western point in Europe, had been the necessary airport stop for American-bound planes since the start of commercial trans-Atlantic aviation. At the end of the 1950s, with the technological developments of the jet engine, Shannon airport was to be removed, in less than a year, from the schedules of many of the airline companies landing there: a likely devastating blow for the local economy. The foundations for the first modern SEZ were laid with a great sense of urgency.

This crisis led to the creation of both the SEZ and a related managing company, SFADCo (Shannon Free Airport Development Company). SFADCo's legal framework gave it considerable freedom of action, and under its terms of reference, the company's mandate was wide enough that it was to contribute to the development of Shannon and its region. Indeed, SFADCo achieved considerable notice in the early days as a developer of tourist sites with the aim of attracting tourists to replace the decline in transit passengers. This included restoration of castles and the popular "rent an Irish cottage" program.

SEZ development was from the outset based on airport-related services, such as repairing and maintaining aircraft, as well as manufacturing, industry, and trading operations, which contributed to the use or development of the airport. Although many of the first operations failed, some emblematic efforts were a great success. The importance at this time was the demonstration effect.

In the following decades, the continued success of the SEZ was ensured by (1) a highly integrated and coordinated approach to development; (2) focus on learning: direct training programs were provided by SFADCo for industry, and skills learned in factories at Shannon flowed subsequently to Irish industry—also, and important for future orientations (such as the set-up of the National Technology Park), partnerships were set up with a specially established university (University of Limerick); (3) trial and error was the norm in setting up new industries and companies, underlining a typically pragmatic approach; and (4) a rapid harmonious social and cultural change at the local level. Thanks to the partnership with the University of Limerick, the SEZ also supports the National Technology Park. Shannon continues to attract investors, more than 50 years after its foundation.

Source: Callanan (2000).

Trade and FDI Flows Attracted by SEZs Constitute Major Channels for Tapping into Global Knowledge and Know-How

Much of the economic and social progress of the past few centuries has been due to, or is associated with, technological innovation. As measured by TFP, the latter factor explains much of the differences in both the level and growth rate of income across countries (Easterly and Levine 2001; GEP 2008). In this regard, one of the problems faced by most developing countries is their inability to generate radical, new-to-the-world innovations. Overall, most of the world's commercial technology and R&D remains highly concentrated in a small number of countries (France, Germany, Japan, the United Kingdom, and the United States), although the nonmember countries of the Organisation for Economic Co-operation and Development's (OECD) share of the world's R&D has been increasing rapidly (OECD 2010). Furthermore, a large share of the world's commercial technology is produced by MNCs, most of which are headquartered in these same high-income countries.

Given the shortage of advanced technological competencies in developing countries, the vast majority of technological progress needs to occur through the adoption and adaptation of preexisting but new-to-the-domestic-market technologies. In this respect, as an effective policy tool to attract FDI and boost trade, SEZs may dramatically increase developing countries' exposure to foreign technologies, know-how, and knowledge.

The main transmission channels of foreign knowledge and technology are trade (imports and exports), the acquisition of foreign technology licenses, and FDI.

- *Imports* of goods and services that include embodied technology, and in particular capital equipment (Coe, Helpman, and Hoffmaister 1997), can be important conduits for the international transfer of technology and diffusion of innovation. The role of capital goods in particular has been supported by a number of empirical studies (Eaton and Kortum 2001; Keller 2004), as well as many case studies (Chandra 2006).

- *Export* contacts, notably with more developed countries, which may include forced adoption of higher standards and new specifications, contact with more demanding consumers, and exposure to new ideas, can constitute a "learning by exporting" effect that may drive domestic innovation. Although empirical studies are ambiguous as to the existence of this effect,[1] a wealth of anecdotal evidence addresses the topic.

- *Acquisition of technology licenses* grants a licensee the right to utilize specific technologies, patents, software, know-how, or product designs to produce them commercially. Licensing enables the rapid acquisition of product and process know-how, also allowing local adaptation and modification. Some studies have found that patent purchases can be more effective than R&D to increase productivity, particularly in developing countries with low R&D productivity, but licensing requires a significant level of technological capability. Interestingly, about three-fourths of the registered payments to the United States for technology sales in 2005 were made by foreign affiliates of U.S. firms (OECD 2009).

- *FDI* is a major source of process technology and learning by doing opportunities for individuals in developing countries. Over the last 15 years, FDI inflows to developing countries have almost doubled as a percentage of GDP. At the same time, the competition, standards, and knowledge of foreign markets that foreign firms bring to the domestic market can have important spillover effects. Spillovers refer here to technology "leakages" from MNCs to local firms in the same industry. Such so-called horizontal spillovers can take place in a number of ways: (1) local firms may be able to learn by observing and imitating; (2) employees may leave MNCs to join local firms, bringing along new technology and management know-how; and (3) MNCs may provide public knowledge and know-how that also can be enjoyed by domestic firms.

The Localized Nature of Innovation Highlights the Importance of SEZs

The fact that innovation tends to be spatially polarized is not new: see Alfred Marshall's "industrial districts" at the end of the nineteenth century; Joseph Schumpeter's "innovation clusters"; Eric Dahmen's "development blocks" and Francois Perroux's "development and growth poles" in the 1950s; and, more recently, economic geographers' and economists' industrial and high-technology agglomerations and "new economic geography." Indeed, research suggests that face-to-face interactions and the constitution of a local community of researchers and entrepreneurs are crucial to the transmission of knowledge and the developments of innovative activities (Storper and Manville 2006). This local dimension of innovation is explicitly taken into account by current innovation policies, which lay increasing emphasis on the creation of "clusters" or "science parks."

Against this backdrop, although in theory the benefits derived from FDI and trade can be obtained at any location in the country, the fact that they may be concentrated in a single geographic location, as is typically the case in SEZs, can be strongly beneficial for innovation. Indeed, the concentration, proximity, and density (Florida and Gates 2001) offered by SEZs, all the more if located close to a city or urban area, may be crucial to facilitate the exchange of knowledge and technologies between people and firms. Overall, in boosting knowledge acquisition from abroad and enabling exchanges between people and firms at the local level, SEZs may constitute an important tool for the development of innovative capacities in developing countries.

The Need for Absorptive Capacity and Local Linkages

By tapping into global knowledge and plugging into the local economy, SEZs can be expected to efficiently foster innovation. Observation suggests, however, that the indirect benefits highlighted above have only been fully exploited in a few, mainly East Asian, SEZs. In the majority of cases, the beneficial impact of SEZs seems to have been restricted to their direct impact on trade flows, and most SEZs never get beyond the basic assembly-type manufacturing activities. In this respect, the success of SEZs in stimulating innovation and encouraging technology transfer appears to depend on the following conditions and features of the domestic economy: (1) domestic technological capabilities, both of firms and of individuals; (2) the partial integration of the SEZs in the local economy (Johansson and Nilsson 1997; Omar and Stoever 2008), and (3) a strategic geographic location for the SEZs.

Increasing Domestic Technological Capabilities

As an extensive empirical and academic literature points out, openness to trade seems to constitute a necessary but not a sufficient condition to bolster local innovation in developing countries. Indeed, even if knowledge and technology are likely to be *transmitted* through trade and FDI, national technological capabilities have been identified as important conditions without which knowledge is not effectively *absorbed* and used domestically. These concepts have been developed by Abramowitz (1994), Kim (1980), and Lall (1992), as well as more recently in Fagerberg, Srholec, and Verspagen (2009).

"Technological capabilities" refer to the ability to develop, search for, absorb, and exploit knowledge commercially (see, notably, Fagerberg,

Srholec, and Verspagen 2009). These capabilities generally are thought to cover (1) the skill level in the economy, including not only general education but also managerial and technical competences; (2) national research and development efforts and technical personnel working in their fields; and (3) the ability of firms to finance their innovative endeavors.

- Training the SEZ workforce on the job and, in parallel, upgrading the national education system can have important benefits for the overall skill level.
- A strong point of many of the more successful SEZs was this concomitant development of an increasingly well-trained SEZ workforce, most often accompanied by major efforts involving the national education system. In 1968, for example, 57 percent of the SEZ workforce in Taiwan had only elementary school training. In 1990, 87 percent had more than elementary training. In the 1970s in the Republic of Korea, 80 percent of the workforce had completed middle school. This proportion was 95 percent in 1990. In terms of gender, these figures are even more dramatic. In the 1970s, only 20 percent of women working in SEZs in the Republic of Korea had completed high school, as compared with more than 95 percent today. Table 8.2 gives examples of on-the-job training provided in some SEZs.

Other initiatives include giving training to local companies outside the SEZs. For example, SFADCo in Ireland provided direct training for local industry outside the SEZs during the early 1960s (Callanan 2000). China, among others, has been more encouraging of joint ventures than inward FDI in its desire to maximize knowledge and technology transfer to local agents (Hoekman and Javorcik 2006). It seems, however, that China's experience may rest on stronger bargaining power of a large economy (Wei 2000). As a consequence of training efforts, a locally high-skilled workforce will be more likely to attract high-technology investments.

In addition to the formal education system and on-the-job training, domestic R&D capacity and technical personnel are important in determining an economy's capacity to absorb technologies from abroad. Gradual buildup of R&D capacity facilitates the imitation and adaptation of foreign technologies and improves the extent to which positive spillovers from FDI and trade accrue to the rest of the economy (Fagerberg 1988). Indeed, a stock of researchers or technical personnel is often necessary to understand and evaluate technology, and the higher

Table 8.2   Training for Workers in SEZs

Country	Training provided
China (Shenzhen)	Three months of on-the-job training for operators (one month for class and two months for production practice); more than 80 adult education institutes (1990) but weak links between needs of enterprises in the EPZ and skills provided.
Republic of Korea (Masan)	Three months of on-the-job training for operators; overseas training for skilled workers (mainly in Japan).
Malaysia	Three months of on-the-job training for operators; Quality Control Cycles with monetary and other incentives (gifts, medals and commendation letters, etc.) for identifying problems and suggesting ways of solving them); little training for computer programming, technical engineering, and design work.
Mauritius	Three months of on-the-job training for operators (trainee status: 75 percent minimum salary); lack of trained intermediate workers.
Philippines	One day to a few weeks of on-the-job training for operators; some firms (Japanese) rotate operators to make them familiar with between 10 and 18 interrelated tasks (three-month rotation).
Sri Lanka	One to three months of on-the-job training for operators.
Taiwan, China (Kaohsiung)	Three months of on-the-job training for operators; cooperative training programs between school/college and the firm in the EPZ. School/college provides the general education and the firms provide special technology training; some overseas training.
Thailand (Lat Krabang)	Three months of on-the-job training for operators; off-the-job training; study and experiment in the classroom and laboratory for some workers; overseas training (at parent company) for core employees in management and technology.

Source: Kusago and Tzannatos (1998).

and more sophisticated the technology, the greater specialization and sophistication needed by researchers. The Republic Korea is an interesting case in this respect, having started with a very low R&D level, which gradually was built up as the country developed, moving from imitation and low value-added manufacturing to high value-added products (see figure 8.1).

Interacting with the Domestic Economy

Many SEZs have remained islands isolated from their host economy, and in consequence, have not played the catalytic role in stimulating innovation played by many of the more successful SEZs. Remaining an island does not imply that the SEZs have not succeeded on some counts: they

Figure 8.1   The Republic of Korea's Gradual Buildup of R&D Capacity

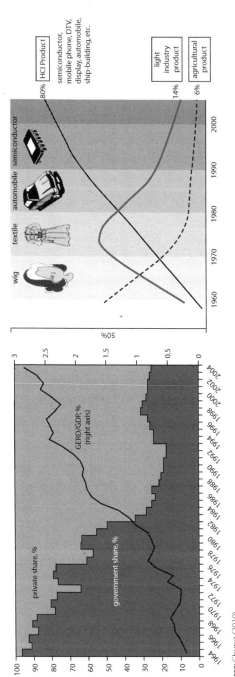

Source: Chung (2010).
Note: DIV =; GERD =; GDP = gross domestic product; HCI = human capital intensive.

often have generated much-needed employment at the local level and have succeeded in attracting FDI and foreign exchange. They have not been able to use this success to stimulate local enterprise upgrading. Gradual interaction of the SEZs with domestic firms, notably through backward linkages and labor circulation, can increase a domestic firm's capabilities to compete, if the business climate outside the SEZs is gradually reformed.

Facilitating backward linkages. Getting SEZs firms to source materials locally—so-called backward linkages—is beneficial to the local economy in terms of increased output and employment and improved production efficiency, technological and managerial capabilities, and market diversification. Lall (1980) notes that such linkages can take several forms. An MNC physically located within an SEZ may help prospective suppliers outside the SEZs set up production capacities, provide technical assistance and information to raise the quality of suppliers' products, or provide training and help in management and organization (UNCTAD 2001). SEZ companies may want to link to local suppliers for multiple reasons, among which are to achieve lower production costs, increase specialization, and better adapt technologies and products to local environments.

Although these linkages can be extremely important, the onus of developing them should not be on the firms inside the SEZs. Experience shows that, when this has been the case, it has not succeeded (see box 8.2). Furthermore, imposing local content and other burdensome requirements is often impracticable because of intense competition between SEZs (FIAS 2008). Host governments, however, can create attractive conditions, facilitate contacts, and provide various direct or indirect incentives that make it cost-effective for foreign companies in SEZs to get supplies from local sources. The Republic of Korea's outsourcing program is one example and, in Shenzhen, SEZ administrators provided individually tailored directories listing prospective domestic suppliers.

Several authors contend that the ease of setting up backward linkages is constrained either by prevalent local industrial development (FIAS 2008; ILO 1998) or by sectoral specialization. Jenkins, Esquivel, and Felipe Larrain (1998) provide a statistically significant econometric link between backward linkages and the country's level of industrialization, although the causality of this link is not demonstrated (Omar and Stoever 2008).[2] In terms of sectoral favoritism, it often is argued that some

Box 8.2

The Development of Backward Linkages: A Successful and Less Successful Example

The Republic of Korea: When the Masan Zone began operations in 1971, domestic firms supplied just 3.3 percent of materials and intermediate goods to firms in the zone. Four years later, they supplied 25 percent and, eventually, 44 percent. Consequently, domestic value added increased steadily from 28 percent in 1971 to 52 percent in 1979. In all, the evidence indicates that the Korean government successfully encouraged backward linkages with local industries and subcontractors. Local companies supplying EPZ firms had preferential access to intermediate and raw materials. The zone administration also provided technical assistance to subcontracting firms.

Dominican Republic: During the 1980s, the share of domestic value added in total output decreased. In the early 1980s, it was between 40 and 45 percent, but toward the end of the decade, it was just 25 to 30 percent. There were few backward linkages between domestic firms and industries in SEZs. One reason was the lack of government interest and incentives. Until 1993, to sell products to firms in these zones, domestic firms needed an export license, which was difficult to obtain. In addition, even though the legislation stated that firms could recover import duties paid for materials used in products sold to EPZ firms, in practice they were almost never able to do so. The Dominican industrial sector's lack of competitiveness with respect to quality, timing of delivery, and price also contributed to the absence of linkages.

Source: Author, based on Jenkins, Esquivel, and Felipe Larrain (1998).

sectors are more receptive to the development of backward linkages than others. Some authors explain that, because of the very nature of manufacturing, the electronics industry should generate more linkages with the domestic economy. Others contend that linkages are difficult to establish in any industry, but particularly in the textile industry (Basile and Germidis 1984; ILO 1998). The accumulated experience of some countries could support these assertions. However, many of the most successful SEZs initially attracted labor-intensive industries with relatively unsophisticated technologies (in textiles and electronics), which required unskilled workers, and then upgraded to more technology-intensive and higher value added sectors. These successful SEZs proved extremely good at moving away from the low-skilled, labor-intensive industries of their first years of operation. New garment industries were not allowed in Taiwan, China's EPZ as of 1974, for example.

Enhancing labor circulation. The literature has paid little attention to the role of labor turnover from SEZs as a channel for the diffusion of technology and processes to the domestic economy. It seems, however, that labor turnover can be significant for transferring technology and managerial know-how to domestic firms. For this reason, some countries (see box 8.3) have used fixed-term nonrenewable two- to five-year contracts for local managers in SEZs. Furthermore, because of a strict labor policy as well as voluntary departure, many employees left SEZs to create rival firms.

Reforming the business climate. Improving the general business climate of the host country is essential for developing a catalyst SEZ (FIAS 2008). Indeed, SEZs' medium- to long-term viability and their capacity to

---

Box 8.3

SEZs and Labor Circulation: A "Domestic Diaspora"?

In the Masan Zone in the Republic of Korea, an estimated 3,000 to 4,000 people received specialized training, either in the zone or abroad (mainly Japan), and half of these employees eventually left the zone to work in local electronic firms.

In Taiwan, China, under government guidance, personnel from firms in the zones were placed at potential suppliers' factories to offer advice on production methods and quality control.

Shannon, Ireland, had high labor turnover between the SEZs and the domestic economy, with many managers leaving to create competing firms outside the SEZs.

In Shenzhen, China, workers were appointed by the government for a three-year term and then were required to leave the zone. Many managers subsequently started their own firms, capitalizing on experience gained in the SEZs. This put competitive pressure on firms within the SEZs to innovate or disappear.

Sources: Callanan (2000); Jenkins, Esquivel, and Felipe Larrain (1998); Leong (2007).

stimulate local dynamics appear to require domestic business reforms when the SEZs is designed or shortly afterward.[3] This ensures that entrepreneurs can set up firms outside the SEZs to collaborate or compete with SEZs companies. Improving the business climate means improving the quality of regulation on such topics as starting a business, dealing with construction permits, employing workers, registering property, getting credit, protecting investors, paying taxes, trading across borders, enforcing contracts, and closing a business (World Bank 2010) (see box 8.4).

The example of Shenzhen offers interesting insights into the technological upgrading of SEZs and the stimulation of innovation in the domestic economy. After testing business climate reforms in the SEZs, the Chinese government launched nationwide reforms to match or emulate the business climate tested within the zone. Exports from the SEZs to the domestic economy were authorized.

The Importance of Strategic Location

Many governments have established SEZs in rural areas, responding to the need to create employment and economic opportunities in these areas. These SEZs, however, have often failed to become catalysts for innovation and technological upgrading.

Box 8.4

A Tale of Two Countries: Investment Climate Reform

India's Kandla, the first SEZ in Asia, was set up in 1965, and the first SEZ in China was set up in 1980. Being the first mover gave little advantage to Kandla, however, and China's SEZs, particularly Shenzhen, have been a phenomenal success.

One major difference between the early Indian and Chinese SEZs is that India had heavily protectionist policies and its share of world trade slipped from 2 percent in the 1950s to less than 0.5 percent in the 1980s. In contrast, China's SEZs were test beds for implementing wide-ranging economic reforms and trade liberalization in the rest of the country. Thus, SEZs in India remained isolated enclaves, whereas SEZs in China were rapidly overtaken and threatened by domestic competitive firms and, to remain relevant, they had to become more technology intensive, become more business friendly, and offer better services to firms.

Source: Leong (2007).

Several studies (FIAS 2008; Wei 2000) have insisted on the importance of the geographic location of the SEZs. Indeed, an SEZ in a city or periurban area has easier access to firms, capital, and skilled labor and can integrate with other firms more easily. For example, while the *maquiladoras* traditionally have purchased no more than 3 percent of their overall material inputs from Mexican sources, the *maquiladoras* of Mexico's three largest metropolitan centers, Mexico City, Guadalajara, and Monterrey, procured 31 percent, 16 percent, and 10.5 percent, respectively, of their inputs from domestic sources (MacLachlan and Aguilar 1998).

Also, the geographical proximity to a city or rapidly developing region has proven important for SEZs to support innovation activities in East Asia: In China, these include Shenzhen (next to Hong Kong, China), Zhuhai (next to Macau SAR, China), Xiamen and Shantou (across the Taiwan Strait opposite Taiwan, China), and Pudong (next to Shanghai). In the Republic of Korea, these include Masan (next to Masan port, not far from Busan). In Taiwan, China, these include Nanzih (next to Kaohsiung) and Taichung (next to Chuanghua).

Overall, the success of SEZs in fostering innovation in developing countries seems crucially determined by the absorption capabilities of the domestic economy. This pleads the case for encompassing targeted innovation policies, aimed at creating optimal conditions to domestically accompany openness to trade and FDI.

A Staged Approach to Building an Innovative SEZ

Domestic technological capabilities and linkages with domestic firms take significant time and effort to build up (Fagerberg, Srholec, and Verspagen 2009). In a context of scarce resources, these often require careful prioritization. Based on examples from some of the most successful Asian cases, most notably Shenzhen, this section advocates a step-by-step strategy for setting up an SEZ and highlights accompanying policy measures aimed at gradually building up technological capabilities and opening up and linking the SEZ to the domestic economy.

SEZ Inception: Infrastructure Development and the Business Environment

The development of a world-class infrastructure and business environment is the first step in the design of an SEZ. This step is all the more important given the fierce international competition to attract manufacturing investment in SEZs. As an example, more than two-thirds of the FDI received by the Shenzhen SEZs went into tourism and real estate development in 1981, and only 16.3 percent went to manufacturing activity. Although industrial growth was the goal of the SEZ, pragmatism prevailed among investors confronted with the poor quality of infrastructure (unreliable water and electricity, lack of housing and communication links), and real estate development also had a shorter return period and smaller profit margins. Lack of efficient legal and financial systems deterred many potential investors from undertaking large-scale manufacturing investments. The government responded to such undesirable outcomes by making massive investments in infrastructure and improvements in the business environment, hence reversing the course of events.

Labor-Intensive Manufacturing

Developing labor-intensive manufacturing activities linked to domestic production capabilities is typically the second step in the development of an SEZ. This step can be one of intense learning and can increase basic technological capabilities, provided that the proper channeling of capital inflows and appropriate regulatory guidance is given.

In 1982, in Shenzhen, the SEZ authorities issued strong guidelines to foreign investors on which sectors FDI should focus. Interestingly, Shenzhen initially aimed to attract high-technology firms, but pragmatically dropped the term "high-technology" for "some technology" in its requirements for manufacturing FDI, which was in greater accord with the absorptive capacity of the area. Small manufacturing (mainly processing and assembly) enterprises in mature industries were set up, based on differential wage costs. Cheap labor combined with guaranteed production capability involved only minor technological adaptation capability. "Exports" of these manufactured products started to be allowed on a restricted basis to the domestic market. Here, the needed technological capability was in adapting the manufactured products to the domestic market: changing the product to suit domestic market conditions and demands, adapting the product or process to take into account special features of local material supply, and adapting products to local conditions (climate, temperature, etc.). Seventy percent of the enterprises in the SEZ were upgraded technologically over a 10-year period (Liu 2002). If the appropriate linkages are not made and technological capabilities are not built up, SEZs may give lackluster results (see box 8.5).

Box 8.5

SEZs in Cambodia

FDI has grown at a high rate over the past decade, with $10.9 billion coming into Cambodia in 2008, playing a key role in employment. The initiatives taken to maximize linkages to the MNCs and foreign-invested enterprises to upgrade the domestic technology and knowledge base have remained scarce. Importantly, the impact of the significant FDI Cambodia receives on technology transfer and spillover appears to be negligible. SEZs are an important part of the country's economic development because they bring infrastructure, jobs, skills, and enhanced productivity. Since 2005, the Royal Government of Cambodia has approved a total of 21 SEZs. Of the 21, only 6 have commenced operations as of early 2010. Virtually no policies, mechanisms, or incentives are in place to encourage foreign firms to engage in technology or knowledge transfer to local companies, or to collaborate with local companies. In interviews with the SEZs in Phnom Penh, it appeared that little interaction existed between firms in the SEZs and local universities or technical institutes; firms occasionally train their low-skilled workers in-house. Highly skilled workers and managers usually are brought in from the respective country of origin. Inputs and technology also are imported.

Source: Author, based on Zeng and White (2010).

Figure 8.2 is a schematic of the transition between an island SEZ, typically one exemplified by many SEZs, in which linkages to the domestic economy are severely limited or inexistent, and a catalyst SEZ, in which technological capabilities are being upgraded and domestic linkages are created.

Technology-Intensive Manufacturing

The third step—transitioning to high(er) technology manufacturing—was gradual in all East Asian SEZs, particularly in view of the fact that technological capabilities take quite some time to build up. In the case of Shenzhen, the transition to technology-intensive manufacturing was brought on naturally by two factors: the cost of land, making it no longer a place for labor-intensive manufacturing industries; and increasing competition from mainland China and other SEZs, including firms set up outside the SEZs by former employees. Through a number of deliberate government policy reorientations, FDI for high-technology firms was

Figure 8.2   Island to Catalyst SEZs

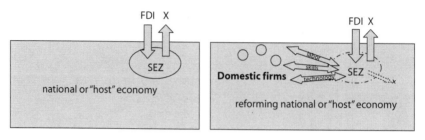

Source: Author.

encouraged by (1) incentives, such as tax holiday extensions, priorities for public utilities, and opening of domestic market; (2) infrastructure support and technology support services, including quality support services through the Shenzhen Quality Assurance Centre and funded by Shenzhen Technology Monitoring Bureau to help manufacturers build quality into their design, management, and production systems; (3) productivity enhancement services (lab facilities, specialized training, consultancies); (4) information services, most notably, the Technology Market Center in 1993, and information on new technology for industrial firms; and (5) strong laws and regulations protecting intellectual property rights (IPR).

In the case of Taiwan, China, the transition to technology-intensive manufacturing was done in part through regulation: New garment industries were not allowed in Taiwan, China's EPZ as of 1974, for example (see table 8.3). Figure 8.3 illustrates the transition between the second and third steps in the development of an SEZ. The figure shows the growing linkages with domestic firms leading to greater competitive pressure from them in the technology-intensive stage.

Conclusion

This chapter has attempted to clarify how SEZs can stimulate innovation and advocate proactive and sequential policies to facilitate domestic absorption of foreign technological know-how.

Developing an SEZ that boosts technological change and innovation can be rewarding for developing-country governments. However, developing an SEZ that drives innovation potentially involves a relatively coordinated set of medium-term policies, many of which attempt to

Table 8.3   Staged Approach to the Development of an SEZ: The Shenzhen Case

Stage	Inception	Labor-intensive	Technology-intensive
Comparative advantage	Incentive package for FDI; location specific advantage	Low-cost labor surplus; location-specific advantage; huge domestic market; incentive package for FDI	Low-cost highly educated labor; accumulated skills and capital; huge domestic market; FDI with advanced technologies
Main products and sectors	Tourism and real estate development	Toys, clothes, and bicycles	Computers, switches, integrated circuits
Source of technology	None	Hong Kong, China	Industrial countries
Role of government	Infrastructure building; Institutional reforms	Help firms find employees nationwide to keep the competitive position; faced with other low-cost competitors	Technology infrastructure building; protection of intellectual property rights

Source: Wei (2000).
Note: FDI = foreign direct investment.

Figure 8.3   SEZs from Linkages and Technological Capabilities to Upgrading

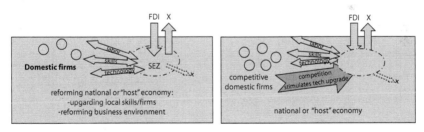

Source: Author.

upgrade domestic conditions (see table 8.4). These policies may include fostering linkages and spillovers between firms in the SEZs and firms outside, in particular, by building domestic capabilities in local firms and training a domestic labor force to take advantage of spillovers. Fostering labor circulation from the SEZs to the domestic economy can generate positive spillover effects. Experience suggests that reforms of the domestic investment climate, to emulate to some extent that of the SEZs, can help domestic firms develop. Finally, it is important to choose the location of the SEZs carefully.

Table 8.4   Some Policies Aimed at Stimulating Innovation Through SEZs

	Policies	Examples
Fostering linkages	Attractive conditions and incentives that make it cost-effective to use local-content	The Republic of Korea; Taiwan, China
Increasing domestic capabilities	Investment in training, technology upgrading of domestic workforce to match; allow and encourage domestic firms to have same access to hardware (machines) to upgrade production (Republic of Korea)	Skills Development Fund (Singapore); Penang Skills Development Center (Malaysia); Satellite Relations Program (Taiwan, China); Intel Corporation (Costa Rica)
Labor circulation	Encouraging placements in local firms by managers inside SEZs, lifting restrictions on labor circulation	Shenzhen, China; Taiwan, China
Accompanying investment climate reforms	Upgrading the overall national investment climate outside the SEZs so domestic firms can flourish	All successful dynamic SEZs
Location	Physical location (proximity to economic hub) and infrastructure linkages are important	All successful dynamic SEZs

Source: Author.
Note: SEZ = special economic zone.

Notes

1. Notably, because firms that export typically make deliberate decisions before exporting in terms of investment training and technology, the before and after effects are likely to be smaller.

2. Some data from Taiwan, China, are interesting in this respect.

3. The World Bank's regular Investment Climate Assessment and *Doing Business* reports can provide useful guidance to necessary national reforms.

References

Abramowitz, M. 1994. *The Origins of the Postwar Catch-up and Convergence Boom in the Dynamics of Technology, Trade and Growth, 1994.* Cambridge, UK: Edward Elgar Publishing.

Aggarwal, A. 2006. "Special Economic Zones—Revisiting the Policy Debate." *Economic and Political Weekly* (November 4).

Aghion, P., and P. Howitt. 1998. *Endogenous Growth Theory.* Cambridge, MA: MIT Press.

Bhagwati, J. 2004. *In Defense of Globalization.* Oxford, UK: Oxford University Press.

Basile, A., and D. Germidis. 1984. *Investing in Free Export Processing Zones.* Paris: Organisation for Economic Co-operation and Development.

Callanan, B. 2000. *Ireland's Shannon Story: A Case Study of Local and Regional Development.* Dublin: Irish Academic Press.

Chandra, V., ed. 2006. *Technology, Adaptation and Exports—How Some Developing Countries Got It Right.* Washington, DC: World Bank.

Chung, S. C. 2010. "Korean Development and Innovation Policy: Any Lessons?" Presentation given at Rapid Innovation Action Learning Workshop, Beirut, Lebanon, July 4–6.

Coe, D. T., E. Helpman, and A. W. Hoffmaister. 1997. "North-South R&D Spillovers." *The Economic Journal* 7 (40): 134–49.

Easterly, W., and R. Levine. 2001. "What Have We Learned from a Decade of Empirical Research on Growth? It's Not Factor Accumulation: Stylized Facts and Growth Models." In *The World Bank Economic Review* 15 (2): 177–219.

Eaton, J., and S. Kortum. 2001. "Technology, Trade and Growth: A Unified Framework." *European Economic Review* 45 (4–6): 742–55.

Fagerberg, J. 1988. "International Competitiveness." *The Economic Journal* 98: 355–74.

Fagerberg, J., M. Srholec, and B. Verspagen. 2009. *Innovation and Economic Development.* Working Paper 32, United Nation University–MERIT, Maastricht.

FIAS (Foreign Investment Advisory Service). 2008. *Special Economic Zones: Performance, Lessons Learned, and Implications for Zone Development.* Washington, DC: FIAS.

Florida, R., and G. Gates. 2001. *Technology and Tolerance: The Importance of Diversity to High-Technology Growth.* Washington, DC: Center on Urban and Metropolitan Policy, The Brookings Institution.

Freeman, C. 1987. *Technology, Policy, and Economic Performance: Lessons from Japan.* New York: Frances Printer Publishers.

Friedman, T.L. 2005. *The World is Flat: A Brief History of the Twenty-First Century.* New York: Farrar, Straus & Giroux.

Global Economic Prospects. 2008. *Technology Diffusion in the Developing World.* Washington, DC: World Bank.

Hahm, S., C. Plein, and R. Florida. 1994. "The Politics of International Technology Transfer: Lessons from the Korean Experience." *Policy Studies Journal* 22 (2): 311–21.

Hoekman, B., and B. Javorcik. 2006. *Global Integration and Technology Transfer.* Washington, DC: World Bank.

ILO (International Labour Organization). 1998. "'Labor and Social Issues Relating to Export Processing Zones.'" Technical background paper for the International Tripartite Meeting of Export Processing Zone-Operating Countries in Geneva, September 28 to October 2, 1998, International Labour Organization, Geneva.

Jenkins, M., O. Esquivel, and B. Felipe Larrain. 1998. *Export Processing Zones in Central America.* Development Discussion Paper No. 646, Harvard Institute for International Development. Cambridge, MA: Harvard University.

Johansson, H., and L. Nilsson. 1997. "Export Processing Zones as Catalysts." *World Development* 25 (12): 2115–28.

Keller, W. 2004. "International Technology Diffusion." *Journal of Economic Literature.*

Kim, L. 1980. "Stages of Development of Industrial Technology in a Developing Country: A Model." *Research Policy* 9 (3): 254–277.

Kusago, T., and Z. Tzannatos. 1998. *Export Processing Zones: A Review in Need of Update.* Social Protection Discussion Paper No. 9802. Washington, DC: World Bank.

Lall, S. 1980. "Vertical Inter-Firm Linkages in LDCs: An Empirical Study." *Oxford Bulletin of Economics and Statistics* 42: 203–06.

Lall, S. 1992. "Technological Capabilities and Industrialization." *World Development* 20 (2): 165–86.

Leong, C. 2007. "A Tale of Two Countries: Openness and Growth in China and India." DEGIT conference paper. Available at http://www.ifw-kiel.de/VRCent/DEGIT/paper/degit_12/C012_042.pdf.

Liu, Z., 2002. "Foreign direct investment and technology spillover: Evidence from China." *Journal of Comparative Economics* 30: 579–602.

MacLachlan and Aguilar. 1998. "Maquiladora Myths: Location and Structural Change in Mexico's Export Manufacturing Industry." *The Professional Geographer* 50 (3): 315–31.

OECD (Organisation for Economic Co-operation and Development). 2005. *Measuring Globalisation: OECD Handbook on Economic Globalization Indicators.* Paris: OECD Press.

OECD. 2007. *Globalisation and Regional Economies: Can OECD Regions Compete in Global Industries?* OECD Reviews of Regional Innovation. Paris: OECD.

Omar, K., and W. Stoever. 2008. "The Role of Technology and Human Capital in the EPZ Life-cycle." *Transnational Corporations* 17 (1) (April): 135–60.

Pack, H., and K. Saggi. 2001. "Vertical Technology Transfer via International Outsourcing." *Journal of Development Economics* 46: 389–415.

Porter, Michael E. 1990. *The Competitive Advantage of Nations.* New York: Free Press.

Saxenian, A. 1999. *Silicon Valley's New Immigrant Entrepreneurs.* San Francisco: Public Policy Institute of California.

Spar, D. 1998. *Attracting High Technology Investment—Intel's Costa Rican Plant.* FIAS Occasional Paper No. 11. Washington, DC: Foreign Investment Advisory Service.

Storper, M., and M. Manville. 2006. "Behaviour, Preferences and Cities." *Urban Studies* 43 (8): 1247–74.

UNCTAD (United Nations Conference on Trade and Development). 2001. *World Investment Report. Promoting Linkages.* Vienna: UNCTAD.

UNCTAD. 2003. *Investment and Technology Policies for Competitiveness: Review of Successful Country Experiences.* Geneva: UNCTAD.

Wei, X. 2000. "Acquisition of Technological Capability through Special Economic Zones (SEZs): The Case of Shenzhen SEZs." *Industry and Innovation* 7 (2): 199–221.

Zeng, Z., and J. White. 2010. "Cambodia's Special Economic Zones." Mimeo. Washington, DC: World Bank.

CHAPTER 9

Early Reform Zones: Catalysts for Dynamic Market Economies in Africa

Richard Auty

Context

This chapter proposes the concept of an Early Reform Zone (ERZ) as a policy tool for restructuring rent-distorted economies in Sub-Saharan Africa. The ERZ is a second-generation SEZ that immediately provides three critical postreform conditions—world-class infrastructure, business-friendly services, and property rights and the rule of law—within distorted economies to rapidly expand a dynamic market economy. Most economies in Sub-Saharan Africa were badly distorted by decades of patronage-driven rent cycling (Ndulu et al. 2008), whether the rent emanated from natural resources, foreign aid (a geopolitical form of rent), or manipulation by governments of relative prices (regulatory rent). The emerging theory of rent cycling demonstrates that patronage-driven rent deployment not only distorts the economy but also entrenches powerful rent-seeking groups that oppose reform and trigger growth collapses (Auty 2010).

The political legacy of rent cycling explains why recovery from the growth collapses of the 1970s and 1980s has been protracted for many Sub-Saharan African economies: rent recipients oppose economic restructuring because it shrinks their scope for rent extraction. The opposition of rent recipients therefore requires that economic reform be expressly complemented by a political strategy to manage the opposition. In contrast to the first-generation EPZs, the ERZ eschews subsidies and is not time constrained. This approach is taken to discourage rent-seeking activity. Moreover, the ERZ also forms part of a specific development strategy to steadily extend reform throughout the economy and simultaneously build a proreform political coalition that, as the relative size of ERZ activity expands, becomes politically strong enough to neutralize the distorted rent-seeking economy.

This chapter argues that the required political dimension can be most effectively provided by the ERZ playing a critical role within a dual-track reform strategy (Lau, Qian, and Roland 2000). In fact, key elements of ERZs can be identified in some first-generation SEZs that were deployed successfully as part of dual-track reform strategies in China, Malaysia, and Mauritius to simultaneously restructure distorted economies and shrink rent-seeking activity through the medium and long term. Most African efforts to deploy SEZs occurred later, but rather than benefiting from the experience of others, they frequently have disappointed because they failed to provide the basic needs of a dynamic competitive economy. Even when fiscal stabilization and trade opening were finally secured in most Sub-Saharan African economies from the late 1990s, the results still were disappointing because reformers neglected to establish a business-friendly environment along with a proreform political coalition. Deficiencies have included unreliable electricity and water services, excess regulation, rent-seeking customs agencies, unsuitable locations, and high-cost, low-productivity labor supplies (Farole 2010). The ERZ expressly seeks to overcome such coordination failure by concentrating activity within geographic zones in which services are provided by a reputable commercially oriented management company that promotes rapid expansion of both the firms and their interests. For those Sub-Saharan African economies that have progressed further with economic reform, ERZs can attract FDI and incubate dynamic internationally competitive firms that eventually will challenge established monopolies in the unreformed sector, forcing them to compete or shut down. The ERZ therefore becomes a catalyst for reform of the initially much larger rent-distorted economy not only through its internal expansion and demonstration effect on adjacent firms in the distorted economy, but also through the establishment of additional ERZs.

The dual-track strategy recently acquired greater interest for African economies because China is contributing to seven economic zones in the continent, partly to encourage the globalization of Chinese firms, and it may extend the total number (Brautigam and Tang 2010). The Chinese experiment is partly a response to the disappointing track record of most, but not all, previous SEZs in Sub-Saharan Africa. Watson (2001) attributes the failure of the continent's EPZs other than Madagascar (and Mauritius) to implementation failures rooted in deficient infrastructure, unstable incentives, and inadequate government services (including export zone management). He might have added macroeconomic instability as a fourth cause of failure because macroeconomic conditions deteriorated in many Sub-Saharan African economies through the 1970s, and improvements in most economies were delayed (by entrenched rent-seeking interests) into the late-1990s.

Cling, Razafindrakoto, and Roubaud (2005) contrast the robust success of EPZs in Madagascar (until recently) with failures elsewhere in the continent, such as Senegal, Cameroon, Kenya, and Zimbabwe. Glick and Roubaud (2006) demonstrate the beneficial employment outcomes of the Madagascar EPZs, which predominantly employ young, semiskilled female workers. The workers earn significantly more than their counterparts in the informal sector and are remunerated at a similar rate to men, improving gender wage equity. Glick and Roubaud also report that EPZ jobs are comparable to (and some superior to) jobs elsewhere in the formal sector, although long hours and high worker turnover restrict the EPZ as a source of long-term employment. However, Cling, Razafindrakoto, and Roubaud (2005) also confirm the importance to successful zones of stability, including a sound macroeconomic environment, which few governments in Sub-Saharan Africa could sustain through the 1970s and 1980s, but more have managed since. Provided that macrostability is achieved, not least in regard to the real exchange rate, ERZs are designed to address the criticisms of first-generation SEZs.

This chapter is presented in four sections. The next defines the ERZ in the context of related spatial policy tools for economic restructuring and identifies, and corrects, a basic confusion in both the terminology of zones and zone objectives. The following section analyzes the successful experiences with first-generation SEZs in China, Malaysia, and Mauritius, noting how their SEZs functioned as catalysts for economywide economic reform. The next section explains how ERZs can avoid the generally disappointing outcomes of first-generation SEZs in Africa. The final section summarizes the policy implications for economic reform in Sub-Saharan Africa.

The Confused Definitions and Aims of Special Economic Zones

The term SEZ embraces a wide range of spatial policy tools that often are defined inadequately so that they elicit much confusion and inaccurate stereotyping. Although ERZs share some characteristics with growth poles and EPZs, which are the two the most common variants of SEZs, they differ from them both in significant ways. Basically, ERZs are geographic areas located within distorted economies, which have yet to establish effective competitive markets. Within the ERZs, postreform conditions (world-class infrastructure, business-friendly services, and property rights and the rule of law) immediately apply. The fundamental objective of ERZs is to quickly establish the conditions of a fully reformed competitive market economy for investors within specific geographic zones inside an otherwise-distorted economy. In contrast to EPZs, which characterized the first-generation SEZs (first appearing in the 1960s), ERZs eschew subsidies because the success of many developing-country SEZs has reduced the risk for second-generation entrants. Experience elsewhere (some of which is elaborated below) shows that if coordination failures are overcome and world-class infrastructure is concentrated in professionally managed ERZs, then new entrants do not require subsidization. The basic point of the ERZ is to establish competitive world-class firms immediately rather than to nurture them from infant status.

In addition, the ERZ is executed as part of an economy-wide dual-track strategy, which adds the essential political component that the reform of distorted economies requires to be effective. The strategy recognizes that the top-down economic reform of such economies is likely to be undermined by the beneficiaries of rent-seeking, because reform extends competitive markets, which reduce their scope for rent-seeking activity. The dual-track reform strategy manages this risk to incumbent governments by using ERZs to kick-start a dynamic market economy, which forms Track 1 and rapidly expands employment, skills, taxes, and exports. Track 1 initially is modest in size, but it builds a proreform political coalition that can eventually take on opponents of reform and neutralize or co-opt them. Meanwhile, reform proceeds slowly in the rent-distorted sector (Track 2) to avoid early confrontation with rent-seekers, which a reforming government is likely to lose. Successful dual-track economic reform in economies as diverse as China, Malaysia, and Mauritius shows that SEZs can grow a dynamic market economy within 15 years to a scale that dominates the total economy, while also nurturing a proreform political coalition capable of managing rent-seeking interests in Track 2.

Compared with alternative spatial policy options, ERZs avoid the problems of overambitious scale that plagued most first-generation growth poles (Parr 1999). The initial wave of growth poles was discredited. Like ERZs, they sought to overcome coordination problems, but they went further by attempting to capture agglomeration economies by concentrating activity geographically. In practice, the optimum scale of growth poles proved so large that it outstripped domestic implementation capacity, squandering the potential economic benefits, as most arrestingly in the case of Republica Bolivariana de Venezuela's *Ciudad Guayana* (Auty 1990, 227–48). Meanwhile, in the theoretical literature, Murphy, Shliefer, and Vishny (1989) clearly do not appreciate the real-world impracticality of the successful coordination of the massive investment required by an industrial push (Auty 1994) that is beloved by balanced-growth enthusiasts. The heyday of first-generation growth poles was in the 1970s when they were extensively, and invariably unsuccessfully, used to revive economic activity in lagging regions (Parr 1999).

The EPZ has proved more resilient than growth poles, but it has had geographically mixed outcomes, with better results in Asia and Central America than in Sub-Saharan Africa and South America (Watson 2001; Jayanthakumaran 2003). For example, cost-benefit analysis undertaken for EPZs in six Asian countries in the 1990s identified positive rates in all of them except for the Philippines, where the Marcos government mistakenly conferred overgenerous subsidies at the outset (table 9.1). But although most first-generation EPZs failed in Sub-Saharan Africa, not all did so.

Five systemic criticisms of EPZs can be easily explained and dismissed because EPZs evolve and mature, which greatly strengthens their economic benefits. The criticisms therefore apply mainly to the many zones in Sub-Saharan Africa that failed to move beyond the early stages. Effectively implemented EPZs that manage to mature neutralize the standard criticisms, namely, that wages are low, skill transfer is negligible, net export earnings are significantly less than gross export earnings, foreign firms squeeze rent from incentives and relocate when the incentives expire, and tax incentives cut government revenue. Because

Table 9.1   Export Processing Zone Performance, Six Asian Economies
(percent)

	Korea, Rep. of	Malaysia	Sri Lanka	Philippines	Indonesia	China
EPZ jobs/total jobs, 1995	n.a.	2.1	4.4	0.3	n.a.	12.0
EPZ foreign profit/ total profit, 1995	n.a.	100.0	60.0	70.0	n.a.	30.0
EPZ exports/total manu- factured exports, 1980s	1.0	49.0	44.0	16.0	n.a.	12.0
EPZ net export/total exports, 1980s	53.2	33.0	27.9	26.2	62.4	16.4
EPZ FDI/total FDI, 1980s	4.0	13.4	73.8	22.6	5.5	11.6
Domestic raw material/ total EPZ raw material	34.0	4.0	5.3	6.0	41.0	n.a.
Economic internal rate of return	15.0	28.0	23.0	−3.0	26.0	10.7

Source: Jayanthakumaran (2003), 59 and 61.
Note: EPZ = export-processing zone; FDI = foreign direct investment; n.a. = not applicable.

SEZs absorb unemployed labor and that is a useful net gain in itself, this feature undercuts the first criticism. The second criticism is inaccurate for EPZs that mature: there is incontrovertible evidence from China, Malaysia, and Mauritius that over the long term, successful EPZs raise skills and productivity, whereas rent-distorted economies struggle. Finally, the ERZ is expressly designed to avoid the three remaining criticisms of EPZs. First, ERZs expand rapidly so that even if value added is a modest share of enterprise revenue, the aggregate value added quickly becomes substantial and linkages proliferate with adjacent Track 2 activity. Second, the ERZ offers a competitive incentive regime rather than subsidies, which may have been necessary for the first-generation SEZs in developing countries but no longer are needed. Consequently, the risk of nurturing rent-seeking is diminished. Third, ERZs generate taxes from the outset in addition to foreign exchange from exports, technology transfer, and skills. In fact, because the five criticisms apply to failed EPZs, in that specific context, they may be correct.

Perhaps most important, ERZs aim not only to create employment, exports, and taxes, but also to incubate dynamic competitive firms capable of rapidly developing and harnessing new ideas to drive welfare improvements, an achievement central to sustaining gains in African welfare. The new competitive enterprises in the Track 1 ERZs generate positive spillovers for adjacent Track 2 activity within the distorted economy.

The central goal of the ERZ is the proliferation of internationally competitive firms throughout the economy. This enables the distorted economy in Track 2 to experience relative decline, and its capital and labor can be absorbed progressively into a modern market economy that expands from Track 1. In contrast to most first-generation SEZs, including growth poles and EPZs, ERZs are not specifically targeted at attracting high-tech activity or at reviving depressed regions but rather at attracting investment by dynamic companies. The ERZ makes no attempt to pick winners in terms of product, source of investment, or intended geographic market.

In the context of Sub-Saharan Africa, the ERZ simply aims to encourage a rapidly expanding number of firms to efficiently employ African land, labor, skills, and capital. To date, companies have been deterred by the absence of the basic conditions required to establish and sustain efficient production in Africa, not least business-friendly regulation and institutions. The ERZ seeks to rectify these shortcomings by establishing such conditions immediately, thereby creating a catalyst for the rapid diffusion of a dynamic market economy capable of sustaining economic growth by raising productivity, an outcome most but not all distorted economies have found elusive (World Bank 2009).

Until the proreform political coalition has grown strong enough to see off opponents of reform, the ERZ is vulnerable to the policy capture that would turn it into just another agency to facilitate rent-seeking activity, as occurred with the Russian SEZs (Tuominen and Lamminen 2009). Most firms within the first-generation Russian SEZs located to escape taxation and showed little interest in being internationally competitive. They did not sustain their activity when the time-constrained subsidies expired. In short, most Russian ERZs simply generated rents for less than dynamic companies. The defense against policy capture is the formation at the outset of a prozone political coalition, which has a vested interest in the success of the zone. The coalition includes not only local workers and local government leaders that stand to gain directly from the ERZ's success, but also investors in the ERZ infrastructure, which for Sub-Saharan Africa include international financial institutions (IFIs) like the Asian Development Bank and World Bank. The participation of the IFIs creates a real risk of painful reprisal should a government fail to ensure that legal contracts are upheld. In addition, recent evidence from Russia with regard to Rosneft's acquisition of some of the Yukos hydrocarbon company's assets indicates that extranational courts can penalize asset confiscation (*Economist* 2010). Finally, WTO membership provides a further means of increasing the risk of painful retaliation for failure to uphold contracts. In the last resort, however, investment risk cannot be entirely eliminated, only minimized and perhaps insured against.

Examples of Successful SEZs

Three cases of successful deployment of SEZs are examined in this section. Mauritius is analyzed as an early pioneer of the dual-track SEZ strategy, demonstrating clearly how SEZs can (1) adjust to changing competitive advantage by improving workforce skills; (2) drive economywide structural change; and (3) strengthen a progrowth political coalition until it outweighs the rival interests that benefit from rent distortion. Malaysia confirms the capacity of economic zones to promote a dynamic market economy and also shows that textile manufacture is not the sole route by which this is achieved. Moreover, Malaysia demonstrates how SEZs can diversify an initially *resource-rich* economy into a manufacturing-driven economy. Mauritius and China have *resource-poor* economies, which rent-cycling theory shows act to strengthen elite incentives to promote sustained economic growth. The case of China most dramatically reveals the strength of the spillover effects from SEZs.

Mauritius: How the Zone's Comparative Advantage Evolved

Mauritius illustrates how an economic zone functioning within a dual-track strategy can dramatically change the fortunes of a small remote economy. As a sugar mono-crop island economy, Mauritius faced a Malthusian situation in the 1960s in the face of rapid population growth and emerging land scarcity. Quickly appreciating the limits of industrialization by import substitution, the government established an SEZ in 1971 primarily to absorb surplus labor. It initially attracted capital from Hong Kong, China, where investors sought to surmount EU and U.S. quotas and tariffs on textile exports by supplying these two major markets from Mauritius. In addition, local sugar planters invested part of a sugar price windfall in 1972–1975 in the SEZ to diversify their options (Findlay and Wellisz 1993). Finally, as part of its Track 2 strategy, the government of Mauritius used some of the extra tax revenue from the sugar boom to undercut radical opposition to market-driven growth by increasing social spending from 6 percent of GDP to 10 percent of GDP through the 1970s. The dual-track policy drove per capita GDP at

6 percent annually through the 1970s and eased the simmering social tension of the 1960s.

Mauritius' SEZ joint ventures of the 1970s gave way in the 1980s to mainly domestic investment, specializing in textiles. Once surplus labor was absorbed and real wages began rising, however, low-value textile items were relocated offshore to Madagascar, allowing Mauritius to focus on higher value products such as textile design, spinning, weaving, and knitting. This outcome flatly contradicts the criticism that SEZs merely employ low-wage labor. At its peak, the Mauritius textile industry was the second-largest world producer of knitted textiles; the third-largest exporter of pure wool tissues, and the fourth-largest exporter of T-shirts to Europe. The zone employed 60,000 workers in 500 firms generating $1.2 billion in exports. A state enterprise serviced the SEZs and included among its functions the provision of such externalities as training, investment credits, and negotiation of trade agreements. In 1985, 14 years after the start-up, the government replaced the SEZ tax holiday with a 15 percent profit tax along with incentives to export for import substitution firms within Track 2. By then, the two tracks had all but merged.

SEZ expansion drove Mauritius per capita GDP at 5.7 percent annually through the 1980s as rapid passage through the demographic transition cut population growth to 1 percent. Manufactured exports rose from one-quarter of the total in 1980 to two-thirds in 1990, ending sugar's dominance. SEZ employment tripled and, by 1990, national unemployment fell to 4 percent from 21 percent, creating labor shortages that strengthened pressure on firms to diversify into more productive activity. By the mid-1990s, Mauritian textile wages were four times those of China and Vietnam and prompted diversification into information technology within the evolving SEZ (Chernoff and Warner 2002). Services increasingly drove the economy: tourist arrivals quintupled to 700,000 in 2003, and financial services rapidly expanded. Moreover, the government used the sustained economic buoyancy to restructure the once-dominant sugar industry as WTO rules phased out sugar's geopolitical rent over 2001–2009.[1]

From 1971 onward, Mauritius' SEZ attracted competitive manufacturing as part of a dual-track economic reform that postponed confrontation with pro-redistribution political forces, including the powerful unions in the initially dominant sugar industry until the dynamic sector was sufficiently strong, both economically and politically, to absorb surplus labor from the lagging sector and also to reform it. Interestingly, Mauritius' experience paralleled that of Malaysia after the Malaysian government established free trade zones in 1971, but electronics were initially the key export product there, rather than textiles.

Malaysia: Zones Facilitate the Shift from Resource-Driven to Skill-Driven Development

Like Mauritius, Malaysia realized the limits of import substitution industrialization well before most other developing economies, and its government embraced export industry, despite the country's richly diversified natural resource endowment. The motivation for change was the inability of infant industry, which proved to be capital intensive, to contribute significantly to unemployment alleviation, which was critical for improving the lagging welfare of the majority native Malay population. From 1968 onward, the government began encouraging export manufacturing because it was more labor intensive. It offered export manufacturers reduced taxation linked to export performance and domestic content; tax deductions on export promotion expenses; accelerated depreciation when more than 20 percent of production was exported; and preferential rates on government export financing and insurance (Salleh and Meyanathan 1993, 9). In 1971, free trade zones were established, which were deemed outside Malaysian territory for the purpose of customs and excise duties. They conferred duty-free imports of capital and inputs for goods that were processed for export. Land within the zones was leased to firms at below-market rates, but firms normally built their own factories rather than leasing them. In addition, company tax relief was provided for specified periods.

Foreign investors in Malaysia through the 1970s were mainly from the United States and Japan, but in the 1980s Taiwan, China, rose to prominence and contributed more than one-third of Malaysia's FDI. Electronics exports were initially a key component in Malaysia's rapid manufacturing expansion. Like Mauritius' textiles, Malaysian electronics initially absorbed cheap labor but subsequently became technologically more sophisticated and, by the late 1980s, they generated one-fifth of all manufacturing employment and half of industrial exports. During 1982–93, the share of manufacturing in Malaysian exports jumped from 22 percent to a dominant 74 percent, and the composition of manufactured exports switched toward telecommunications (Islam and Chowdhury 1997, 228). The resulting growth in the contribution of exports to industrial output steadily reduced the economywide average effective rate of protection from 45 percent in 1969 (itself modest by developing-country standards at the time) to 31 percent in 1979 and

17 percent in 1987 (Edwards 1990), just 16 years after the SEZs were established. The Mahathir government rashly launched a heavy industry drive in the early 1980s, just as the Republic of Korea was reacting strongly against that policy and the social and economic costs it had imposed on the majority of the population. Much Malaysian heavy industry was prone to rent-seeking and required prolonged adjustments to mitigate the worst consequences. Fortunately, the export manufacturing sector proved sufficiently resilient to absorb the costs of Malaysia's ill-judged heavy industry drive. Malaysia not only confirms the viability of the dual-track strategy and the speed with which economywide reform can be achieved but also demonstrates that the strategy can work in a natural resource–abundant economy as well as in resource-poor economies like Mauritius and China.

China: The Mechanism of the SEZ Spillover to the Rent-Distorted Sector

China provides a sterner test of the viability of the dual-track strategy in a strongly distorted economy within which central planning had repressed markets for three decades. Although the Chinese economy was less distorted than that of the USSR when their respective governments commenced reforms (de Melo, Denzier, Gelb, and Tenev 2001), the process of economic reform still encountered strong vested interests within the dominant state-owned industrial sector. This opposition prompted the Chinese reformers to eschew top-down big-bang reform for gradual reform that first reformed agriculture and then, using SEZs in the southeastern coastal region, reformed industry to create employment and attract foreign investment, notably from the adjacent economic agglomerations Hong Kong SAR, China, and Taiwan, China. China also clearly illustrates the demonstration effect of the SEZs on firms in the adjacent rent-distorted economy.

The Chinese SEZs were formally established in 1980 to restructure the economy by tapping into foreign investment and expertise. The government aimed to test a controlled economic liberalization after three decades of central planning and economic autarky. China initially established four zones on the coast: three in Guangdong province close to Hong Kong SAR, China, at Shenzhen, Zhuhai, and Shantou; and one at Xiamen in Fujian, close to Taiwan, China. The number of zones increased through the 1980s and 1990s to 200 with varying structures, ranging from free commercial zones to free industrial zones and technology parks. Of all China's principal regions, the neglected southern coastal region initially was well placed to sustain dual-track reform. The south coast region had little obsolete industrial capital because of neglect under central planning; it was well located to capture spillover effects from the adjacent dynamic market economies of Hong Kong, China, and Taiwan, China; and as a resource-poor region, the absence of natural resource rents incentivized provincial and local governments to promote wealth creation so they could provide employment and eventually expand the tax base.

Throughout the 1980s, the SEZs combined lower central taxation with enhanced infrastructure investment to attract foreign capital investment first to the original reform zones and then to additional zones established along the coast (Litwack and Qian 1998). From the early 1990s, the tax benefits were removed from the zones, although investment in superior infrastructure continued to be concentrated, albeit in a larger set of zones. From 1994, taxation was equalized across regions, and government attention shifted from the coast to stimulating the lagging interior regions. Moreover, government efforts also sharply intensified to reform the large SOEs (the principal consumers of regulatory rent) in Track 2 (Farole 2010), which no longer dominated industrial production but a decade earlier had received a disproportionately high share of capital investment and had been sufficiently powerful politically to discourage top-down economic reform.

The SEZ strategy contributed strongly to China's rise to become a leading world exporter of manufactured goods and the principal recipient of FDI among the developing economies. During 1979–95, the SEZs helped China attract 40 percent of all FDI to developing countries, of which the coastal areas received 90 percent. Guangzhou alone drew 40 percent of Chinese FDI, which with the two other local SEZs, lifted the local share of FDI to 50 percent. Importantly, the gains were made rapidly: whereas the south coast region occupies 5 percent of China's land area and held 19 percent of the population, by the mid-1990s, it generated 32.7 percent of national GDP, which represented a gain in share of 8.5 percent of national GDP during 1980–1995 (Golley 1999). China experimented not only with economic incentives but also with different forms of enterprise. The rise of new more flexible enterprises resulted by the mid-1990s in the expansion of township and village enterprises (TVEs), which were basically local devices to absorb surplus rural labor in self-supporting employment. TVEs accounted for two-fifths of China's manufactured output, mostly for the domestic market. In addition, however, joint ventures grew to 15 percent of manufactured output, but they generated half of all China's consumer goods and two-fifths of its exports; MNCs produced half of all exports, worth 9 percent of GDP (Gang 2001).

The SEZ experiment began to transform the Track 2 economy. It rapidly turned the Zhu Delta around Guangzhou into the second of three major Chinese agglomerations, with the established zone in the Chang Delta centered on Shanghai and the third in the Bohai Triangle. The agglomerations began exerting beneficial spillover effects on local SOEs. Johnston (1999) shows that provinces hosting one of the three agglomerations also hosted dynamic competitive manufacturing, whereas provinces outside the agglomerations did not, including coastal provinces outside the three agglomerations. Table 9.2 demonstrates that agglomerations developed shares of non-SOEs and profits in excess of their share of urban population. Interestingly, however, the profitability of SOEs in the agglomeration provinces was disproportionately higher than that of SOEs elsewhere. The higher ratio of viable SOEs in the agglomerations confirms positive spillover effects from adjacent market enterprises. The ratio of the share of SOE profits to the share of SOEs in the interior regions remote from the three agglomerations is significantly lower (see table 9.2), with the exception of three resource-based activities (Henan oil and coal, Heilongjiang oil, and Yunnun tobacco).

Aslund (1999) argues that such rapid extension of local competition as occurred in China reduces scope for rent-seeking by government officials. Because growing competition between firms in adjacent authorities shrinks the regulatory (government-created) rents, local officials thereby acquire an incentive to pass residual claims, for example, from underemployed workers, on to enterprise managers to avoid incurring onerous social support charges (Li, Li, and Zhang 2000). Officials need to improve efficiency incentives for local enterprises so that they can bear the extra

Table 9.2   Ratio of Firms, Workers and Profits to Urban Population Share, Chinese Regions, 1996

	Urban population (%)	Non-state enterprise ratios			State enterprise ratios		
		Firms	Workers	Profits	Firms	Workers	Profits
Coast south	27.25	1.15	1.20	1.88	0.78	0.60	0.97
Coast north	23.35	0.82	1.00	0.99	0.83	0.98	1.35
Center	43.45	1.01	0.90	0.54	1.19	1.21	1.33
West	4.95	0.91	0.80	0.18	1.59	1.47	0.20

Source: Johnston (1999), 13.

social responsibilities, which can be achieved by replacing SOEs with more efficient private firms (including MNCs) or initially at least with profit-sensitive cooperatives like the TVEs. The pressure for proefficiency change is sensitive to the tax rate, however, which exerts an inverse-U effect, because high taxes repress the incentives of management to be efficient, whereas low taxes diminish government interest in boosting enterprise efficiency (the fruits of which yield taxes).

The final part of the competitive spatial dynamic triggered by SEZs worked by encouraging the non-SOE managers to demand both legislation to fully safeguard private property rights and independent courts to enforce contracts that are free of government manipulation (Li, Li, and Zhang 2000). Consistent with this thesis, Li, Li, and Zhang (2000) show that privatization spreads faster in cases in which competition is most intense, that is, in simple undifferentiated products and in the presence of sharply falling transport costs, which characterized the south coast region in the 1980s and 1990s. Li, Li, and Zhang (2000) also find that privatization occurs faster among lower tiers of government. In the absence of scale economies in local enterprises, local TVEs face intensifying competition sooner than large national SOE monopolies, thereby facilitating entry by new small firms. Additionally, local officials have less administrative and legal leverage with which to protect firms than higher tiers of government. However, the relevance of this particular facet of Chinese reform for natural resource-rich African economies (which most are) is potentially undercut by the fact that, as a resource-poor economy, the Chinese elite had a strong incentive to grow the economy by efficient use of capital and labor, rather than by relying on politically driven (and personally enriching) rent cycling (Auty 2010). This is why the case of resource-rich Malaysia is particularly instructive for African economies.

Most critically, in all three successful country cases, the first-generation SEZs proved effective catalysts for establishing or sustaining dynamic market economies (Track 1) that acquired the capacity to transform lagging sectors within the initially dominant rent-distorted economy (Track 2), an outcome that all three countries achieved within the space of just 15 to 20 years.

The Potential Role of ERZs in Sub-Saharan Africa

ERZs set the bar higher for potential investing companies than the first-generation SEZs by eschewing subsidies and encouraging efficient and competitive enterprises from the outset. Rather than subsidizing firms through an "infant" start-up phase, Fafchamps, El Hamine, and Zeufack (2008) find from research in Morocco that firms thrive by learning from meeting foreign demand, which is discerning, rather than by "production learning" as a consequence of first reducing costs in the domestic market. This approach in turn results in export firms commencing overseas sales shortly after their start-up. These firms also benefit from some degree of foreign ownership, and most importantly from being productive at the outset rather than following an infant industry learning curve. A well-executed ERZ is designed to reduce the risk for second-generation SEZ firms, although that risk is systematically reduced by the very success of first-generation SEZs.

Economic geography reinforces the rationale for promoting ERZs within the economies of Sub-Saharan Africa because ERZs can help them to tap into spillovers from overseas urban agglomerations that their own economies will be unable to generate for several decades. Few economies in Sub-Saharan Africa apart from South Africa and Nigeria are likely to grow cities of a sufficient size and economic structure to capture the agglomeration economies. However, the smaller Sub-Saharan African economies can build links to such agglomerations just as Mauritius did in the 1970s with Hong Kong, China; and Malaysia did with Japan and the United States. In contrast, the sheer scale of the Chinese market allowed that country to quickly promote its own agglomerations, although it did so by initially tapping into spillovers from Hong Kong, China (Zhu Delta) and Taiwan, China (Zhang Delta). The smaller African economies can benefit from agglomeration spillover effects if clusters of same-firm activities emerge within ERZs that secure localization economies. Localization economies are more specialized than the agglomeration economies and enhance the efficiency of firms by achieving the modest thresholds required to sustain local pools of specialized labor and services, and specific production inputs, and also by providing high exposure to innovative ideas. Viewed within this spatial context, the ERZ is an effective vehicle to nurture the localization economies and confer an advantage over African economies that lack ERZs. Consequently, the spillover from the agglomerations is not through physical proximity, because such effects attenuate rapidly, but rather from contact with firms in such agglomerations as their suppliers, which can create localization economies through which best business practice and standards diffuse to the local economy.

In this context, control of operating conditions appears to underlie the Chinese strategy of systematically expanding SEZs in Africa (World Bank 2010) rather than any conscious intention to establish catalysts of reform in rent-distorted economies. Brautigam and Tang (2010) identify multiple objectives for the Chinese economic zones, which center on facilitating export diversification by Chinese companies. The advantages for China include (1) helping inexperienced small and midsize firms gain overseas experience; (2) facilitating China's domestic restructuring by relocating mature industries offshore; (3) surmounting barriers to Chinese exports to Europe and North America; (4) tapping into economies of scale for overseas investment; and (5) creating markets for Chinese-made machinery. Chinese firms receive incentives that include grants, long-term loans plus subsidies on loans, and subsidies on up to one-third of some preparation costs. Host governments are also expected to extend concessions, such as tax holidays, duty waivers, and relaxed labor laws, which they have done with different levels of enthusiasm in different countries. Although the zones are open to domestic and non-Chinese foreign firms as well as Chinese firms, the latter have tended to dominate. Most zones remain in an early stage of development and maturation is projected at a decade. Chinese firms report problems arising from policy fluctuations, deficient service provision, and inadequate infrastructure beyond the zones. African agencies express concern over potential abuses, such as relabeling products made in China for export and labor exploitation.

A further policy option for those African economies in which mining is important is to harness the potential to create ERZs presented by major mining projects operated by international mining companies. International mines resemble ERZs by functioning as enclaves of efficiency within underperforming economies. The massive scale of the sunk investment made in mining renders it imperative for the mining company to negotiate, as a precondition of such investment, conditions of operation that ensure the efficient application of capital, labor, and technology. Such mines and oil wells can form the nucleus of ERZs through a modification of the standard corporate social responsibility policy. Experiments by, among others, BP in Azerbaijan (Auty 2006) suggest that if international mining firms reorient their corporate social policies away from filling gaps in infrastructure that central governments should provide, and instead substitute the encouragement of new enterprise formation around the mining area, then the mineral enclave effectively expands into an ERZ. BP shared infrastructure and gave advice to new entrants, while also assisting with finance and legal guidance. The mining area nurtures new economic activity that can continue to operate after mining is exhausted, helping to sustain the local economy. The proposed shift in corporate social responsibility policy encourages local entrepreneurs to establish both mine-related and unrelated businesses. The policy helps to build local social capital (BP cooperated with the Open Society Foundation to achieve this in Azerbaijan) within the mining region to strengthen the lobbying capacity of local governments and businesses for legitimate central government assistance.

Conclusions: ERZs and Economic Reform in Sub-Saharan Africa

Effective economic reform of rent-distorted political economies demands a political component to overcome policy capture by rent recipients. This chapter argues that African governments can achieve this through a variant of the dual-track strategy, within which second-generation SEZs, defined as ERZs, play a critical role. Elements of such a strategy can be detected in successful reforming economies as diverse as resource-poor Mauritius and China and resource-abundant Malaysia. The dual-track strategy postpones confrontation with the rent-seeking opponents of reform in the rent-distorted economy (Track 2), and it accelerates the emergence of a dynamic market economy within ERZs, which comprise Track 1. The Track 1 ERZs immediately provide world-class infrastructure, effective business-friendly services and incentives, and institutional safeguards for property rights and the rule of law. The effective coordination and delivery of this efficient business environment mean that, unlike the first-generation SEZs, the ERZ firm does not require subsidies. The successful expansion of dynamic internationally competitive firms in Track 1 also builds a strong proreform political coalition that can eventually neutralize rent-seeking elements and confer strong and positive spillover effects on economic activity in Track 2.

Mauritius demonstrates the basic dynamic of ERZs, which Malaysia confirms, and China most clearly shows the beneficial spillover effects of ERZs on the distorted economy in Track 2. SEZ activity in all three economies achieved sufficient scale to accomplish radical restructuring within 15 to 20 years of their launch. Given the many obstacles to business formation in Sub-Saharan African economies that are the legacy of decades of economic distortion, the ERZ seeks to kick-start the emergence of a dynamic market economy. The ERZ geographically concentrates the principal components of a business-friendly environment and leaves the rest of the economy to progress through subsequent spillover effects.

Most economies in Sub-Saharan Africa are too small to develop cities large enough to create agglomeration economies. The ERZ can build localization economies that link to global agglomerations in North America, Europe, and Asia, and thereby provide access to the stimulus to raise productivity that such agglomerations generate. In this way, the ERZ not only facilitates reform but also diffuses productivity-driven growth throughout the reformed economy. Ironically, the ERZ turns the much-criticized economic enclave into a virtue by first tapping into the advantages of the enclave to incubate dynamic competitive firms in isolation from the distorted economy and subsequently allowing the enclave through its spillover effects to gradually incorporate the rest of the economy into global best practice.

Note

1. Mauritian sugar production costs under the Commonwealth Sugar Agreement were 25 percent above world levels and reform aimed to cut them from US$0.40/kilogram to US$0.26/kilogram by increasing the average factory size, mechanizing cane production, and releasing marginal land for tourism and information technology (IMF 2002).

References

Aslund, A. 1999. "Why Has Russia's Economic Transformation Been So Arduous?" Paper to the World Bank Annual Conference on Development Economics, April 28–30, 1999, Washington, DC.

Auty, R. M. 1990. *Resource-based Industrialization: Sowing the Oil in Eight Oil-Exporting Economies.* Oxford, UK: Oxford University Press.

Auty, R. M. 1994. "Industrial Policy Reform in Six Large Newly Industrializing Countries: The Resource Curse Thesis." *World Development* 22: 11–26.

Auty, R. M. 2006. "From Mining Enclave to Economic Catalyst: Large Mineral Projects in Developing Countries." *Brown Journal of World Affairs* 13 (1): 135–45.

Auty, R. M. 2010. "Elites, Rent Cycling and Development: Adjustment to Land Scarcity in Mauritius, Kenya and Cote d'Ivoire." *Development Policy Review* 28 (4): 411–33.

Brautigam and Tang. 2010. "China's Investment in African Economic Zones". Mimeo. January, 2010, World Bank.

Chernoff, B., and A. M. Warner. 2002. *Sources of Fast Growth in Mauritius: 1960–2003*. Cambridge, MA: Harvard Centre for International Development.

Cling, J. P., M. Razafindrakoto, and F. Roubaud. 2005. "Export Processing Zones in Madagascar: A Success Story Under Threat?" *World Development* 33 (5): 785–803.

de Melo, M., C. Denzier, A. Gelb, and S. Tenev. 2001. "Circumstance and Choice: The Role of Initial Conditions and Policies in Transition Economies." *World Bank Economic Review* 15 (1): 1–31.

Economist. 2010. "Yukos Haunts Rosneft: A Spectre of Litigation." *The Economist.* March 25, 2010.

Edwards, C. 1990. *Protection and Policy in the Malaysian Manufacturing Sector.* Vienna: UNIDO.

Fafchamps, M., S. El Hamine, and A. Zeufack. 2008. "Learning to Export: Evidence from Moroccan Manufacturing." *Journal of African Economies* 17 (2): 305–55.

Farole, T. 2010. *Second Best? Investment Climate and Performance in Africa's Special Economic Zones.* World Bank Policy Research Working Paper No. 5447, Washington, DC: World Bank.

Findlay, R., and S. Wellisz. 1993. *Five Small Open Economies: The Political Economy of Poverty, Equity and Growth.* New York: Oxford University Press.

Gang, F. 2001. "The Chinese Road to the Market: Achievements and Long-Term Sustainability." In *Transition and Institutions,* edited by A. G. Cornia and V. Popov, 78–93. Oxford, UK: Oxford University Press.

Glick, P., and F. Roubaud. 2006. "Export Processing Zone Expansion in Madagascar: What Are the Labor Market and Gender Impacts?" *Journal of African Economies* 15 (4): 722–56.

Golley, J. 1999. *Regional Development and Government Policy in China's Transitional Economy.* UNU/WIDER Research in Progress 20. Helsinki: UNU/WIDER.

IMF (International Monetary Fund). 2002. *Mauritius: Selected Issues and Statistical Appendix.* IMF Staff Country Report 02/144. Washington, DC: International Monetary Fund.

Islam, I., and A. Chowdhury. 1997. *Asia-Pacific Economies.* London: Routledge.

Jayanthakumaran, K. 2003. "Benefit-Cost Appraisals of Export Processing Zones: A Survey of the Literature." *Development Policy Review* 21 (1): 51–65.

Johnston, M. F. 1999. "Beyond Regional Analysis: Manufacturing Zones, Urban Employment and Spatial Inequality in China." *China Quarterly* 161: 1–21.

Lau, L. J., Y. Qian, and G. Roland. 2000. "Reform without Losers: An Interpretation of China's Dual-Track Approach to Transition." *Journal of Political Economy* 108: 120–43.

Li, S., S. Li, and W. Zhang. 2000. "The Road to Capitalism: Competition and Institutional Change in China." *Journal of Comparative Economics* 28: 269–92.

Litwack, J., and Y. Qian. 1998. "Balanced or Unbalanced Development: Special Economic Zones as Catalysts for Transition." *Comparative Economics* 26 (1): 117–41.

Murphy, K., A. Shliefer, and R. Vishny. 1989. "Industrialisation and the Big Push." *Journal of Political Economy* 97 (5): 1003–26.

Ndulu, B. J., S. A. O'Connell, J.-P. Azam, R. H. Bates, A. K. Fosu, J. W. Gunning, and D. Njinkeu. 2008. *The Political Economy of Economic Growth in Africa 1960–2000*. Cambridge, UK: Cambridge University Press.

Parr, J. B. 1999. "Growth Pole Strategies in Regional Economic Planning: A Retrospective View. Part 2. Implementation and Outcome." *Urban Studies* 36 (8): 1247–68.

Salleh, I. M., and S. D. Meyanathan. 1993. *Malaysia: Growth, Equity and Structural Transformation*. Washington, DC: World Bank.

Tuominen, K., and E. Lamminen. 2009. *Russian Special Economic Zones*. Turku: Turku School of Economics.

Watson, P. L. 2001. *Export Processing Zones: Has Africa Missed the Boat? Not Yet.* Washington, DC: World Bank.

World Bank. 2009. *From Privilege to Competition: Unlocking Private-Led Growth in MENA*. Washington, DC: World Bank.

World Bank. 2010. *China's investment in African Special Economic Zones: Prospects, Challenges and Opportunities.* Economic Premise No. 5. Washington DC: World Bank.

CHAPTER 10

Planned Obsolescence? Export Processing Zones and Structural Reform in Mauritius

Claude Baissac

Introduction

This case study first summarizes the conditions within which the Mauritius Export Processing Zone (MEPZ) was established and the initial policy objectives at its root. It then reviews the major national policy changes that occurred in the early 1980s and how these affected the zone. Following this review, it provides an overview of the MEPZ's performance since its early days and explores the current challenges being faced by the program. Finally, it analyzes the relationship between the MEPZ and broad economic reforms and develops conclusions.

The Policy Environment

Context and Objectives

Following independence in 1968, Mauritius chose a social-democratic path, with a welfare state providing free universal education and health care. Economic production, however, remained in the hands of a narrow elite, highly concentrated in the sugar sector. The MEPZ was created in

1971 in the context of an import-substitution development strategy meant to decrease the economy's heavy reliance on sugar exports, which accounted for 75 percent of exports at the time, and the macroeconomic vulnerabilities this created. Within the broader economic strategy, MEPZ was very much an ad hoc and secondary instrument focused on absorbing surplus labor, with unemployment standing at more than 20 percent and the labor force growing at 3 percent per year. There had been widespread concerns over the long-term socioeconomic and political viability of the island, and these concerns fed into policy formulation and political arrangements.

The exact origin of the MEPZ idea is somewhat disputed. According to Dommen and Dommen (1999) it originated in a Swiss-Mauritian entrepreneur, José Poncini, who opened a factory assembling watch jewels from imported components using imported machinery in 1965. Poncini obtained permission from the Mauritian authorities that all imports would escape duties provided the final product would be exported. This was the catalyst for the creation of the MEPZ some six years later. Paturau (1988) argues that the key initiator was Professor Lim Fat of the University of Mauritius, who proposed the creation of an EPZ in a lecture after a visit to Taiwan, China, in 1969.

If the role of economic entrepreneurs has been widely acknowledged, so are those of Prime Minister Seewoosagur Ramgoolam and Foreign Minister Gaëtan Duval. Duval had been leader of the main opposition party, the *Parti Mauricien Social Democrate* (PMSD), and opposed independence out of concerns it would jeopardize the position of his constituencies, the French and Creole ethnic minorities. In 1969, the PMSD joined Ramgoolam's Mauritian Labor Party to form a coalition government, until both parties were defeated by Paul Beranger's party in 1982, the *Mouvement Militant Mauricien* (MMM).[1] Although Ramgoolam advocated import-substitution, Duval, concerned about further economic marginalization for the Creoles, strongly supported a labor-intensive, export-oriented approach. This demand contributed to support for the passing of the Export Processing Zone Act.[2] As Roberts (1992, 100) notes, regardless of its paternity, "Whoever first brought up the idea of an EPZ for Mauritius, the (Government of Mauritius) is clearly responsible for the steps that led to its creation."

Initial investors were primarily Hong Kong, Chinese firms seeking to bypass European tariffs and quotas by taking advantage of the country's preferential access to the European market. European firms soon joined in, attracted by the country's bilingual population (French and English).

From the start, domestic firms invested significantly in the zone, at first in joint ventures with foreign firms. This investment was allowed by government to limit capital flight. Domestic investment originated from the sugar rent, which resulted from the European guaranteed prices and a series of bumper crops. The zone experienced rapid initial growth, with export growth averaging 9 percent per year between 1972 and 1977. By 1977, the MEPZ employed nearly 20,000 and generated about 50 percent of domestic capital investment.

Economic Crisis and Restructuring

From the mid-1970s, however, government expenditures increased significantly—by about 18 percent per year—notably, through large-scale public sector hiring, wage increases, and food subsidies in the context of serious political instability.[3] The currency rose as the country experienced the effects of Dutch disease, resulting from escalating sugar prices. As sugar prices declined after 1975 and the international economic situation combined to hit the economy hard, the government deficit rose rapidly. Investment dried up, growth collapsed to less than 2 percent in 1979, and foreign reserves all but disappeared.

In 1978, the government called the IMF for emergency assistance. A series of bad crops hurt sugar production badly and more emergency measures were required, including devaluation. In 1981, the World Bank intervened in a context of continued economic crisis and political instability. Stabilization and structural adjustment programs targeted the budget deficit and mounting public debt. The productive sector was liberalized. The economy decisively turned away from import-substitution to export-led growth by the 1982 socialist government.

With this move, the EPZ became a pillar of the development strategy. The objective was a diversified economy initially based on three private sector-led pillars: (1) sugar, (2) the MEPZ, and (3) tourism. This strategy paid off, and the MEPZ experienced explosive growth from 1983 onward (see overview of performance section below). In 1985, it overtook sugar as the primary export earner and employer. Employment in the MEPZ reached nearly 90,000 in 1989, helping to reduce unemployment to less than 3 percent from more than 14 percent in 1984. Principal export markets were France, Germany, Italy, and the United Kingdom. Later, with the implementation of the African Growth and Opportunity Act, the U.S. market became an import destination for Mauritian exports.

From the late 1980s onward, the government actively promoted new sectors while pursuing improved efficiency in existing ones. For instance, in the sugar industry, it encouraged consolidation, despite the negative impact on employment. Tourism was significantly expanded, with new hotels, investment in the flag carrier Air Mauritius, and extensive promotion. The government also pushed for greater productivity in the EPZ.

The launch of the offshore financial sector and the free port in the early 1990s, and then the Cybercity/ICT initiative in the early 2000s and the integrated resort scheme in the mid-2000s, represented continuation in the launch of specialized economic tools capable of ensuring balanced growth, employment, and sustainability in changing international trade and investment conditions.

Overview of MEPZ Performance

The government produces regular in-depth data on the economy and the EPZ. This section highlights the MEPZ's key performance indicators since 1973.[4]

Firms and employment demographics have been closely related over the life of the zone, with average employment per firm remaining between 130 and 200, showing a progressive decline over time (see figure 10.1). The curve shows a number of distinct phases: (1) rapid

Figure 10.1 Employment Data

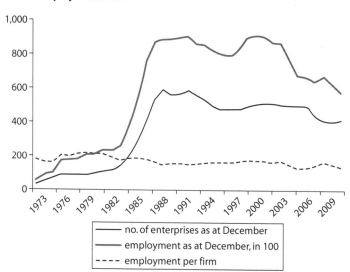

no. of enterprises as at December
employment as at December, in 100
- - - - employment per firm

Source: Government of Mauritius, *Mauritius Productivity and Competitiveness Indicators: 1999–2000* (Port Louis, Mauritius: Central Statistical Office, 2010).

growth until 1976, (2) slow growth between 1976 and 1983, (3) explosive growth between 1983 and 1988, (4) stabilization between 1989 and 1991, (5) decline between 1992 and 1997, (6) recovery in 1998–2002, and (7) continuous decline since 2003. As at December 2009, employment was at its lowest level since 1986.

Investment (in 1982 prices, starting in 1979) shows greater variability within the same general trend (see figure 10.2): (1) decline between 1979 and 1982; (2) explosive growth between 1983 and 1989; (3) decline between 1990 and 1992; (4) cycles of recoveries and declines between 1993 and 2003; (5) strong recovery between 2004 and 2007, that year being the highest recorded; and (6) collapse with the global economic crisis in 2008 and 2009.

Export performance (see figure 10.3) and value added in constant prices (1982) again has followed a similar general trend.[5] Value added peaked at 3.2 billion rupees in 2001.

Sectoral data are available only since 1992. The most remarkable facts are (1) the absolute dominance of the apparel sector; (2) its continued decline in relative and absolute terms in relation to the number of firms, employment, and exports; and (3) the absence of one or several sectors compensating for this decline. Indeed the growth of emerging sectors

Figure 10.2   Investment Data

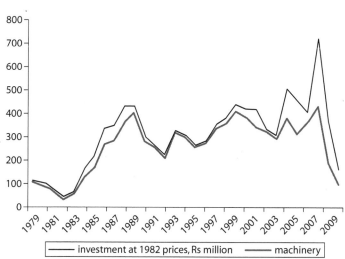

Source: Government of Mauritius, *Mauritius Productivity and Competitiveness Indicators: 1999–2000* (Port Louis, Mauritius: Central Statistical Office, 2010).

Figure 10.3   Exports

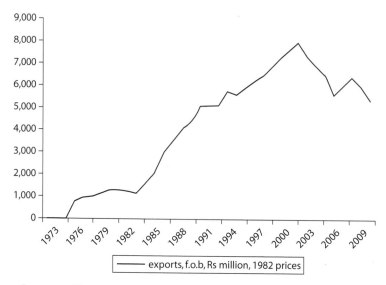

Source: Government of Mauritius, *Mauritius Productivity and Competitiveness Indicators: 1999–2000* (Port Louis, Mauritius: Central Statistical Office, 2010).

such as fish products, and to a lesser extent gems and jewelry, has so far proven insufficient, notably in terms of export performance and employment.

Figure 10.4 clearly illustrates the dependency of the MEPZ on the apparel sector. Not surprisingly, as the Mauritian economy has continued to diversify over the past decade the MEPZ has declined in relation to the rest of the economy. Manufacturing as a whole, which is highly concentrated in the MEPZ, represented 24 percent of GDP in 1998; it declined to just 18.6 percent by 2006.

Although these figures indicate secular decline, closer analysis shows that nuance may be required in interpreting the implications of these trends for the future of the MEPZ. For example, evidence indicates that the productivity of labor has not declined when measured through the zone's export intensity (exports and employment). As shown in figure 10.5, export intensity has increased steadily since 1987, although it decreased during the early part of the boom. This suggests that efficiency in labor utilization decreased as labor costs were low, given its abundance. Data show the same trend when measuring the productivity of labor through value added. It follows a curve closely aligned to that of export intensity. The productivity of firms shows a similar trend.

Figure 10.4   Sectoral Share of Exports

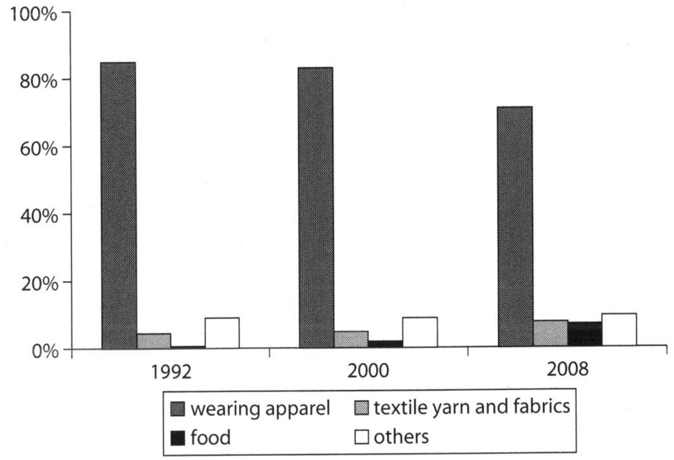

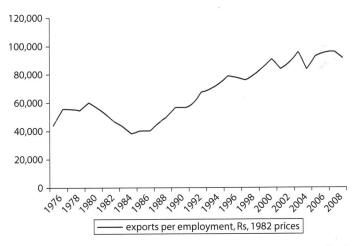

Source: Government of Mauritius, *Mauritius Productivity and Competitiveness Indicators: 1999–2000* (Port Louis, Mauritius: Central Statistical Office, 2010).

Figure 10.5   Exports per Employment

Source: Government of Mauritius, *Mauritius Productivity and Competitiveness Indicators: 1999–2000* (Port Louis, Mauritius: Central Statistical Office, 2010).

Similarly, the export productivity of investment has shown resiliency, as demonstrated in figure 10.6. This indicator experienced rapid decline in 1979–1981, remained low in the early part of the boom years, and subsequently recovered. It fell after 2000, but recovered from 2004 onward. The government's drive toward greater productivity (see box 10.1),

Figure 10.6   Measures of Export Productivity

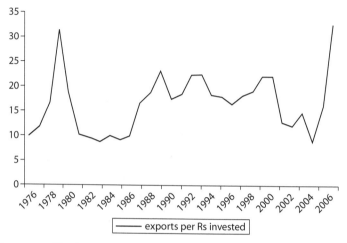

Source: Government of Mauritius, *Mauritius Productivity and Competitiveness Indicators: 1999–2000* (Port Louis, Mauritius: Central Statistical Office, 2010).

Box 10.1

Targeting Productivity Improvements in the EPZs

The government of Mauritius created the Export Processing Zone Development Authority (EPZDA) in 1992 to support technology acquisition, skills development, and efficiency improvement. EPZDA, together with the Mauritius Export Development and Investment Authority (MEDIA), was absorbed in the Mauritius Industrial Development Authority in 2000, replaced in 2005 by Enterprise Mauritius. Also, in 1999 the government launched the National Productivity and Competitiveness Council (NPCC), a tripartite body whose goal is to "stimulate and generate productivity and quality consciousness and drive the productivity and quality movement in all sectors of the economy with a view to raising national output and achieving sustained growth and international competitiveness" (NPCC Act of 1999). In 2003, the government launched the Textile Emergency Support Team, cochaired by government and business, and focused on restructuring the industry through (1) productivity enhancements; (2) financial management and debt restructuring; and (3) international marketing.

Source: Author.

which increased in 1992, clearly has had an impact as export intensity in 2008 was 2.4 times and the export productivity of investment was 3.4 times that of 1985.

Today's Challenges

Current challenges to the export processing zone include (1) relatively low and unstable FDI, (2) rising labor and operating costs, (3) increased competition from LDCs in a liberalizing trade environment, and (4) absence of an industrial sector capable of replacing apparels as an employment-intensive alternative.

FDI

FDI has rarely exceeded 5 percent of GDP. Even during the MEPZ boom years, it exceeded this mark only in 1990 and 1991. On the one hand, it is possible, given the evidence that the presence of multinationals fosters technology transfers, that this low attraction of FDI has affected the performance of the MEPZ, and the island's growth and development path as a whole. On the other hand, it is possible that this lack of FDI has exerted pressure on the government and the domestic sector to acquire technology through other means, including contract manufacturing, joint ventures, vocational training, and the acquisition of up-to-date production technologies. This is supported by data. Indeed, although FDI has been low, domestic private sector investment has never been below 15 percent of GDP since 1985 and has often been over 20 percent.

Cost Structure

Unlike many countries that have embarked on EPZ strategies, Mauritius has not been aggressive in seeking to keep real wages low through labor market and exchange rate policies. Mauritius' wages were 25 percent of those of Hong Kong, China, and Singapore in the early 1980s. They have increased rapidly since then. For instance, wages in the EPZ more than doubled between 1992 and 2004, although they remained lower than in the rest of the economy. In 2002, Mauritius' labor costs were significantly higher than those of major apparel producers.[6] To partly compensate, a regional division of labor between Mauritius and Madagascar has developed since the 1990s, controlled by Mauritian firms.[7] Labor costs in Madagascar were one-third of those in Mauritius. This overseas expansion of Mauritian firms has continued, with apparel groups operating in South and East Asia.

From a competitiveness standpoint, Mauritius long benefited from wise utilization of the preferential trade agreements it secured from the American and European markets. It capitalized on the African, Caribbean and Pacific Sugar Protocol from 1975 to September 2009, when it expired. It also capitalized on the MFA, which expired in January 2005. Although it actively opposed the end of these frameworks, it also sought to prepare its industries for the new order, as well as its economy—notably through productivity-enhancing measures and the launch of new sectoral initiatives (such as the Cybercity and the conversion of least productive sugar-producing lands to other uses). Nevertheless, the competitiveness of Mauritius' apparel industry has declined, notably for lower cost and higher volume items. From 2003 on, the MEPZ lost some key foreign investors and more than 25,000 jobs. Most of these investors transferred their operations to China. The recovery of exports and investment in 2004, however, shows some resiliency as a result of markets diversification, notably toward the European Union and regional markets like South Africa and Madagascar.

Diversification

Efforts to diversify *within* the EPZ have had limited success, and the zone's core activities have remained largely concentrated on apparel. Endeavors to increase textile manufacturing have born limited results. Diversification has essentially taken place "outside" of the MEPZ, although the fish-product sector, part of an expanding cluster called the seafood hub, has shown remarkable growth. With an economic value added of more than US$320 million in 2007, it combines activities such as licensing and services of fishing vessels, aquaculture, exports of unprocessed fish and processed fish, and more. Inside the MEPZ, the focus has been specialization and increased productivity. Most of the diversification has taken place outside of manufacturing and processing altogether, particularly in the growth of the services sector, including ICT services, financial services, and the well-established tourism sector.

Although challenges exist, there is evidence of adjustment outside the traditional MEPZ sector and of resiliency within it. This is supported by Ancharaz's (2009) detailed analysis of Mauritius' revealed comparative advantage against China for the island's 10 main apparel exports for the period 2000–2007. It managed to maintain competitiveness, and in some cases to increase its competitiveness, in products like knitted T-shirts and shirts, blouses, and shirt blouses. While other products have suffered, new products have emerged. Thus, evidence indicates that the diversification failure has been somewhat mitigated by the productivity gains and the growth of Mauritian-owned companies that have attained autonomy from the foreign companies they used to be partners with. Today, Mauritius is the world's second producer of knitwear, the third exporter for pure wool garments, and the fourth supplier of T-shirts to the European market.

The MEPZ and Economic Reform

Although the MEPZ started in the early 1970s and achieved impressive results during its first decade, it rose to international prominence during its "boom" time of the mid-1980s, attracting much policy attention and becoming a valued subject of research and analysis. The question of the relationship between the MEPZ and economic reform has also been well researched, notably, since the late 1980s. The Mauritius case has attracted the attention of distinguished institutions and economists, who have explored this relationship both for the sake of assisting the island's economic development and that of deriving useful generalizations.

In considering the many assessments of the MEPZ, it is possible to summarize the key question many researchers have attempted to answer as follows: *Was the MEPZ a manifestation of reform, or was it the cause of it?*

Setting aside the question of the cost benefit of the MEPZ and its net contribution to Mauritius' relatively rapid economic growth (cf. Gulhati and Nallari 1990; Jaycox 1992; Sawkut et al. 2009; World Bank 1989), perhaps the most important impact of the MEPZ was in the political economic context, as a catalyst for reforms in the country. For these perspectives, the EPZ is a manifestation of this export-oriented strategy, formulated and implemented by a strongly developmental state.

This export-oriented approach has been taken up by previous researchers. For example, Kearney (1990) argued Mauritius' economic success could be attributed to its government having replicated the strategy of the so-called newly industrializing countries (NICs), with policy makers being "pragmatic, bold, innovative, and closely attentive to the NIC experience" (Kearney 1990, 207), and the government being the country's "leading entrepreneur." To Meisenhelder (1997, 288), the export-oriented strategy chosen by government cannot be reduced to structural adjustment, but rather it represents an indigenous reform endeavor that is the expression of the existence of a developmental state, characterized by "a capable and relatively autonomous state bureaucracy . . . it was local bureaucrats—with the help from academics and the Meade report—who recognized the potential of export-led industrialization for the creation of economic growth, and who used state authority and resources to implement it."

This theme of the Mauritius developmental state has been a regular feature. Carroll and Carroll (1997) note the essential role of a competent bureaucracy, capable of formulating policies (either in response to demands or in anticipation of them), obtaining support, and implementing them. Evidence of this is found in the political and legislative process that established the MEPZ and described above in "The policy environment." It is worth mentioning that the government—once Ramgoolam was won to the cause—worked with little initial support from its own ranks, including labor and business, and needed to address resistance to the project. Particularly opposed to the EPZ solution were the sugar barons, who were at the helm of the largest sector of the economy, and the virulent MMM, for different reasons. Although the first group was concerned about the negative consequence of the EPZ on labor supply and cost, the second opposed further inserting Mauritius within the international capitalist system. In addition to convincing these groups that the EPZ would "ultimately benefit all Mauritians" (Roberts 1992, 101), the government had to win assent from the legislature.

In addition to its strategic role, government and the state apparatus took a central role in implementing the EPZ and adapting it over the years. As described by Bheenick and Shapiro (1991),

> The government soon realized that it would have to strengthen the capacity of the Ministry of Commerce and Industry to make the EPZ approach work. To bolster its staff size and expertise, assistance was secured under bilateral and multilateral foreign aid programmes. This facilitated the creation of new cells for projects evaluation, monitoring, investment promotion, export marketing, funding of projects, and provision of insurance to protect exporters against defaults by importers. While foreign consulting firms were initially used, they were replaced as soon as Mauritian authorities gained needed experience. (264–65)

Measures taken included the creation within the Ministry of Industry of an Industrial Coordination Unit in charge of simplifying the investment process in the EPZ, and later, MEDIA, a parastatal organization whose mission was to promote exports, engage in investment promotion, develop and operate industrial estates, and plan and implement export-oriented manufacturing.

Dommen and Dommen (1994, 25) have argued that, in all, the choice of export-oriented growth and its early implementation through the MEPZ led to an increase in state involvement in economic management. Although the Ramgoolam government of the 1970s was keen on leaving "the choice of industry to the imagination of the private sector, limiting Government's role to setting the legal and policy environment, the Jugnauth government has been willing to take initiatives in pointing directions for the private sector."

From this perspective, it is evident that the creation of the MEPZ represented reform: it constituted the principal policy instrument through which the island transitioned from an import-substitution growth model to a dual economic regime.

Although this is undoubtedly true, one should not overstate the case of a "grand reform strategy." As indicated in "The policy environment," the MEPZ was at inception a "problem-solving tool" given the specific function of absorbing labor surplus within an economic (and political economic) enclave. Evidence of that exists in the fact that the two development plans of the period (1971–1975 and 1975–1980) do not give any clear indication of a shedding of a replacement of import-substitution with export-oriented growth. Furthermore, evidence is provided by the fact that protection remained high. According to Subramanian (2009),

> During the 1970s and 1980s, Mauritius remained a highly protected economy: the average rate of protection was high and dispersed. In 1980, the average effective protection exceeded 100 per cent, and although this diminished by the end of the 1980s, it was still very high (65 per cent). Moreover until the 1980s, there were also extensive quantitative restrictions in the form of import licensing, covering nearly 60 per cent of imports... An alternative scheme of classification that has been devised in the IMF ranked Mauritius as one of the most protected economies in the early 1990s. (15)

This is a critical part of the story of the political economy impact of the zones. MEPZs did not represent liberalization across the board; rather, they coexisted with a strategy of import-substituting industrialization. Indeed, this was the necessary political balance required to appease the traditional industrial elites that opposed reform. As Rodrik (2004) notes,

The creation of the EPZ generated new profit opportunities, without taking protection away from the import-substituting groups. The segmentation of labor markets was particularly crucial in this regard, as it prevented the expansion of the EPZ (which employed mainly female labor) from driving wages up in the rest of the economy, and thereby disadvantaging import-substituting industries. New profit opportunities were created at the margin, while leaving old opportunities undisturbed. (12)

If there was a grand reform strategy toward export-oriented growth, it was piecemeal and pragmatic—spurred in part by the following:

- The structural reforms of the late 1970s and early 1980s.[8] Restraints on government expenditures and the reform of the incentive structure played a key role in the post-1984 prosperity.
- The success of the nontraditional export sector (i.e., the EPZ). And this strategy did not simply equate to lesser state intervention.

For Rodrik (2004), the island's development path has represented an incarnation of the transitional growth model combining "elements of orthodoxy with unorthodox institutional practices," a path shared with the likes of China; the Republic of Korea; and Taiwan, China.

Conclusion

Static versus Dynamic Impact
Conventional economic assessments and cost-benefit analyses, while useful in their own right, may be too narrow in their focus when trying to assess the MEPZ situation. This is because they fail to quantify some of the critical dynamic impacts that successful zones programs can catalyze, particularly those involving political-economic processes of reform.

Ultimately, it is speculation to imagine a counterfactual scenario for Mauritius, but it is not counterintuitive to advance the hypothesis that without the MEPZ, or with a "cheaper" MEPZ, or with an MEPZ with higher wages in the 1970s and 1980s, it is probable that its growth rate would have been lower. Beyond the reduced static impact, its dynamic impact would have been less. This in turn would probably have had negative consequences on the island's overall strategy of diversification, would have maintained high dependency on sugar, and may have led to continuing Dutch disease, capital flights, and sociopolitical instability.

This is not to say that resources could not have been better utilized. Evidence suggests that they could have been. But excluding the dynamic perspective, the analysis thus misses the key point of the Mauritian experience: the impact of the MEPZ on the island's path from colonial monoculture to a sustainable, diversified economy operating within the international economic system achieving high rankings in political, economic, and social governance. The zone has played an immense role in the secular transformation of the island, attracting FDI, generating massive technology transfers, integrating Mauritius into global commodity chains, and leading the way toward the creation of a series of growth poles (the Freeport, the International Banking Center, the Integrated Resort Scheme, the Cybercity, the new SEZ, etc.) whose combined effect has been enormous.

Also of fundamental importance has been the contribution of the zone to political stability, through the provision of employment and the creation of a "virtuous cycle" of growth and development. Overall, the MEPZ has acted as an important contributor to transforming the island into Africa's premier country in many comparative rankings. It has consistently ranked first in the Mo Ibrahim Index on African Governance. It has topped the World Bank's *Doing Business Index* in Africa, improving its global position to 17 in 2010. The social benefits of these changes have been enormous, and some part of these benefits is directly and indirectly imputable to the MEPZ.

The Long-Term View

Indeed, the MEPZ represents one phase in the island's secular path, but it is one that has been critical to its long-term development. The island's economy has experienced four principal phases in its economic history since the mid-19th century: (1) export-oriented colonial monoculture (before the mid-1950s); (2) a mix regime of import substitution and export monoculture (between the mid-1950s and circa 1981); (3) export-led growth (between circa 1981 and circa 2005); and (4) toward the open economy, the "duty-free island" initiative (since circa 2005).

The latest strategy represents a radical break with the previous paradigm that provided a set of sector-specific special regimes and associated infrastructure while the domestic economy remained relatively protected by tariff barriers, quotas, restrictions on investment and activities, and a relatively high tax burden. This evolution aims at turning Mauritius toward the Singapore and Hong Kong, China, model, in which the entire economy creates a low-tax environment acting as a trade, financial, tourism, and specialized-manufacturing platform. This latest restructuring is critical, as the new international trading order and the global recession have affected Mauritius hard: the national growth rate has been below 5 percent for three consecutive years for the first time in a generation.

This restructuring is progressive, with tax and trade measures being implemented slowly. One such policy has been the harmonization of the tax regime, whereby EPZ and domestic corporate tax rates have been aligned at 15 percent. Another is trade policy, through which the average tariff has decreased from 19.9 percent in 2001 to 6.6 percent in 2007. In the intervening period, however, tariffs have increased for some commodities manufacturing in Mauritius.[9]

As for the future, it is likely that even as the world economy recovers the apparel industry will not return to Mauritius in the numbers observed in the past. Although this will present a significant challenge, adaptation to changing international conditions is in the makeup of the MEPZ, and the relative decline of the zone has been integrated into government policy and private sector strategy. Thus, while the size of the MEPZ will continue to decline in absolute and relative terms, it will increase its focus on specialized and high-end products, with Mauritian firms continuing to lead the way. If it is unlikely that other sectors of the MEPZ will compensate for the decline in firms and employment, sectors outside of the MEPZ will partially do so. For instance, the food-processing industry has experienced significant growth. So, too, have financial services, whose share of GDP has been more than 10 percent since 2003. This is more than tourism.

Some will see in the relative decline of the MEPZ proof of its nonsustainability, but this decline also may be interpreted as the very proof of its success. The MEPZ will have achieved the secular role it was assigned in the early 1980s, following its unexpected growth in the 1970s. The MEPZ it will have played a key catalytic role at two levels: (1) it fostered high private domestic investment in export-oriented nontraditional manufacturing, which resulted in a dynamic private sector opened to the world economy and investing in foreign countries (including in EPZs and SEZs) to maintain its competitiveness; and (2) it encouraged the government to commit to further economic diversification and progressively open the economy to trade and investment. China's choice of the island as a location for one of its five African Trade and Economic Cooperation zones is testimony to its unique position in Africa.

It is worth quoting Subramanian (2009):

> In the face of these challenges, the question often posed is: what will Mauritius do next? What industries or services will replace the inevitable decline of

sugar and clothing? While these may be interesting questions, they are almost certainly the wrong ones for outsiders to ask. The key point is that Mauritius has reached a stage of development and maturity and sophistication that, long before the outside world had even recognized the looming challenges, the Mauritian domestic system had started the necessary processes to confront them. Whether Mauritius upgrades into high-value added financial services or information technology (this is already happening), one can be confident that Mauritius will figure out a way. The world can, in fact, stop worrying about Mauritius because it has demonstrated the ability to worry for itself. (22)

Notes

1. Political parties did and continue to have either English or French names, depending on their main constituencies and sources of ideological inspiration. MMM used Creole, and not French, as its political language.

2. The 1971 *4-year Plan for Social and Economic Development, 1971–1975*, the first of a long series of such plans, explicitly recognized the limited impact and scope of ISI: "Industrialisation, apart from the processing of agricultural crops—sugar and tea—for export, has been almost wholly geared to meeting the requirements of the small domestic market and therefore limited in scope" (pp. v–vi).

3. The governing coalition of the MLP and PMSD confronted the MMM from 1971 on with expansionary social spending on the one hand and repression on the other, declaring a state of emergency that was lifted only in 1975. At the time, the MMM was calling for the nationalization of the sugar industry and radical social changes.

4. The prices used here are constant prices, based on 1982 value in Mauritian rupees. Although this provides a "real" perspective into the performance of the zone, it significantly undervalues its performance at current prices.

5. No data are available for 1973–1976 constant prices.

6. According to the Economist Intelligence Unit (cited by Ancharaz 2009), Mauritius labor costs in the clothing industry were US$1.25 per hour, versus US$0.39 in Bangladesh, between US$0.68 and US$0.88 in China, US$0.77 in Egypt, US$0.38 in India, US$0.38 in Kenya, US$0.33 in Madagascar, US$2.45 in Mexico, US$1.38 in South Africa, and US$0.48 in Sri Lanka.

7. In 2000, it was estimated that two large Mauritian firms, Floreal and CMT, employed 9,000 workers in Malagasy EPZ factories.

8. Bowman (1991, 122) advanced that "the sustained commitment of the Mauritian government and the political opposition to the structural adjustment program set the stage for a resounding economic performance in the middle and late 1980s."

9. Footwear, apparel, sugar products, and beverages, for instance.

References

Ancharaz, V. 2009. "David V. Goliath: Mauritius Facing Up to China." *European Journal of Development Research* 21 (4): 622–43.

Bheenick, R., and M. O. Shapiro. 1991. "The Mauritian Export Processing Zone." *Public Administration and Development* 11: 263–67.

Bowman, L. 1991. *Mauritius: Democracy and Development in the Indian Ocean.* Boulder, CO: Westview Press.

Carroll, B. W., and T. Carroll. 1997. "State and Ethnicity in Botswana and Mauritius." *The Journal of Development Studies* 33 (4): 464–86.

Dommen, B., and E. Dommen. 1999. *Mauritius: The Roots of Success. A Retrospective Study, 1960–1993.* Oxford, UK: James Currey.

Government of Mauritius. 1999. *National Productivity and Competitiveness Act 1999.* Act No. 9 of 1999, 14 May, 1999.

Government of Mauritius. 2010. *Mauritius Productivity and Competitiveness Indicators: 1999–2009.* Port Louis: Central Statistical Office.

Gulhati, R., and R. Nallari. 1990. *Successful Stabilization and Recovery in Mauritius.* Washington, DC: World Bank.

Jaycox, E. V. 1992. "Sub-Saharan Africa: Development Performance and Prospects." *Journal of International Affairs* 46 (1): 81–95.

Kearney, R. C. 1990. "Mauritius and the NIC Model Redux: Or, How Many Cases Make a Model?" *Journal of Developing Areas,* 24 (2): 195–216.

Meisenhelder, T. 1997. "The Developmental State in Mauritius." *The Journal of Modern African Studies* 35 (2): 279–97.

Paturau, J. M. 1988. *Historie economique de l'ile Maurice.* Port Louis: Le Pailles.

Roberts, M. W. 1992. *Export Processing Zones in Jamaica and Mauritius. Evolution of an Export-Oriented Model.* San Francisco: Mellen Research University Press.

Rodrik, D. 2004. *Getting Institutions Right.* CESifo DICE Report, Cambridge, MA: Harvard University.

Sawkut, R., V. Sannassee, and S. Fowdar. 2009. "The Net Contribution of the Mauritian Export Processing Zone Using Cost-Benefit Analysis." *Journal of International Development* 21: 379–92.

Subramanian, A. 2009. *The Mauritian Success Story and Its Lessons.* UNU-WIDER Research Papers No. 2009/36. Helsinki: UNU-WIDER.

World Bank. 1989. *Mauritius, Managing Success.* Washington, DC: World Bank.

PART III

Social and Environmental Sustainability: Emerging Issues for SEZs

CHAPTER 11

The Gender Dimension of Special Economic Zones[1]

Sheba Tejani

Introduction

It is impossible to discuss the full developmental and social consequences of SEZs[2] without considering the gender dimension. Women constitute more than 50 percent and in some cases 90 percent of employment in SEZs in developing countries. Given such high levels of female employment in SEZs and the important role of SEZs in developing-country exports, we can fairly conclude that export-oriented industrialization over the past 30 years has been a distinctly gendered process. The purpose of this chapter is to describe and explain the remarkable degree of "feminization"[3] of work in SEZs in the recent era of export-oriented industrialization. The following section discusses the scholarly literature on trade and the feminization of labor. The third section offers a synthetic theory of feminization, building on the extensive research on industrial upgrading in global value chains. The fourth section reviews the evidence of the female intensity of SEZ employment. The fifth section presents the main characteristics of the quality of female employment in SEZs, and the sixth section attempts to explain recent trends of the defeminization of labor in manufacturing. The final section discusses the policy implications of the analysis and concludes.

Background on Trade and Gender

The link between trade openness and gender was first made when women were drawn into paid employment in manufacturing in unprecedented numbers in Puerto Rico, Ireland, and the East Asian first-tier NICs as they pursued export-oriented growth in the 1960s and 1970s. As these countries promoted light, labor-intensive manufacturing industries, such as textiles, clothing, leather, and footwear in EPZs, the female share of employment rose in may cases to well over 70 percent, a much higher proportion than in the economy as a whole. Later, as developing countries in Southeast Asia, South Asia, Latin America, and Eastern Europe adopted export-oriented industrialization, trade expansion became strongly associated with a demand for female labor. Industrialization in low-income countries was characterized as both "female-dependent as well as export-led" (Joekes 1999, 36; also see Joekes 1995). Kusago and Tzannatos (1998), for instance, report the high proportion of female labor in SEZs in the Republic of Korea, Malaysia, Mauritius, Philippines, and Sri Lanka in the late 1980s and early 1990s. Joekes (1999, 35) sums up the situation: "In effect, in developing countries, new job openings for women have been dependent on the expansion of production for exports, and formal sector manufacturing employment opportunities for women in developing countries are now concentrated in production for exports."

In fact, it was argued that trade liberalization, rising international competition, and labor deregulation had led to a "global feminization of labor" in which women were being substituted for men across sectors and employment categories (Standing 1989, 1999). A number of other studies confirmed these findings of a positive correlation between greater trade openness or export orientation and the feminization of labor (e.g., see Cagatay and Berik 1990; Cagatay and Ozler 1995; Ozler 2000; Wood 1991).

Many of the women employed in export-oriented manufacturing were previously agricultural or informal workers, such as in East Asia, or were entering the labor force for the first time as in Latin America (Horton 1999). Although the wages they earned might have been lower than men, paid employment allowed women relatively stable access to cash income that otherwise might not have been available in the informal or agricultural sector. Women's entry into export-oriented manufacturing thus has been described as a double-edged and contradictory phenomenon, in which some structures of gender inequality have eroded even as others have been constructed anew (Elson 2007, 8). Evidence indicates that access to paid employment increased women's self-confidence and assertiveness and led to an improvement in their influence and standing in the household (Jayaweera 2003, cited in Elson 2007; Kabeer 2000; Zhang 2007). Factory employment afforded women opportunities to exit the sphere of familial control as well as situations of domestic violence, to gain financial independence, and to expand their personal autonomy and life choices. But social norms dictate that women do not always control the income they earn, and paid work adds to the household work for which women assume primary responsibility, leaving them less time for rest and leisure. Besides, women generally remained confined to low-paid and low-productivity activities in export-oriented manufacturing that had harsh working conditions and few opportunities for advancement. These issues are explored further below.

Reasons for the Feminization of Labor[4]

What are the reasons for this feminization of export-oriented production? One view is that the gender wage gap[5] has led to a high demand for female labor in an environment of rising international competition. Early observers commented that firms preferred women for export-related production because they provided cheap labor and because gender stereotypes attributed women with dexterity ("nimble fingers"), docility, and submissiveness—traits that employers considered desirable for labor intensive work (Elson and Pearson 1981).[6] Standing (1989, 1999) claimed that employers seeking to expand exports hired women to lower labor costs in the face of severe international competition, to raise flexibility in response to fluctuations in product demand, and to minimize the bargaining power of workers on issues of working conditions, overtime, workplace safety, and collective bargaining.

More recently, Seguino (2000a) has shown the gender wage gap to be particularly relevant to the rapid export and GDP growth of East Asian countries for the period 1975 to 1995.[7] She shows in some detail that "[l]ow female wages have spurred investment and exports by lowering unit labor costs and providing the foreign exchange to purchase capital and intermediate goods which raise productivity and growth rates" (Seguino 2000a, 27). In a cross-country study, Busse and Spielman (2006) find that gender wage inequality is positively correlated with comparative advantage in labor-intensive production or that countries with a higher gender wage gap have higher exports of such goods. Mitra-Kahn and Mitra-Kahn (2007) report that the relationship between gender wage inequality and growth for 20 developing countries is nonlinear: during the early stages of export-oriented (and labor-intensive) industrialization, wage inequality is positively related to growth, but at later stages, it may hurt growth. Ghosh (2002, 20) argues that the feminization of labor in East Asia was highly dependent on the "relative inferiority of remuneration and working conditions" of women. As evident in table 11.1, a substantial gender wage gap still exists in the manufacturing sector in many countries, although it has mostly narrowed over time.

Apart from the gender wage gap, gender norms and stereotypes segment workers into particular types of economic activities on the basis

Table 11.1   Female Wages as a Percentage of Male Wages in Manufacturing

Country	1985	1990	1998	2001
Transition Economies				
Bulgaria			73	70[6]
Georgia			63	63
Hungary			69[5]	73[6]
Latvia			88	84
Asia				
Hong Kong SAR, China		69	61	65
Malaysia	49	50	63[4]	
Myanmar	99		96	112[5]
Republic of Korea	47	50	56	58
Singapore		55	58	59
Sri Lanka	70	88	83	86
Indonesia				92
Philippines			80	90
Thailand		64[2]		72
Latin America				
Costa Rica	74.	74	80	81[6]
El Salvador	81	94	75	92
Brazil	51[1]	54	59	61
Mexico			71	70
Middle East				
Bahrain	83	62	45	44[5]
Egypt, Arab Republic of	68	68	69	75[e]
Jordan	62	57	60	68[e]
Sub-Saharan Africa				
Botswana			54	52[6]
Kenya	76	73	48	
Swaziland	72	88	87[3]	

Source: UNCTAD (2004), table 5; expanded by author using ILO (2009).
Note: 1 = 1988; 2 = 1991; 3 = 1995; 4 = 1997; 5 = 1999; 6 = 2000.

of sex and contribute to the feminization of export-oriented production. The segmentation of occupations by sex remains a pervasive and global phenomenon.[8] Mechanisms such as the gender-typing of jobs as "masculine" or "feminine," differentiating the abilities and roles of workers on the basis of sex during recruitment and promotion, and devaluing the work done by women both create and reproduce social hierarchies in the workplace. Thus, the belief that women are dexterous, docile, and unsuitable for "heavy" or technical work leads to their recruitment in labor-intensive activities that have lower pay and fewer opportunities for advancement.[9] Gender hierarchies that elevate males to "breadwinner" status while designating females as secondary income earners also confine women to low-wage and insecure jobs while placing men in positions with better prospects (Seguino, Berik, and Rodgers 2010, 6). Women have rapidly closed the gender gap in education at the primary and secondary level so the argument that they lack the necessary skills to perform in higher skill occupations is not a sufficient explanation for this segmentation (for an exploration of this issue, see Tejani and Milberg 2010). Instead, persistent discrimination against women in the labor market is the more likely explanation.

The argument can then be made that export-oriented industrialization became female dominated because its sectoral composition was low value added and labor intensive, which lent itself to the segmentation of work by sex. This is confirmed by Caraway (2007, 155) who shows that feminization in the aggregate is the result of the balance of employment between labor- and capital-intensive sectors in manufacturing and that early export-oriented industrialization was female intensive because it was labor intensive. In fact, the segmentation of women within labor-intensive export industries, in which the price elasticity of demand is high, can keep women's wages artificially low by restricting their bargaining power (Seguino 2000b, 1214). Historically, too, the feminization of labor has been associated with a downgrading of status and pay in such professions as clerical work (Horton 1999, 574), nursing, and teaching.

In sum, the feminization of SEZ production is attributed to three broad factors in the literature: women's relative "cheapness" owing to the gender wage gap, rising international competition, and gendered norms and stereotypes that segment work by sex and assign women to low-skill and low-paying work.

Finally, we focus here on the impact of gender inequality on trade to explain why export-oriented production has been female intensive, although the causality can run in both directions in the literature. A number of studies find that increasing trade openness leads to a fall in gender inequality (see Black and Brainerd 2004; Brainerd 2000; Gray, Kittilson, and Sandholtz 2006; Oostendorp 2004), whereas others find that it hurts women in terms of employment, wages, and education (see Baliamoune-Lutz 2006; Berik, Rodgers, and Zveglich 2004; Chamarbagwala 2006; Kongar 2007; Kucera and Milberg 2000; Menon and Rodgers 2008).

The Role of SEZs

Where do SEZs fit in this picture? The purpose of SEZs is to generate employment, attract FDI and new technology, provide foreign market access, and earn foreign exchange through the expansion of exports. The attractiveness of traditional EPZ models to foreign (and in some cases domestic) firms were the elimination of tariffs on imported inputs and exports, low or zero taxation of profits, and the provision of a less stringent regulatory environment with respect to labor laws or at least their relaxed enforcement (Milberg and Amegual 2008, 7). Women were the "unintended beneficiaries"[10] of early zone development in Puerto Rico and Ireland. These countries were among the first to experiment with the export growth model and explicitly oriented their industrialization plans to reduce male unemployment, with Ireland legally requiring at least 75 percent male employment in all new investments, a condition that eventually had to be dropped (Caraway 2007, 19). The Border Industrialization Program that created *maquiladoras* in Mexico was also initially established to generate employment for male agricultural workers returning from the United States to northern Mexico (Caraway 2007, 19). Ironically, in all three cases, zone employment became highly female-intensive.

In subsequent SEZ promotion, however, governments actively sought and facilitated the hiring of women for light manufacturing jobs (Caraway 2007, 20; Lutz 1988), including publicizing the virtues of "oriental female" workers in investment brochures (Elson and Pearson 1981, 93) and ensuring that their wages remained low. As Salzinger (2003, 10, 11, 15) argues, official and global corporate rhetoric at the time firmly established the "trope of productive femininity" in the labor-intensive industries of SEZ production, so that the feminized East Asian model was deliberately emulated in other countries. This trope of productive femininity has currency to this day, as SEZs, which continue to specialize in light manufacturing, also remain largely female dominated.

As SEZs have upgraded their productive activities over time, however, their female intensity of employment has tended to decline. This decline highlights the fact that the feminization of employment is a historically specific and contingent phenomenon in which women tend to predominate in some occupations during particular periods in time.[11] Some other limits to the feminization of labor include worker resistance, including the actions of male-dominated unions that seek to exclude women from formal employment,[12] a closing gender wage gap that may result in a falling demand for female labor, and the willingness of males to accept "feminized" or insecure, low-paying and flexible positions (in this regard, see Barrientos, Kabeer, and Hossain 2004, 6).

The Economics of Female-Intensive Production in SEZs

In this section, we develop a more general argument about the role of women in SEZ employment, by linking feminization to the changing structure of world trade that has occurred with the evolution of global value chains (GVCs). Production has become increasingly fragmented and internationalized, with different activities being carried out in disparate locations and coordinated increasingly through GVCs. Kaplinsky (1998, 13) describes a GVC as "the full range of activities that are required to bring a product from its conception, through its design, its sourced raw materials and intermediate inputs, its marketing, its distribution and its support to the final consumer." The rapidly growing share of intermediate goods in world total merchandise trade is evidence of this phenomenon. For the period 1988 to 2006, world trade of total merchandise tripled (grew by 300 percent), while the intermediate goods component of total merchandise trade quadrupled (grew by 400 percent) (WTO 2008, chart 13, 102).

But what drives a firm's decision to subctontract? Milberg (2004, 60–61) suggests that firms engage in arm's-length subcontracting, rather than intrafirm trade, when the expected cost savings from the former exceed rents from internalization, which is more probable when intermediate product markets are, or can be made, highly competitive.[13] Fostering downstream competition allows lead firms to shave supplier margins, keep supply conditions flexible, and transfer risks onto producers, perpetuating asymmetric market structures that distribute value added across the chain in a highly skewed fashion.[14] When externalization itself fosters competition among suppliers, the asymmetry of market structures can be considered endogenous to the lead firm's strategies (Milberg 2004, 61).

SEZ policies have no doubt spurred this trend of externalization among transnational firms by offering the institutional set-up in developing countries within which costs can be kept low. But developing countries are integrated into GVCs at the low value added segment and "tend to have the most commodified, fragmented and cost-driven portion of the production system," whereas lead firms situated mostly in industrial countries retain the high value added segments (Gereffi 2005, 47). This asymmetry persists over time for a number of reasons: significant entry barriers at higher ends of the chain, capital mobility and the credible threat of firm exit when costs (including wage costs) rise, and low tariffs (especially through SEZs) (Milberg 2004, 67). Despite the notable success of first-, and to a lesser extent, second-tier East Asian NICs in upgrading industrially,[15] most SEZ production remains concentrated in textiles and electronics (Milberg and Amengual 2008). In fact, the entry of a large swathe of developing countries into these low value added activities has led to a "fallacy of composition" effect (Milberg and Amengual 2008, 27), resulting in a flood of imports into industrial countries and rapidly falling prices[16] (Gereffi 2005, 12). The fact that developing countries still face falling terms of trade despite having switched to manufactures to avoid the commodity trap that Prebisch (1950) and Singer (1950) warned of approximately 60 years ago is perhaps emblematic of the global asymmetry in trading relations.[17]

How is gender implicated within this asymmetrical market structure? Given their position in GVCs, producers in developing countries are under great pressure to deliver high-quality products at low cost and under tight shipping deadlines to lead firms (Barrientos 2001, 5). With just-in-time delivery systems and seasonal demand peaks, GVCs also demand a high degree of supply flexibility on the part of producers. The feminization of labor in SEZs plays a critical role in meeting the demands of lead firms in GVCs and protecting their rents by providing a relatively cheap and flexible source of labor for suppliers. As Barrientos (2001, 8) points out, producers located at the weakest positions in the value chain hierarchy are the most likely to use female labor to deal with the risks of price fluctuations and supply volatility. Gender discrimination crowds women into the low value added segment of the chain and puts them in the position of effectively absorbing those risks. Thus, a link exists between the asymmetry of market relations between lead firms and suppliers in GVCs and the segmentation of women in labor-intensive industries generally located in SEZs. Although employment in GVCs can

*gender segmenta-
tion*

provide women much-needed income-earning opportunities, the structural import of gender segmentation within the value chain hierarchy cannot be denied.

Because of women's position within the structure of GVCs, they are particularly vulnerable to fluctuations in export demand and job loss. In the present crisis, female workers who form part of the flexible workforce in labor-intensive industries have been particularly hard-hit with the decline in exports in apparel, footwear, and electronics (Sirimanne 2009, 6). The segment of export activity in which women are concentrated is also highly competitive: China's low unit costs in apparel have seriously undermined the industry in Mexican *maquiladoras* (Sargent and Matthews 2008) with the result that female intensity in EPZ employment has markedly declined. A number of low-income countries, including some in Africa, have experienced a decline in export output with the end of the MFA, with many low-skilled female workers losing jobs as a result (ILO 2005).

Evidence on Gender in SEZs

Exports and Employment

As mentioned in chapter 1, there has been a virtual explosion of SEZs in developing countries since 1975 with the most rapid expansion taking place in the last 20 years. In 2006, 130 countries operated 3,500 zones and employed roughly 66 million people around the globe, with China alone employing 60 percent of all workers (Boyenge 2007). More recently, India passed a controversial SEZ law that is estimated to add another 250 zones and 150,000 workers to that number (Murayama and Yokota 2008, 23). At the same time, zone models have expanded from being manufacturing assembly-type operations to ones that are dedicated to services such as high-tech, finance, logistics, and even tourism (ILO 2008, 2). SEZs are being used to capture markets in business services, IT, and IT-enabled services in countries that have higher skilled workforces, such as India, Russia, and China, although they are not particularly employment intensive (Milberg and Amengual 2008, 7). In terms of scope, SEZs might be enclave type or focused on a single industry, such as jewelry or leather; focused on a single commodity, such as coffee; or house only a single factory or company (ILO 2003, 2).

Table 11.2 presents zone exports as a percentage of total exports for 2002 and 2006 for a selection of countries. Zone exports account for a bulk of total exports for most of the countries reported. Countries such

Table 11.2   SEZ Exports as a Percentage of Total Exports

Country	2000	2006	Change (Percent points)
Philippines	87	60	−27
Malaysia	83	83	0
Mexico	83	47	−36
Kenya	80	87	7
Gabon	80	80	0
Macao SAR, China	80	80	0
Zimbabwe	80	80	0
Vietnam	80	80	0
Dominican Rep.	80	80	0
Tunisia	80	52	−28
Mauritius	77	42	−35
Morocco	61	61	0
Bangladesh	60	76	16
Costa Rica	50	52	2
Haiti	50	50	0
Madagascar	38	80	42
Sri Lanka	33	38	5
Cameroon	32	33	1
Maldives	13	48	35
Colombia	9	40	31

Source: Boyenge (2003, 2007).
Note: The global crisis that started in 2008 has significantly affected export volumes in some of these countries.

as Bangladesh, Madagascar, Colombia, and the Maldives experienced a significant expansion of zone-related exports even during this brief period, whereas the Philippines, Mexico, Tunisia, and Mauritius experienced the reverse trend. Employment in SEZs also expanded moderately in Bangladesh, Malaysia, Honduras, and Nicaragua, while it stayed stable in most other countries except for Mexico, Sri Lanka, and the Dominican Republic (see table 11.3). Despite the rapid expansion of zones, in most regions, direct employment in SEZs does not account for a significant proportion of total employment globally at 0.2 percent (Engman, Onodera, and Pinali 2007, 29). However, their social impact can be significant in pockets of unemployment or underemployment (Engman, Onodera, and Pinali 2007, 29), as well as in smaller countries such as Bangladesh, Sri Lanka, and Mauritius, where the SEZ share of total employment is substantial (Aggarwal 2007, 7). In China, the growth of SEZ employment alone contributed to 49 percent of total employment growth from 1995 to 2005 (ILO 2008, 5), highlighting the strategic use of zones in generating employment in the country.

Table 11.3   Total Employment and Female Share of Employment in SEZs

| Country | 2000–2003 | | 2005–2006 | | Change over the period | |
	Total employment	Percent female	Total employment	Percent female	Total employment (%)	Female share (%)
Bangladesh	2,138,341	62	3,438,394	85	0.6	23
Mexico	1,906,064	60	1,212,125	60	−0.4	0
Philippines	820,960	74	1,128,197	74	0.4	0
Sri Lanka	461,033	78	410,851	78	−0.1	0
Malaysia	322,000	54	491,488	54	0.5	0
Dominican Republic	181,130	53	154,781	53	−0.2	0
Honduras	106,457	67	353,624	75	2.3	8
Guatemala	69,200	70	72,000	70	0.0	0
Nicaragua	40,000	90	340,000	90	7.5	0
Korea, Republic of	39,000	70	39,000	70	0.0	0
Malawi	29,000	51	29,000	51	0.0	0
Kenya	27,148	60	38,851	60	0.4	0
Jamaica	20,000	90	20,000	90	0.0	0
Panama	14,900	70	18,000	70	0.2	0
Haiti	10,000	69	10,000	69	0.0	0
Cape Verde	1,141	88	1,180	88	0.0	0

Source: Boyenge (2003, 2007).

SEZs remain highly female intensive in general with countries such as Bangladesh, Jamaica, and Nicaragua displaying a female share of employment close to 90 percent. For the period 2000–2003, the average female share of employment in SEZs in the sample of countries in table 11.3 was 69 percent; this increased slightly to 71 percent because of a rise in the number of women employed in Bangladesh and Honduras in 2005–06. When compared with the share of female employment in nonagricultural employment, the high female intensity of SEZs is all the more revealing (see figure 11.1) and the segmentation of women in export-related employment is quite starkly evident. In countries such as Bahrain and Morocco, the female share of employment is low in comparison to other regions, although it is still high relative to female nonagricultural employment; a fact explained by sociocultural norms that keep female labor force participation there low. In India, female employment in SEZs has shown a declining trend from 1981 (46.5 percent) to 2003 (36.9 percent), although it is still much higher than formal sector employment

Figure 11.1   Female Share of SEZ Employment and Nonagricultural Employment, 2005–06

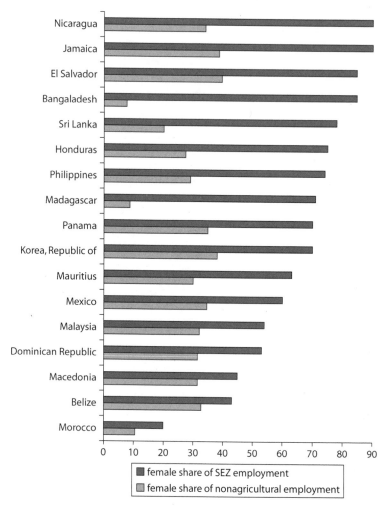

female share of SEZ employment
female share of nonagricultural employment

Source: Author's illustration, based on Boyenge (2007) and ILO (2010).
Note: SEZ = special economic zone.

for women in the economy (Aggarwal 2007, 20–21). Some authors attribute the low proportion of women in Indian SEZs to the willingness of male workers to take up the same positions (Murayama and Yokota 2008, 25). Although the exact proportion of women working in SEZs in China is not available, Fu and Gao (2007, 33) find that the share of female employees in foreign-funded enterprises (most of them situated in SEZs) has fluctuated between 50 and 55 percent from 1995 to 2005, while the

Figure 11.2   Female Share of SEZ Employment and Nonagricultural Employment in African Countries, 2009

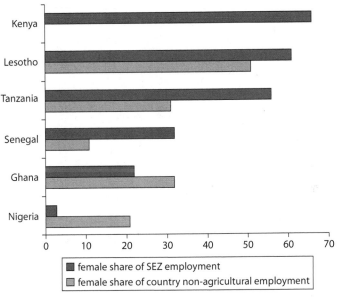

Source: World Bank 2009–10.
Note: SEZ = special economic zone.

ratio of·female to male workers employed in all enterprises dropped from 40 to 36.5 percent during the same period. Ngai (2004, 30) reports that young migrant female workers accounted for around 90 percent of workers in light manufacturing industries in the Shenzhen SEZ.

Figure 11.2 presents more recent data on the female intensity of SEZs in African countries separately. Zones in Kenya, Lesotho, and Tanzania are female dominated with the median shares of female employment at around 60 percent. Ghana and Nigeria are noteworthy in that they are the only two countries in our sample for which the female share of employment in SEZs is lower than that in nonagricultural employment as a whole.

Sectoral Distribution of Female Employment

As mentioned earlier, the predominant exports from SEZs are textiles, garments, electrical, and electronic goods (Cling and Letilly 2001, 12; ILO 2003, 3), which explains their continuing female intensity.[18] The distribution of women's employment across SEZs in 10 countries, including six in Africa, shows a clear pattern in figure 11.3: Women

Figure 11.3   Female Share of Employment in SEZs by Sector, Select Countries, 2009

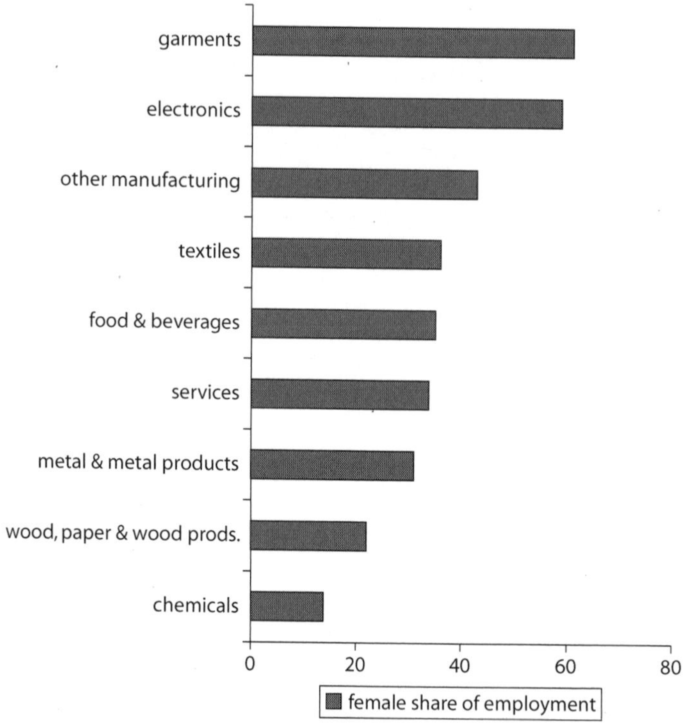

Source: World Bank 2009–10.
Note: The countries across which data are pooled include Bangladesh, Dominican Republic, Honduras, Ghana, Kenya, Lesotho, Nigeria, Tanzania, Senegal, and Vietnam.

predominate in light industries that are gender-typed as female, such as garments, electronics, and textiles, while their share of employment is reduced quite starkly in chemicals, wood products, and metals. The lack of comprehensive statistics on female employment disaggregated by sector and industry in SEZs globally poses a challenge, although case studies provide ample evidence at the country or SEZ level of the concentration of women in particular activities.

In general, women tend to predominate in the low-paying and low value added segment of export production. In Madagascar, for instance, 64 percent of the enterprises in SEZs were in the textiles and clothing industry and they engaged a workforce that was 71 percent female (ILO 2005, 47). Similarly, in Bangladesh, the female share of employment in the garment industry of the Dhaka EPZ was 72 percent, while it was 23 percent in the nongarment industry (Zohir 2001, 13). In Sri Lanka,

76 percent of the female respondents in a survey of EPZs were employed in garments or textile factories and a similar proportion were engaged in low-status positions, such as machine operators, packers, and helpers (Hancock, Middleton, and Moore 2009, 15). Cling and Letilly (2001, 13) report that employment in textiles and clothing in SEZs comprised 77 percent of employment in Tunisia, 66 percent in Sri Lanka, 55.5 percent in Mauritius, and 49 percent in Madagascar in the mid-1990s. Electronic goods predominate in SEZ production in relatively higher income countries, such as the Republic of Korea; Taiwan, China; Malaysia; and Mexico (Cling and Letilly 2001, 13), where they also form a high proportion of female employment. In terms of occupation, women generally have generally been concentrated in low-skill, assembly-type jobs in SEZs, while their share of managerial positions has been relatively much lower, as seen in figure 11.4.

Figure 11.4   Female Share of Employers and Managers, Select Countries, 2009

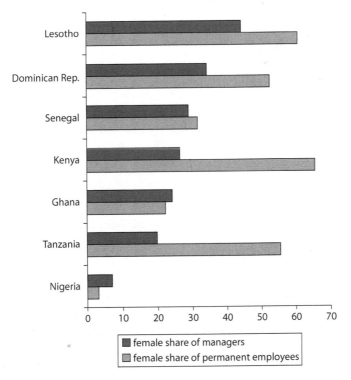

Quality of Female Employment in SEZs

Flexibility of Employment

Employment in export industries has provided women previously unavailable formal earning opportunities, especially in China, where young female workers who flock to the cities in search of work have earned the epithet of "factory girls" (Chang 2008). In many cases, especially for low-skill workers, no alternate employment opportunities were available, such as in the Vishakhapatnam SEZ in India (Aggarwal 2007, 19), or self-employment did not provide a stable source of income even though it paid more (Fussell 2000). Yet, the irony is that even this form of "stable" formal employment has been flexible and informal to a degree. In the Shenzhen Zone in China, young female migrant workers lack the right to stay in the city and cannot be classified as formal workers no matter how long they have worked in the zone. They remain classified as peasant workers and have "ambiguous citizenship rights and weak bargaining power" (Ngai 2004, 30).

In fact, formal employment in the zones has layers of informality. In the Noida EPZ in India, employment conditions and wage levels resemble those of the urban informal economy (Murayama and Yokota 2008, 29), whereas in the Madras EPZ, female workers are paid wages far below the minimum wage. Fu and Gao (2007, 32) find that the number of development zones in China has a strong correlation with the share of informal employment in different regions. In addition, recruitment in SEZs is not always a formal process, and the rights of workers with respect to recruitment and dismissal are not always respected (ILO 2008, 5, 6). Employees in zones also tend to have a high rate of turnover with an average career of no more than five years because of the use of fixed-term contracts and the intensive nature of work (ILO 2003, 7).

Wages and Working Conditions

SEZs have been created as islands of duty-free, tax-free export-oriented production in developing countries, but they were also known to offer a more relaxed environment with respect to labor regulation to attract foreign investment. Labor laws within SEZs now appear to be the same as in the rest of the country, although some countries such as Algeria, Cameroon, and Mauritius have exceptions in their national legislation with respect to issues such as overtime, wages, and duration of work in SEZs, while others, such as Djibouti, Panama, and Zimbabwe, have different labor laws altogether (ILO 2008, 7). Still, in an ILO (2001) survey, approximately 28 percent of respondents in 19 countries reported that laws within SEZs differed in some way from those outside, including more overtime work, lack of retirement provisions, less favorable leave terms, exemption from occupational safety provisions, and prolonged temporary contracts (cited in Engman, Onodera, and Pinali 2007, 30). Although there has been some movement forward in harmonizing laws within and outside zones, the main problem in SEZs remains government indifference toward the enforcement of laws and the lack of resources or capacity for monitoring and supervision (Milberg and Amengual 2008, 58–9). For instance, Vietnam's labor laws, which were drafted in consultation with the ILO, include the strongest protection for workers' rights and for gender equality in the region, but the lack of enforcement and monitoring means that many of those provisions simply remain on paper (Farole 2010).

We present some general characteristics with respect to work and working conditions in SEZs, although considerable variations exist between countries, zones, and industries. First, SEZs offer higher or similar wages and benefits as compared with other sectors of the economy, but the gender wage gap as well as other forms of discrimination persist. Second, SEZs are characterized by much longer and frequently illegal working hours as compared with other sectors of the economy (Milberg and Amengual 2008, 61). Third, the rights to freedom of association and collective bargaining are seriously impaired (ICFTU 2004). We will discuss each by turn as well as discuss gender-related concerns.

Based on country studies, the ILO (2008, 6) reports that wages in SEZs appear to be at the same level or higher for equivalent work in the rest of the economy. Studies on Bangladesh, Madagascar, Costa Rica, Honduras, and Sri Lanka indicate that wages in zones generally tend to be higher than in sectors outside zones, although which control group is being used for the comparison is critical (for a summary, see Milberg and Amengual 2008). However, wage and nonwage discrimination against women is a continuing reality within SEZs (ILO 2008, 4).[19] This is the case for, instance, in SEZs in Honduras where women earn less than men for comparable work (Ver beek 2001) and in Madagascar where the average female wage is lower than the male, with the gap rising from 8 percent for low-skill work to 20 percent for managerial positions (ILO 2008, 4). In Bangladesh, women not only earned less than men because of their segregation in low-skilled work, but more women also left their jobs for reasons of low pay than did men (Zohir 2001). The question remains as to whether employers in SEZs provide workers with a livable wage even if they do comply with minimum wage laws (Milberg and Amengual 2008, 35).

 Excessive overtime appears to be an endemic feature of employment in SEZs. Overtime work is often mandatory because of the requirements of GVCs, seasonal demand peaks, and stringent shipping deadlines. Refusal to comply with long hours of work can result in dismissal or retaliation (ILO 2008, 6). In Madagascar, female employees in the zone worked for 209 hours in a month on average, as compared with 168 hours in the non-EPZ private sector and 147 hours in the public sector (Glick and Roubaud 2006). Based on the Fair Labor Association's workplace code of ethics, garment factories display the most number of violations with respect to hours of work, overtime compensation and wages[20] followed in second place by noncompliance on health and safety codes (Rodgers and Berik 2006, 62).[21]

 Perhaps the most critical issue with regard to employment in SEZs, and one that has a bearing on all the others, is the restriction of the right to freedom of association and collective bargaining. Although most countries legally recognize the rights of workers to join unions, severe limitations are frequently placed on these rights in practice. Workers are unable to organize effectively due to the discrimination and harassment they face from employers when they engage in union-related activities, including unfair dismissal and suspension, blacklisting of union members, and even physical violence (Gopalkrishnan 2007, 1). It is also difficult in many cases for existing unions to gain physical access to firms and workers inside SEZs (ILO 2003, 8) and repression of union-related activity is widespread, as studies on Dominican Republic, Guatemala, Jamaica, and Sri Lanka have shown (Milberg and Amengual 2008, 33).

Gender-based discrimination in SEZs also comes in the form of hiring and benefits, career development, and women workers' rights in relation to working hours, pregnancy, maternity leave, and children (ILO 2003, 9). Firms in SEZs have displayed a tendency to employ young, unmarried women and to discriminate against married women and women with children, although the profile of SEZ employees has changed to some extent over time. Mexico is an infamous example of firms in SEZs requiring women to take pregnancy tests before recruitment, a practice that was eventually prohibited by law (ICFTU 2004, 12). This practice still appears to be in force in the Dominican Republic; however, in the Philippines, women have been made to resign after becoming pregnant and have not been allowed to return to work subsequently (ICFTU

2004). There are frequent reports of sexual harassment and abuse[22] in SEZs and even mandatory HIV screening requirements in some cases (ICFTU 2004).

Some Initiatives to Improve Compliance on Labor Issues in SEZs

Different efforts have been made to address some of the persistent problems with respect to the quality of employment in SEZs as well as to enhance compliance and monitoring of labor laws. They have enjoyed varying degrees of success. We briefly present three noteworthy initiatives here.

Under the U.K. Ethical Trade Initiative and the U.S. Apparel Industry Partnership, both multistakeholder initiatives, lead firms in the North have adopted voluntary codes of conduct to work with suppliers that observe certain minimum labor standards, which has helped improve labor conditions in some value chains (see Barrientos 2000; Smith and Barrientos 2005). For instance, in Lesotho, working conditions in textiles and clothing factories improved notably as global buyers imposed codes of conduct on suppliers and monitored their enforcement in factories (Farole 2010). Still there are limits to private and voluntary regulation and monitoring and they cannot be a substitute for broader developmental strategies that address issues of labor law compliance in supplier countries (Barrientos 2000, 559).

To improve compliance on social and labor issues, the Bangladesh Export Processing Zones Authority (BEPZA) initiated a Labor Counselor Program in 2005 by which it recruited 67 counselors to pay visits to factories within the EPZ and to work with management on the correct implementation of labor laws and compensation practices. Perceived more as facilitators rather than regulators, the counselors also arbitrated informally between workers and management and reported existing problems to the BEPZA. It is reported that better implementation of the law through the program led to a 32 percent increase in the wages of the workers and to fewer worker grievances (Farole 2010).[23]

The ILO runs a well-known Better Factories Programme in Cambodia through which it monitors the compliance of garment firms on national labor laws and international core labor standards. It publishes the findings of the ILO monitors and gives firms a chance to improve their compliance, after which it conducts a reevaluation and identifies by name the firms that do not remedy their violations in publicly available reports (Milberg and Amengual 2008, 38). Because the reports are available to international buyers who are making sourcing decisions, it acts as a pressure point for producers to comply (see www.betterfactories.org for more information on this program). Berik and Rodgers (2010) find that the program has achieved modest improvements in working conditions in garment factories in the country.

Defeminization of Employment

The link between export orientation and the feminization of labor has been critiqued and refined by researchers who argue that it is not export orientation per se, but rather the type of manufacturing that takes place within these sectors that matters for female employment. As we have seen, an overlap exists between the types of industries located within SEZs, the quality of employment in terms of low wages and flexibility, and the female intensity of employment. This raises the question of whether the gains in women's employment are sustainable over time and what factors contribute to the defeminization of labor that has been noted in some countries.[24] A number of reasons have been identified in the literature for this defeminization, including industrial upgrading, closing of the gender wage gap, cyclical factors such as recessions, and outsourcing to home-based workers, which leads to statistical defeminization. We will consider each of these in turn bearing in mind that one or more of these factors might be acting to produce the given outcome at any time.

Industrial upgrading can be defined as the ability of producers "to make better products, to make products more efficiently, or to move into higher-skilled activities" (Pietrobelli and Rabellotti 2006, 1) and studies on upgrading generally tend to focus on the technological content of production and on value added (Milberg 2008, 6).[25] For our purposes, the shift of output to more capital- and technology-intensive sectors as well as the production of higher value added products within a sector can have implications for the distribution of employment by sex for a number of reasons. First, as described earlier, the gender-typing of jobs as masculine and feminine leads to discrimination against women when industrial upgrading involves heavy, capital-intensive, or skilled work. Second, women lack access to on-the-job training and retraining to upgrade their skills when the skill requirements of the job change. This is partly due to their segmentation in what is considered unskilled work and partly because employers view women as "unstable workers," who will withdraw from the labor force as domestic obligations mount (Jayasinghe 2001, 72, 73). Third, gender biases operate to segment young women and girls into more "feminine" vocations in the education system, while reserving the heavy, technical, and often better-paid professions for men.

Thus, Fussell (2000, 65) notes that as production became more technologically intensive in Mexican *maquiladoras* between 1983 and 1999, the number of female operatives declined from 77 percent to 41 percent, although total employment in *maquiladoras* grew rapidly during the period. Jomo (2009) identifies the rise of skill-intensive manufacturing and the likely gender-typing of new industrial jobs as the reason for defeminization of export-oriented manufacturing in North and Southeast Asia in the 1990s. Jayasinghe (2001, 77), in a study on the Caribbean, explains the predominance of male export workers in Trinidad by the fact that its major exports were minerals, fuels, and chemicals and work in these industries was considered heavy and more skilled. Further, because the few women who are employed are concentrated in low-skill processing jobs, where labor costs are of critical importance, they are rapidly losing employment as a result of mechanization. Caraway (2007, 149) finds a statistically significant and negative relationship between capital intensity and female employment in manufacturing for a sample of countries in East Asia and Latin America from the late 1950s to mid-1990s.

Tejani and Milberg (2010) find that both the defeminization of labor in manufacturing in Southeast Asia and the feminization of labor in Latin America over the period 1985 to 2006 are driven by shifts in manufacturing labor productivity and capital intensity. As proxies for industrial upgrading, both capital intensity and labor productivity have a statistically significant and negative relationship with the female intensity of employment in manufacturing over the period. Figure 11.5 reproduces the relationship between the female intensity of employment and manufacturing productivity for relevant countries.

Other scholars have argued that the feminization of labor "creates conditions for its own unravelling over time" because the wage differentials that drive feminization tend to decrease over time as the labor market tightens and demands for better work conditions and security gain momentum (Ghosh 2002, 25). That is, the demand for female labor is contingent on its relative cheapness; once this incentive to hire women disappears, firms prefer to employ men. Murayama and Yokota (2008, 16–17) attribute the steady decline of the female share of employment in the Masan SEZ in the Republic of Korea from 85 percent in 1972 to 62 percent in 2001 to massive worker resistance led by young female

Figure 11.5   Female Intensity of Manufacturing Employment and Manufacturing Value Added per Worker, Average Annual Growth, Southeast Asia and Latin America, 1985–2006

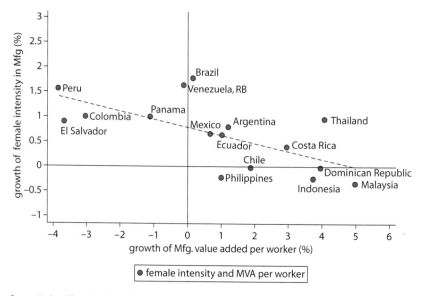

Source: Authors' illustration, based on ILO (2009) and World Bank (2009).
Note: MVA = manufacturing value added.
Fitted Line: $Y = 0.86 - 0.13X$ (Adj. Rsq.= 0.24; t-stat = −2.38).
Data availability varies by country. Please contact author for details.

workers in the late 1980s, which led to rapid wage increases across the board. Additionally, the rise of capital- and technology-intensive production in the zone displaced female workers who were employed in labor-intensive industries. Similarly, as the supply of female workers willing to work for low wages in Mexican *maquiladoras* in the 1980s boom fell because of a tightening labor market, managers were forced to recruit men for the same jobs (Salzinger 2003, 11).

Rubery (1998) argues that female employment is procyclical and that women act as a flexible "buffer" labor force to be roped into the workforce when required and released when not. The buffer explanation implies that women are employed in larger numbers in periods of expansion and are laid off during recessions, providing one explanation for defeminization. Such a buffer role is concentrated in particular occupations in industries that face competitive pressures and greater demand fluctuations. Kucera (2001) shows this buffer role of female workers in the 1960s and 1970s in Germany and Japan.[26]

The defeminization of labor in SEZs could be related to the greater informalization of work and outsourcing to home-based workers as a result of the cost pressures on suppliers that are integrated into GVCs.[27] In the fashion garments chains, for instance, suppliers outsource the work to intermediaries who hire mostly home-based, and largely female, workers for the job. Thus, women who were formerly employed in SEZ factories now could be located in the informal sector and working for lower wages with no benefits, outside the ambit of regulatory structures and unrecorded in labor force surveys (Carr, Chen, and Tate, 136). Thus, defeminization in this case is a statistical artifact and the result of productive activities of home-based workers going unrecorded. We discuss some policy measures to address defeminization in manufacturing in the concluding section.

Conclusion and Policy Implications

Without doubt, export-oriented industrialization has created new opportunities for women by drawing many into paid employment for the first time. The high degree of female intensity in light manufacturing industries in SEZs attests to this fact. Women have, at the same time, served as a source of competitive advantage for firms competing in the international market because of (1) a persistent wage gap that makes women a cheaper source of labor and (2) a high degree of occupational sex segmentation that perpetuates the wage gap. Within the framework of GVCs, this segmentation by sex serves the asymmetry of market structures between lead firms situated in the rich countries and producers in poor countries and distributes value added in a highly skewed fashion.

Because women's employment has been contingent largely on their disadvantages in the labor market, rather than the abatement of gender-based discrimination, the gains made in the initial phases of export-oriented industrialization might not be sustainable. There is clear evidence of a defeminization of export labor in countries that have upgraded their industrial structures and, in some cases, where the gender wage gap has closed.

The feminization of SEZ labor has been a double-edged phenomenon: it has provided women jobs and access to income that has earned them other kinds of freedom, but these jobs have been poorly paid and insecure; they have generally not led to promotion; and when countries have upgraded their industries, they have hired fewer women. SEZ work remains highly segmented with women crowded in a few industries in low value added, assembly-type operations with conditions of work that include long working hours, impediments to the freedom of association, sexual harassment, and other forms of gender-based discrimination. These conditions have severely limited the gains that could have otherwise been made.

Further, with the scaling up and expansion of the SEZ model to incorporate a variety of activities, including information processing, financial services, and logistics among others, the gender dimension of employment in the zones is likely to be affected. In service-oriented SEZs, the nature of work and skill profile of workers is expected to be quite different from the traditional EPZ model, which involves mostly blue-collar work. Women have generally benefited in terms of employment gains from the increasing share of services in output (see GET 2009), but evidence suggests that service activities also tend to be segmented by gender. Mitter (2003, 10–13) finds that women predominate in the low-skilled segments of IT and IT-enabled services in a number of developing countries. Kelkar, Shrestha, and Veena (2002, 70–71) also highlight the segmentation of women in low-skilled jobs in the IT-enabled service industry in India, such as in call centers and medical transcription centers. In a study of firms engaged in high-tech production in the Philippines, McKay (2006, 231) predicts that women will have little access to the high-skilled jobs that are finally being created in the industry as a result of entrenched gender norms.

What policy conclusions do we draw from these developments? The policy implications for SEZs can be inferred at two different levels: (1) protecting the rights of all workers in the zone and (2) addressing the various forms of gender-based discrimination that women workers face in particular. Perhaps the most important step in this regard would be to remove existing barriers to the right of freedom of association in SEZs so that workers can engage in collective bargaining and can organize to access the full range of their rights. Because trade unions have traditionally been hostile to the inclusion of gender concerns, this will require a change in their culture and a larger role and voice for women. National labor laws also need to be brought in line with international labor standards to raise standards for all workers in general.

Given that zones cover a limited geographic area and generally are governed by a centralized zone authority, they can be used to spearhead innovative labor reforms that can serve as models for the rest of the country. The ILO's Decent Work Programme, which promotes fundamental rights at work, social security, social dialogue, and tripartism, can be implemented within an SEZ as a pilot initiative. Such proposals have already been made in the case of Sri Lanka and Indonesia (see Sivananthiram n.d.). For targeted interventions in persistent problem areas, the ILO's Factory Improvement Program has enjoyed success in enhancing productivity and reducing overtime work in factories in Sri Lanka and Vietnam and has led to broad gains in job quality (Milberg and Amengual 2008, 56). The zone authority can enforce more regular labor and gender audits within the zone area by obtaining support from other stakeholders, including international agencies and local NGOs, and take steps to build the capacity of firms to properly implement labor laws, as the Labor Counselor Program did in Bangladesh in 2005. Furthermore, to address the vertical gender segmentation evident in export-oriented employment, zone authorities can stipulate targets for women's representation in supervisory and managerial positions in SEZ firms and can undertake affirmative action policies to promote women entrepreneurs within the zone. Providing accessible childcare and schooling facilities, creating proper mechanisms to handle sexual harassment complaints, and enforcing equal remuneration legislation and maternity or paternity leave can address some of the persistent problems with respect to gender discrimination in SEZs.

It is important for policy makers to recognize that although industrial upgrading is a laudable policy goal to promote economic growth and development, it has gender consequences. National programs that promote upgrading and diversification of exports must address this gender dimension. Steps must be taken to update women's skills through on-the-job training programs to ensure advancement and retention when industries upgrade their products or processes. Zone authorities, along with other stakeholders, can cofinance or offer firms partial rebates for training schemes for higher-skilled positions that mandate the participation of women. The ComMark Trust funded such an initiative in the textile and clothing industry in Lesotho and successfully increased the participation of Basotho workers in supervisory positions (see Farole 2010). Zone authorities can institute awards to spotlight firms that have integrated women into technical, high-skilled, or traditionally masculinized work to generate incentives to change social norms and make these firms more attractive to international buyers. Further, governments need to actively promote institutions that reduce gender segmentation in the labor market. Because segregation begins in the educational system, addressing systematic biases in admission policy and instruction so that women have better access to technical education and vocational training would be a step in this direction.

Finally, the present financial crisis and the collapse of export demand in the European Union and United States reveal some of the pitfalls of pursuing export-oriented growth, and rising levels of international trade liberalization undercut some of the incentives to establish SEZs in the present environment (see Cattaneo, Gereffi, and Staritz 2010). It is important in this context to improve the quality of work for women, even as their role in the late-20th-century wave of industrialization inevitably shifts.

Notes

1. The author is greatly indebted to William S. Milberg, Professor and Chair of Economics, New School for Social Research, who provided valuable inputs and advice at every stage of this paper. Thanks are also due to Tom Farole and Cornelia Staritz, who provided helpful comments on an earlier draft. Any errors or deficiencies remain the sole responsibility of the author.

2. I use the generic term special economic zone or SEZ to denote a wide variety of free zones, including export processing zones, free trade zones, and wide area zones using the typology outlined in chapter 1 of this book. Most SEZs remain concentrated in manufacturing-related activities, although services increasingly are being incorporated into the model.

3. Feminization here refers to the rising share of female employment in total employment.

4. This section draws partially on Tejani and Milberg (2010).

5. Or the ratio of female to male wages for similar work.

6. In what came to be known as the "international division of labor" literature, scholars argued that cheap female labor in developing countries was not just incidental in a system of global production, but pivotal to ensuring transnational profits and competitiveness. An entrenched system of gender subordination lay at the heart of women's relative disadvantage in the labor market, which firms seized on to make profits. Further, it was argued, the gendered division of labor in the patriarchal household provided a blueprint for women's integration into the labor market, confining them to low-paid, labor-intensive work (Elson and Pearson 1981; Fernandez Kelly 1989).

7. See Seguino (2000b) for the impact of gender inequality on growth through the channel of exports and investment for a group of semi-industrialized countries in Asia and Latin America from 1975 to 1995.

8. About one-half of the workers in the world are in occupations that can be classified as "male" or "female" based on the fact that at least 80 percent of

workers therein belong to a single sex. Further, not only are male-dominated occupations much more numerous than female, the latter "tend to be less valuable with lower pay, lower status and fewer advancement possibilities as compared to 'male' occupations" (Anker 1998, 407).

9. But contrary to the belief that female workers are inherently compliant and productive, Salzinger (2003, 10) contends that ideal workers are "produced" through repeated invocation in managerial discourse and shop-floor practices that employ gendered strategies to enhance productivity. Thus, female workers do not innately display the required "feminine attributes" that can be put to use in production, but rather, those attributes are elicited and performed because they serve productive interests in the factory, with multiple possibilities for disruption and resistance.

10. I borrow this term from Madani (1999), though I use it in a different spirit.

11. See Strom (1989) for a description of the process by which U.S. office work became feminized in the early 20th century; also see Walsh (1997).

12. Caraway (2007, 133), for instance, highlights the role of unions in keeping the female share of employment in manufacturing in Latin America traditionally low.

13. In turn, firms will internalize production processes that protect rents accruing from firm-specific and knowledge-based assets, which are possible to maintain only in an oligopolistic industry with firms that enjoy economies of scale and market power (Milberg 2004, 60–1).

14. The structure of GVCs is by no means homogenous. See Gereffi, Humphrey, and Sturgeon (2005) for the different forms of governance and Milberg (2004) for an anatomy of cost markups and value added in GVCs.

15. Gereffi (1999) documents the shift from assembly activities to "full-package production" and supplier-oriented production in developing countries.

16. For the rise in imports and precipitous decline in prices of clothing in the United States, see Heintz (2006, 508).

17. Ironically, the current commodities boom means a complete reversal of the Prebisch-Singer predictions.

18. This does not necessarily imply a lack of dynamism, however, as upgrading can occur within an industry to full package production (Milberg and Amegual 2007, 9) and to more technologically intensive products.

19. A recent meta-analysis of the gender wage gap showed that a fall in the gender wage gap worldwide was due to the increased labor market productivity of females even as the discriminatory component of the wage gap held steady (Weichselbaumer and Winter-Ebmer 2003).

20. China fares particularly poorly on this count as compared with Asia and other regions (Berik 2006, 62.)

21. The recent fire in a garment factory in the Ashulia Industrial Zone in Bangladesh that killed 25 people and injured more than a 100 is a grim reminder of these poor safety standards ("Bangladesh Factory Fire Kills 25," December 15, 2010).

22. The ICFTU (2004) reports complaints of harassment in Bangladesh, Dominican Republic, Kenya, and Mexico.

23. More recently, however, Bangladesh has been the site for great labor unrest as garment factory workers in EPZs in Dhaka and Chittagong protested the fact that firms have not implemented overdue pay hikes ordered by the government. The protests turned violent as police clashed with the protestors leading to the death of three people and dozens of injuries ("Three killed, dozens hurt in Bangladesh clashes," December 12, 2010).

24. Barrientos, Kabeer, and Hossain (2004, 5) summarize declining trends in the female share of employment for a number of countries.

25. In the GVC literature, upgrading can mean moving to a more advantageous position in the chain by making higher value added products or performing more valuable functions. And upgrading can include process, product, functional, or intersectoral upgrading (see Milberg and Winkler 2008, 6–7, and references therein).

26. On the other hand, downturns might motivate the search for cost-saving solutions leading to the substitution of male workers with female workers and a rising feminization of labor. In gender-segmented occupations, female employment would be related more to secular trends in sectoral structures rather than to cyclical factors (Rubery 1988). It is beyond the scope of this chapter to identify which of these hypotheses might be operating within a given period of time, although they provide a useful framework for thinking about defeminization.

27. See Chen, Sebstad, and O'Connell (1999) for a discussion of the limitation of official statistics on the informal sector.

References

Aggarwal, A. 2007. *Impact of Special Economic Zones on Employment, Poverty and Human Development*. Working Paper No. 194. New Delhi: Indian Council for Research on International Economic Relations.

Anker, R. 1998. *Gender and Jobs: Sex Segregation of Occupations in the World*. Geneva: International Labor Office.

Arndt, S., and H. Kierzkowski. 2001. "Introduction." In *Fragmentation: New Production Patterns in the World Economy*, edited by S. Arndt and H. Kierzkowski, 1–16. New York: Oxford University Press.

Baliamoune-Lutz, M. 2006. "Globalisation and Gender Inequality: Is Africa Different?" *Journal of African Economies* 16 (2): 301–48.

"Bangladesh Factory Fire Kills 25." 2010. *Wall Street Journal Asia*, December 15. Available at http://online.wsj.com/article/SB10001424052748704706940045 76019490529039646.html (accessed December, 15, 2010).

Barrrientos, S. 2001. "Gender Flexibility and Global Value Chains." *IDS Bulletin* 32 (3): 83–93.

Barrientos, S., N. Kabeer, and N. Hossain. 2004. *The Gender Dimensions of the Globalization of Production*. Working Paper No. 17. Geneva: Policy Integration Department, World Commission on the Social Dimension of Globalization, International Labor Office.

Berik, G. 2000. "Mature Export-Led Growth and Gender Wage Inequality in Taiwan." *Feminist Economics* 6 (3): 1–26.

Berik, G., and Y. Rodgers. 2010. "Options for Enforcing Labor Standards: Lessons from Bangladesh and Cambodia." *Journal of International Development* 22 (1): 56–85.

Berik, G., Y. V. Rodgers, and J. E. Zveglich. 2004. "International Trade and Gender Wage Discrimination: Evidence from East Asia." *Review of Development Economics* 8 (2): 237–54.

Black, S., and B. Brainerd. 2004. "Improving Equality? The Impact of Globalization on Gender Discrimination." *Industrial and Labor Relations Review* 57 (4): 540–59.

Boyenge, J. P. S. 2003. *ILO Database on Export Processing Zones*. Sectoral Activities Department. Geneva: International Labour Organization.

Boyenge, J. P. S. 2007. *ILO Database on Export Processing Zones (Revised)*. Sectoral Activities Programme, Working Paper 251. Geneva: International Labour Organization.

Brainerd. E. 2000. "Changes in Gender Wage Differentials in Eastern Europe and the Former Soviet Union." *Industrial and Labour Relations Review* 54 (1): 138–62.

Busse, M., and C. Spielman. 2006. "Gender Inequality and Trade." *Review of International Economics* 14 (3): 362–79.

Cagatay, N., and G. Berik. 1990. "Transition to Export-led Growth in Turkey: Is There a Feminisation of Employment?" *Review of Radical Political Economics* 22 (1): 115–34.

Cagatay, N., and S. Ozler. 1995. "Feminization of the Labor Force: The Effects of Long-Term Development and Structural Adjustment." *World Development*: 23 (11): 1883–94.

Caraway, T. L. 2007. *Assembling Women: The Feminization of Global Manufacturing*. Ithaca, NY: ILR Press.

Carr, M., M. A. Chen, and J. Tate. 2004. "Globalization and Home-based Workers." *Feminist Economics* 6 (3): 123–42.

Cattaneo, O., G. Gereffi, and C. Staritz. 2010. *Global Value Chains in a Postcrisis World: A Development Perspective.* Washington, DC: World Bank.

Chamarbagwala, R. 2006. "Economic Liberalization and Wage Inequality in India." *World Development* 34 (12): 1997–2015.

Chang, L. T. (2008). *Factory Girls: From Village to City in a Changing China.* New York: Spiegel & Grau.

Chen, M., J. Sebstad, and L. O'Connell. 1999. "Counting the Invisible Workforce: The Case of Homebased Worker." *World Development* 27 (3): 603–10.

Cling, J., and G. Letilly. 2001. *Export Processing Zones: A Threatened Instrument for Global Economy Insertion?* Document de Travail, DT/2001/17. Development et insertion internationale, Paris.

Engman, M., O. Onodera, and E. Pinali. 2007. *Export Processing Zones: Past and Future Role in Trade and Development.* OECD Trade Policy Working Paper No. 53. Paris: Trade Committee, OECD.

Elson, D. 2007. "International Trade and Gender Equality: Women as Achievers of Competitive Advantage and as Sources of Competitive Advantage." Paper prepared for International Symposium on Gender at the Heart of Globalization, March 21–23, 2007, Paris.

Elson, D., and R. Pearson. 1981. "'Nimble Fingers Make Cheap Workers': An Analysis of Women's Employment in Third World Export Manufacturing." *Feminist Review* 7 (Spring): 87–107.

Farole, T. 2010. "Case Studies on Special Economic Zones." Mimeo. Washington, DC: World Bank.

Feenstra, R. 1998. "Integration of Trade, Disintegration of Production." *Journal of Economic Perspectives* 12 (4): 31–50.

Fernandez Kelly, P. 1989. "Broadening the Scope: Gender and International Economic Development." *Sociological Forum* 4 (4): 611–35.

Fu, X., and Y. Gao. 2007. *Export Processing Zones in China: A Survey.* Geneva: International Labour Organization.

Fussell, E. 2000. "Making Labor Flexible: The Recomposition of Tijuana's Maquiladora Female Labor Force." *Feminist Economics* 6 (3): 59–79.

Gereffi, G. 1999. "International Trade and Industrial Upgrading in the Apparel Commodity Chain." *Journal of International Economics* 48 (1999): 37–70.

Gereffi, G. 2005. *The New Offshoring of Jobs and Global Development.* ILO Social Policy Lectures. Geneva: International Institute for Labour Studies.

Gereffi, G., J. Humphrey, and T. Sturgeon. 2005. "The Governance of Global Value Chains." *Review of International Political Economy* 12 (1): 78–104.

GET (Global Employment Trends). 2009. *Global Employment Trends for Women.* Geneva: International Labour Organization.

Ghosh, J. 2002. "Globalisation, Export-Oriented Employment for Women and Social Policy: A Case Study of India." *Social Scientist* 30 (11/12): 17–60.

Glick, P., and S. Roubaud. 2006. "Export Processing Zone Expansion in Madagascar: What Are the Labor Market and Gender Impacts?" *Journal of African Economies* 15 (4): 722–56.

Gopalkrishnan, R. 2007. *Freedom of Association and Collective Bargaining in Export Processing Zones: Role of the ILO Supervisory Mechanism.* Working Paper No. 1, International Labour Standards Department. Geneva: International Labour Office.

Gray, M., M. C. Kittilson, and W. Sandholtz. 2006. "Women and Globalization: A Study of 180 Countries, 1975–2000." *International Organization* 60: 293–333.

Hancock, P., S. Middleton, and J. Moore. 2009. "Export Processing Zones (EPZs), Globalisation, Feminised Labour Markets and Working Conditions: A Study of Sri Lankan Workers." *Labour and Management in Development* 10: 1–22.

Heintz, J. 2006. "Low-Wage Manufacturing and Global Commodity Chains: A Model in the Unequal Exchange Tradition." *Cambridge Journal of Economics* 30: 507–20.

Horton, S. 1999. "Marginalization Revisited: Women's Market Work and Pay, and Economic Development." *World Development* 27 (3): 571–82.

ICFTU (International Confederation of Free Trade Unions). 2004. *Behind the Brand Names.* International Confederation of Free Trade Unions.

ILO (International Labour Organization). 2001. *Follow-up and Promotion on the Tripartite Declaration of Principles Concerning Multinational Enterprises and Social Policy: (a) Seventh Survey on the Effect Given to the Tripartite Declaration of Principles Concerning Multinational Enterprises and Social Policy.* Analytical report of the Working Group on the reports submitted by governments and by employers' and workers' organizations, GB.280/MNE/1/1. Geneva: International Labour Organization.

ILO. 2003. *Employment and Social Policy in Respect of Export Processing Zones (EPZs).* Committee on Employment and Social Policy, Document No. GB.286/ESP/3. Geneva: International Labour Office.

ILO. 2005. *Promoting Fair Globalization in Textiles and Clothing in a Post-MFA Environment.* Geneva: International Labour Organization.

ILO. 2008. *Employment and Social Policy in Respect of Export Processing Zones (EPZs).* Committee on Employment and Social Policy, Document No. GB.301/ESP/5. Geneva: International Labour Office.

ILO. 2009. *LABORSTA Internet*. Geneva: International Labour Organization. http://laborsta.ilo.org/STP/guest (accessed January 2009).

ILO. 2010. *Key Indicators of the Labor Market*. Geneva: International Labour Organization. http://kilm.ilo.org/KILMnetBeta/default2.asp (accessed September 2010).

Jayasinghe, D. 2001. "'More and More Technology, Women Have to Go Home." *Gender and Development* 9 (1): 70–81.

Jayaweera, S. 2003. "Continuity and Change: Women Workers in Garments and Textile Industries in Sri Lanka." In *Tracking Gender Equity Under Economic Reforms: Continuity and Change in South Asia*, edited by S. Mukhopadhyay and R. Sudarshan, 196–226. New Delhi: Kali for Women.

Joekes, S. 1995. *Trade-Related Employment for Women In Industry and Services in Developing Countries*. Occasional Paper 5, United Nations Research Institute for Social Development. Geneva: United Nations Development Programme.

Joekes, S. 1999. "A Gender-Analytical Perspective on Trade and Sustainable Development." In *U.N. Development, Trade, Gender and Sustainable Development*, Papers prepared in support of the themes discussed at the Pre-UNCTAD X Expert Workshop on Trade, Sustainable Development and Gender (Geneva, 12–13 July 1999), 33–59. Geneva: UNCTAD.

Jomo, K. S. 2009. "Export-Oriented Industrialisation, Female Employment and Gender Wage Equity in East Asia." *Economic and Political Weekly* (January): 41–54.

Kabeer, N. 2000. *The Power to Choose: Bangladeshi Women and Labour Market Decisions*. London: Verso.

Kaplinsky, R. 1998. *Globalisation, Industrialisation and Sustainable Growth: The Pursuit of the Nth Rent*. IDS Discussion Paper No. 110. Sussex, UK: Institute of Development Studues.

Kelkar, G., G. Shrestha, and N. Veena. 2002. "IT Industry and Women's Agency: Explorations in Bangalore and Delhi, India." *Gender, Technology and Development* 6 (1): 63–84.

Kongar, E. 2007. "Importing Equality or Exporting Jobs? Gender Wage and Employment Differentials in US Manufacturing." In *The Feminist Economics of Trade*, edited by I. van Staveren, D. Elson, C. Grown, and N. Cagatay, 215–36. New York: Routledge.

Kucera, D. 2001. *Gender, Growth and Trade: The Miracle Economies of the Postwar Years*. London and New York: Routledge.

Kucera, D., and Milberg, W. 2000. "Gender Segregation and Gender Bias in Manufacturing Trade Expansion: Revisiting the 'Wood Asymmetry'." *World Development* 28 (7): 1191–1210.

Kusago, T., and Z. Tzannatos. 1998. *Export Processing Zones: A Review in Need of an Update*. Discussion Paper Series, No. 9802. Washington, DC: World Bank.

Lutz, N. M. 1988. "Images of Docility: Asian Women and the World Economy." In *Racism, Sexism and the World-System*, edited by J. Smith, 57–74. New York: Greenwood.

Madani. D. 1999. *A Review of the Role and Impact of Export Processing Zones*. PREM-EP. Washington, DC: The World Bank.

Mehra, R., and S. Gammage. 1999. "Trends, Counter-trends and Gaps in Women's Employment." *World Development* 27 (3): 533–50.

McKy, S. C. 2006. "Hard Drives and Glass Ceilings: Gender Stratification in Hi-tech Production." *Gender and Society* 20 (2): 207–35.

Menon, N., and Y. M. Rodgers. 2008. "International Trade and the Gender Wage Gap: New Evidence from India's Manufacturing Sector." *World Development* 37 (5): 965–81.

Milberg, W. 2004. "The Changing Structure of Trade Linked to Global Production Systems: What Are the Policy Implications?" *International Labour Review* 143 (1–2): 45–90.

Milberg, W., and Amengual. 2008. *Economic Development and Working Conditions in Export Processing Zones: A Survey of Trends*. Working Paper 3, ILO. Geneva: International Labour Office.

Milberg, W., and D. Winkler. 2008. "Measuring Economic and Social Upgrading in Global Production Networks." Concept Note prepared for DFID grant "Capturing the Gains: Economic and Social Upgrading in Global Production Networks." London: U.K. Department for International Development.

Mitra-Kahn, B. H., and T. Mitra-Kahn. 2007. "Gender Wage Gaps and Growth: What Goes Up Must Come Down." Unpublished manuscript.

Mitter, S. 2003. "Globalization and ICT: Employment Opportunities for Women." Paper commissoned for Gender Advisory Board Policy Research Programme, "Gender Dimensions of Science and Technology Policy: Research in New Critical Issues." United Nations Commission on Science and Technology for Development.

Murayama, M., and N. Yokota. 2008. *Revisiting Labour and Gender Issues in Export Processing Zones: The Case of South Korea, Bangladesh and India*. IDE Discussion Paper No. 174. Japan: Institute of Developing Economies.

Ngai, P. 2004. "Women Workers and Precarious Employment in Shenzhen Special Economic Zone, China." *Gender and Development* 12 (2): 29–36.

Oostendorp, R. H. 2004. *Globalization and the Gender Wage Gap*. World Bank Policy Research Paper No. 3256, April. Washington, DC: World Bank.

Ozler, S. 2000. "Export Orientation and Female Share of Employment: Evidence from Turkey." *World Development* 28 (7): 1239–48.

Pietrobelli C., and R. Rabelloti. 2006. "Clusters and Value Chains in Latin America: In Search of an Integrated Approach." In *Upgrading to Compete: Global Value Chains, Clusters, and SMEs in Latin America,* edited by C. Pietrobelli and R. Rabelloti, 1–40. Washington, DC: Inter-American Development Bank.

Prebisch, R. 1950. *The Economic Development of Latin America and its Principal Problems.* New York: United Nations.

Rodgers, Y., and G. Berik. 2006. "Asia's Race to Capture Post-MFA Markets: A Snapshot of Labor Standards, Compliance and Impacts on Competitiveness." *Asian Development Review* 23 (1): 55–86.

Rubery, J. 1988. *Women and Recession.* London: Routledge and Kegan Paul Ltd.

Salzinger, L. 2003. *Genders in Production: Making Workers in Mexico's Global Factories.* Berkeley and Los Angeles: University of California Press.

Sargent, J., and L. Matthews. 2008 "China versus Mexico in the Global EPZ Industry: Maquiladoras, FDI Quality and Plant Mortality." *World Development* 37 (6): 1069–82.

Seguino, S. 2000a. "Accounting for Gender in Asian Economic Growth." *Feminist Economics* 6 (3): 27–58.

Seguino, S. 2000b. "Gender Inequality and Economic Growth: A Cross-Country Analysis." *World Development* 28 (7): 1211–30.

Seguino, S., G. Berik, and Y. M. Rodgers. 2010. *An Investment that Pays Off: Promoting Gender Equality as a Means to Finance Development.* Gender Study. Berlin: Friedrich Ebert Stiftung International.

Singer, H. W. 1950. "The distribution of gains between investing and borrowing countries." *American Economic Review, Papers and Proceedings* 5: 473–85.

Sirimanne, S. 2009. "Emerging Issue: The Gender Perspectives of the Financial Crisis." Written Statement, Commission on the Status of Women, Fifty-third Session, March 2–13, New York.

Sivananthiram, A. n.d. "Promoting Decent Work in Export Processing Zones (EPZs) in Sri Lanka." Available at http://www.ilo.org/public/english/dialogue/epz.htm (accessed September 2010).

Smith, S., and S. Barrientos. 2005. "Fair Trade and Ethical Trade: Are There Moves towards Convergence?" *Sustainable Development* 13: 190–98.

Standing, G. 1989. "Global Feminization through Flexible Labor." *World Development* 17 (7) : 1077–95.

Standing, G. 1999. "Global Feminization Through Flexible Labor: A Theme Revisited." *World Development* 27 (3): 583–602.

Strom, S. H. 1989. "'Light Manufacturing': The Feminization of American Office Work, 1900–1930." *Industrial and Labor Relations Review* 43 (10): 53–71.

Tejani, S., and W. Milberg. 2010. *Global Defeminization? Industrial Upgrading, Occupational Segmentation and Manufacturing Employment in Middle-Income Countries.* SCEPA Working Paper Series 2010-1. New York: Schwartz Center for Economic Policy Analysis.

"Three Killed, Dozens Hurt in Bangladesh Clashes." 2010. BBC, December 12. Available at http://www.bbc.co.uk/news/world-south-asia-11978254 (accessed December 12, 2010).

UNCTAD. 2004. *Trade and Gender: Opportunities and Challenges for Developing Countries.* Edited by A. Tran-Nguyen and A.B. Zampetti. United Nations Conference on Trade and Development. New York and Geneva: United Nations.

Ver Beek, K. A. 2001. "Maquiladoras: Exploitation or Emancipation? An Overview of the Situation of Maquiladora Workers in Honduras." *World Development* 29 (9): 1553–67.

Walsh, M. 1997. "Women's Place in the American Labour Force, 1870–1955." *History* 82 (268): 563–81.

Weichselbaumer, D., and R. Winter-Ebmer. 2003. *A Meta-analysis of the International Gender Wage Gap.* Discussion Paper No. 906. Bonn: Institute for the Study of Labor (IZA).

Wood, A. 1991. "North-South Trade and Female Labour in Manufacturing: An Asymmetry." *Journal of Development Studies* 27 (2): 168–89.

World Bank. 2009. *World Development Indicators Online.* Washington, DC: World Bank. http://databank.worldbank.org/ddp/home.do?Step=12&id=4&CNO=2 (accessed January 2009)

World Bank. 2009–10. *SEZ Surveys.* International Trade Department. Washington, DC: World Bank.

WTO (World Trade Organization). 2008. *World Trade Report 2008: Trade in a Globalizing World.* Geneva: World Trade Organization.

Zhang, H. 2007. "China's New Rural Daughters Coming of Age: Downsizing the Family and Firing up Cash-Earning Power in the New Economy." *Signs: Journal of Women in Culture and Society* 32 (3): 671–98.

Zohir, S. C. 2001. *Gender Balance in the EPZ: A Socio-economic Study of the Dhaka Export Processing Zone in Bangladesh.* Bangladesh: Bangladesh Institute of Development Studies.

CHAPTER 12

Low-Carbon, Green Special Economic Zones

Han-Koo Yeo and Gokhan Akinci

Introduction

The climate change agenda has emerged as a core development challenge of our time as it became obvious that countries cannot continue a development paradigm of the past depending on heavy fossil-fuel and greenhouse gas (GHG) emissions. Deep cuts in global emissions are required to hold the increase in global temperature below 2 degrees Celsius (2°C), and this will not be possible to meet without full participation by all the countries.

There has been a growing consensus that all the countries have to participate in global efforts to fight climate change in accordance with the principle of "common but differentiated responsibilities and respective capabilities," as clearly stipulated in the Article 3 of the United Nations Convention on Climate Change. The Copenhagen Accord, which came out of the Climate Change Summit in December and to which more than 100 countries have committed, states in Article 5 that developing countries will implement nationally appropriate mitigation actions and shall communicate such actions.

To developing countries, development and climate change are two interlinked challenges, neither of which can be sacrificed. These countries have to lift 1.4 billion people out of poverty by building factories, power plants, roads, buildings, and transport systems, while ensuring that they comply with environmental sustainability and significantly reduce their carbon footprints along the way. The Copenhagen Accord reflects such need in Article 2, bearing in mind that social and economic development and poverty eradication are the first and overriding priorities of developing countries and that a low-emission development strategy is indispensible to sustainable development.

In this regard, exploring new ways to pursue low-carbon and green growth, a new development paradigm, is a big task ahead. This new development paradigm is meant to decouple economic growth from further increases in GHG emissions. This paradigm also seeks to create jobs based on the development and deployment of clean technologies. It is important to come to a common understanding that shifting to a low-carbon, green economy does not mean sacrificing competitiveness and economic growth; but rather, is an investment in long-term sustainable economic development.

Low-Carbon, Green SEZs: Overview

Special Economic Zones

SEZs have played an important role in advancing industrial development, attracting FDI, and creating jobs in developing countries for the last 30 years. As climate change agenda emerges as one of the core development challenges, governments, developers, and companies around the world are increasingly demanding that SEZs also contribute to environmental sustainability and GHG mitigation. Governments like China and India already are developing guidelines and policies for green zones, and many others like the Republic of Korea and Thailand are focusing on systematic development of eco-industrial parks.

In fact, in many countries, industrial zones are major contributors to GHG emissions from manufacturing, energy generation and consumption, buildings, and transportation. For instance, in the Republic of Korea, about 650 industrial parks account for 63 percent of industrial emissions in the nation, according to the Korea Industrial Complex Corporation. This exemplifies the challenges as well as the opportunities that SEZs face in addressing climate change. In other words, more than 3,000 SEZs around the globe can provide one of the best opportunities to tackle climate change and reduce GHG emissions in a systematic and measurable way.

What Is a Low-Carbon, Green SEZ?

There has been a strong trend to develop more environmentally sustainable SEZs over time, reflecting the private sector's increasing awareness of and demands for environmental sustainability. Lately, as climate change agenda adds more emphasis on the environmental dimension of SEZs, similar terminologies, such as Pollution Control Zone, Environment Compliance Zone, Eco-industrial Zone (Park), Low-carbon Zone, Green Zone and others, are being used interchangeably without clear distinctions. This section attempts to define "low-carbon, green SEZ" and identifies its key attributes, within the spectrum of environmentally sustainable zones (see figure 12.1).

The *environment compliance zone* or *pollution control zone* could be considered as an early stage form of zones in this spectrum. Its main emphasis is on the implementation of effective measures for pollution control and environmental compliance, such as air pollution control, centralized services for sewage and wastewater treatment, hazardous waste collection and disposal, and environmental training programs for zone managers and company operations. Implementation of environmental management tools such as International Organization for Standardization (ISO) 14001 Environmental Management System (EMS) may be one of the systematic programs to consider in these zones.

Eco-industrial zones (parks) goes beyond simple environmental management to reduce the negative impact of pollution. This is a more advanced concept in terms of environmental sustainability. Its purpose is to manage the whole resource, energy, and environmental impact in an

Figure 12.1   Spectrum of Environmentally Sustainable Zones

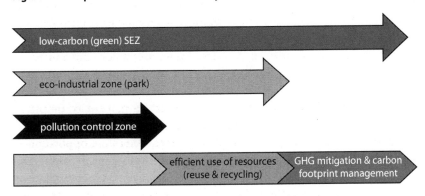

Source: Authors.
Note: GHG = greenhouse gases; SEZ = special economic zone.

integrated manner. The *Eco-industrial Park Handbook* (Ernest 2001) developed by the Asian Development Bank states that "[a]n Eco-Industrial Park is a community of manufacturing and service businesses located together on a common property. Members seek enhanced environmental, economic, and social performance through collaboration in managing environmental and resource issues" (1). Therefore, eco-industrial zones reuse and recycle resources within industrial zones and clustered or chained industries, so that resources will circulate fully in the local production system. Also known as industrial symbiosis, zone networks are established between companies in the zone to exchange waste from one company to another to be reused in another production process.

Low-carbon, green SEZs is the most comprehensive and advanced concept in terms of environmental sustainability. Pollution control and environment management as well as reuse and recycling of resources in terms of industrial symbiosis, are important ingredients of low-carbon, green SEZs. However, this concept goes further to more actively manage carbon footprint. Generally, low-carbon, green SEZs can be defined as SEZs that are designed, developed, and operated in a low-carbon, green, sustainable way, and hence they reduce the carbon footprint and effectively address climate change mitigation in the process of their economic and industrial activities in the SEZ. Some of the main attributes of low-carbon, green SEZs include, but are not limited to, energy supply in part using renewable energy sources; energy-efficiency measures, including use of energy-efficient production methods for industries; construction of buildings and factories using "green building codes"; waste-reuse and recycling systems inside and outside the zone; promotion of climate-friendly investment into the zone and clean technology R&D and deployment; and carbon finance mechanisms that can be utilized to build the zone and many others.

Why Low-Carbon, Green SEZs?

Low-carbon, green SEZs build on the proven concept of SEZs, to play a catalytic role by trying out new low-carbon, green measures in an SEZ setting, and if proven valid, roll out into nationwide initiatives. Its clustering of companies and industries in an SEZ could provide multiple advantages not only to apply different components of a climate-friendly policy and investment regime, but also to target existing zones or future zones. On one hand, the low-carbon, green zone maximizes the effectiveness of environmental infrastructure for industry, which otherwise could be expensive for individual companies. On the other hand, single zone management for hundreds of companies from a low-carbon, green perspective allows for a huge synergy effect in various forms, such as the efficient use of low-carbon management expertise, the steep learning curve, and peer pressure to do what is right that does not exist outside the zone.

Low-carbon, green SEZs could be a useful platform to materialize a low-carbon development strategy that developed and developing countries tend to have consensus on in international climate change negotiations. It is expected that in the near future GHG emission from developing countries will surpass that from developed countries. As SEZs have effectively driven industrial development and growth in the developing world (but following an old, high-carbon development path), this new trend of low-carbon, green SEZs could be a shortcut to achieve a low-carbon development path in developing countries around the world in a concrete and realistic way.

Low-Carbon (Green) SEZ Framework

Low-carbon, green SEZs can take many different forms across a wide spectrum of countries. Low-carbon green, SEZs have five core components (see figure 12.2):

* *GHG Mitigation Target:* The economic activities inside the SEZ are aligned with concrete action plans for mitigation. As such, a low-carbon, green SEZ can establish a goal and commitment to GHG mitigation at the center of its overall strategy (e.g., SEZ-wide 30 percent reduction

Figure 12.2   Main Components of a Low-Carbon, Green SEZ Framework

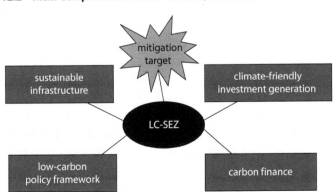

Source: Authors.
Note: LC-SEZ = low-carbon, green special economic zone.

by 2020, renewable energy mix of 15 percent). The first step is to develop a baseline using basic GHG accounting rules and inventory systems making it possible to monitor how much GHG emission comes from which source and how much emission reduction potential exists in each sector.

- *Sustainable Infrastructure:* Planning, designing, and building a zone infrastructure using energy-efficient, resource-saving, and low-carbon methods would provide ample opportunities to reduce the carbon footprint. Some sources for GHG reduction include renewable energy, energy efficiency, green buildings, and a waste reuse and recycling system.

- *Climate-Friendly Investment Generation:* Low-carbon, green SEZs can generate a streamlined and low-risk environment that fills in the gaps in the national legal framework to attract new, climate-friendly investment and technologies. To do so, it is also important to develop relevant investment promotion tools and methodologies to incorporate green elements in terms of green business targeting, incentives, intellectual property protection, and marketing strategy.

- *Low-Carbon Policy Incentives and Regulations:* Putting the right public policy framework in place is a critical success factor for low-carbon, green SEZs. Some best practices include eliminating trade and nontrade barriers on climate-friendly products, instituting green building codes, and establishing renewable energy or energy-efficiency laws (e.g., Brazil, China, India), which introduce a feed-in tariff system, renewable portfolio standards (RPS) and energy-efficiency standards, tax reduction for green high-technology investment, and R&D support.

- *Carbon Finance:* A carbon finance mechanism, such as a clean development mechanism (CDM), can provide the potential to channel new source of funding to develop low-carbon, green SEZs in middle-income as well as low-income countries.

GHG Mitigation Target

A low-carbon, green SEZ needs a clear goal and commitment to GHG mitigation at the center of its overall strategy. Under the general direction of a low-carbon development strategy, all the economic activities inside the SEZ need to be aligned with concrete action plans for mitigation. A mitigation goal can be set up in many different forms to accommodate the different circumstances found in each SEZ. For instance, Incheon Free Economic Zone in the Republic of Korea plans to set the goal of

achieving an SEZ-wide 30 percent reduction of GHG by 2020 compared with its business-as-usual (BAU) scenario. A more ambitious target
could be an absolute amount of GHG reduction compared with the
emission level at a certain point in the past (e.g., 30 percent reduction by
2020 compared with its 2005 level). SEZs with a contained expectation
could consider more modest targets, limiting the scope and extent of the
target to certain sectors (e.g., 10 percent energy-efficiency improvement
by 2020, or 15 percent of power supply from renewable energy source
by 2020). In terms of time, the SEZ can set up a short-term (2015),
midterm (2020), or long-term (2050) target for more visible outcomes.

The first step to introduce GHG mitigation components into all parts
of the SEZ is to establish a GHG inventory system to monitor, report, and
verify how much GHG is being emitted from which sources, and to
determine how much GHG reduction can be achieved through what
kinds of methods from which sources (see figure 12.3).

The SEZ authority needs to develop a GHG inventory guideline,
referring to the GHG inventory guideline established by the
Intergovernmental Panel on Climate Change and other internationally
recognized institutions such as World Resources Institute, and verify the

Figure 12.3   Trajectory of GHG Emission and Mitigation Target

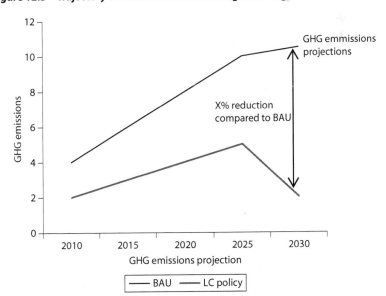

Source: Authors.
Note: BAU = business as usual; GHG = greenhouse gas; LC = low carbon.

accuracy and credibility of such data. By nature, GHG emission data are closely linked to energy generation and consumption data, which makes integrated management of such data sets more efficient. Companies and institutions above a certain level of annual GHG emission in an SEZ should be required to monitor and report their GHG emission data on an annual basis to the appropriate authority. According to the Copenhagen Accord (Article 5), developing countries are supposed to communicate mitigation actions, including national inventory reports, every two years. The SEZ authority also needs to carry out an analysis of how much GHG emission is projected by a certain point (e.g., 2020) according to its current SEZ development plan (the base scenario) and to identify how much GHG emission reduction potential exists in each sector through a diverse set of mitigation measures (the policy scenario). Such analysis may need top-down macroeconomic modeling exercises as well as bottom-up surveys. Generally, most GHG emissions in an SEZ come from energy consumption, such as electricity, heating, cooling, industrial process, transportation, and water and waste disposal (see figure 12.4).

Figure 12.4   Example: Some SEZ GHG Emission Structures by Sector

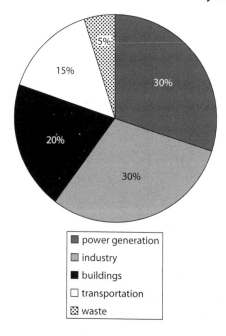

Source: Authors.
Note: GHG = greenhouse gas; SEZ = special economic zone.

Therefore, opportunities for GHG mitigation in an SEZ could lie in renewable energy generation, energy efficiency and conservation, green buildings, a sustainable transportation system, water and waste reuse, and recycling systems.

Sustainable Infrastructure

Planning, designing, and building zone infrastructure in energy-efficient, resource-saving, waste-recycling ways from the outset could provide ample opportunities to reduce an SEZ's carbon footprint. **Energy supply and demand, green buildings, and waste recycling systems** are important examples. Such infrastructure investment would be sustainable only when medium- and long-term social and economic benefits surpass incremental cost increases in the short term. For instance, making buildings in China more energy efficient would add 10 percent to construction costs but would save more than 50 percent on energy cost (Shalizi and Lecocq 2009). Integrated zero-emission building designs, which combine energy-efficiency measures with on-site power and heat from solar power and biomass, are technically and economically feasible, and their costs are falling (Brown, Southworth, and Stovall 2005).

First, in terms of **energy supply** infrastructure, providing some portion of electricity through **renewable energy** is an important element of low-carbon, green SEZs. To meet the 450 parts per million, 2°C goal, most developing countries would need to boost their production of renewable energy. It is important to identify suitable sources of renewable energy, such as biomass, solar, wind, hydro, and geothermal, for certain SEZs in the context of national circumstances. For instance, in India, wind power would be one of easier options for SEZs, taking into account that the nation has the fifth-largest installed wind power capacity in the world. As a second-best option, when renewable energy is not readily available in terms of technical or financial feasibility, even increasing the average efficiency of coal-fired power plants can reduce GHG emission. For instance, China has increased the average efficiency of coal-fired power plants by 15 percent over the last decade to an average of 34 percent. Replacing small-scale coal-fired power plants with large-scale efficient plants over the last few years reduced annual CO_2 emissions by 60 million tons. An SEZ could commit to a certain target for renewable energy supply, which would be higher than the national average. According to India's *Guidelines for Energy Conservation in SEZ* (October 27, 2010), 100 percent of organic waste generated within SEZs should be used for in-situ power generation or vermi-composted, as applicable. Also, external lighting in common spaces may comply with the requirement that at least 10 percent of the installed load should be solar powered during the first year of operation, and the installed load must be extended by at least 5 percent annually until a target of 50 percent is achieved. The use of incandescent lamps is not allowed. The *Vision and Roadmap for Haiti* (May 23, 2010) prepared by the Private Sector Economic Forum of Haiti and presented to the government of Haiti states that in five years, 15 percent of energy needs to come from renewable energy sources, mostly in housing and industrial parks.   ·

In the short term, the largest and cheapest source of emission reduction is increased **energy efficiency** on both the supply and demand side in power, industry, buildings, and transport. Energy efficiency offers the biggest source (approximately 60 percent) of emission reduction, according to the International Energy Agency. A range of measures can be taken, from simply replacing road lights with energy-efficient light-emitting diode lights (LEDs) to bringing new energy-efficient technologies to industrial processes and managing the load profiles of individual industrial production. Some examples include energy-efficient process equipment, industrial air conditioning, electrical power, power transmission and distribution, heating and cooling of industrial and commercial space, and lighting. For instance, in India, a large potential exists to reduce the 29 percent losses in transmission and distribution to a level closer to the world average of 9 percent, which will smooth out peak demand and lessen the pressure to build more fossil-fueled power plants.

Buildings provide good opportunities for GHG mitigation. For some large-scale SEZs with many factories and commercial and residential buildings, emissions from the building sector account for a considerable portion of total emissions. Putting energy-efficient measures into the design and planning stage, such as energy-efficient heating and cooling systems, insulation, natural ventilation, and efficient lighting, could effectively reduce emissions in a sustainable way. For existing buildings, a dramatic change would not be possible; however, retrofitting some older buildings into more energy-efficient buildings actually could make business sense in that long-term energy saving would be greater than the upfront investment (as seen in many of the recent retrofitting examples in high-income countries). An appropriate set of incentive programs could facilitate such investment. The SEZ authority needs to employ administrative action programs, such as green building codes, that can be enforced during the building review process to ensure that buildings

across the zone as a whole meet minimum standards and reduce the carbon footprint.

Waste reuse and recycling is a quick win through which companies
can reap the concrete benefits upon implementation. Recycling can be
done at the individual company level, but when it is done across multiple
companies in low-carbon, green SEZs, the benefits can be maximized. For
instance, a textile company, SAE-A Trading Co., installed an incinerator
in a Nicaragua factory to utilize regenerated heat energy. The company
completed combustion of fabric wastes and utilized steam generated by
heating water during the ironing process to generate energy, which helped
the company save energy costs and reduce GHG emission. The Republic
of Korea applies the industrial symbiosis concept to its industrial parks
(see figure 12.5). It transforms industrial parks into comprehensive and
collective networks of waste, energy, and information exchanges.

Figure 12.5   Example of Industrial Symbiosis Networking Map, Republic of Korea

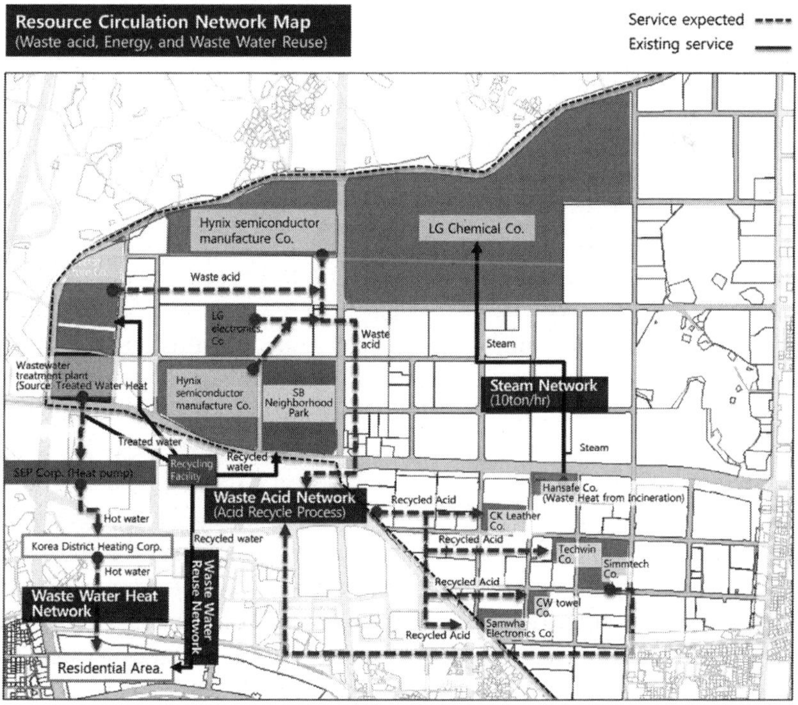

Source: Ban, Young Un (2010).

In terms of infrastructure planning, design, and construction, these actions and measures could be enforced during the master planning and reviewing process at the initial stage of an SEZ. The role of the SEZ authority is critical as a facilitator as well as a regulator to ensure that this happens.

Climate-Friendly Investment Generation

When basic infrastructure such as roads, electricity, and water are complete and ready, the focus turns to investment generation, which will create business and job opportunities. To put it in a broader context of current global climate change negotiations, the implication of a low-carbon, green SEZ is quite significant. The Copenhagen Accord states that developed countries commit to a goal of jointly financing US$100 billion a year by 2020 to developing countries with combined sources from the private and public sector. This commitment means that a significant portion of investment generation to mitigate GHG emission could materialize in a setting like a low-carbon, green SEZ, considering that an SEZ has a more favorable investment climate in developing countries. In reality, such investment flows from developed to developing countries could take the form of FDI. In 2007, FDI accounted for 12.6 percent of the total gross fixed capital formation in electricity, gas, and water in developing countries, which was three times the amount of multilateral and bilateral aid (Brewer 2008).

There is an encouraging sign in the global market that the flow of climate-friendly, low-carbon investment is rapidly increasing lately. According to *World Investment Report* 2010 by UNCTAD, low-carbon FDI is significant and its potential is huge.

The cost curve in figure 12.6 shows what actions or investment would be most cost-effective in delivering GHG mitigation to fully capture opportunities across sectors. The key issue would be how to make an attractive investment environment to facilitate and generate investment in diverse sectors to realize GHG mitigation opportunities.

Climate-friendly or green investment can be roughly defined as investment aiming to increase the use of clean energy from renewable sources, improve energy efficiency, or reduce the carbon footprint in the production of products or provision of services. Investment in renewable energy or energy efficiency is a good example. MNCs have invested massively in renewable industry of developing countries, such as photovoltaic production in India (BP Solar), ethanol in Brazil (Archer Daniels Midland and Cargill), and wind power in China (Gamesa and Vestas). According

Figure 12.6   Global Greenhouse Gas Mitigation Marginal Cost Curve Beyond 2030 Business-as-Usual

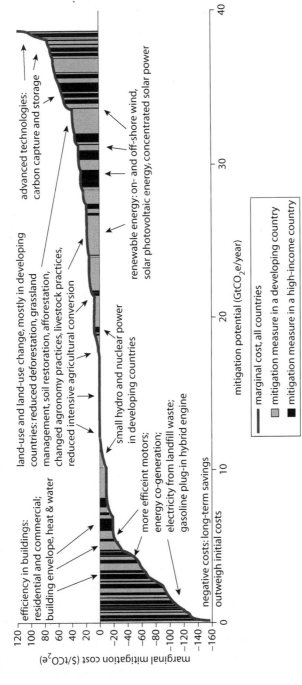

Source: World Bank, *World Development Report 2010.*

Note: The bars represent various mitigation measures, with the width indicating the amount of emission reduction each measure would achieve and the height indicating the cost, per ton of avoided emissions, of the measure. Tracing the height of the bars creates a marginal mitigation cost curve.

to *fDi Markets* data (Brownell 2009), between January 2003 and August 2009, there have been more than 1,400 cross-border greenfield investment projects in renewable energy. In terms of energy-efficiency investment, energy service companies (ESCOs) could provide energy-efficiency services (such as energy auditing), recommend energy-saving measures, provide financing to clients, and serve as project aggregators. ESCOs are not just limited to the high-income-country environment. In China, for example, after a decade of capacity building supported by the World Bank, the ESCO industry grew from three companies in 1997 to more than 400, with US$1 billion in energy performance contracts in 2007 (World Bank 2008). Such investment in renewables and energy efficiency is expected to grow as more developing countries race toward a low-carbon development path. Conversely, investment in traditional industries such as steel, chemicals, and textiles can be "greened" by bringing in more energy-efficient or clean technologies to reduce GHG emission and by "greening" some parts of the value chain with low-carbon technologies. For instance, a steel company, POSCO, is introducing a new eco-friendly FINEX technology and processes in building a new steel plant in India. FINEX, which POSCO has developed, is an environmentally friendly iron-making process that allows the direct use of iron ore fines and non-coking coal as feedstock. As a result, the emission of pollutants will be drastically reduced, to levels of only 4–8 percent of traditional steel production processes.

To institutionalize the carbon factor into the investment decision process, the SEZ authority may require that all investment projects report GHG emission estimation throughout the project life cycle. Currently, all new real sector projects in IFC require GHG estimation before they can receive approval.

Attracting green FDI could draw in domestic investors in this area, developing further linkages with local suppliers. Clean technology transfer and deployment is one of the most important issues enabling developing countries to build capacity and fight climate change. In fact, an attractive investment climate for FDI could be critical to accelerating technology transfer and absorption (Goldberg, Branstetter, Goddard, and Kuriakose 2008). The Copenhagen Accord (Article 11) emphasizes establishing the technology mechanism to accelerate technology development and transfer. To maximize spillover of low-carbon technologies, low-carbon, green SEZs could explore the "clean technology center" concept, in which companies, local universities, and research institutes collaborate to develop, transfer, and deploy clean technologies through a PPP model.

This kind of center can become a center of excellence for innovation, knowledge sharing, and training for local companies and institutions. Such initiatives need to be coordinated with national technology policies and programs, and can pursue international collaboration in joint R&D with public support from developed countries.

For effective investment promotion efforts, it is important to incorporate the green aspect into the investment promotion tools and methodologies that have been developed so far. These aspects include identifying target industries and businesses through competitive market analysis, developing coherent marketing strategies, and implementing marketing campaigns, including investor relations activities. In many countries, however, such incorporation is not an easy task because most government agencies dealing with climate change and energy policies are different from those in charge of investment promotion and generation.

Low-Carbon Policy Incentives and Regulations

An integrated policy approach to providing an enabling business environment for low-carbon, green SEZs cannot be overemphasized. Putting in place an appropriate set of public policies, including incentives and regulations, is a critical success factor for low-carbon, green SEZs. In the early stage of market development, the role of the public sector can make or break the success of the project. The policy framework for low-carbon, green SEZs can be categorized as basic, legal, regulatory, incentive, or institutional (see figure 12.7). Some of these issues can be applied at the SEZ level, whereas others need to be applied as national policy initiatives.

Basic Policy Framework

Fostering an environment for free trade and investment should be included in a basic policy framework. Eliminating trade and nontrade barriers on climate-friendly products or services could be a strong merit of a low-carbon, green SEZ. For instance, in Egypt, the average tariffs on photovoltaic panels are 32 percent, 10 times the 3 percent tariff imposed in high-income member countries of OECD. In Nigeria, potential users of photovoltaic panels face nontariff barriers of 70 percent in addition to a 20 percent tariff. Considering that the absorption of technologies normally occurs through imports of equipment, tariff barriers could restrict local learning of these technologies. Conversely, low-carbon, green SEZs need to apply the extraterritoriality principle—that is, they should be treated as outside the domestic customs territory, but eligible for

Figure 12.7   Low-Carbon, Green SEZ Policy Framework

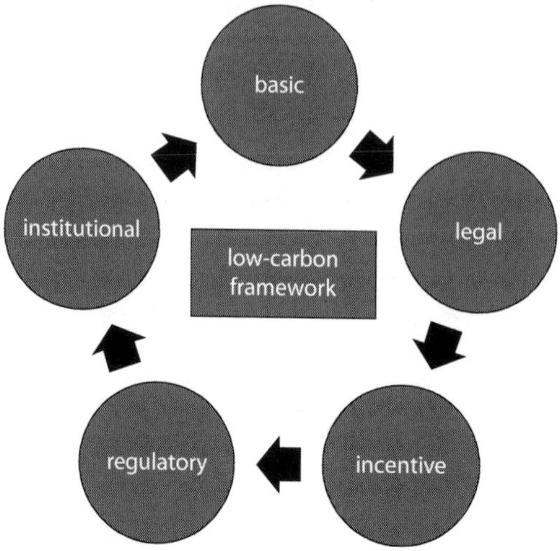

Source: Authors.

national certificates of origin and to participate in trade and market access agreements.

To facilitate local capacity building and technology transfer, a weak IPR regime could be an obstacle for middle-income countries. Weak IPR enforcement discourages foreign subsidiaries from increasing the scale of their R&D activities and foreign venture capitalists from investing in promising domestic enterprises (Branstetter, Fisman, and Foley 2005). Low-carbon, green SEZs could absorb foreign technologies and facilitate technology cooperation with foreign companies by providing a more predictable and stable IPR environment.

Legal Framework

Developing a conducive legal framework is fundamental to ensuring a transparent and predictable business environment for SEZs as well as for climate change mitigation. Currently, most countries with SEZ programs have SEZ legislation in place, and many high-income and middle-income developing countries have completed or are legislating comprehensive climate change law. In addition, many countries have established renewable energy or energy-efficiency laws (e.g., Brazil, China, India). These laws institutionalize incentives and regulations to promote renewable energy or energy-efficiency programs. Considering the generally accepted best practices for a legal framework surrounding climate change, renewable energy, energy efficiency, and SEZs, the key issue is how to incorporate low-carbon, green SEZ components into the current legal framework. Different countries may have different solutions. One solution is to incorporate low-carbon aspects into SEZ laws. Low-carbon elements could be required for SEZ approval and designation. Another solution is to include a low-carbon aspect in general climate change legislation. The contents of climate change legislation vary depending on countries, but some (such as the Republic of Korea's Low-Carbon, Green Growth Basic Law) stipulate a basis for developing a low-carbon industrial cluster or complex. More fundamentally, countries need to legally define the meaning of "low-carbon" or "green" to prevent confusion or overexpansion. These terms might be used frequently to determine the beneficiaries of diverse incentives or regulations.

Regulatory Framework

According to conventional wisdom, environmental regulations could contribute to creating markets and advancing technological innovation versus suffocating businesses. For instance, the state of California—known for its superior leadership in environmental performance and energy efficiency—has pioneered one of the strongest regulations for its environment in advance of other states in the United States. Of course, regulation alone cannot claim all the credit, because regulations need to be supplemented with incentives for consumers and producers. Some of best practices that can be applied to a low-carbon, green SEZ include energy-efficiency standards for sectors, green building codes, climate change impact assessment, and RPS. For utilities, RPS means that some portion of power supply should come from renewable sources. The SEZ authority may require that investors disclose their GHG emission estimation for investment projects above a certain level, and that businesses as well as buildings monitor and report annual GHG emission data. In a country where comprehensive climate change mitigation measures already are being taken, low-carbon, green SEZs could follow suit, but could aim higher than the national average.

Incentive System

In many countries, SEZs have diverse incentive systems in place, including corporate tax reductions or exemption; duty-free importation of raw materials, capital goods, and intermediate inputs; no restrictions or taxes on capital and profits repatriation; tax relief for foreign workers and executives; exemption from most local and indirect taxes; financial support; and so on. Also, many countries operate incentives to encourage investment in green industry, such as renewable energy and energy efficiency. Therefore, to promote low-carbon investment and actions in SEZs, incorporating diverse incentives developed for different purposes into a coherent low-carbon, green SEZ incentive scheme is a key issue. When foreign investors bring in high-tech green capital equipment, intermediary parts, or materials, customs tariff and tax could be exempted. Indonesia introduced green initiatives in April 2010, stating that it would reduce the net tax base by 5 percent annually for the next six years on the total investment in renewable energy. Foreign investors will receive a lower tax rate on all dividend payments. Companies involved in construction will not be charged value added tax or import duty on machinery and equipment used for such projects. For renewable energy and energy efficiency for which it is hard to make the business case in the absence of government incentives, feed-in tariffs for renewable energy investment and tax credits for energy-efficiency investments are critical. Feed-in tariff laws require mandatory purchases of renewable energy at a fixed price, such as those in Germany, Kenya, Spain, and South Africa, producing the highest market penetration rates in a short period. Investors consider these laws to be the most desirable and conducive to creating local industries because of their price certainty and administrative simplicity.

Several financial incentives to consider include reducing upfront capital costs through subsidies; reducing capital and operating costs through investment or production tax credits; improving revenue streams with carbon credits; and providing financial support through concessional loans and guarantees. Prioritizing R&D funds for projects in a low-carbon, green SEZ, or mass procurement of energy-efficient green products, could provide substantial incentives. In Uganda and Vietnam, the bulk procurement of 1 million compact fluorescent lamps in each country substantially reduced the cost of the lamps and improved product quality through technical specifications and warranty; once installed, they cut peak demand by 30 megawatts.

Institutional Framework

An institutional champion, such as a dedicated agency in charge of climate change policy, is essential to coordinate multiple stakeholders and promote and manage relevant policy issues. In a low-carbon, green SEZ, a dedicated department in charge of low-carbon initiatives needs to be established inside the SEZ authority. Because low-carbon initiatives are multidisciplinary, involving energy, environment, buildings, transportation, and so on, such a department needs to be established as a control tower overlooking all relevant functions. Its main mission will be to make a low-carbon master plan, lead the implementation process, and coordinate among different departments.

Carbon finance. A carbon-pricing mechanism is needed in developing countries to signal that investment in high-carbon projects will yield lower returns. This mechanism is needed to internalize externalities regarding environmental and climate problem. The carbon market will provide a cost-effective way to reduce emissions from MNCs and direct investment flow to low-income countries through its offset mechanism. Low-carbon, green SEZs can channel new source of financing through the carbon finance mechanism and facilitate investment in climate-friendly investment.

Using Market Instruments: Clean Development Mechanisms

Market mechanisms can encourage private investment in GHG mitigation. Although some uncertainty remains after 2012 when the first commitment period under the Kyoto Protocol ends, the CDM is one of the most prominent market instruments related to developing countries. CDMs enable low-carbon projects in developing countries to generate and trade carbon credits (Certified Emission Reductions, or CERs). For instance, a German power utility may acquire CERs by investing in renewable energy projects in Chile, or a Japanese steel company may acquire CERs by investing new clean mitigation technology in its Vietnamese steel projects. The CDM has triggered more than 4,000 recognized emission reduction projects since 1997 when CDM was conceived by Kyoto Protocol, but a small group of middle-income countries such as Brazil, China, India, and the Republic of Korea have dominated 75 percent of these carbon credit supplies. In the ongoing United Nations Framework Convention for Climate Change (UNFCCC) negotiations, the CDM reform agenda is one of the hottest topics on the table. The debate includes such issues as how to rectify the unequal distribution of CDM projects across developing countries and how to scale up the CDM scheme to have a greater impact on global mitigation.

From the low-carbon, green SEZ angle, CDM provides the potential to channel a new source of funding to develop low-carbon, green SEZs in middle- and low-income countries. The CDM scheme could be fully explored and utilized in many sustainable infrastructure projects. For example, as long as credible baseline and methodologies are developed,

Table 12.1   Some Examples of CDM Projects of IDA Countries

Host country	Investor	Project	Emission reduction
KENYA	Ormat Technologies (United States)	Geothermal expansion	177,600 t CO_2e/yr
UGANDA	Global Development Forum Suez, Chubu Electric Power Co., BP Alternative Energy, Deutsch Bank, etc.	Nile electrification	36,210 t CO_2e/yr
NIGERIA	Atmosfair gGmbH, Lernen-Helfen-Leben e.V. (Germany)	Energy-efficient fuel wood stoves replacement	31,309 t CO_2e/yr
SENEGAL MAURITANIA MALI	IBRD acting as a trustee for the Spanish Carbon Fund	Félou regional hydro-power	188,282 t CO_2e/yr
TANZANIA	Consorzio Stabile Globus (Italian)	Landfill gas recovery and electricity generation	202,271 t CO_2e/yr

Source: Compiled by authors based on data from UNFCCC.
Note: IBRD = International Bank for Reconstruction and Development; IDA = International Development Association; t CO_2e/yr = tons of carbon dioxide emissions per year.

building wind farms, deploying solar panels in buildings, changing street-lights into energy-efficient LEDs, retrofitting old buildings into more energy-efficient ones, improving manufacturing processes into energy-efficient ones, and recycling wastes to generate energy could create potential CDM projects. CDM projects increasingly are expanding to lower-income countries. Also, to overcome the limitation of individual project-based CDM, the concept of bundling multiple projects into one broader CDM program is being explored for scaling up.

Voluntary Carbon Market

Whereas CDM is a market mechanism based on the Kyoto Protocol, developing countries (more accurately, non–Annex I countries without mandatory compliance obligations according to the convention) could explore developing a voluntary carbon market domestically. A voluntary carbon market could be designed as a national, subnational, or private scheme in which participating companies voluntarily reduce GHG emission and get carbon credits (but different from CERs) from the appropriate authorities, and participants could trade their carbon credits. For instance, the Republic of Korea developed a voluntary carbon market by creating the Korea Certified Emission Reduction (KCER) program in 2005. In the national program, companies can voluntarily reduce GHG emissions and receive KCERs after the reduction is verified by the national authority. The Korean government provides incentives by purchasing KCERs for a certain price according to a guideline. Companies are compensated for their voluntary mitigation actions, such as investing in clean technologies and facilities, and the program encourages other companies to take early actions of mitigation, although they are not obliged to do so. Through the KCER scheme, an estimated 5.6 million tons of carbon dioxide emissions (t CO_2e) was reduced by 2009. Another example of a privately initiated voluntary carbon market is the Chicago Climate Exchange (CCX). The CCX is a private-sector-initiated, voluntary cap-and-trade program with members participating voluntarily but according to a legally binding contract. Its members represent 17 percent of the companies in the Dow Johns Industrial Average, including Ford, DuPont, Motorola, Sony, IBM, and Nike. Approximately 80 million t CO_2e of offset credits have been issued to date.

A low-carbon, green SEZ could become the centerpiece of voluntary carbon market development in the country. As CDM transactions in the SEZ gain steam, further potential to develop local voluntary carbon market could be explored. As China's representative low-carbon city, Jilin City, considers establishing a carbon exchange, hosting a carbon exchange in the low-carbon, green SEZ could promote the local carbon market.

Synergy between FDI and CDM

Although CDM is the principal instrument for catalyzing mitigation in developing countries, the CDM is unique in that it very much depends on a regulatory framework because it has to go through a lengthy and often bureaucratic approval process both domestically and internationally. Only after the final approval goes through the United Nations CDM Executive Board will CDM projects be permitted and CERs generated accordingly. Such an administrative process inherently brings the problem of incompetent institutional capacity of developing countries to implement CDM projects. The interlinkage and similarity between FDI and CDM has been overlooked, however, as well as the possible synergy to be created between them in terms of institutional capacity building (see table 12.2). For instance, if a Danish utility company makes FDI to build a wind farm in Cameroon through a CDM instrument, the investment could be classified as FDI as well as CDM. Although CDM is not the same as FDI, many of the tools and experiences developed under the FDI regime, such as targeting, competitive analysis, marketing,

Table 12.2   Interlinkage between CDM and FDI

Project design and formulation	The structure of information required for the project design document of the CDM is the same as that required for FDI
National approval	The national approval is similar to the approval given within the ambit of the Investment Facilitating Committee
	As the FDI projects, the technical review of projects can often involve the ministries and bureaus of the relevant sector
	The legal framework required for FDI would also apply to CDM
Validation/registration	For validation and registration a designated operational entity will review the project design document. A validation exercise by outside expects could also accompany many FDI-related projects.
Project financing	Generally, FDI comes in based on equity shares of a company, whereas CDM is based on projects
Monitoring/Verification/certification	Monitoring, verification and verification functions are carried out as required by EIAs or by specific requirements of particular industries
Issuance of CERs	CERs can be sold in the international carbon market, which will generate additional returns for MNCs

Source: Authors.
Note: CDM = clean development mechanism; CER = certified emission reduction; EIA = environmental impact assessment; FDI = foreign direct investment; MNCs = multinational companies.

and investor aftercare, could be used for CDM projects. One business executive from Sierra Leone has pointed out that existing channels handing FDI matters in developing countries could be made to handle CDM matters as FDI and CDM are interlinked (Keili 2003).

Low-Carbon, Green SEZs around the World: Current Status and Future Trends

Several countries are exploring ways to implement low-carbon, green SEZs in various forms, but with the common denominator of GHG mitigation and environmental and carbon footprint management. No clear industry model or leadership has been established for low-carbon, green SEZs. Some initiatives are emerging as pioneers in this area, with some of them expanding even further into low-carbon cities or eco-city initiatives.

Since the 1960s, a few industrial parks or cities in Europe such as Denmark and Sweden have evolved toward eco-industrial parks (EIPs). One of the most successful cases of EIP is the Kalundborg EIP in Denmark. The Kalundborg industrial symbiosis (IS) was started out of business motivation to reduce costs by seeking income-producing uses for "waste" products. This EIP model gradually developed over decades, turning into a complex web of symbiotic interactions. In Kalundborg IS, firms have saved US$160 million by 2001 ($15 million in annual savings), with return on the total investment reaching $75 million in the 18 projects established up to the end of 1998; therefore, the average payback time for all projects was less than five years (Sakr, Baas, El-Haggar, and Huisingh 2011). By 2001, at least 40 similar projects in the United States and 60 in Asia, Europe, South America, Australia, and South Africa have been initiated.

As SEZs have proven to be a successful model for China, low-carbon, green SEZs are also drawing a lot of policy attention as low-carbon growth pilots. A road map to transform Jilin City in northeast China to the first low-carbon SEZ (city) is underway in a partnership between the European Union and China, with participating institutions from U.K.'s Chatham House, E3G and the Chinese Academy of Social Sciences, Energy Research Institute, and Jilin University. According to the *Washington Post* (November 29, 2010), China's National Development and Reform Commission has listed 13 cities and provinces as pilot low-carbon areas to help reach the country's carbon intensity target, which is expected to feature heavily in the 12th Five-Year Plan (2011–2015). Hangzhou, capital of East China's Zhejiang province, for example, aims to reduce carbon intensity by about 35 percent by 2015 and 50 percent by 2020. India has also been quite active in rolling out its green SEZ initiatives. India's Ministry of Commerce put forward Guidelines for Energy Conservation in SEZ in October 2010, which covers a wide range of measures to push for energy efficiency, renewable energy usage and environment management.

The Republic of Korea is also gearing up for its green growth agenda through low-carbon cities and low-carbon SEZ initiatives. For instance, Korea's Incheon Free Economic Zone (IFEZ) set a new low-carbon, green vision with its "Low Carbon IFEZ 30" Plan, and a GHG mitigation target: 30 percent reduction compared to BAU by 2020 (15 percent reduction compared to BAU by 2014). IFEZ made a low-carbon master plan in December 2009 and organized a "GHG Mitigation TF" to spearhead its low-carbon strategy and plan, overarching all different departments in the SEZ authority.

As such, concrete actions toward low-carbon, green SEZs are being taken in these countries. Developing country GHG emissions are expected to grow above the world average at 2.7% annually between

2001 and 2025, and surpass emissions of industrialized countries near 2018 (Source: Energy Information Administration (EIA), International Energy Outlook, 2003). China, India, and Korea have clearly signaled that SEZs will have a growing role as components of their low-carbon, green growth path. As an instrument of trade and investment policy, SEZs have played a catalytic role in processes of industrialization, diversification and trade integration in developing countries. It is expected that SEZs will evolve to continue to play a similar role in low-carbon and green growth with more and more countries following suit to incorporate this new approach into their development models.

References

Asia Business (in Korean). Dec. 8, 2009. "Incheon Free Economic Zone aims to reduce GHG emissions 30% by 2030." http://www.ajnews.co.kr/view.jsp?newsId=20091208000189.

Ban, Young Un. 2010. "Eco-industrial Park Strategies in Korea." Regulatory Reform for Green Growth conference, Seoul, Korea, November 4–5.

Branstetter, L., R. Fisman, and C. F. Foley. 2005. *Do Stronger Intellectual Property Rights Increase International Technology Transfer? Empirical Evidence from U.S. Firm-Level Data.* Working Paper No. 11516. Cambridge, MA: National Bureau of Economic Research.

Brewer, T. L. 2008. *International Energy Technology Transfer for Climate Change Mitigation: What, Who, How, Why, When, Where, How Much . . . and the Implications for International Institutional Architecture.* Working Paper No. 2048. Venice: CESifo.

Brown, M. A., F. Southworth, and T. K. Stovall. 2005. *Toward a Climate-Friendly Built Environment.* Arlington, VA: Pew Center on Global Climate Change.

Brownell, G. Global outlook: "Renewable energy—Just a load of hot air?" *Foreign Direct Investment* (fDI): December 2009.

Chatham House and E3G, 2008. "Low Carbon Zones: A transformational agenda for China and Europe." December 2001. London: Chatham House.

Chatham House, Chinese Academy of Social Sciences,Energy Research Institute, Jilin University, and E3G. 2010. "Low Carbon Development Roadmap for Jilin City." March 2010. London: Chatham House.

Christensen, J. 1999. Proceedings of the Industry & Environment Workshop, held at the Indian Institute of Management, Ahmedabad.

Climate Action Reserve. Available at http://www.climateactionreserve.org/resources/climate-change-facts/.

Copenhagen Accord. Available at http://unfccc.int/home/items/5262.php.

Goldberg, I., L. Branstetter, J. G. Goddard, and S. Kuriakose. 2008. *Globalization and Technology Absorption in Europe and Central Asia.* Washington, DC: World Bank.

Haiti Private Sector Economic Forum. 2010. *Vision and Roadmap for Haiti.* Prepared by the Private Sector Economic Forum, Final Draft version presented to government of Haiti.

India Ministry of Commerce and Industry. 2010. *Guidelines for Energy Conservation in SEZ.*

International Energy Agency, World Energy Outlook 2009. Available at http://www.iea.org/speech/2009/Tanaka/WEO2009_Press_Conference.pdf.

International Organization for Standardization (ISO). Avvailable at http://www.iso.org/iso/iso_14000_essentials.

Keili, Andrew K. 2003. Executive Director, Cemmats Group Ltd. Sierra Leone.

Korea Industrial Complex Corporation. 2011, March 21. Executive interviews. http://www.kicox.or.kr/main/main.jsp.

Li Jing, 2010. "Industrial zones come clean due to green drive." *Washington Post* (November 29).

Lowe, E. A. 2001. *Eco-industrial Park Handbook for Asian Developing Countries. A Report to Asian Development Bank.* Oakland, CA: Environment Department, Indigo Development.

POSCO website. http://posco-india.com/website/press-room/posco-completes-commercialization-of-finex-technology.htm.

Sae-A Trading Co. website. http://www.sae-a.com/.

Sakr, D. L. Baas, S. El-Haggar, and D. Huisingh. 2011. "Critical Success and Limiting Factors for Eco-Industrial Parks: Global Trends and Egyptian Context." Journal of Cleaner Production 19(11): 1158–1169

Shalizi, Z., and F. Lecocq. 2009. *Economics of Targeted Mitigation Programs in Sectors with Long-Lived Capital Stock.* Policy Research Working Paper No. 5063. Washington, DC: World Bank.

United Nations Conference on Trade and Development. 2011. *World Investment Report* 2010. New York and Geneva. United Nations.

UNFCCC (United Nations Framework Convention for Climate Change). Available at http://unfccc.int/2860.php.

World Bank. 2008. *The Development of China's ESCO Industry, 2004–2007.* Washington, DC: World Bank.

World Bank. 2010. *Eco2 Cities: Ecological Cities as Economic Cities.* World Bank's New Urban Development Initiative. Washington DC: World Bank.

World Bank. 2010. *World Development Report 2010, Development and Climate Change.* Washington, DC: World Bank.

World Bank, FIAS. 2008. *Special Economic Zones, performance, lessons learned and implications for zone development.* Washington DC: World Bank.

Index

A

Adamjee EPZ, Bangladesh, 28
Adapting Singapore Experience Office, 108
ADOZONA (Dominican Association of
    Free Zones), 166, 172, 173, 175
AFTA (Association of Southeast Nations
    (ASEAN) Free Trade Area), 133
Agreement on Subsidies and
    Countervailing Measures (SCM),
    WTO, 172
Algeria-China Jiangling Economic and
    Trade Cooperation Zone,
    79–80, 92
Amapala Free Zone, Honduras, 48
Andean Community, 133
apparel sector
    Bangladesh garment industry, 26
    in the Dominican Republic, 160,
        168–169, 170f, 173
    labor laws and women, 264
    in Mauritius, 232, 233f
ASEAN (Association of Southeast
    Nations), 41, 133
Asian Development Bank, 286
Association of Southeast Nations
    (ASEAN) Free Trade Area
    (AFTA), 133, 150
Australia, 133–134

B

Bahrain, 257
Bangladesh EPZs (BEPZs)
    background, 25–26
    challenges faced by
        diversification of the industrial
            base, 41
        reform of existing regime, 41–43
        wage and conditions
            competitiveness, 38–40
    country overview, 9–10
    domestic market linkages, 31–33
    Economic Zones Act, 26, 42, 43
    employment, 31
    exports, 30–31
    female share of employment,
        31, 257
    firms and investment, 29–30
    garment industry status, 26
    historical development of, 27–29
    key success factors
        administrative regime efficiency, 36
        incentives, 36–38
        investment climate, 34–35
        market size, 34
        serviced land and infrastructure,
            35–36
        wages, 34

Bangladesh EPZs (BEPZs) (*continued*)
    labor law compliance, 265
    labor laws and women, 263
    local market restrictions, 33
    private EPZ, 42
    sectoral distribution of female
        employment, 260
Bangladesh Export Processing Zone
        Authority (BEPZA), 27, 265
Bangladesh Investment Climate
        Fund (BICF), 38
Bangladesh Small and Cottage Industries
        Corporation (BSCIC), 27
Beranger, Paul, 228
Better Factories Programme,
        Cambodia, 265
Border Industrialization Program,
        Mexico, 252
BSCIC (Bangladesh Small and Cottage
        Industries Corporation), 27

C

CACM (Central American Common
        Market), 133
CADF (China-Africa Development
        Fund), 70, 74
CAFTA (Central American Free
        Trade Agreement), 176
Cambodia, 199
carbon emissions
    financing, 301
    policy incentives and
        regulations, 297, 298*f*
    voluntary market, 302–303
Caribbean Basin Economic Recovery
        Expansion Act (CBI II)
        (1990), 56, 176
Caribbean Basin Initiative (CBI), 55–56
Caribbean Basin Trade Partnership Act
        (CBTPA), 49, 56, 176
CCECC (China Civil Engineering
        Construction Corp.), 78
CDM (clean development mechanisms),
        301–302
CEMAC (Economic and Monetary
        Community of Central Africa), 134
Central American Common Market
        (CACM), 133
Central American Free Trade Agreement
        (CAFTA), 176

Chambishi multi-facility economic
        zone, 73–74
Chicago Climate Exchange (CCX), 303
China
    African SEZs (*see* China's overseas SEZs)
    current status of green SEZs, 306
    female share of employment, 258
    flexibility of employment
        for women, 262
    Singapore EPZ (*see* China-Singapore
        (Suzhou) Industrial Park)
China-Africa Development Fund
        (CADF), 70, 74
China-Africa Investment Ltd., 79
China Civil Engineering Construction
        Corp. (CCECC), 78
China-Nigeria Economic and Trade
        Cooperation Zone, 78
China Nonferrous Mining Co.
        (CNMC Group), 73
China Pakistan Enterprise Zone, 86
China-Singapore (Suzhou) Industrial
        Park (SIP)
    aligning interests of stakeholders,
        113–114
    background, 101–102
    competition from neighboring industrial
        parks, 111–112
    competitive advantage issues, 112
    current situation, 102–104
    customs handling support, 115
    development and operations lessons, 119
    development costs challenges, 110–111
    economic indicators, 121*t*
    employee pension fund system, 114–115
    Free Trade Zone development
        milestones, 116–117
    government leadership, 114
    key success factors, 113
    knowledge-sharing process, 107,
        109–110, 119–120
    macroeconomic challenges, 112–113
    misalignment of government and
        stakeholder incentives, 111
    partnership structure, 105–107, 108*f*,
        117–119
    policy incentives, 114
    political and economic strategies,
        104–105
    timeline and major milestones, 122–124
    training for officials, 109

China-Singapore Joint Steering Council
(JSC), 105
China-Singapore Suzhou Industrial Park
Development Co., Ltd. (CSSD),
102, 106
China's overseas SEZs
Algeria-China Jiangling, 79–80, 92
background, 11, 70–71
benefits for African economies, 95
benefits for Chinese enterprises, 95
current situation, 72–73
developers disappointment with
government support, 94
development and management, 87–89
domestic concern about Chinese
investment, 94–95
dual-track strategy for ERZs
background to SEZs, 217–218, 222
economic results, 218–219
privatization support, 220
reduction in opportunities for rent-
seeking, 219–220
transforming of the rent-distorted
economy, 219
Egypt Suez, 74–76, 88–89, 90, 92
enterprise interest in the zones, 91–92
enterprise requirements, 89–90
establishment process, 80–81
Ethiopia, 76–77, 88, 91, 92
experience to date, 70, 91–92
financing challenges, 92
history, 71–72
investments structure, 84–85t
labor requirements, 90–91
Mauritius Jinfei (see Mauritius
Jinfei Economic and Trade
Cooperation Zone)
Nigeria Lekki, 78–79, 87–89, 90
Nigeria Ogun-Guangdong, 79, 92
objectives, 69, 71, 222
partnership framework elements, 95–96
strategy and financial
commitments, 83–87
support mechanisms, 82–83
tender process, 81–82
Zambia-China, 73–74, 88–90, 91
zones list, 96–97t
Chinese CCNC Group, 79
Chittagong EPZ, Bangladesh, 28,
31, 35, 40
Choloma free zone, Honduras, 48

CIC (Investment Climate Advisory
Services), 148–149
Ciudat Guayana, Venezuela, 211
clean development mechanisms
(CDM), 301–302
Closer Economic Relations
Agreement (Australia and
New Zealand), 133–134
CNMC (China Nonferrous Mining
Co. Group), 73
CNZFE (Consejo Nacional de Zonas
Francas de Exportación), 164
CODEVI FZ, Dominican Republic, 174
Comilla EPZ, Bangladesh, 28
ComMark Trust, Lesotho, 271
Common Market for Eastern and Southern
Africa (COMESA), 133, 150
Consejo Nacional de Zonas Francas de
Exportación (CNZFE), 164
Copenhagen Accord, 283, 284,
290, 294, 296
coproduction, 174
Costa Rica, 191
CSSD (China-Singapore Suzhou
Industrial Park Development
Co., Ltd.), 102, 106
CS-SIP Land Corporate, 107

D

Daewoo Company, 27
Decent Work Programme, ILO, 270–271
DEDO (Duty Exemptions and Drawback
Office), Bangladesh, 33
Dhaka EPZ, Bangladesh, 28, 31,
35, 40, 260
Doha Round, 130
Dominican Association of Free Zones
(ADOZONA), 166, 172, 173, 175
Dominican Republic-Central American
Free Trade Agreement
(DR-CAFTA), 49, 56, 176
Dominican Republic's free zones
apparel sector, 160, 168–169, 170f, 173
background, 162–166
backward linkages failures, 178, 194
compatibility issues with
WTO, 171–172
competitiveness challenges, 165–166
country overview, 14–15
current situation, 164, 175–176

Dominican Republic's free
  zones (*continued*)
  employment, 171
  exports, 168–171
  factors driving early growth, 163–165
  failure to integrate with the local
    economy, 177–178
  forward linkages promotion
    initiatives, 173
  impact on economic growth, 165
  impact on GDP and FDI growth,
    159–160, 166–167, 167*f*
  investment, 167–168
  job creation, 179
  labor force training and wages, 178–179
  labor laws and women, 264
  overreliance on trade
    preferences, 176–177
  policy reforms attempted, 161
  production sharing, 174
  profile, 164
  recent decline in, 166
  structural upgrades shortcomings,
    173, 175
  threats to the FZ-based economic
    model, 160–161
  wage incentives, 172–173
DR-CAFTA (Dominican Republic-Central
  American Free Trade Agreement),
  49, 56, 176
DuShu Lake Innovation District of Science
  and Technology, SIP, 102
Duty Exemptions and Drawback Office
  (DEDO), Bangladesh, 33
Duval, Gaëtan, 228

E

Early Reform Zones (ERZs)
  Asian zone performance statistics, 212*t*
  basis of failures of SEZs, 208
  China's dual-track strategy, 217–220
  compared to growth poles, 211
  compared to SEZs, 210
  concept of, 15–16
  creation of competitive
    enterprises, 212–213
  criticisms of, 211–212
  dual-track reform strategy role,
    208–209, 210–211
  failure of Africa's, 209
  fundamental objective, 210

goal of, 213
Madagascar, 209
Malaysia, 216–217
Mauritius, 214–216
need for a prozone political
  coalition, 213
rent cycling issues, 207–208
Sub-Saharan Africa role, 220–224
East African Community
  (EAC), 133, 138, 142,
  148–149, 150
Eastern High-Tech Industrial Zone, SIP, 102
ECCI (Egypt-Chinese Corporation
  for Investment), 74
Eco-industrial Park Handbook, 286
eco-industrial zones/parks (EIZ/Ps),
  286, 304–306
Economic and Monetary Community of
  Central Africa (CEMAC), 134
Economic Community of West African
  States (ECOWAS), 150
Economic Zones Act (2010), Bangladesh,
  26, 42, 43
EDB (Singapore Economic Development
  Board), 107
EFTA (European Free Trade
  Association), 133
Egypt-Chinese Corporation for Investment
  (ECCI), 74
Egypt Suez Economic and Trade
  Cooperation Zone, 74–76,
  88–89, 90, 92
EIPs (eco-industrial zones/parks), 286,
  304–306.
energy service companies (ESCOs), 296
Enterprise Mauritius, 234
Environmental Management
  System, ISO, 285
environment compliance zone, 285
EPZDA (Export Processing Zone
  Development Authority),
  Mauritius, 234
ESCOs (energy service companies), 296
Ethiopia Eastern Industrial Park, 76–77,
  88, 91, 92
European Economic Community, 133
European Free Trade Association
  (EFTA), 133
Export Processing Zone (EPZ) Act,
  Bangladesh, 38
Export Processing Zone (EPZ) Act,
  Mauritius, 228

Export Processing Zone (EPZ) Law,
    Honduras, 48–49, 55
Export Processing Zone Development
    Authority (EPZDA), Mauritius, 234

F

Factory Improvement Program, ILO, 271
Fair Labor Association, 264
Fat, Lim, 228
feminization of labor
    advantages for employers, 249
    beginnings of link between trade
        and gender, 248
    defeminization of employment factors
        cyclical economic influences, 268–269
        gender wage gap, 267–268
        industrial upgrading, 266–267, 268f
        outsourcing to home-based
            workers, 269
    economics of female-intensive
        production, 253–255
    exports and employment, 255–256
    factors attributed to, 251
    female share of employment,
        31, 257–259
    female wages as a percent of male
        wages, manufacturing, 250t
    flexibility of employment, 262
    gender wage inequality's relationship
        to growth, 249–250
    initiatives to improve compliance on
        labor issues, 265–266
    labor laws and women, 263–264
    policy conclusions and
        recommendations, 270–272
    pros and cons of, 248–249, 269–270
    restrictions on unions and, 264
    sectoral distribution of female
        employment, 259–261
    segmentation of occupations
        by sex, 251
    SEZs role in, 17–18, 252–253
    wages and working conditions, 262–265
FIDE (Foundation for Investment and
    Development of Exports), 58–59
FINEX technology, 296
Foreign Investment (Promotion and
    Protection Act) (1980),
    Bangladesh, 27, 37
Forum on China-Africa Cooperation
    (FOCAC), 70

Foundation for Investment and
    Development of Exports
    (FIDE), 58–59
free trade agreements (FTAs), 130
Free Zone Law, Dominican Republic, 172
Free Zone Law, Honduras, 48
Fruit of the Loom, 54
Fund for the Promotion of Exports
    and Investments, Dominican
    Republic, 173

G

garment industry. See apparel sector
GCC (Gulf Cooperation Council),
    133, 150
gender dimension of SEZs. See
    feminization of labor
General Agreement on Tariffs and
    Trade (GATT), 129
Ghana, 259
Gildan, 54, 65
green house gas (GHG) mitigation
    target, 288–291
green SEZs. See low-carbon, green SEZs
growth poles, 211
Grupo M, 160, 174
Guangdong Xinguang International
    Group, 79
Gulf and Western Corporation, 162
Gulf Cooperation Council
    (GCC), 133, 150

H

Haier, 72, 83–84, 86
Haiti, 173, 174
Hanes, 54
Honduras free zones
    background, 47–48, 65–67
    challenges faced by
        crime, 62
        efforts to increase productivity, 62
        existing privileges discouragement of
            reform, 64
        global economic downturn, 61
        international competition, 62
        macroeconomic climate, 61–62
        product diversification, 63–64
        vocational training, 64, 65
    employment, 53–54
    female share of employment, 257

Honduras free zones (*continued*)
  firms and investment, 49, 51*t*, 52
  historical development of, 48–49
  incentives summary, 50–51
  key success factors
    agglomeration support, 57–58
    domestic investors attracting
      of FDI, 60
    domestic private sector, 59–60
    infrastructure and services support, 57
    institutional support in marketing and
      promotion, 58–59
    legal framework, 55
    preferential trade agreements, 55–57
  labor laws and women, 263
  local market linkages, 54
  overview, 10–11
  production and exports, 52–53

I

IFC (International Finance
  Corporation), 40
Incheon Free Economic Zone,
  Republic of Korea, 289
India
  current status of green SEZs, 306
  female share of employment, 257, 258
  flexibility of employment
    for women, 262
Indonesia, 147
Industrial Relations Ordinance (1969),
  Bangladesh, 38
INFOTEP, 175, 179
innovation support through SEZs
  background, 183–184
  backward linkages facilitation
    need, 192, 194–195
  business climate reform
    requirement, 196
  direct and indirect benefits, 184–185
  domestic technological capabilities
    requirement, 189–192
  evolution of first modern SEZ, 186
  FDI flows as a source of technology
    and learning, 188
  influence derived from local-level
    concentration, 188–189
  labor circulation enhancement need, 195
  policies summary, 202*t*
  R&D capacity and personnel
    requirement, 190, 192, 193*f*

  steps in building an innovative SEZ
    infrastructure and business
      environment development,
      197–198
    labor-intensive manufacturing
      development, 198–199
    staged approach summary, 201*t*
    technology-intensive manufacturing
      development, 200
  strategic location importance, 196–197
  training programs and, 190, 190*t*
  transmission of foreign
    knowledge and technology,
    187–188
Instituto Politécnico Centroamericano, 65
Integrated Free Trade Zone (IFTZ),
  SIP, 102, 115
Interamericana Products International, 160
International Finance Corporation
  (IFC), 40
Investment Climate Advisory Services
  (CIC), 148–149
Ireland
  feminization of labor, 252
  first modern SEZ, 186, 195
Ishwardi EPZ, Bangladesh, 28

J

Jamaica, 257
Japan International Cooperation Agency
  (JICA), 70
Jiangling Free Trade Zone, 76, 79–80.
  See also Algeria-China Jiangling
    Economic and Trade
    Cooperation Zone
JinFei. *See* Mauritius Jinfei
  Economic and Trade
  Cooperation Zone
Jinji Lake-Rim Central Business
  District, SIP, 102
JSC (China-Singapore Joint Steering
  Council), 105
Jurong Town Corporation (JTC), 105

K

Kandla, India, 196
Karnaphuli EPZ, Bangladesh, 28
Kenya
  female share of employment, 259
  regional trade agreements in, 142–143

Korea Certified Emission Reduction
    (KCER), 303
Kunshan Economic and
    Technological Development
    Zone, 111
Kyoto Protocol, 301, 302

L

labor
    Bangladesh's cost advantage, 34, 38
    gender dimension of (*see* feminization
        of labor)
    innovation in SEZs and, 195, 198–199
    requirements in China, 90–91
    training and wages in Dominican
        Republic, 178–179
    women and laws, 263–264
Labor Counselor Program, Bangladesh, 38,
    40, 265, 271
La Ceiba free zone, Honduras, 48
Lagos, Nigeria, 78
La Romano Zone, Dominican
    Republic, 162
Lekki Free Trade Zone (LFTZ), Nigeria,
    78–79, 90, 92, 93
Lesotho, 259, 265
low-carbon, green SEZs
    basic policy framework, 297–298
    carbon finance, 301
    clean development mechanisms,
        301–302
    climate-friendly investment
        generation, 294–297
    core components overview, 287–288
    current status worldwide, 304–307
    defined, 285–286
    GHG mitigation target, 288–291
    incentive system, 299–300
    institutional framework, 300–301
    international agreements, 283–284
    legal framework, 298–299
    low-carbon policy incentives and
        regulations, 297, 298f
    new focus on green zones, 284–285
    potential benefits of, 286–287
    regulatory framework, 299
    sustainable infrastructure, 291–294
    synergy between FDI and
        CDM, 303–304
    voluntary carbon market, 302–303
Lusaka subzone project, Zambia, 74

M

Madagascar
    EPZs success, 209
    labor laws and women, 263, 264
    sectoral distribution of female
        employment, 260
Madras EPZ, India, 262
Malaysia
    growth triangle, 147
    sectoral distribution of female
        employment, 261
    shift from resource to skill-driven
        development, 216–217
    training for workers in SEZs, 191t
maquila, 48. *See also* Honduras free zones
Maquila Association of Honduras, 61
Masan Zone, Republic of Korea
    defeminization of employment
        factors, 268
    labor circulation enhancement, 195
Mauritian Labor Party, 228
Mauritius Export Development and
    Investment Authority
    (MEDIA), 234
Mauritius Export Processing
    Zone (MEPZ)
    apparel sector dependency, 232, 233f
    background and objectives, 227–229
    contribution to political
        stability, 241, 242
    diversification and competitiveness
        challenges, 236–237
    dual-track SEZ success, 214–216
    economic crisis and restructuring
        history, 229–230
    employment demographics, 230–231
    export-oriented approach
        results, 237–238
    export performance, 231, 232f
    export productivity, 233–235
    FDI challenges, 235
    future prospects, 241–243
    government leadership role, 238–239
    investment data, 231, 233–235
    labor and operating cost
        structure, 235–236
    labor productivity, 232, 233f
    overview, 16–17
    phases in its economic history, 241
    political economy impact, 239–240
    preferential trade agreements, 236

Mauritius Export Processing
    Zone (MEPZ) (*continued*)
  sectoral distribution of female
    employment, 261
  static versus dynamic impact, 240–241
  training for workers in SEZs, 191*t*
Mauritius Industrial Development
    Authority, 234
Mauritius Jinfei Economic and Trade
    Cooperation Zone
  background, 77–78
  Chinese workers employed, 90–91
  development and management, 87, 88
  foreign investors requirement, 89
  investment incentives, 86–87
  zone status, 91
McKinsey cost curve, 294, 295*f*
MEDIA (Mauritius Export Development
    and Investment Authority), 234
Mercosur, 141, 142
Mexico
  defeminization of employment
    factors, 268
  feminization of labor, 252
  labor laws and women, 264
  regional trade agreements in, 141, 142
MFA (Multi-Fiber Arrangement), 6
MIGA (Multilateral Investment Guarantee
    Agency), World Bank, 38
mining and ERZs, 222–223
Ministry of Commerce, China
    (MOFCOM), 73, 81, 83, 86
MMM (*Mouvement Militant
    Mauricien*), 228
Mongla EPZ, Bangladesh, 28
Morocco, 257
Mouvement Militant Mauricien
    (MMM), 228
Multi-Facility Economic Zones (MFEZs),
    Zambia, 74
Multi-Fiber Arrangement (MFA), 6
Multilateral Investment Guarantee Agency
    (MIGA), World Bank, 38

N

NAFTA (North American Free Trade
    Agreement), 56, 133, 138, 176
Nanjing Jiangning Development Zone,
    Nigeria, 83
National Productivity and Competitiveness
    Council (NPCC), Mauritius, 234

New Zealand, 133–134
Nicaragua, 257
Nigeria Lekki Economic and Trade
    Cooperation Zone
  background, 78–79
  Chinese workers employed, 90
  development and management, 87–88
  female share of employment, 259
  foreign investors requirement, 89
Nigeria Lekki Free Trade Zone (LFTZ),
    78–79, 90, 92, 93
Nigeria Ogun-Guangdong Economic
    and Trade Cooperation
    Zone, 79, 92
Noida EPZ, India, 262
North American Free Trade Agreement
    (NAFTA), 56, 133, 138, 176

O

Ogun-Guangdong Economic and Trade
    Cooperation Zone, 79, 92
Omoa Free Zone, Honduras, 48
Organisation for Economic
    Co-operation and Development
    (OECD), 186
Overseas Private Investment
    Corporation (OPIC), 38

P

Panapak Electronics, 86
Parti Mauricien Social Democrate
    (PMSD), 228
Philippines
  labor laws and women, 264–265
  training for workers in SEZs, 191*t*
Pingxiang Coal Group (PKCC), 80
PMSD (*Parti Mauricien Social
    Democrate*), 228
pollution control zone, 285
Poncini, José, 228
POSCO, 296
Presidential Table for the Promotion
    of Exports, Dominican
    Republic, 175
Private EPZ Act (1996), Bangladesh, 42
production sharing, 174
Puerto Cortés free zone, Honduras, 48

Q

Qiyuan Group, 76, 77

R

Ramgoolam, Seewoosagur, 228
Regional Industrial Parks Initiative,
    Singapore, 104
regional trade agreements (RTAs)
    in Africa and the Middle East, 132*f*
    Asian growth triangles, 147–148
    benefits to member countries, 129–130
    challenge of incorporating
        SEZs into, 128
    competitiveness of local producers, 136
    competitive positioning of SEZ, 137
    EAC export processing zones, 148–149
    evolution of intra-RTA trade, 135*f*
    factors determining effectiveness of, 134
    financial incentives, 145–146
    growth in number of, 130, 131*f*, 132
    in Kenya, 142–143
    in Mexico, 141
    performance, 133–134, 135*f*
    policy trends, 133
    promotion of regional economic
        integration, 136–137
    regulations and handbooks
        available, 150
    regulatory framework, 144–145
    in SADC, 143
    strategic framework, 146–147
    synergies with SEZs, 127–128
    tariff-reduction purpose, 129
    tariff-related issues response,
        138–139, 140*f*
    tariff-related measures
        summary, 151–153*t*
    trade triangulation, 136
    in Uruguay, 141–142
rent cycling
    dual-track strategy that
        addresses, 219–220
    issues in ERZs, 207–208
Republic of Korea
    awareness of emissions issues, 284
    backward linkages facilitation, 194
    current status of green SEZs, 306
    defeminization of employment
        factors, 268
    EPZ in Bangladesh, 284
    GHG mitigation target, 289
    innovation support in SEZs,
        190, 192, 193*f*
    labor circulation enhancement, 195
    sectoral distribution of female
        employment, 261
    training for workers in SEZs, 191*t*
Ruba General Trading Company, 86
rules of origin, 139
Russia, 213

S

SACU (Southern African Customs
    Union), 143
SADC (Southern African Development
    Community), 143, 150
SAFE (Security and Accountability for
    Every Port), 57
San Pedro Sula, Honduras, 58
SCM (Agreement on Subsidies and
    Countervailing Measures),
    WTO, 41, 172
Sectoral Promotion Program, Mexico, 141
Security and Accountability
    for Every Port (SAFE),
    Honduras, 57
Shannon, Ireland, 186, 195
Shannon Free Airport Development
    Company (SFADCo), 186
Shanxi Coking Coal Group, 77
Shenzhen, China
    backward linkages facilitation, 192
    business climate reform, 196
    female share of employment, 259
    flexibility of employment
        for women, 262
    labor circulation enhancement, 195
    labor-intensive manufacturing
        development, 198
    staged approach summary, 201*t*
    technology-intensive manufacturing
        development, 200
    training for workers in SEZs, 191*t*
Singapore. *See* China-Singapore (Suzhou)
    Industrial Park
Singapore Economic Development Board
    (EDB), 107
Singapore-Suzhou Township
    Development Co., 106
SIP. *See* China-Singapore (Suzhou)
    Industrial Park
SIPAC (Suzhou Industrial Park
    Administrative Committee), 106
SIP Ecological Science Hub, 102
SIP Provident Fund System (SPF), 114

Software Project Office (SPO),
    Singapore, 108
South Asian Free Trade Agreement
    (SAFTA), 133
Southern African Customs
    Union (SACU), 143
Southern African Development
    Community (SADC), 143, 150
special economic zones (SEZs). *See also*
    specific countries
    areas for growth opportunities, 15
    benefits, 8–9
    challenges faced, 6
    critical policy issues, 7
    early reform zones concept, 15–16
    elements needed to achieve dynamic
        economic benefits, 13–14
    environmental policy and, 18–19
    ERZs and (*see* Early Reform Zones)
    exports and employment, 255–256
    gender dimension of labor (*see*
        feminization of labor)
    growth in number of new zones, 5–6
    innovation support from (*see* innovation
        support through SEZs)
    lessons in zone development, 11–12
    policy objectives, 3–4
    regulatory issues overview, 12–13
    role in economic growth, 4–5
    role in international trade, 3
    RTAs and (*see* regional trade
        agreements)
    shift away from traditional model, 6–7
    success factors, 10
    success record, 4
    types and definition, 1, 2*t*, 3
Special Fund for Economic and
    Technological Cooperation, 82
SPF (SIP Provident Fund System), 114
Sri Lanka
    sectoral distribution of female
        employment, 260–261
    training for workers in SEZs, 191*t*
Sub-Saharan Africa and SEZs. *See also*
    Early Reform Zones
    agglomeration spillover effects, 221
    economic benefits of approach, 220–221
    economic reforms possible, 223–224
    objectives for Chinese economic
        zones, 222
    policy options involving mining, 222–223

Suez Economic and Trade Cooperation
    Zone, 74–76
sustainability in SEZs. *See* low-carbon,
    green SEZs
sustainable infrastructure in a SEZ
    buildings, 292–293
    energy efficiency, 292
    energy supply, 291–292
    waste reuse and recycling, 293–294
Suzhou. *See* China-Singapore
    Industrial Park (SIP)
Suzhou Industrial Park Administrative
    Committee (SIPAC), 106
Suzhou New and Hi-Tech Development
    Zone, 111, 112, 113
Suzhou Taihu National Tourism and
    Vacation Zone, 111

T

Taiwan, China
    labor circulation enhancement, 195
    sectoral distribution of female
        employment, 261
    technology-intensive manufacturing
        development, 200
    training for workers in SEZs, 191*t*
Taiyuan Iron and Steel Company, 77
Tanzania, 259
tariff-jumping, 128
TEDA (Tianjin Economic-Technological
    Development Area) Investment
    Holdings, 74, 83
Tela free zone, Honduras, 48
Temporary Importation Regulations
    Law, Honduras, 48
Textile Emergency Support Team,
    Mauritius, 234
Thailand, 147, 191*t*
Tianjin Economic-Technological
    Development Area (TEDA)
    Investment Holdings, 74, 75–76, 83
Tianli Group, 77
township and village enterprises (TVEs),
    China, 218
Tunisia, 261
twin-planting, 174

U

UEMOA. *See* West African Economic
    and Monetary Union

U.K. Ethical Trade Initiative, 265
United Nations Convention on Climate
    Change, 283
United Nations Framework Convention for
    Climate Change (UNFCCC), 301
Uruguay, 141–142
U.S. Apparel Industry Partnership, 265
Uttara EPZ, Bangladesh, 28

V

Vietnam, 263
Vishakhapatnam SEZ, India, 262
voluntary carbon market, 302–303

W

West African Economic and Monetary
    Union (WAEMU), 138, 150
women and SEZs. *See* feminization of labor
Workers Association and Industrial
    Relations Act (2004),
    Bangladesh, 38
World Bank, 38, 40, 148, 213, 229, 296
World Trade Organization (WTO), 26, 41,
    112, 129, 130, 172, 213–214

Y

Yangcheng Lake Tourism
    Resort, SIP, 102
Yangyang Asset Management, 76
Yonggang Group, 76, 77
Youngone Corporation, 28, 42

Z

Zambia-China Economic
    and Trade Cooperation
    Zone
    background, 73–74
    Chinese workers employed, 90
    development and management, 88
    foreign investors requirement, 89
    zone status, 91
Zhangjiagang Bonded Area, 111
Zhangjiagang Free Trade Zone, 77, 83
Zhongding International
    Group, 79–80
ZOLI, Puerto Cortés, Honduras, 59
Zona Industriales de Procesamiento (ZIPs),
    Honduras, 49
zonas francas especiales (ZFEs), 165